W9-AEA-732

THE FATHERS
OF THE CHURCH

A NEW TRANSLATION

VOLUME 117

THE FATHERS OF THE CHURCH

A NEW TRANSLATION

EDITORIAL BOARD

Thomas P. Halton
The Catholic University of America
Editorial Director

Elizabeth Clark
Duke University

Robert D. Sider
Dickinson College

Joseph T. Lienhard, S.J.
Fordham University

Michael Slusser
Duquesne University

David G. Hunter
University of Kentucky

Cynthia White
The University of Arizona

Kathleen McVey
Princeton Theological Seminary

Rebecca Lyman
Church Divinity School of the Pacific

David J. McGonagle
Director
The Catholic University of America Press

FORMER EDITORIAL DIRECTORS
Ludwig Schopp, Roy J. Deferrari, Bernard M. Peebles,
Hermigild Dressler, O.F.M.

Carole Monica C. Burnett
Staff Editor

BR
60
,F3
J4713
2008

ST. JEROME

COMMENTARY ON MATTHEW

Translated by

THOMAS P. SCHECK
Ave Maria University

THE CATHOLIC UNIVERSITY OF AMERICA PRESS
Washington, D.C.

JAN

JAN

26 !

26 '09.

;
;

Copyright © 2008
THE CATHOLIC UNIVERSITY OF AMERICA PRESS
All rights reserved
Printed in the United States of America

The paper used in this publication meets the minimum requirements of the
American National Standards for Information Science–Permanence of Paper
for Printed Library Materials, ANSI z39.48—1984.

LIBRARY OF CONGRESS CATALOGING-IN-PUBLICATION DATA
Jerome, Saint, d. 419 or 20.
[Commentariorum in Evangelium Matthei libri quatuor. English]
Commentary on Matthew / St. Jerome ; translated by Thomas P. Scheck.
p. cm. – (The fathers of the church ; v. 117)
Includes bibliographical references (p.   ) and indexes.
ISBN 978-0-8132-0117-7 (cloth : alk. paper)   1. Bible. N.T. Matthew–
Commentaries.   I. Scheck, Thomas P., 1964–   II. Title.
BR65.J473C6413 2008
226.2'077–dc22
2008011349

Dedicated in friendship and affection to
Father Ken Kuntz, Pastor of St. Mary's Catholic Church,
Iowa City, Iowa

CONTENTS

INDICES

ACKNOWLEDGMENTS

I am grateful to Dr. Ralph McInerny, Director of the Jacques Maritain Center at the University of Notre Dame, who awarded me a post-doctoral fellowship for the 2004–5 academic year. Much of the present work is the fruit of that year of research. Craig Gibson, my Latin teacher at the University of Iowa, assisted in the translation of Jerome's Preface. Carl Beckwith offered valuable criticisms of the Introduction. The Staff Editor, Carole Monica Burnett, offered wise and learned counsel, as did my friend and colleague Jay Martin of South Bend.

ABBREVIATIONS

ACC   Ancient Christian Commentary on Scripture. Ed. Thomas
C. Oden. Downers Grove, Intervarsity.

ANF   Ante-Nicene Fathers. 1890. Reprint. Grand Rapids: Eerdmans,
1994.

CBQ   Catholic Biblical Quarterly.

CCSL   Corpus Christianorum, Series Latina. Turnhout and Paris.

CSEL   Corpus Scriptorum Ecclesiasticorum Latinorum. Vienna.

CWE   Collected Works of Erasmus. Toronto: University of
Toronto Press, 1974–.

DCB   *A Dictionary of Christian Biography.* Ed. W. Smith and
H. Wace. 4 vols. London, 1887.

EEC   *Encyclopedia of the Early Church.* Ed. A. Di Berardino. 2 vols.
New York: Oxford University Press, 1992.

Ep.   Epistle.

FOTC   Fathers of the Church. Washington, DC: The Catholic
University of America Press, 1947–.

GCS   Die griechischen christlichen Schriftsteller der ersten drei
Jahrhunderte. Leipzig: J. C. Hinrichs, 1897–1949. Berlin:
Akademie-Verlag, 1953–.

HTR   *Harvard Theological Review.*

JBL   *Journal of Biblical Literature.*

JTS   *Journal of Theological Studies.*

LCL   Loeb Classical Library.

M   Migne.

NJBC   *The New Jerome Biblical Commentary.* Ed. R. E. Brown,
J. A. Fitzmyer, R. E. Murphy. Englewood Cliffs, NJ:
Prentice Hall, 1990.

NPNF   A Select Library of Nicene and Post-Nicene Fathers of the
Christian Church. 1890. Reprint. Grand Rapids: Eerdmans,
1994.

NT   New Testament.

NTA	*New Testament Apocrypha.* Ed. E. Hennecke and W. Schneemelcher.
NTS	*New Testament Studies.*
OT	Old Testament.
PG	Patrologiae Cursus Completus: Series Graeca. Ed. J.-P. Migne. Paris, 1857–66.
PL	Patrologiae Cursus Completus: Series Latina. Ed. J.-P. Migne. Paris, 1878–90.
SC	Sources chrétiennes. Paris: Cerf.
TU	Texte und Untersuchungen zur Geschichte der altchristlichen Literatur. Berlin, 1882–.
VC	*Vigiliae Christianae.* Amsterdam: North-Holland Pub. Co., 1947–.

SELECT BIBLIOGRAPHY

Texts and Translations

Jerome

Archer, G., trans. *Jerome's Commentary on Daniel*. Grand Rapids: Baker, 1958.

Bonnard, E., ed. *Saint Jérôme: Commentaire sur S. Matthieu*. 2 vols. SC 242, 259. Paris: Cerf, 1977, 1979.

Ewald, M. L., trans. *The Homilies of Saint Jerome*. 2 vols. FOTC 48, 57.

Heine, R. E. *The Commentaries of Origen and Jerome on St. Paul's Epistle to the Ephesians*. Oxford Early Christian Studies. Oxford and New York: Oxford University Press, 2002.

Hurst, D., and M. Adriaen, eds. *Sancti Hieronymi Presbyteri. Commentariorum in Mathaeum libri iv*. CCSL 77. Turnhout: Brepols, 1969.

Migne, J.-P., ed. PL 26: 15–218.

Simonetti, M., ed. *Matthew 1–13. Matthew 14–28*. ACC, New Testament 1a, 1b. Downers Grove: Intervarsity Press, 2001–2.

Origen

Klostermann, E., and E. Benz, eds. *Origenes Matthäuserklärung I*. Die griechischerhaltenen Tomoi (Origenes Werke, X). Leipzig, 1935.

———, eds. *Origenes Matthäuserklärung II*. Die lateinische Übersetzung der Commentariorum Series (bearbeitet von U. Treu) (Origenes Werke, XI). Berlin, 1976.

———, eds. *Origenes Matthäuserklärung III*. Fragmente und Indices (Origenes Werke, XII/1). Leipzig, 1941.

Klostermann, E., and L. Fruchtel, eds. *Origenes Matthäuserklärung III*. Fragmente und Indices (zweite durchgesehene Auflage besorgt von U. Treu) (Origenes werke, XII/2). Berlin, 1968.

Secondary Works

Balas, D. "Marcion Revisited: A 'Post-Harnack' Perspective." In *Texts and Testaments: Critical Essays on the Bible and Early Church Fathers*. Ed. W. E. March. San Antonio: Trinity University Press, 1980. Pp. 95–108.

Bardy, G. "Jérôme et ses maîtres hébreux." *Revue Bénédictine* 46 (1934): 145–64.

Brown, D. *Vir Trilinguis: A Study in the Biblical Exegesis of Saint Jerome.* Kampen: Kok Pharos Publishing House, 1992.

Campenhausen, H. von. *The Fathers of the Church.* Peabody, MA: Hendrickson, 2000.

Cavallera, F. *Saint Jérôme: Sa vie et son oeuvre.* 2 vols. Paris, 1922.

Clark, E. *The Origenist Controversy: The Cultural Construction of an Early Christian Debate.* Princeton, 1992.

———. "The Place of Jerome's Commentary on Ephesians in the Origenist Controversy." *VC* 41 (1987): 154–71.

Courcelle, P. *Late Latin Writers and their Greek Sources.* Trans. H. E. Wedeck. Cambridge, MA: Harvard University Press, 1969.

Daniélou, J. *A History of Early Christian Doctrine.* Volume 1: *The Theology of Jewish Christianity.* Trans. and ed. John A. Baker. Chicago: The Henry Regnery Company, 1964.

Encyclopedia of the Early Church. Ed. A. Di Berardino. 2 vols. New York: Oxford University Press, 1992.

Fokke, G. "An Aspect of the Christology of Erasmus of Rotterdam." *Ephemerides Theologiae Lovanienses* 54 (1978): 161–87.

Erasmus, Desiderius. *Patristic Scholarship: The Edition of St Jerome.* Edited, translated, and annotated by James F. Brady and John C. Olin. Collected Works of Erasmus 61. Toronto: University of Toronto Press, 1992.

Farkasfalvy, D. "Theology of Scripture in St. Irenaeus." *Revue Bénédictine* 78 (1968): 318–33.

Hale Williams, Megan. *The Monk and the Book: Jerome and the Making of Christian Scholarship.* Chicago: University of Chicago Press, 2006.

Hennecke, E., and W. Schneemelcher, eds. *New Testament Apocrypha.* 2 vols. Trans. R. Wilson. Philadelphia: Westminster, 1959.

Hilary of Poitiers (Hilaire de Poitiers). *Sur Matthieu (In Matthaeum I & II).* Ed. J. Doignon. SC 254, 258. Paris: Cerf, 1978–79.

Kamesar, A. *Jerome, Greek Scholarship, and the Hebrew Bible.* Oxford: Oxford University Press, 1993.

Kelly, J. N. D. *Jerome: His Life, Writings, and Controversies.* New York: Harper & Row, 1975.

Klijn, A. F. J., and G. J. Reinink. *Patristic Evidence for Jewish-Christian Sects.* Leiden: Brill, 1973.

Lardet, P. *L'Apologie de Jérôme contre Rufin: Un Commentaire.* Leiden: Brill, 1993.

Largent, A. *Saint Jerome.* Translated by Hester Davenport. With preface by George Tyrrell. London: Duckworth; New York: Benziger, 1900.

Layton, R. A. *Didymus the Blind and his Circle in Late-Antique Alexandria.* Urbana: University of Illinois Press, 2004.

———. "From 'Holy Passion' to Sinful Emotion: Jerome and the Doctrine of *Propassio.*" In P. M. Blowers, et al., eds. *Dominico Eloquio—In Lordly Eloquence: Essays on Patristic Exegesis in Honor of Robert Louis Wilken.* Grand Rapids: Eerdmans, 2002. Pp. 280–93.

Lienhard, J. "Origen and the Crisis of the Old Testament in the Early Church." *Pro Ecclesia* 9.3 (2000): 355–66.

Lightfoot, J. *The Apostolic Fathers*. 5 vols. Peabody, MA: Hendrickson, 1989.

Lubac, Henri de. *Medieval Exegesis*. Volume 1: *The Four Senses of Scripture*. Trans. M. Sebanc. Grand Rapids: Eerdmans, 1998. Originally published as *Exégèse médiéval, 1. Les quatre sens de l'écriture*, 1959.

———. *Medieval Exegesis*. Vol. 2 : *The Four Senses of Scripture*. Trans. E. M. Macierowski. Grand Rapids: Eerdmans, 2000. Originally published as *Exégèse médiéval, 2. Les quatre sens de l'écriture*, 1959.

———. *History and Spirit: The Understanding of Scripture according to Origen*. Trans. A. Nash. San Francisco: Ignatius, 2007. Originally published as *Histoire et esprit: L'Intelligence de l'Ecriture d'après Origène*. Editions Montaigne: Paris, 1950.

Madigan, Kevin. "*Christus Nesciens?* Was Christ Ignorant of the Day of Judgment? Arian and Orthodox Interpretation of Mark 13:32 in the Ancient Latin West." *Harvard Theological Review* 96.3 (2003): 255–78.

Malley, William J. *Hellenism and Christianity: The Conflict between Hellenic and Christian Wisdom in the* Contra Galilaeos *of Julian the Apostate and the* Contra Julianum *of St. Cyril of Alexandria*. Rome: Università gregoriana editrice, 1978.

Margerie, Bertrand de. *An Introduction to the History of Exegesis*. Volume 2: *The Latin Fathers*. Petersham, MA: St. Bede, 1995.

McGuckin, J., ed. *The Westminster Handbook to Origen*. Louisville: Westminster John Knox Press, 2004.

McHugh, John. *The Mother of Jesus in the New Testament*. Garden City: Doubleday, 1975.

Metzger, Bruce M. *A Textual Commentary on the Greek New Testament*. Stuttgart: United Bible Societies, 1971. Corrected edition, 1975.

Murphy, F. X. *Rufinus of Aquileia (345–411): His Life and Works*. Washington, DC: The Catholic University of America Press, 1945.

———, ed. *A Monument to Saint Jerome*. New York: Sheed & Ward, 1952.

———. "Saint Jerome." New Catholic Encyclopedia. 2d ed. Washington, DC. 7.756–59.

O'Connell, John P. *The Eschatology of Saint Jerome*. Dissertationes ad Lauream 16. Pontificia Facultas Theologica Seminarii Sanctae Mariae ad Lacum. Mundelein, Illinois, 1948.

Olin, J. "Erasmus and Saint Jerome: The Close Bond and its Significance." *Erasmus of Rotterdam Society Yearbook* 7 (1987): 33–53.

Plummer, A. *An Exegetical Commentary on the Gospel According to Matthew*. London: Robert Scott, 1911.

Quasten, J. *Patrology*. 4 vols. Utrecht-Antwerp: Spectrum, 1975.

Reese, A. "'So Outstanding an Athlete of Christ': Erasmus and the Significance of Jerome's Asceticism." *Erasmus of Rotterdam Society Yearbook* 18 (1998): 104–17.

Scheck, Thomas P. *Origen and the History of Justification: The Legacy of Origen's Commentary on Romans*. Notre Dame: University of Notre Dame Press, 2008.

Scheerin, D. "St. John the Baptist in the Lower World." *VC* 30 (1976): 1–22.

Souter, A. "Greek and Hebrew Words in Jerome's Commentary on St. Matthew's Gospel." *HTR* 28 (1935): 1–4.

———. "Notes on Incidental Gospel Quotations in Jerome's Commentary on St. Matthew's Gospel." *JTS* 42 (1941): 12–18.

Steinmann, Jean. *Saint Jerome and his Times.* Trans. R. Matthews. Notre Dame: Fides Publishers, 1959.

Sutcliffe, E. F. "Jerome." In *The Cambridge History of the Bible.* Volume 2: *The West from the Fathers to the Reformation.* Ed. G. W. H. Lampe. Cambridge: Cambridge University Press, 1969. Pp. 80–101.

Tracy, J. "Humanists Among the Scholastics: Erasmus, More, and Lefèvre d'Etaples on the Humanity of Christ." *Erasmus of Rotterdam Society Yearbook* 5 (1985): 30–51.

VanLandingham, Chris. *Judgment & Justification in Early Judaism and the Apostle Paul.* Peabody, MA: Hendrickson, 2006.

Vessey, M. "Jerome." In *Augustine through the Ages: An Encyclopedia.* Ed. A. D. Fitzgerald. Grand Rapids: Eerdmans, 1999. Pp. 460–62.

Weedman, Mark. *The Trinitarian Theology of Hilary of Poitiers.* Leiden: Brill, 2007.

INTRODUCTION

INTRODUCTION

Aureum flumen habet, locupletissimam bibliothecam habet quisquis unum habet Hieronymum. "It is a river of gold, a well-stocked library, that one acquires who possesses Jerome and nothing else."[1]

1. General Introduction

St. Jerome (347–420) is one of the four Doctors of the Latin Church, alongside St. Augustine (d. 430), St. Ambrose (d. 397), and Pope St. Gregory the Great (d. 604).[2] Much of his fame rests upon the important role he played in the translation of the Bible that became known in later centuries as the Latin Vulgate. Under the patronage of Pope Damasus (d. 384), Jerome systematically revised existing Latin versions of the four Gospels and the Psalter, though he did not touch the New Testament Epistles. Later in his life Jerome produced extensive translations of the Old Testament based directly on the Hebrew.[3] The resulting version of the Bible was destined to become a theological classic in the West. Jerome's dedication in mastering the original languages of Scripture would be an inspiration to later generations of scholars, especially during the Renaissance and Reformation.[4] Jerome was

1. Erasmus of Rotterdam (1466–1536), *Ep.* 396 (Allen 2.220). This letter forms the dedicatory epistle addressed to Archbishop William Warham in Erasmus's *Edition of St. Jerome* (1516). For an English translation of the prefatory documents, see Desiderius Erasmus, *Patristic Scholarship: The Edition of St. Jerome,* ed. J. Brady and J. Olin, CWE 61 (Toronto: University of Toronto Press, 1992).

2. This list was formally ratified by Pope Boniface VIII on September 20, 1295.

3. For a succinct account of Jerome's work on the Vulgate, see H. Sparks, "Jerome as Biblical Scholar," in *The Cambridge History of the Bible,* 1. *From the Beginnings to Jerome,* ed. P. Ackroyd and C. Evans (Cambridge, 1970), 510–41.

4. Cf. E. Rice, *Saint Jerome in the Renaissance* (Baltimore: Johns Hopkins, 1985).

certainly one of the most learned of the Latin Fathers, but he was not a bishop, nor did he take a synthetic view of theological questions, as did his contemporary Augustine, and for these reasons Augustine's theological legacy was far greater.[5] In contrast with Augustine, however, Jerome had mastered both the Greek and the Latin theological traditions, and he was deeply influenced by the literature from both streams. Among the Latin Church's scriptural commentators, Jerome is pre-eminent. His outstanding ecclesiastical learning led the Council of Trent to speak of him as "the greatest doctor in explaining the Sacred Scriptures."[6] In the seventeenth century, the learned Scripture scholar Richard Simon expressed the opinion that Jerome's commentaries were the most thorough and instructive of his works:

In his knowledge of Hebrew, Chaldean, Greek and Latin, Jerome possessed the necessary qualities for properly interpreting the Scriptures in a greater degree than all the other Fathers. Not only had he read and examined the Greek versions in Origen's "Hexapla," but he had also frequently conferred with the most erudite Jews of his day, and he rarely took any steps in his scriptural work without first consulting them. In addition to this he had read every author, both Greek and Latin, who had written upon the Bible before him, and finally, he was well versed in profane literature.[7]

Popes Benedict XV[8] and Pius XII[9] warmly commended Jerome's Scripture scholarship to Catholic scholars, though these exhortations were not universally received.[10] Yet Jerome's im-

---

5. J. P. O'Connell, *The Eschatology of St. Jerome* (Mundelein, IL: Pontificia Facultas Theologica Seminarii Sanctae Mariae ad Lacum, 1948), i, says: "[Jerome] was not a theologian but an exegete and a polemist. He has left us no methodical and comprehensive studies of theological questions."

6. *Doctor Maximus in Exponendis Sacris Scripturis;* cited by F. X. Murphy, "Saint Jerome," New Catholic Encyclopedia, 2d ed., 7.759.

7. *Critical History of the Old Testament* (1685), book 3, chap. 9, cited in A. Largent, *Saint Jerome,* trans. H. Davenport with preface by G. Tyrrell (London: Duckworth; New York: Benziger, 1900), 146.

8. *Spiritus Paraclitus* = Encyclical of Pope Benedict XV on St. Jerome, September 15, 1920 (*Acta Apostolicae Sedis* 12:385–420).

9. *Divino afflante Spiritu* (Sept. 30, 1943). Note that this date is St. Jerome's Feast Day.

10. For example, the American Scripture scholar Raymond E. Brown, "The Problems of the *Sensus Plenior,*" *Ephemerides Theologicae Lovanienses* 43 (1967):

portance endures, since, as Murphy has observed, Jerome is "an indispensable witness to the mind of the Church in dealing with the Word of God."[11]

2. Jerome's Life and Works

Jerome was probably born in 347.[12] He names his hometown as Stridon,[13] a village in the western Balkans under northern Italian influence. It was near Emona,[14] between the Roman provinces of Dalmatia and Pannonia. Although his parents were Christians,[15] he was not baptized as an infant, in keeping with a common custom of the time.[16] At the age of twelve he was sent to Rome to complete his literary studies. For the next eight years he acquired a thorough education in grammar, the humanities, rhetoric, and dialectics. In Rome Jerome studied under Aelius Donatus, who was the most famous teacher of literature of the period.[17] Jerome became a passionate enthusiast for Latin literature and Ciceronian eloquence and honed his skills

---

463, wrote: "I think we must recognize that the exegetical method of the Fathers is irrelevant to the study of the Bible today."

11. F. X. Murphy, "Saint Jerome," New Catholic Encyclopedia, 2d ed., 7.759.

12. There is still scholarly disagreement about this date. In 1945 F. X. Murphy, *Rufinus of Aquileia* (Washington, DC: The Catholic University of America Press, 1945), 2, declared that the result of Cavallera's study on Jerome was that it is all but certain now that Jerome was born in 347. And yet J. N. D. Kelly, *Jerome: His Life, Writings, and Controversies* (New York: Harper & Row, 1975), 1 and 337–39, dates Jerome's birth sixteen years earlier, in 331. Kelly's dating is based on the testimony of Prosper of Aquitaine (390–455), who knew Jerome personally and recorded that he died at the age of ninety-one. Very recently, Megan Hale Williams, *The Monk and the Book* (Chicago: University of Chicago Press, 2006), 268, argues for the later date.

13. *Vir. ill.* 135; cf. *Ep.* 66.14. The exact location of Stridon is not known.

14. Emona is present-day Ljubljana/Laibach in Slovenia.

15. J. Gribomont, in J. Quasten, *Patrology*, 4.195, suggests that Jerome's parents were even "pious" Christians, on the evidence that Jerome's brother and sister followed him into monastic life.

16. Rufinus of Aquileia, Basil the Great, Gregory Nazianzus, Ambrose, John Chrysostom, and Augustine, all born of Christian parents, were baptized as adult believers. F. X. Murphy, *Rufinus of Aquileia*, 6, describes this as "a sad, if not cynical, concession of the day to the follies of youth."

17. Jerome writes in his *Chronicle* for the seventeenth year of Constantius

as a young scholar by transcribing a great number of Latin authors for his personal library. Jerome's own letters, written in a pure and vigorous Latin, rank alongside the epistolary collections of Cicero, Seneca, and Pliny the Younger as the most celebrated in Latin literature.[18] Jerome also learned the rudiments of Greek, though his eventual mastery of the Greek language would only be attained later, after living in the East for many years.

In Rome, it is probable that Jerome allowed himself some experience of the *dolce vita*, "since he was not yet baptized."[19] Yet he did not break off his ties with his Christian friends with whom he was accustomed to visit on Sundays the tombs of the apostles and martyrs.[20] At the age of eighteen or nineteen, Jerome experienced a deeper religious conversion and asked for baptism, which he received in Lent 367, possibly from Pope Liberius. Later that year he traveled to Gaul, where, in Trier, he made a decision to pursue the monastic life. Here he made copies of some works by Hilary of Poitiers (d. 368), for example, *De synodis* and some Scripture commentaries, including one on Matthew's Gospel that is cited in the preface of the present work. Jerome moved to Aquileia in northeastern Italy, where he studied theology and lived as an ascetic for seven years. In 374 he began living as a hermit in the desert of Chalcis, a region located slightly east of Syrian Antioch. During this period Jerome was exposed to controversy about some heretical views on the Trinity. His *Ep.* 15 to Pope Damasus describes these Eastern

---

(354): "Victorinus the teacher of rhetoric and Donatus the grammarian, my teacher, are considered illustrious in Rome." Cited from R. Helm (Leipzig, 1913), 239, in F. X. Murphy, *Rufinus of Aquileia*, 8, n. 35. Aelius Donatus's two treatises on Latin grammar dominated European learning until the twelfth century. He also wrote commentaries on Terence and Virgil. See G. Conte, *Latin Literature: A History* (Baltimore: The Johns Hopkins University Press, 1999), 627–28.

18. Cf. F. Wright, trans., *Select Letters of St. Jerome*, LCL 262 (Cambridge, MA: Harvard University Press, 1991), xiii. St. Teresa of Avila (1515–1582) experienced her religious conversion through reading St. Jerome's letters. St. Francis de Sales commended them in his *Introduction to the Devout Life*.

19. J. Gribomont, in J. Quasten, *Patrology*, 4.213.

20. *In Hiez.* 12.244–53.

controversies, which he never seems to have attempted to understand fully.[21] He also made the acquaintance of a converted Jew named Baranina, who introduced him to the Hebrew language. Jerome was the first Latin Christian to attempt to learn the original languages of the OT and would eventually master both Hebrew and Aramaic (Chaldean). A famous incident in his life occurred at Chalcis. Jerome dreamed that he stood before the judgment seat of Christ. In the vision he was accused of being a Ciceronian rather than a Christian and was ordered to be flogged. In the midst of the scourging, he begged Christ for mercy and vowed never to touch pagan literature again. Jerome recounts the experience in *Ep.* 22.30 to Eustochium. The story would become a reference point for later theorists of Christian literary culture.[22]

Jerome went to Antioch in 379 and was ordained a priest by Bishop Paulinus. In Antioch he wrote his first controversial work, *The Dialogue against the Luciferians.* He also repeatedly heard lectures there from Apollinaris of Laodicea, the son of Apollinaris the Elder and an Alexandrian grammarian, who had mastered Greek literature and philosophy and had written an important apologetic work in thirty books, *Against Porphyry.* In *Ep.* 84.3, Jerome said that he had learned biblical interpretation from Apollinaris, though he distanced himself from Apollinaris's heterodox understanding of the Incarnation. Certainly the influence of "Alexandrian" methods of exegesis would influence Jerome in a decisive way. Yet the fact that Jerome learned *Alexandrian* methods of biblical interpretation in *Antioch,* a city famous for producing scholars who preferred a more literal approach to the Scriptures, suggests that traditional scholarly cari-

---

21. Cf. T. Lawler, "Jerome's First Letter to Damasus (ep. 15)," in *Kyriakon,* Festschrift J. Quasten II (Münster, 1970), 548–52.

22. Cf. M. Vessey, "Jerome," in *Augustine through the Ages: An Encyclopedia,* ed. A. D. Fitzgerald (Grand Rapids: Eerdmans, 1999), 460. On the (slim) evidence that Jerome's writings from the 370s "know nothing of this incident," Hale Williams, *The Monk and the Book,* 26–27, dismisses Jerome's account of his dream as probably the saint's own fabrication. She adds: "At best, it may be a literary elaboration of an incident that had originally borne none of the heavy freight of meaning it later acquired."

catures that posit a radical dichotomy between the Antiochene and Alexandrian schools of exegesis stand in need of revision.[23] From Antioch Jerome went to Constantinople, where he became a pupil of Gregory Nazianzus (d. 389), who encouraged Jerome to study Origen's scriptural exegesis. Jerome did so and would draw upon and indeed appropriate Origen's exegesis for the rest of his life. More than that, Jerome took Origen's comprehensive pattern of life, scholarship, and asceticism as a model for his own. Jerome's fluency in Greek is proven by the fact that at this time he undertook a translation of Origen's *Homilies on Jeremiah, on Ezekiel,* and *on Isaiah.* He also translated Eusebius's *Chronicle* of world history.

The Latin Vulgate

In 382 Jerome was drawn back to Rome where, at the invitation of Pope Damasus, he undertook a revision of the Old Latin versions of the Psalms and the Gospels based on the Greek text.[24] For the OT translations from the Hebrew and Aramaic that were carried out later in Bethlehem, Jerome's stated aim was that of "restoring" the text to its original purity. This may be too high a claim, since the Hebrew exemplars he used were not originals.[25] In any case, Jerome based his OT translations not on the LXX, which was itself a translation, but on the Hebrew exemplars. Jerome's "improved" version of the Bible provoked howls of indignation from many churchmen, who preferred the

23. Cf. K. Froehlich, *Biblical Interpretation in the Early Church* (Philadelphia: Fortress, 1984), 20–21.

24. In his Preface to the Gospels, Jerome addresses Damasus as "the most blessed pope" (*beatissimo papae*) and says that the Pope is compelling (*cogis*) him to do this task (PL 29: 525; NPNF, Second Series, 6.487–88). M. Vessey, "Jerome," 460, depicts Jerome as the instigator of the whole project: "At Rome, under Pope Damasus (d. 384), [Jerome] . . . announced a revision of the Latin New Testament for which he claimed a papal commission." Hale Williams, *The Monk and the Book,* 50–52, amasses a large amount of evidence that confirms the intimate and subservient nature of Jerome's relation to Pope Damasus.

25. The LXX was made from a much older, and at times much purer, Hebrew text than the one in use at the end of the 4th century. Modern textual critics hold the LXX in much higher esteem than did Jerome. For an excellent discussion, see Hale Williams, *The Monk and the Book,* 67–73.

traditional Old Latin readings.[26] This is precisely what Jerome predicted would happen. The Old Latin OT that Jerome's version threatened to replace was a translation of the Septuagint (LXX), which was the Greek translation of the OT that had been produced originally in Alexandria beginning in the third century B.C. The LXX version had been used by the apostles themselves and their successors and was widely believed to be a divinely inspired translation.[27] To base his new Latin translation on "the Hebrew truth," as Jerome did, was interpreted by Jerome's critics as an attack on the Bible that was in use in the Christian liturgies. Also under criticism was Jerome's apparent rejection of the Alexandrian canon of the OT. The books that had been added in the Alexandrian canon, that is, the deutero-canonicals, such as Wisdom, Tobit, Sirach, Judith, Maccabees, Additions to Daniel and Esther, and Baruch, had been in use in the Christian churches for centuries and contained some of the most beloved stories in the OT. Moreover, some of these works, such as Sirach, Maccabees, and Tobit, had Hebrew or Aramaic exemplars. Yet, taking the judgments of contemporary Jews as his authority and criterion for canonicity, Jerome ridiculed the belief that these books were divinely inspired and at times suggested that they were to be excluded from the canon of Scripture.[28]

On the question of the Western canon, the Catholic Church endorsed the views of Jerome's critics (Augustine, Rufinus) and adopted the Alexandrian (Septuagint) canon. In Jerome's defense it can be said that his motive in favoring the Hebrew canon of the OT was at least in part a missionary one: He believed that evangelization of the Jews would be thwarted if Christians cited Scriptures that the contemporary Jews did not accept as

---

26. Rufinus attacked Jerome's efforts in *Apology* 2.32–35. Augustine's concerns are expressed in *Epp.* 28, 71, 82, but his final verdict and a generous tribute to Jerome are found in *De civitate Dei* 18.43. Jerome defended his project against Rufinus in *Apology* 2.34–35 and against Augustine in *Ep.* 75.

27. Cf. Irenaeus, *Adv. haer.* 3.21.3; cited by Eusebius in *HE* 5.8; Augustine, *De civitate Dei* 15.23. The original story about the inspiration of the LXX is found in Pseudo-Aristeas.

28. For a good discussion, see Hale Williams, *The Monk and the Book,* 81–95.

authoritative.[29] Moreover, Jerome's theory about the authority of the Hebrew canon was not consistent with his actual practice. In his correspondence he continued to cite as Scripture texts from the Septuagint canon.[30]

While Jerome was secretary and adviser to Pope Damasus,[31] he wrote an important work of controversial theology, *Against Helvidius,* in which he defended the Church's belief in Mary's perpetual virginity.[32] Ten years later, he also wrote *Against Jovinian,* which was aimed to refute Jovinian's theses, which were as follows: (a) that all states of life—virginity, widowhood, and marriage—were of equal merit; (b) that a perfect Christian life was possible without fasting, abstinence, or other ascetical practices; and (c) that all the saints will enjoy equal remuneration in heaven.

Jerome was a zealous apostle of the ascetic life. The term "asceticism" derives from the Greek word for "training."[33] Although the term is Greek, the reality of a religiously-motivated asceticism is embedded in the Bible and Jewish tradition. To say nothing of the Hebrew prophets[34] and the early Church,[35] the Jewish Essenes of the first century B.C., who produced the Dead

29. Cf. *Pref. in Ios.; Pref. in Is.; Pref. in Psalm.; Adv. Rufin.* 3.25. Origen made a similar argument in his *Letter to Africanus,* not in order to dismiss the Alexandrian canon, but to justify his text-critical project, *The Hexapla.*

30. For discussions of Jerome's view of the canon, see D. Brown, *Vir Trilinguis: A Study in the Biblical Exegesis of Saint Jerome* (Kampen: Kok Pharos Publishing House, 1992), 62–86; P. Skehan, "St. Jerome and the Canon of the Holy Scriptures," in F. X. Murphy, ed., *A Monument to Saint Jerome* (New York: Sheed & Ward, 1952), 257–87; E. F. Sutcliffe, "Jerome," in *The Cambridge History of the Bible,* 2: *The West from the Fathers to the Reformation* (Cambridge: Cambridge University Press, 1969), 80–101.

31. This function explains why Jerome is often depicted in art with a red cardinal's hat (sometimes hanging on the wall). In actual fact, the office of cardinal in its modern sense did not develop until centuries after Jerome's life. The artistic depiction of Jerome in his monastic cell with a lion at his feet is a legend based on his time in the desert.

32. M. Vessey, "Jerome," 460, seems to miss the main point of this work when he depicts it as a continuation of Jerome's "passionate campaign for ascetic values."

33. That is, *askēsis.*

34. Cf. Ex 34.28; 1 Kgs 19.8.

35. Cf. Acts 4.32 and 18.18; 1 Cor 9.27.

Sea Scrolls, practiced communal ownership of property, voluntary celibacy, religious fasting and prayer, withdrawn communal life, and disciplined study of Scripture.[36] Jerome's view of the ascetic life advocated a link between authentic Christian spirituality and an appropriate measure of voluntary self-denial. The chief tenet of asceticism was to place God ahead of the things of this world. Jerome was inspired in particular by the example of John the Baptist, Jesus, and the apostles.[37] Consequently he embraced a life characterized by self-control, poverty, fasting, and celibacy. For Jerome the Christian life was a rigorous spiritual contest or warfare against "the world, the flesh, and the devil."[38] His theological outlook emphasized that the Christian's heavenly rewards depend on one's divinely enabled earthly merits and the achievement of spiritual victory over the devil. Such ideals made Jerome, on the one hand, a hero and patron of monasticism in subsequent centuries,[39] and, conversely, a figure who was despised by the Protestant Reformers.[40]

During his sojourn in Rome, Jerome translated Origen's *Homilies on the Song of Songs,* which he dedicated to Pope Damasus. He then became embroiled in controversy with his brother monks and priests as a result of the insulting and defamatory style of his satirical writings. The situation became so serious that after Damasus's death in December 384, an official ecclesiastical inquiry was conducted and Jerome was condemned in

36. Cf. Josephus, *BJ* 7.

37. Cf. Mk 1.13; Mt 3.4; 4.2; 5.28; 8.20; 19.11–12, 21, 23–30; Lk 8.3; 9.58–62; 16.13; Acts 3.6; 4.32. See also John Chrysostom, Hom. 15 on Acts.

38. Cf. 1 Cor 9.24–27; 2 Cor 10.3–6; Eph 6.10–20; Jas 4.4.

39. Interestingly, it was precisely Jerome's form and standards of asceticism that the Augustinian priest Erasmus of Rotterdam found worthy of retrieval and emulation in the 16th century. These ideals included the practice of corporal chastisements for past sins, voluntary celibacy and chastity, fasting, zeal for sacred study, self-denial, and love of God and neighbor. See A. Reese, "'So Outstanding an Athlete of Christ': Erasmus and the Significance of Jerome's Asceticism," *Erasmus of Rotterdam Society Yearbook* 18 (1998): 104–17.

40. For example, Martin Luther wrote: "Jerome can be read for the sake of history, but he has nothing at all to say about faith and the teaching of true religion." LW 54:33f. = WA, Tischreden 1: p. 106, no. 252. See T. Scheck, *Origen and the History of Justification: The Legacy of Origen's Commentary on Romans* (Notre Dame: University of Notre Dame Press, 2008), 176–77, 185.

a formal judgment that was delivered orally. Thus in 385 the atmosphere in Rome had become so hostile toward Jerome that he was requested to leave the city altogether.[41] After traveling to Palestine and visiting the holy sites, Jerome made a brief visit to Egypt, where he stayed for thirty days with Didymus the Blind (d. 398). Soon he would publish his own translation of Didymus's *Treatise on the Holy Spirit*.[42] In 385 Jerome settled in Bethlehem, where he set up a monastery for men. He was within range of Caesarea and made trips there to consult its magnificent library, which included a copy of Origen's *Hexapla*, a work Jerome would use to assist him in his biblical translations. The period during which Jerome lived in Bethlehem until his death in 419/420 was very productive. In 393 he wrote a literary and biographical survey of Christian writers, *De viris illustribus*, "On Famous Men." This pioneering work of patrology was modeled on Suetonius's *Lives* and to this day is indispensable for much of our knowledge of the literature of the Church's early centuries. It also reveals Jerome's personal likes and dislikes (compare his preference for the rigid and ascetic Tertullian with his disparagement of Ambrose). Also during the Bethlehem years, Jerome undertook his great translation of the OT from Hebrew (390–406), and the writing of his biblical commentaries.[43] He also continued his famous epistolary exchanges, and later combated the Pelagian heresy.

---

41. Cf. J. N. D. Kelly, *Jerome: His Life, Writings and Controversies*, 113.

42. Jerome's motive for undertaking this translation was base: He aimed to show Latin readers that Ambrose, whom he intensely disliked, had plagiarized much of his own book on the Holy Spirit from Didymus. Jerome's motive in translating Origen's *Homilies on Luke* was also to embarrass Ambrose. Cf. J. N. D. Kelly, *Jerome: His Life, Writings and Controversies*, 143.

43. Hale Williams, *The Monk and the Book*, 66, rightly calls Jerome's commentaries on the Hebrew prophets his greatest achievement as a biblical scholar. "No other patristic writer, either in Greek or in Latin, came close to equaling the comprehensiveness of Jerome's exegesis of the Prophets." They comprise a major focus of Hale Williams' fine study. Similarly, Erasmus of Rotterdam, *Ep.* 1334, described them as Jerome's greatest works. Because these works are still buried in Latin, they are, unfortunately, largely unknown today.

3. The Origenist Controversies

The various controversies over Origenism occurred during this latter period of Jerome's life.[44] The first Origenist controversy was instigated by Epiphanius (d. 403), the impetuous bishop of Salamis in Cyprus and heresiologist. In 393 Epiphanius initiated a campaign dedicated to securing a formal denunciation of Origen as a heretic. When his monk Atarbius presented himself at Jerome's and Rufinus's monasteries, in Bethlehem and on the Mount of Olives respectively, demanding their signatures on the formal abjuration of Origen, Jerome signed his name on the document, whereas Rufinus threatened to drive off Epiphanius's satellite by violence if need be. This enraged Jerome against both Rufinus and Bishop John of Jerusalem, who supported his priest Rufinus. Jerome and Epiphanius falsely accused John and Rufinus of adhering to Origen's dubious doctrines. In reality, Rufinus and John were following the pattern set by Basil, Gregory Nazianzus, and Athanasius in seeing fit to use Origen's writings for the spiritual benefits and the tremendous advantages they possessed for the theologian, while distinguishing carefully between the tenable and untenable among Origen's positions. According to this irenic approach, Origen's errors were attributed to the vastness of his pioneering effort rather than to any maliciousness or heretical obstinacy.

A public conflict ensued in Jerusalem in the Church of the Resurrection between the bishops John and Epiphanius. When John remained steadfast in his refusal to submit to Epiphanius's campaign, Epiphanius denounced him as a heretic and forcibly ordained Paulinian, Jerome's younger brother, a priest in John's diocese. (Epiphanius would later replicate this uncanonical procedure in John Chrysostom's diocese and play a key role, along with Bishop Theophilus of Alexandria, in having Chrysostom, Patriarch of Constantinople, deposed and exiled.)

44. See the still indispensable historical study by F. X. Murphy, *Rufinus of Aquileia,* 59–157, and E. Clark, *The Origenist Controversy: The Cultural Construction of an Early Christian Debate* (Princeton: Princeton University Press, 1992).

Epiphanius's pretext was that Jerome's monks could not continue receiving Communion from priests whose bishop (John of Jerusalem) was a heretic. In response, John of Jerusalem barred Jerome's and Paula's religious from the Basilica of the Nativity. Eventually, through the mediating efforts of Paulinian, Jerome's brother, and through Melania's influence, at the Easter Mass in 397 in the Church of the Resurrection, a temporary reconciliation occurred between Jerome, Rufinus, and John of Jerusalem.[45] Unfortunately, another, even more embittered, Origenist controversy broke out in late 398 as a consequence of Rufinus's translation of Origen's work, *Peri Archōn*. In this later controversy, Jerome became the collaborator of the unscrupulous bishop Theophilus of Alexandria. In the service of this man, Jerome endeavored to defame John Chrysostom and Rufinus of Aquileia with charges of heresy. In the case of Rufinus, Jerome's attacks were largely effective in damaging Rufinus's reputation in the Latin Church in subsequent centuries. This obtained in spite of the fact that Augustine refused to take sides with Jerome in the dispute and lamented the way in which these fruitless quarrels shattered friendships between orthodox churchmen.[46]

The puzzling ambiguity of the entire controversy over "Origenism" in the West is revealed by the fact that Rufinus, with the approval of his bishop, continued to translate Origen's works into Latin and publish these translations in Rome during and immediately after the official condemnation of "Origenism" in 401.[47]

---

45. Cf. F. X. Murphy, *Rufinus of Aquileia*, 78.

46. Cf. Augustine, *Ep.* 73 to Jerome (404 A.D.): "Where is the friend who may not be feared as possibly a future enemy, if the breach that we deplore could arise between Jerome and Rufinus? Oh, sad and pitiable is our portion!" NPNF, First Series, 1.331. Cf. Augustine, *Ep.* 82.1.

47. In 400, Theophilus, bishop of Alexandria, condemned Origenism at a council held at Alexandria. The imperial authority confirmed the condemnation and proscribed Origen's works. Theophilus then sent a letter to Pope Anastasius in Rome, detailing these proceedings. Anastasius issued a condemnation of the propositions contained in Theophilus's document along with other propositions of Origen that were contrary to the Catholic faith. He communicated these decisions to Simplician, Bishop of Milan. Eusebius of Cremona served as the messenger between the Pope and the Bishop of Milan. Cf. F. X. Murphy, *Rufinus of Aquileia*, 128–29.

This activity did not provoke a word of protest.[48] Von Campen-hausen claimed that there was hardly any real excuse for Jerome's agitation over the potential rise of "Origenism" in the West. For it was just in the West, which Jerome tried to stir up against Origen, that there was not the slightest ecclesiastical cause for this. "It was only his own interests, by no means unselfish, his private embarrassments, entanglements, and whims which forced him, almost against his will, to this public polemic and heresy-hunt. Jerome cannot be excused in this case."[49] Likewise, F. X. Murphy judged that the controversy between Jerome and Rufinus was needless, since the two men agreed on their attitude toward Origen.[50] I concur with this assessment and would only add that if Jerome indeed exceeded the limits of moderation in his polemical zeal for orthodoxy during these controversies, this does not obscure his brilliance as a translator, theologian, and Scripture scholar.[51]

4. Jerome's *Commentary on Matthew*

Date and Dedicatee

Jerome's *Commentary on Matthew* was written in Bethlehem in March 398.[52] In terms of the Origenist controversies, it is thus positioned about one year after the resolution of the first controversy and a few months before the outbreak of a subsequent phase of the controversy, which was occasioned by Rufinus's translation of Origen's *Peri Archōn* in late 398. Jerome's dedi-

---

48. Cf. J. N. D. Kelly, *Jerome: His Life, Writings and Controversies*, 256. For a similar assessment, see C. Hammond, "The Last Ten Years of Rufinus' Life and the Date of His Move South from Aquileia," *JTS* 28 (1977): 372–429.

49. *The Fathers of the Church* (Peabody, MA: Hendrickson, 2000), 178–79.

50. *Rufinus of Aquileia*, 110.

51. The story is told of a Renaissance pope, looking at Jerome's portrait, in which the saint is holding a stone with which to strike his own breast as a sign of his voluntary penance. The pope said it was well for Jerome that he held his stone, for without this he could scarcely be considered a saint. Cf. D. Farmer, *The Oxford Dictionary of Saints,* Third Edition (Oxford: Oxford University Press, 1992), 253.

52. Cf. J. Quasten, *Patrology,* 4.235. Jerome refers to it in *Ep.* 73.10 to Evangelus (398).

catee was Eusebius of Cremona,[53] a priest-friend of Jerome to whom he also dedicated his *Commentary on Jeremiah*. During the first Origenist controversy, Jerome had translated for this same individual, unschooled in Greek, Epiphanius's letter of self-vindication against John of Jerusalem. Eusebius was also the messenger of Pope Anastasius who communicated to Bishop Simplician of Milan the Roman approval of the condemnation of Origenism by the Synod of Alexandria.

Jerome reports in the preface that Eusebius was about to set sail for Italy. He requested from Jerome an historical commentary on the Gospel of Matthew to provide him reading material and spiritual sustenance for the voyage. Jerome wrote the work in haste and completed it within two weeks. Upon his arrival in Rome, Eusebius would become a principal instigator of another Origenist controversy, when in late 398 he purloined a draft copy of Rufinus's translation of Origen's *Peri Archōn* and stirred up charges against Rufinus based on it.[54] From Italy Eusebius remained in contact with Jerome for another twenty years. He later sent Jerome books related to the Pelagian controversy.[55]

General Observations

Jerome dictated his *Commentary on Matthew* over the course of two weeks. The work shows signs of hasty composition, such as, at times, extreme brevity and numerous inaccurate citations from the Bible and Josephus. Jerome's commentary is not very extensive. He translates the text of Matthew's Gospel in the lemma and then paraphrases or explains the words with brief glosses and commentary notes. Souter has made a study of the use of the text of Matthew's Gospel in Jerome's commentary. The most interesting result is the observation that this text is not identical with the Vulgate revision made by Jerome himself (and critically edited by Wordsworth and White). Souter reports that of 104

---

53. Cremona is located in northern Italy in Lombardy on the Po, east southeast of Milan.

54. Rufinus describes this in *Apology* 1.19–20. See the letter of Pammachius and Oceanus to Jerome, which appears in Jerome, *Ep.* 83. Cf. F. X. Murphy, *Rufinus of Aquileia*, 97–98.

55. See Jerome's *Ep.* 143 to Alypius and Augustine; *Prologue to Commentary on Jeremiah*.

incidental quotations, only 33 harmonize with the Vulgate text while the other 71 are definitely different. The situation is the same with respect to Jerome's use of the other Gospels. Souter draws the following conclusion: "From all this it is clear that Jerome had no particular respect for his own revision . . . even when he was writing a commentary on a Gospel."[56]

In his explanation of Matthew's text, Jerome occasionally relies on Josephus, Origen, or Eusebius for information about geographical or historical details, but he also shows evidence of a personal knowledge of the biblical sources, of the topography of Palestine, and of current traditions, both Jewish and Christian. In an influential article, G. Bardy argued that Jerome took from Origen all of what he claimed to know firsthand from the Jews.[57] Hale Williams has faulted Bardy for analyzing a very limited number of instances of Jerome's use of Jewish interpretation. Sometimes Bardy distorts the evidence by neglecting to notice the way Jerome adds important details to the Jewish traditions presented by Origen, which suggests that he had independent access to the Jewish materials.[58] Kamesar's recent study confirms that Jerome's very real knowledge of Jewish textual and historical scholarship formed the backbone of his own Scripture scholarship.[59]

Jerome examines the details in the text that seem interesting to him in themselves, or for what he read about them in his sources, or for what he knew about them from personal experience or hearsay. He passes over many other details and sometimes expresses regret that he does not have time to develop his interpretations further. When he does expand his notes and

56. A. Souter, "Notes on Incidental Gospel Quotations," *JTS* 42 (1941): 13. It appears to me that Souter's research has important implications for later theological controversies. For example, when Erasmus of Rotterdam in 1516 published a fresh Latin translation of the Greek NT, he was attacked by conservative theologians for diverging from "Jerome's Vulgate." It appears that Jerome himself did not hesitate to diverge from his own Vulgate readings.

57. G. Bardy, "Jérôme et ses maîtres hébreux," *Revue Bénédictine* 46 (1934): 145–64. J. Gribomont follows this judgment in J. Quasten, *Patrology*, 4.235.

58. Hale Williams, *The Monk and the Book*, 227–28.

59. A. Kamesar, *Jerome, Greek Scholarship, and the Hebrew Bible* (Oxford: Oxford University Press, 1993), 193–95.

bring in multiple interpretations for a single biblical passage, his explanations remain "streamlined and concise."[60] In spite of the brevity of Jerome's historical exposition, the commentary is an eminent work.[61] As Simonetti has observed, the distinguishing feature of Jerome's exegesis is his ability to balance the requirements of both literal and spiritual interpretation: "Despite the speed of composition and the resulting disconnected and rhapsodic nature of many interpretations, he has on the whole succeeded in expressing his exegetical message, although perhaps not at its best."[62] Jerome's commentary contains some memorable glosses, such as his paraphrase of the response of Jesus to John at the Lord's baptism: "You baptize me in water, in order that I might baptize you for my sake in your blood" (3.15). Even scholars who generally think that Jerome has little to offer modern exegesis have expressed admiration of his eloquent explanation of the parable of the mustard seed (Mt 13.31–32).[63] While it is to be regretted that Jerome did not write at greater length on Matthew's Gospel, what he has set down is dense, Spirit-filled exegesis that draws on all canonical Scripture and is governed by the Church's Trinitarian Rule of Faith.

Jerome is quite aware of the verbal differences between the four Gospels, but he unhesitatingly affirms the truthfulness, inerrancy, reconcilability, and historicity of them all.[64] Jerome sees

---

60. M. Simonetti, *Matthew 1a* (ACC), xlv.

61. Two recent patristic scholars render a different judgment. C. Moreschini and E. Norelli, *Early Christian Greek and Latin Literature: A Literary History*, volume 2: *From the Council of Nicea to the Beginning of the Medieval Period* (Peabody, MA: Hendrickson, 2005), 313, write of Jerome's commentary: "This work is likewise of no great importance: it was written in haste in little over a month [*sic*] and without any depth; even the rather plain style reflects the haste." The error in the quotation proves that these scholars are not really familiar with the work. These same scholars, vol. 2, p. 150, likewise say that John Chrysostom's exegetical homilies on Romans "show little theological depth."

62. *Matthew 1a* (ACC), xlv.

63. Cf. J. Steinmann, *Hieronymus: Ausleger der Bibel. Weg und Werk eines Kirchenvaters* (Leipzig: St. Benno, 1958), 247.

64. Cf. pref (2); 1.1; 1.4ff.; 1.16; 2.5; 3.3; 12.40; 13.35; 17.1; 21.4f.; 23.35f.; 26.8–9; 27.9f.; 27.32; 27.44. Jerome's affirmation follows from his belief in the divine authorship of Scripture. Cf. L. Schade, *Die Inspirationslehre des Heiligen Hieronymus* (Freiburg: Herder, 1910), 48–83.

no reason to deny that the Gospel accounts are firmly rooted in reliable tradition. Indeed, he asserts that it is precisely the concern for writing historical truth (*historiae veritas*) that distinguishes the canonical Gospels from the heretical ones (Pref. 1). Jerome believes that both internal and external evidence points to the first Gospel being written by the apostle Matthew, a former tax-collector, who is also named Levi. Jerome claims that Matthew "published a Gospel in Judea in the Hebrew language, chiefly for the sake of those from the Jews who had believed in Jesus and who were by no means observing the shadow of the Law, since the truth of the Gospel had succeeded it." In *Vir. ill.* 3 Jerome adds that afterwards Matthew's Gospel was translated into Greek, but no one knows by whom. Jerome's source here is Eusebius (*HE* 3.24, 39; 5.8; 6.25), who in turn based his remarks on ancient tradition recorded by Irenaeus, who received his information orally from disciples of the apostles. A strong case for Matthean authorship can still be made. In a very recent commentary on the Greek text of Matthew, J. Nolland dates the composition of the Gospel to the late 60s, which he describes as "well within the life span of the eyewitnesses and of many apostolic figures."[65] Gundry dates the Gospel to the same decade and identifies the author as the apostle Matthew, as does R. T. France.[66]

5. Sources of Jerome's Exposition: Origen

In the Preface, Jerome cites the works he has read and from which he has excerpted. Among the Greek writers he names Origen, Theophilus of Antioch, Hippolytus, Theodore of Heraclea, Apollinaris of Laodicea, and Didymus of Alexandria. Among the Latins he cites the works of Hilary, Victorinus, and Fortunatianus. Of these works, the only ones that have survived are the

65. *The Gospel of Matthew: A Commentary on the Greek Text* (Grand Rapids: Eerdmans, 2005), 4.

66. Cf. R. Gundry, *Matthew: A Commentary on his Literary and Theological Art* (Grand Rapids: Eerdmans, 1982), 599–622; R. T. France, *The Gospel of Matthew* (Grand Rapids: Eerdmans, 2007), 15, 19. See also L. Morris, *The Gospel According to Matthew* (Grand Rapids: Eerdmans, 1992), 12–15.

commentary of Hilary and a part of that of Origen.[67] It appears that Jerome's most important source was Origen.[68]

Among the Greek Fathers, Origen (185–254) wrote the first systematic commentary on Matthew in the 240s. Origen's monumental work enhanced the status of the first Gospel, which was already very high, and contributed to ensuring its pre-eminence.[69] Of the twenty-five books of Origen's *Commentary on Matthew,* eight survive in Greek (books 10–17), which comment on Mt 13.36–22.33. More of the work survived in an anonymous Latin translation of the late fifth or early sixth century.[70] Jerome's work, with its extensive excerpts from Origen throughout, thus provides us access to many of Origen's no-longer-extant interpretations. For the most part Jerome appropriates Origen positively. He values him highly as both a literal and a spiritual interpreter of Scripture and essentially sets forth Origen's exegesis as his own. He integrates the prominent Origenian theme of the divine goodness, that is, the view that the God of the OT is good and gracious and is the same as the God of the NT, in opposition to the claims of the Gnostics.[71] Moreover, Jerome imitates Origen's ability to link up parts of Scripture and to trace NT word usage to its sources in the OT.

On the other hand, a comparison of Jerome's *Commentary on Matthew* (398) with his earlier *Commentary on Ephesians* (386), reveals that Jerome's work on Matthew exhibits a more open hostility toward some of Origen's interpretations and speculations. In the earlier work on Ephesians, Jerome had incautiously transmitted many of Origen's controversial opinions as his own, without a word of reproach. This left him exposed to the criticism of being hypocritical in his subsequent denunciation

---

67. J. Quasten, *Patrology,* 4.235.

68. M. Simonetti, *Matthew 1a* (ACC), xliv, states that Hilary seems to have been little used by Jerome, but that the surviving fragments of Theodore and Apollinaris indicate points of contact with Jerome's commentary.

69. Cf. E. Massaux, *The Influence of the Gospel of Saint Matthew on Christian Literature before Saint Irenaeus* (Macon: Mercer University Press, 1990).

70. For nice summaries of Origen's work on Matthew, see M. Simonetti, *Matthew 1a* (ACC), xlii–xliii; J. McGuckin, ed., *The Westminster Handbook to Origen* (Louisville: Westminster John Knox Press, 2004), 30.

71. Cf. 5.1; 10.1; 10.40; 11.30; 13.1–2; 17.7.

of Origen. Rufinus's *Apology* (400) aimed to demonstrate that Jerome expressed or implied approval of all the material he had adopted from Origen in the *Commentary on Ephesians*. Rufinus produced seventeen passages in succession that showed that Jerome had not dissociated himself from the very points of doctrine that he later denounced as heresy.[72] Rufinus also observed that whereas Origen had put forward his speculations cautiously and hesitantly, Jerome, in contrast, had repeated these things abruptly and decisively.[73] Rufinus's intention was not to deny or defend Origen's errors or even to accuse Jerome of heresy. Rather, it was to expose Jerome's vacillation and to demonstrate that Jerome's accusations against Rufinus would also land on Jerome himself. For Jerome, who was now accusing Rufinus of "spreading Origen's blasphemies throughout the world" by his new Latin translation of *Peri Archōn*, had also published translations of some of Origen's works and had even set forth Origen's "blasphemies" in his very own commentaries, such as the one on Ephesians. Rufinus was compelled to expose these matters because of the gravity of the charges that Jerome and others were now making against Rufinus's orthodoxy.

In response to this, Jerome wrote his *Apology against Rufinus* (402), in which he endeavors to show that he cited more interpreters than Origen in that *Commentary on Ephesians*.[74] Jerome says that he often placed divergent interpretations side by side, and that in such cases he could not be supposed to be expressing agreement with both views. Therefore, he says, readers of his *Commentary on Ephesians* should assume the same negative attitude toward the interpretation of Origen that he has subsequently adopted, even in cases where he gives the view of Origen only.[75] Some scholars, like E. Clark[76] and the present writ-

---

72. Cf. F. X. Murphy, *Rufinus of Aquileia*, 138–57; E. Clark, *The Origenist Controversy*, 121–25; R. Heine, *The Commentaries of Origen and Jerome on St. Paul's Epistle to the Ephesians*, Oxford Early Christian Studies (Oxford and New York: Oxford University Press, 2002).

73. Rufinus, *Apology* 1.43; cf. 2.42.

74. The definitive study of Jerome's *Apology* is by P. Lardet, *L'Apologie de Jérôme contre Rufin* (Leiden: Brill, 1993).

75. Jerome, *Apology* 1.21–28.

76. *The Origenist Controversy*, 124; 141.

er, regard Jerome's argument here as disingenuous, but others, like J. P. O'Connell, have defended Jerome's method.[77]

These polemics between Rufinus and Jerome are still in the future (400–402) when Jerome writes his *Commentary on Matthew* in 398. Jerome, however, has already passed through the first Origenist controversy, and it is noticeable that he is no longer reluctant to express doctrinal criticisms of Origen, though he always does so anonymously. These turn out to pertain to Origen's speculations about the pre-existence of souls and particularly of the soul of John the Baptist, the possible future salvation of the devil, the possibility of sinning and falling when in the heavenly state, and the nature of the resurrection body.[78] Jerome also reproaches Origen for apparently trusting in certain apocryphal traditions, especially the suggestion deriving from the *Protevangelium of James* that Joseph, the husband of Mary, had children by a previous marriage (cf. 12.49).

E. Clark seems to think that Jerome's criticism of Origen was riveted on the concept of hierarchy in the afterlife. She writes:

It is significant that the central issue so exercising Jerome in these two commentaries [*Commentary on Jonah* (396), *Commentary on Matthew* (398)] is one with deep resonances in his recent fight against Jovinian. It was, indeed, in the Jovinianist controversy that Jerome had adamantly affirmed a hierarchy in the afterlife based on the degrees of merit accumulated by humans in this life–a merit calculated by the stringency of ascetic renunciation.[79]

Clark misunderstands the Catholic doctrine of merit here, as something human beings can "accumulate" and "calculate," rather than as a duty performed to which God's favor is owed. She even interprets Jerome's rejection of Origen's views concerning the future restoration of the devil as an outgrowth of his (Jerome's) doctrine of merit. This appears to be a highly dubious interpretation. The issue Clark has chosen as a "central issue" to Jerome is not justified by the evidence found in this commentary. J. P. O'Connell seems nearer to the truth when he identifies the corporal resurrection as the point of dispute aris-

---

77. *The Eschatology of Saint Jerome*, 8–12.
78. See on 6.10; 6.26; 7.23; 8.29; 16.14; 18.24; 23.35–36; 25.46; 26.24.
79. *The Origenist Controversy*, 129.

ing from the Origenist controversy that colors Jerome's commentary.[80] In my judgment it is difficult to identify a "central issue" that troubles Jerome about Origen's theology in the present commentary. It seems better to speak of a cluster of dubious Origenian speculations.

It is worth emphasizing, however, that even at the height of his anti-Origenist period and later in his life, Jerome was never embarrassed by the fact that he relied on Origen's exegesis in his own. In *Ep.* 85 to Paulinus of Nola (A.D. 400) Jerome endorsed Origen's defense of the free choice of the will found in *Peri Archōn* (which was supposedly the most dangerous of Origen's works). To explain the meaning of the hardening of Pharaoh's heart, Jerome recommended Origen's work for study.[81] Earlier in his career (392), Jerome responded to critics who accused him of dependence on Origen in his own exegetical writings in these words:

> They say that I made excerpts from Origen's works, and that it is illegitimate to touch the writings of the old masters in such a way. People think that they gravely insult me by this. For myself, however, I see in this the highest praise. It is my express desire to follow an example of which I am convinced that it will please all men of discernment and you too.[82]

The fact that Jerome's later OT commentaries also display massive assimilation of Origen's exegesis seems to confirm that Jerome did not substantially differ from his ecclesiastical adversaries such as Rufinus and Ambrose in his approach to appropriating Origen. All such defenders of the Catholic faith adopted Origen's best exegetical and spiritual insights and rejected only the errors and un-catholic speculations found in Origen's thought.

---

80. *The Eschatology of St. Jerome,* 40.

81. E. Clark, *The Origenist Controversy,* 35, remarks that Jerome's nonchalance in suggesting that Paulinus read the *Peri Archōn* at the very height of the Origenist controversy casts doubt on the importance of theology in Jerome's attack on Origenism. This generalization wrongly assumes that Jerome made no distinctions between Origen's theological views.

82. *Comm. Mich. II prol.,* PL 25: 1189.

6. Jerome's Exegetical Method

Eusebius of Cremona had requested of Jerome a brief "historical" interpretation of the Gospel of Matthew.[83] Jerome replies by saying that this is what he has composed, but from time to time he has mingled in the flowers of the spiritual understanding. A fully finished work in which he will "place a very beautiful roof upon the foundations that have been laid," he has reserved, he says, for a future date—a promise never fulfilled. Jerome employs allegorical interpretations of the Gospel text especially in passages dealing with Jesus' physical and geographical movements and in the interpretation of Jesus' parables. Jerome's allegories are far more controlled than Origen's, from whom they derive, but even their presence in the commentary may surprise the uninitiated modern reader. Therefore, some things should be said about Jerome's method of biblical interpretation.

Essentially patristic exegesis endeavors to be a perpetuation of the interpretive methods and principles that are established or implicit in the writings of the New Testament itself. Paul in particular and the author of Hebrews give clear examples of allegorical interpretation of the OT, as do the Gospels, Revelation, and the Catholic Epistles.[84] The early Christian Fathers were devoted pupils of such masters.[85] Unfortunately, the fidelity of ancient Christian exegesis to these NT patterns of interpretation has been largely ignored in scholarship until recently. Instead, patristic exegesis is often depicted as "arbitrary" or as a Hellenistic corruption. The sources of patristic exegesis are more readily traced to Philo, the Mishnah, or Neo-platonic allegory of Homer than to Paul. While these links undoubtedly exist, they are not as fundamental as the NT practice, and it would be negligent to ignore the NT as the principal paradigm for the Fathers. H. de Lubac has effectively confronted what he de-

---

83. Cf. Preface (5).

84. Cf. 1 Cor 9.9, 10.4; Gal 4.24; Eph 5.31–32; Heb 7; 9.5; Lk 24.27; Rv 14.8; 1 Pt 2.6–8.

85. The classic study is H. de Lubac, *History and Spirit: The Understanding of Scripture according to Origen* (San Francisco: Ignatius, 2007).

scribes as a seemingly invincible scholarly ignorance that would persist in describing as "Philonism" or "Platonism" in the work of the Fathers what is often in reality fidelity to Paul, John, and the teaching of the Letter to the Hebrews.[86] Along similar lines, J. McGuckin recently wrote with respect to Origen: "Time after time the source of Origen's particularly nuanced biblical interpretations of the Old Testament text can be explained on the basis of the Pauline or Johannine text through which he is reading the old narratives."[87]

Doubtless the Church Fathers would have been puzzled by the judgment of scholars who think that it is impermissible for Christians to emulate the apostles' practice of scriptural exegesis. For example, R. Longenecker writes: "Our commitment as Christians is to the reproduction of the apostolic faith and doctrine, and not necessarily to the specific apostolic exegetical practices. . . . we cannot assume that the explication of their methods is necessarily the norm for our exegesis today."[88] However valid this decision may be, it is plainly arbitrary when compared with the Fathers, for whom the apostolic faith, doctrine, and exegetical practice went together.

Essentially the patristic method advocates using a two-level approach to interpreting the biblical texts: the literal/historical meaning and the spiritual meaning.[89] Yet even this generalization needs to be nuanced, since everything depends on which Scriptural texts are being interpreted and what the text actually says. A fundamental distinction needs to be made between the exegesis of the OT and of the NT: within the OT, one should distinguish patristic interpretation of the Pentateuch from that of the prophets; and within the NT, the interpretation of the Epistles of St. Paul should be distinguished from that of the Gospels, since the letters of Paul are usually interpreted quite literally by the Fa-

---

86. *Medieval Exegesis*, 1: *The Four Senses of Scripture,* trans. M. Sebanc (Grand Rapids: Eerdmans, 1998), 150; also *History and Spirit,* 77–86.

87. *The Westminster Handbook to Origen,* 10–11.

88. *Biblical Exegesis in the Apostolic Period* (Grand Rapids: Eerdmans, 1974), 198.

89. The latter is also called the allegorical, mystical, anagogical, and tropological interpretation.

thers. A controlling principle of all patristic exegesis is that the Fathers will support Christian interpretations of the text, as opposed to Jewish or heretical interpretations.[90] If the establishment of the Christian interpretation turns on the assertion of the literal meaning of the original text, then the literal sense will be insisted upon, even of the OT, and the allegorical meaning will be rejected. With very few insignificant exceptions, the literal factuality of historical events recorded in Scripture is never called into question. But the ancient Fathers aimed to find deeper Christological and ecclesiological applications in their interpretations, since Jesus claimed that the OT writings and events were prophecies and shadowy types pointing to himself.[91] Moreover, the Gospels interpret themselves allegorically,[92] and the Letter to the Hebrews practices the mystical interpretation of the OT.[93] Furthermore, Paul declared that the OT texts were written down primarily for the Christian's instruction and edification.[94]

Literal Interpretation

The first level of interpretation involves the historical/philological explanation of the text and the concrete meaning of the words. This is always the presupposition and basis for the allegorical/mystical meaning. In order to ascertain the literal meaning of Matthew's text, Jerome employs his extensive knowledge of Scripture, Palestinian geography, and history (both secular and ecclesiastical). He also takes advantage of his knowledge of languages, Greek, Hebrew, Aramaic, and Latin, as well as textual criticism, Jewish tradition and customs, philosophy, and the antecedent Christian interpretive tradition. To determine the literal meaning Jerome repeatedly emphasizes that the interpreter needs to be completely "rooted" (*haerere*) in the context of the words.[95] For Jerome the danger of erroneous and het-

90. Consider Jerome's exegesis at 22.41–44, where the contrast between Jewish and Christian interpretation of Ps 110 can be clearly seen.

91. Cf. Lk 4.21; Lk 10.18–19; cf. Ps 91.13; Is 14.12; Jn 3.14.

92. Cf. Lk 1.51–53, 68–71, with the rest of Luke-Acts.

93. Cf. Heb 7.

94. Cf. Rom 4.23–24; 15.4; 1 Cor 10.11.

95. Cf. 5.19, 25–26; 10.29–31; 12.30; 12.35–36; 12.43, 45; 16.15–16; 18.21–22; 20.1–2.

erodox interpretations arises precisely when the interpreter ignores the context (cf. 10.29–31). Jerome tends to associate Origen (whom he never identifies by name) with failing at times to pay strict attention to the context and with launching into questionable allegories. For example, at 25.13 Jerome criticizes Origen's interpretations of Jesus' parables in these words:

I always warn the wise reader not to subscribe to superstitious interpretations and those that are spoken "line by line" [*commatice*] by people who fabricate things by their own arbitrary will. Instead, let the reader consider what precedes, what is in the middle, and what follows. And let him connect to one another all the things that are written.

This passage seems to be directed against Origen, since in his Preface (4), Jerome refers to Origen's "line by line" (*commaticum*) interpretation of Matthew. Thus for Jerome the context needs to be strictly examined and should function as a stringent control on all secondary exegesis. Jerome explicitly states: "An unrestrained and sweeping use of allegorical interpretation is not allowed to us" (11.16–19). An interpreter is at fault, Jerome says, if he wants to understand obscure things plainly or plain things obscurely (15.15–16).

In addition to context, the interpreter needs to be acquainted with biblical word usage.[96] Jerome is convinced that Helvidius's big mistake is found precisely in his failure to know this.[97] Jerome also accuses the pagan critics of Christianity with being unfamiliar with Scriptural word usage (cf. 1.16). In the present commentary, Jerome is often satisfied with setting forth the literal meaning, as he promised his dedicatee. Sometimes, however, Jerome branches out into more developed spiritual levels of interpretation. The goal of this movement is to edify the souls of believers further through exhortation and to equip them for spiritual battle.

Spiritual Interpretation

The quest for a spiritual interpretation is based explicitly on the pattern of Christ, who concealed a spiritual meaning in his

---

96. Cf. 7.21; 14.9; 15.46; 26.18.
97. Cf. 1.16; 1.18; 1.24–25; 12.49. On Helvidius, see below.

teachings and declared that the OT prefigured himself.[98] In addition, it is hardly doubtful that the evangelists themselves intended their readers to detect symbolic typological patterns in the narratives about Jesus, as any modern commentary will point out. For Jerome the application of this pattern addresses the devotional, practical, and ecclesiastical needs of his readers. Whereas the literal explanation is precise and does not permit arbitrary deviations (even if there may be various possible interpretations of a given text), the allegorical interpretation, on the other hand, is freer and subject only to the one law that it must have a pious meaning in view.[99] The criteria by which spiritual interpretations are to be judged is whether they edify and whether they are sympathetic with the doctrine of the Church. Jerome will often offer more than one such interpretation, and he asks readers to accept the one that pleases them best (cf. 13.33). In this same passage he admits that doubtful allegorical interpretations cannot be used to advance the authority of Church dogma. From this, de Margerie plausibly suggests that Jerome viewed his spiritual exegesis as an "adaptive contemplation, based on a previously and independently known doctrine and meant to enhance the understanding and appreciation of that doctrine."[100] It was thus possible for Jerome to shift from literal to spiritual exegesis "without wondering whether or not it was necessary to discern a strictly determined typology indicated by God himself in revelation."[101]

To illustrate Jerome's method, we can consider his comments on Mt 10.9–10. After explaining the passage historically, Jerome offers a spiritual interpretation of the disciples' equipment for their mission: "take no gold" applies to the avoidance of the perverse teachings of heretics and philosophers; "wear no sandals" means to live an unencumbered holy life; and so forth. Another example of the movement from historical to spiritual interpretation is Jerome's explanation of the "cleansing of the Tem-

---

98. Cf. 13.4; 13.35; 15.13; 14.19; 16.8–12; 23.4; 24.24; 27.46.

99. Cf. Jerome, *Comm. Abac.* 1.2.

100. *An Introduction to the History of Exegesis*, 2: *The Latin Fathers* (Petersham, MA: St. Bede, 1995), 134.

101. Ibid.

ple," when Jesus expels the money-changers from the Temple precincts (Mt 21.12–13). Again, Jerome first offers an historical explanation of the event, the gist of which is Jesus' condemnation of the avarice of the Jewish priests. In great detail Jerome explains the historical situation and the mechanics of the greedy practices devised by these historical contemporaries of Jesus. Then Jerome makes a transition to the "mystical understanding." Here he applies the story to the Church and to the soul of the believer. Jerome says that "Jesus daily enters the Church" and expels greedy bishops, priests, deacons, and laymen. He holds them guilty of the crime of buying and selling. Finally, Jerome exhorts the individual believer, including himself:

May there not be business in the house of our heart. May there not be the commerce of selling and buying. May there not be desire for donations, lest an angry and stern Jesus enter and cleanse his own temple in no other way but with a whip that he administers in order to make a house of prayer out of a den of thieves and a house of business.

In the spiritual interpretation, then, what we often essentially have is a homiletical exhortation to the Christian. What Jesus said and did back then is made to speak to Jerome's contemporaries. It is easy to verify that homiletical exhortation is a driving impulse behind Jerome's movement from literal to spiritual interpretation by comparing his exegesis here with its more expanded form that is found in his homilies.[102]

This suggests that for Jerome biblical exegesis is a specifically Christian exercise. We recall that exegesis was born and developed in the office of the liturgy, around the sacred readings that had to be commented upon, and that exegetes were often preachers.[103] The context of their task was ecclesiastical, and they took as a given the need for sympathy with the faith of the Church. Exegesis was aimed at the edification of the believer. Jerome's commentary is thus an inextricable complex of historical explanation of the text (literal interpretation) combined with homiletical exhortation (spiritual interpretation). To be

102. Abundant references to Jerome's homilies will be found in the footnotes.

103. H. de Lubac, *Medieval Exegesis*, 2.28.

sure, the allegorical movement is more than homiletical exhortation, but it is not less. For all these reasons, it is fundamentally asymmetrical to make a one-to-one comparison between patristic exegesis and "modern" exegesis, since the latter generally makes use of altogether different principles of methodology and goals. Modern exegetes persist in objecting to the Fathers' approach to interpretation and in asserting that a text's meaning should be restricted to its historical referent. This misguided criticism neglects the ecclesiastical context of the ancient genre. When moderns further complain that the Fathers were only interested in history as parable, a defense of the Fathers might wish to remind readers that the Fathers almost always assume the literal historicity of the biblical narratives. Further, one might raise the question whether it really follows that the restriction of a passage's meaning to its historical referent equates to taking history seriously. Indeed, one might reverse this judgment and assert that history is only taken seriously when the exegete takes the full symbolic potential of an event into consideration.[104]

7. Themes of Jerome's *Commentary on Matthew*

The Revelation of the Triune God

Jerome's commentary has been reproached for lacking a central coherent theme.[105] Yet one can find motifs that run through the work like scarlet threads from beginning to end. One of these is the revelation of the Triune God. For Jerome, the encounter with the historically incarnated Son of God, Jesus Christ, who comes to us in the preaching of the Church, has revealed the Trinity to us. (This does not imply, of course, that the Trinity was not foreshadowed in the OT.) At 1.1 Jerome says that Matthew's proclamation of the Incarnation begins with fleshly matters, "so that through the man we might begin to become acquainted with God." The mystery of the Trinity is shown in the Lord's baptism, when God's Son was revealed to the world (3.16). The

---

104. I am indebted to my colleague, Peter Martens, for this insight.
105. Cf. M. Simonetti, *Matthew 1a* (ACC, xlv).

whole Trinity is at work in Jesus' ministry of exorcism, where Jerome comments: "If then the Son is the hand and arm of God, and the Holy Spirit is his finger, then there is one substance of the Father and of the Son and of the Holy Spirit" (12.28). Jerome supports Trinitarian interpretations of Jesus' parables and words.[106] He finds the whole Trinity active in the divine revelation to Peter that enabled his confession of Jesus as the Son of God.[107] The Trinity was signified in the three tabernacles (17.4). Finally, Jerome declares that baptism is given in the name of the Trinity so that there may be one gift from those whose divinity is one (28.19). Thus Jerome begins and ends his commentary with a Trinitarian emphasis.[108] Though Jerome's technical language reflects his post-Nicene theology, this particular theological accent also owes a great deal to his exegetical master, Origen.[109]

Heaven as a Reward to the Victors

Another recurrent theme is Jerome's emphasis that heaven is a reward paid out to those who are victorious in the Christian contest. O'Connell has identified the unifying thought of Jerome's teaching on heaven to be the idea of reward.[110] He notes the significant fact that Jerome never presents the beatific vision of God (cf. 1 Cor 13.12) as the cause of heavenly happiness. Jerome seems to have considered this vision, which is so fundamental to Augustine's conception of heaven, and subsequently to that of Thomas Aquinas, as one of the less important elements of the heavenly life. Jerome's concept of heavenly

106. Cf. 13.33; 15.32.

107. Cf. 16.17; 22.41–44.

108. This Trinitarian motif is, of course, embedded in the structural framework of Matthew's Gospel. See L. Morris, *The Gospel According to Matthew,* 748: "That the early followers of Jesus thought of God as triune seems clear from the passages that speak of the three together (e.g., Rom. 8:11; 1 Cor. 12:4–6; 2 Cor. 13:14; Gal. 4:6; Eph. 4:4–6; 2 Thess. 2:13, etc.). That God is a Trinity is a scriptural idea." These Trinitarian formulations are most easily explained if they go back to Jesus himself.

109. See C. Kannengiesser, "Divine Trinity and the Structure of *Peri Archōn,*" in *Origen of Alexandria: His World and His Legacy,* ed. C. Kannengiesser and W. Petersen (Notre Dame, IN: University of Notre Dame Press, 1988), 231–49.

110. J. P. O'Connell, *The Eschatology of Saint Jerome,* 102–18.

life is intimately linked to his concept of the Christian's earthly life. Jerome recognizes that the theme of God's rewarding and punishing according to one's deserts is a major emphasis in the proclamation of Jesus.[111] For Jerome this is a motive for Christians to rejoice in the midst of persecutions and to fear committing sin (cf. 5.12; 11.11). Jerome makes clear that when Christ returns, the opportunity for merit, that is, good works and justice, will disappear (25.10). But since the soul enjoys its reward immediately after death, the implication is that death is the end of the Christian contest.[112] In short, in his *Commentary on Matthew* Jerome repeatedly emphasizes that God prefers to reward our merits gained on earth rather than to make an outright gift of eternal happiness to us. It appears that Origen's anti-Gnostic theology of merit and free will has contributed to the shape of Jerome's theology here.

Polemic against the Heretics

Jerome sustains a polemic against the heresies of the past and present.[113] In the name of ecclesiastical peace, Jerome has made the adversaries of the Church his own adversaries.[114] Jerome frequently mentions two sets of heretics: Marcion, Valentinus, and Manicheus, who founded heresies that have traditionally been categorized as "Gnostic," and Arius and Eunomius, who are rep-

111. In the present commentary, the term "reward" is found at 5.12; 6.2; 6.5; 8.29; 10.12–13; 10.41; 10.42; 11.9; 11.30; 14.14; 14.16; 14.17; 16.22–23; 16.28; 18.19–20; 18.21–22; 19.5; 19.12; 19.14; 19.19; 19.27; 20.13; 24.40–41; 24.44–46; 25.9; 25.26–28; 25.29; 25.31–33. "Merit" occurs at 2.12; 7.22–23; 10.2; 11.9; 13.17; 18.5; 20.13; 20.23; 21.14; 22.11–12; 26.8–9; 27.61; 28.9. For what appears to be a strikingly similar interpretation of reward and punishment in the OT and in St. Paul's writings, see C. VanLandingham, *Judgment & Justification in Early Judaism and the Apostle Paul* (Peabody, MA: Hendrickson, 2006), 175–241.

112. This teaching distinguishes Jerome from Origen, who denied that death was the term of the Christian's probation. Cf. J. P. O'Connell, *The Eschatology of St. Jerome*, 8.

113. My principal secondary source for the following brief treatments is A. Di Berardino, ed., *Encyclopedia of the Early Church*, 2 vols. (New York: Oxford University Press, 1992).

114. Cf. Jerome, *Against the Pelagians*, Prol. 2: "I have never spared heretics, and I have done my best to make the enemies of the Church my own." NPNF, Second Series, 6.449.

resentative of the fourth-century Trinitarian heresy of Arianism. Jerome's depiction of the heretics, although generally correct, is stereotyped and polemical. Yet he correctly understands that the heretical trio of Marcion, Valentinus, and Manicheus were united in their denial of the Incarnation, in their adhesion to docetism,[115] in their denial of the free choice of the will in salvation, and in their faulty view of the OT and its God.

Marcion, Valentinus, and Manicheus

Marcion of Sinope in Pontus was reputedly the son of the bishop of Sinope, who came to Rome and founded a heretical sect in the 140s.[116] Scandalized by the problem of evil and other philosophical problems, Marcion's response was to reject his former faith.[117] He thought out a doctrinal system based on the irreconcilability of justice and grace, Law and Gospel, Judaism and Christianity, the God of the OT and the Father of Jesus. Marcion posited two deities, a good non-judicial God (the Father of Jesus), who is not to be feared, and a just but inferior god (the Creator of the world, who is the God of the OT and of the Jews), in whom resides the grounds of fear, anger, severity, judgment, vengeance, and condemnation.[118] Marcion so emphasized the absolute newness of the dispensation brought by Jesus that he repudiated the OT in its entirety and denied that it predicted the coming of Jesus or spoke about the good Father proclaimed by Jesus. Moreover, he taught his followers that the received form of the NT had been corrupted by Judaizing Christians, whom he identified as the Catholics of his day.[119] He "edited" the Gospel of Luke and ten of Paul's letters and made these documents the canon of his church. But he removed Luke's name from the Gospel material (since Paul was the only apostle Marcion recognized) and excised texts within these writings that he found incompatible with his own preconceived theolo-

---

115. The term "docetism" derives from the Greek word, *dokein*, "to seem or appear." Docetists denied the Incarnation of Christ, saying that he only *appeared* to be human. This heresy is combated in the NT itself. Cf. 1 Jn 4.2.

116. Epiphanius, *Haer.* 42.2.

117. Cf. Tertullian, *De carne Christi* 2; *Adversus Marcionem* 1.2.

118. Cf. Tertullian, *Adv. Marc.* 4.8.

119. Cf. ibid. 1.20; 4.2–7.

gy. In this way he endeavored to sever the link between what he regarded as the original core of his new religion and Old Testament Judaism.[120] That Marcion denied free will is an inference drawn by the orthodox Fathers on his behalf from the observation that Marcion railed against the Creator God and held the Creator to be responsible for the evil in the world.[121]

Valentinus was an Egyptian heretic of the second century who spread Alexandrian Gnosticism in Rome between 135 and 160. He, too, rejected the traditional identification of the Christian God with the Creator of the OT and taught a sort of natural predestination which divided humanity into three categories. The Redeemer, Jesus, saves people from the world by giving them saving knowledge, or *gnosis* (from which Gnosticism derives its name), which is available only to the "spiritual" (*pneumatikoi*). The second kind of nature is the "soulish" (*psychikoi*) and refers to ordinary members of the Church, who can achieve some kind of salvation by faith and good works. The third group is the rest of mankind, or the "natural" (*hylikoi*) who have no chance at redemption.[122]

Manicheus, or Mani/Manes (215–276), was the founder of Manichaeism, which threatened the Church for many centuries and even claimed the young Augustine as one of its adherents. Manicheus came from Persia and is reported to have died of torture in prison while chained up by the wrists.[123] He desired to blend Christianity, Zoroastrianism, and elements of Buddhism together.[124] Manicheus likewise preached an extreme dualism of

120. Cf. D. Balas, "The Use and Interpretation of Paul in Irenaeus's Five Books *Adversus haereses*," *The Second Century* 9 (1992): 27–39.

121. Cf. Tertullian, *Adv. Marc.* 2.5–8; 4.41; Scheck, *Origen and the History of Justification*, 23–29.

122. The above account is drawn from Irenaeus, *Adv. haer.* 1.6; Tertullian, *Against the Valentinians* 29–30. Although the Nag Hammadi discoveries have increased our knowledge of these heretical groups, the accuracy of Irenaeus's and Tertullian's depiction of Valentinus's system has not been conclusively disproven. Cf. M. van den Broek, "The Present State of Gnostic Studies," *VC* 37 (1983): 47–71.

123. Cf. S. Lieu, *Manichaeism in the Late Roman Empire and Medieval China: A Historical Survey* (Manchester, 1985).

124. For evidence of Manicheus's dependence on the Gnostic *Gospel of Thomas*, see Preface (1) n. 3.

two independent and absolutely opposed eternal principles, of good and of evil (cf. 8.31). Like Marcion he denied that Jesus was prophesied in the OT, and said that the good God was characterized by light while the material world was inherently dark and corrupt. Manicheus believed that Jesus and other teachers came to release souls of light from imprisonment in material bodies. The Old Testament was the product of the forces of darkness. Manicheus also denied the free choice of the will in salvation.

A. Viciano observes that Manichaeism had an unusual capacity for syncretism with other religions. As it spread throughout the Roman Empire, it adapted to certain aspects of Christianity, particularly to the theology of the heretic Marcion, whose cosmology was dualistic whereas his Christology was permeated by Gnostic elements.

Such coincidence with Manichaean doctrine, along with the fact that Marcionism, like Manichaeism, was organized as a church, facilitated such syncretism. Moreover, Mani himself admired Marcion in so far as their respective interpretations of the epistles of Paul had many points in common.[125]

Jerome is not concerned with pointing out that Marcion, Valentinus, and Manicheus do not represent identical elements of heretical religion. The Valentinians, for example, used the OT and all four canonical Gospels in an eclectic fashion to support their doctrines about the divine emanations that eventually produced the material world. Unlike Marcionism, some forms of Basilidean and Valentinian Gnosticism were antinomian and believed in an ingrained election that gave the followers a license to commit sin.[126] On the other hand, these schools do share enough in common to make it legitimate for Jerome to associate them closely. For the common denominator of all Gnostic systems, including Marcion's special form, is their polytheistic or dualistic tendency. These heretics univocally denied the one God as unique source of all creation, revelation, and

125. "Mani (216–276) and Manichaeism," in C. Kannengieser, ed., *Handbook of Patristic Exegesis: The Bible in Ancient Christianity,* vol. 1 (Leiden: Brill, 2004), 658.

126. Cf. Clement of Alexandria, *Strom.* 3; Irenaeus, *Adv. haer.* 2.32.

grace. They all accepted Christ but denied his real Incarnation and introduced plurality into the Divinity.[127] For Jerome, as for all the anti-Gnostic Church Fathers, Irenaeus, Clement, Origen, Tertullian, there is one God from whom all miracles, divine interventions, and revelation come.

Jerome confronts Marcion's and Manicheus's rejection of the OT by insisting that Jesus himself sanctified the OT; he did not repudiate it.[128] Jerome criticizes Marcion and Manicheus for mangling the OT and insists upon the unity of the character and being of God throughout Scripture.[129] At 5.39–40 Jerome cites Lam 3.27–30 to good effect, namely, to prove that the precept "to turn the other cheek" was given by the God of the OT before it was articulated by Jesus. It is worth noting that many of these OT connections were first identified by Origen.[130]

Since these heretics rejected the Creator God and the inherent goodness of the material world, they were also unanimous in their denial of the Incarnation. They viewed Christ as a phantom-like nature and not a real human being. Docetists believed that Jesus "seemed" human but in fact passed through Mary like water through a pipe, receiving nothing from her body. Marcion's version of docetism is slightly different: he claimed that Jesus suddenly appeared in full-grown adult form in the semblance of a human body.[131] In either case the Incarnation is denied: Mary was not the real mother of Jesus, Jesus was not truly descended from David, Jesus did not have real human flesh, nor did he rise physically from the dead. Jerome rejects such views at 9.27, 14.26, and 21.18–20. He cross-examines the followers of Marcion and Manicheus by asking them how Jesus could be called a son of David if he was not born in the flesh, as a descen-

---

127. Cf. D. Farkasfalvy, "Theology of Scripture in St. Irenaeus," *Revue Bénédictine* 78 (1968): 321.

128. Cf. 13.45–46; 14.18.

129. Cf. 9.27; 4.17; 5.39–40.

130. Cf. J. Lienhard, "Origen and the Crisis of the Old Testament in the Early Church," *Pro Ecclesia* 9.3 (2000): 355–66.

131. Cf. Irenaeus, *Adv. haer.* 1.27; Tertullian, *Adv. Marc.* 1.19.2. In *De carne Christi*, Tertullian distinguishes three different heretical approaches to the body of Jesus: that of Marcion, that of Apelles, and that of Valentinus. Much of Jerome's presentation can also be found in Tertullian's work.

dant of David. At 12.49 Jerome critiques Marcion's docetic interpretation of Jesus' words about his relatives;[132] and at 14.26 and 17.2 he reproaches a docetic interpretation of Jesus walking on the sea and of the Transfiguration.

Jerome stands in line with the antecedent Christian tradition in his affirmation of the freedom of the will, his rejection of fate, and his repudiation of the doctrine of an irresistible natural predestination to life and death. He attacks Valentinus's doctrine of natures at 13.4–5, 15, and his comments at 5.45 are obviously directed against determinism: "If one becomes a son of God by keeping God's commands, then he is not a son by nature but by his own choice."[133] Jerome's words in 27.4 are significant in showing that in Jerome's view, not even Judas Iscariot was destined for death, since Christ was hoping for his repentance. Jerome says that those who attribute Judas's damnation to an unalterable destiny ingrained in his evil nature need to explain how it is that he was able to repent. In Jerome's view Judas had been a "good tree," but through a bad use of his free will, he converted himself into an "evil tree" when he betrayed the Savior (7.18). Repeatedly, Jerome defends the free choice of the will in salvation, damnation, and the attainment of perfection.[134]

Arius and Eunomius

A second heretical pair referred to by Jerome represents the Trinitarian heresy called Arianism.[135] Arius (260–336) was a priest from Alexandria whose doctrine was condemned at the Council of Nicaea in 325.[136] After the death of Constantine in 337, Arianism regained ascendancy. Arius asserted that Christ

132. A similar refutation is found in Tertullian, *Adv. Marc.* 4.19.

133. Similar arguments are found at 7.18; 13.4–5, 15; 15.13; and 27.4.

134. Cf. 11.30; 19.11, 21; 20.28; 21.33; 21.37–36.

135. Modern scholarship would not speak of "Arianism" as a monolithic entity, but of plural forms of subordinationist Christianity.

136. The Nicene-Constantinopolitan Creed, which describes God's Son as "begotten, not made, one in being (*homoousios*) with the Father" is directed against Arius's teaching. Important modern studies of the Arian crisis include M. Simonetti, *La crisi ariana nel IV secolo* (Rome, 1975); R. Williams, *Arius: Heresy and Tradition* (London: Longman and Todd, 1987).

is a creature in the proper sense of that word, and as such does not share in the divine nature. Arius believed that the Father created the Son *in time*, and, therefore, the Son has not always existed. The notorious Arian affirmation was: "There was a time when he (the Son) was not (did not exist)."[137] Eunomius of Cyzicus (bishop, 360–364) was the greatest exponent of radical Arianism in Jerome's day.[138] His apologies for "Arianism" were refuted in detail by Basil and Gregory of Nyssa. Jerome alludes to or openly attacks Arius and Eunomius frequently, and his spirited Nicene orthodoxy is reflected throughout.[139]

It is also against the counter-claims of Arius and Eunomius that Jerome directs his defense of Jesus' foreknowledge and omniscience. According to Jerome, the Arians based their argument that Jesus could not be equal in nature to the Father on the text where Jesus seems to profess ignorance of the hour of his second coming (Mt 24.36). The Arians claimed that He who knows and he who does not know cannot be equal.

It is true that Jesus' admission of ignorance in Mt 24.36 posed a serious and embarrassing problem for orthodox defenders of the deity of Christ. Indeed, one of Jerome's tactics is to question the passage (Mt 24.36) at the text-critical level. R. Vaggione has observed that one of the things that most outraged Nicenes about the non-Nicene portrait of Christ was the extent to which they played down the passages describing Christ's glory at the expense of those describing his humiliation:

---

137. Arius, *Ep. ad Alex.*; cited by J. N. D. Kelly, *Early Christian Doctrines*, rev. ed. (San Francisco: Harper and Row, 1978), 228. According to M. Simonetti, "Arius," EEC 1.77, at first Arius stated (in his letter to Eusebius) that the Son had been created from nothing by the work of the Father; later he avoided speaking like this because of the scandal it caused, and spoke of the Son's generation from the Father. "But he continued to consider this generation as creation."

138. For a sensitive treatment of him, see R. Vaggione, *Eunomius of Cyzicus and the Nicene Revolution*, Oxford Early Christian Studies (Oxford and New York: Oxford University Press, 2000); cf. M. Wiles, "Eunomius: Hair-splitting Dialectician or Defender of the Accessibility of Salvation?" in R. Williams, ed., *The Making of Orthodoxy: Essays in Honour of Henry Chadwick* (Cambridge: Cambridge University Press, 1989).

139. Cf. 1.20; 11.27; 14.33; 21.37–36; 24.36; 26.37; 27.54.

The passages in question were those in which he was seen praying, displaying fear, anguish, or ignorance, hunger, fatigue, or thirst, recognizing his subordination or assigning limits to his authority. We can gauge their effectiveness by the vehemence of the response. For in Nicene eyes there could be only one reason for such a tack: to deny the divinity of the Son and make him equivalent to any other creature. Non-Nicenes, naturally, took it all quite differently.[140]

Jerome's defense makes use of several arguments. He first observes that Scripture attests that Jesus, as the Word of God, made all time. How, then, could he be ignorant of a part of which he knows the whole? (24.36). Jerome also notes that the Arian thesis can only be sustained by remaining silent about other texts that contradict this position. And in fact, there are multiple texts in the Gospels where Jesus exercises foreknowledge and omniscience, or in which his omniscience is implied.[141]

Another line of argument used by Jerome is given at 21.37. The householder in Jesus' parable, who represents God the Father, appears to be ignorant and mistakenly thinks that the tenants will respect his son. By a strict interpretation, Jerome argues, the householder's (God the Father's) knowledge of the future is deficient. Whatever answer the Arians give on the Father's behalf, Jerome invites them to give this answer as well on the Son's behalf. Also, Jerome uses the argument that the posing of questions does not imply that the questioner is ignorant of the answer.[142] Jerome's exposure of the weaknesses and inconsistencies in the Arian position seems more effective than his own explanation of Jesus' words in Mt 24.36. He seems to suggest that Jesus, as the Word of God, indeed knew the day and the hour of his return, but he kept this knowledge hidden, because it was not expedient for the disciples for him to reveal it. For the disciples' uncertainty about the time of judgment would be an incentive to virtue. God *is said* to be uncertain, so that free will may be preserved.[143]

---

140. R. Vaggione, *Eunomius of Cyzicus and the Nicene Revolution*, 107–8.

141. Cf. 17.27; 26.13; 28.20.

142. Cf. 22.20–21.

143. Cf. 24.42, 44–46; 21.37. K. Madigan, *"Christus Nesciens?* Was Christ Ignorant of the Day of Judgment? Arian and Orthodox Interpretation of Mark 13:32 in the Ancient Latin West," *HTR* 96.3 (2003): 267–70, describes Jerome's

Helvidius

Texts from the Gospel of Matthew played a key role in the heresy of Helvidius (fl. 380s). Helvidius was a Roman layman and, according to Gennadius,[144] a disciple of the Arian bishop Auxentius of Milan (the predecessor of Ambrose).[145] Helvidius denied Mary's post-partum virginity and claimed that Mary gave birth to a large number of sons and daughters in addition to Jesus, since he believed Joseph and Mary had normal marital relations after the birth of Jesus. Jerome, on the other hand, interpreted the Lord's "brothers" to refer to his cousins, that is, children not of Mary but of her sister. He based this view on the textual link between Mt 13.55 and 27.55. Jerome's explanation can be contrasted with that of Epiphanius of Salamis and Hilary of Poitiers, who saw Jesus' "brothers" as step-brothers, that is, children of Joseph from a previous marriage.

In *Against Helvidius* Jerome reproduces Helvidius's arguments at length. From what we read there, it is clear that Helvidius possessed no more than a rudimentary understanding of scriptural language. For example, from the words "*before* they came together" (Mt 1.18), Helvidius saw the implication that afterward Joseph and Mary must have "come together" carnally. In the description of Jesus as Mary's "firstborn" (Mt 1.25), Helvidius surmised that there must have been a "second-born," "third-born," and so on. When he encountered the conjunction "until" in Mt 1.25, Helvidius drew the conclusion that after Jesus' birth, Joseph must have later "known" Mary in the sexual sense. And in the term "the Lord's brothers" (Mt 12.46), Helvidius found evidence for biological brothers of Jesus.

---

commentary as a work "not noted for either doctrinal originality or profundity" (267). He particularly dismisses Jerome's reply to the Arians on the subject of Christ's ignorance as logically incoherent, triumphalist, and "altogether unconvincing." Madigan does not explain why he finds Jerome's arguments unconvincing.

144. *Vir. ill.* 32.

145. G. Jouassard, "La personalité d'Helvidius," in *Mélanges Saunier* (Lyon, 1944), 139–56, casts doubt on the historicity of Helvidius's connection to the Arian bishop. My colleague Carl Beckwith, who also thinks that the link with Auxentius is polemical, not historical, informs me that Auxentius was extremely powerful and had a large following, but that the popularity and attraction to him was not necessarily a result of his anti-Nicene views.

In the *Commentary on Matthew,* Jerome refers to Helvidius multiple times.[146] Usually he simply refers the reader to his earlier, more detailed writing.[147] The strength of Jerome's interpretation of these matters stems from his mastery of scriptural word usage. Being fluent in Hebrew and Aramaic, Jerome knew firsthand that these languages used "brother" and "sister" to describe varying degrees of blood relationships.[148] The term once coined passed into the Greek NT, which in fact nowhere says that these "brothers" and "sisters" were sons and daughters of Mary. As for Jesus being described as Mary's "firstborn," Jerome recognized that this was a technical term for the male who opened the womb and was especially consecrated to God.[149] The biblical term implied nothing about subsequent children. And with regard to the words in Mt 1.25 that "Joseph knew her not until . . . ," Jerome understood that this preposition was only intended to establish Mary's virginity at the time of Jesus' birth. It was not concerned with what followed.[150]

Chiliasm

At Mt 19.29–30 Jerome mentions the heresy of chiliasm, or millenarism. As usual he adopts the tactics of a polemicist and makes no distinction between orthodox and unorthodox forms of this doctrine. Chiliasm was very widespread among early orthodox Christian writers. It was advocated by Papias, Ps-Barnabas, Justin, Irenaeus, Tertullian, Victorinus, Lactantius, and Apollinaris. According to the orthodox form of chiliasm, Christ at his second coming will establish an earthly millennial kingdom in which there will be a first resurrection *on the earth* for 1000 years.[151] The essential affirmation is of an intermediate

---

146. Cf. 1.20; 1.24–25; 12.49; 13.55.

147. For an excellent recent treatment of Mary's perpetual virginity in the NT, the Fathers, and modern theology, see Paul Haffner, *The Mystery of Mary* (Chicago: Liturgical Training Publications, 2004), chap. 6. For an explication of Jerome's view of the brothers of Jesus, see J. McHugh, *The Mother of Jesus in the New Testament* (Garden City: Doubleday, 1975), chap. 8.

148. E.g., Gn 13.8; 29.12; Lv 10.4; 1 Chr 23.22f.

149. Cf. Ex 13.2; Lk 2.23.

150. Cf. Dt 34.6; 2 Sm 6.23; 1 Mc 5.54; Mt 28.20.

151. Cf. Rv 20.1–10. For a good discussion of chiliasm, see J. Daniélou, *A*

stage in which the risen saints are still on earth and have not yet entered into their final state. Of the early Fathers who supported this doctrine, none of them made any reference to the continuance of procreation during the messianic reign. In contrast, the view of the heretic Cerinthus was that the millennium would be a time of material pleasures in which procreation continues.

In at least fifty passages in his writings, mostly in his commentaries on the prophets, Jerome discusses the error of chiliasm; yet he describes it only in its most extreme form, the form that made the best foil for his own position.[152] O'Connell notes that Jerome's method of treating millenaristic exegesis differs from his method of treating other errors. For in regard to other errors, even Origenism, Jerome often fails to indicate that the exegesis he gives is not his own or not approved by him. Yet, when there is an instance of millenaristic exegesis, Jerome never fails to make clear that such teaching is unacceptable. Jerome does not consider this error exclusively Christian, for he often engages Jewish proponents of an earthly messianic kingdom, yet he does not distinguish the Jewish and Christian forms. Jerome's hostility toward this doctrine seems excessive when we recall that Christian chiliasm did not advocate indulgence in material pleasures (such as procreation) during the millennial kingdom and therefore can hardly be accused of that for which Jerome seems to hold it responsible.

Further Theological Themes

Fifteen Miracles

Jerome enumerates fifteen miraculous signs in the course of his exposition of Matthew's Gospel, neglecting to specify the fourteenth. The catalogue consists in the following: (1) the leper (8.1–3); (2) the centurion's servant (the first paralytic, in 8.6, 13, 23); (3) Peter's mother-in-law (8.15); (4) the expulsion of demons from those brought to Jesus (8.16); (5) the calming

---

History of Early Christian Doctrine, 1: *The Theology of Jewish Christianity,* trans. and ed. John A. Baker (Chicago: The Henry Regnery Company, 1964), 379ff.

152. See J. P. O'Connell, *The Eschatology of Saint Jerome,* chap. 4.

of the wind and sea (8.23–26); (6) the healing of the demoniac in the country of the Gerasenes (8.23; 8.32); (7) the paralytic on the mat (8.23; 9.2–8); (8) the hemorrhaging woman (9.22); (9) the ruler's daughter (9.25); (10) the two blind men (9.27–30); (11) the mute man (9.32–33); (12) the giving of power to the apostles for working signs (10.1); (13) the man with the withered hand (12.9–13); (14) the blind and mute demoniac (12.22; Jerome forgets to identify this one as the fourteenth and says that three signs were accomplished simultaneously in this man); (15) the daughter of the Canaanite woman (15.21–28). Jerome does not tell us why he lists only fifteen miraculous signs, or what significance he finds in this number. From Augustine, we know that the number fifteen signifies the harmony between the two Testaments, because it is made up of seven, a number characteristic of the Old Testament (the Sabbath was the seventh day), and eight, a number proper to the New Testament (the Resurrection occurred on the eighth day of the week).[153] Jerome is of course aware of many other miraculous signs done by Jesus (21.21). Interestingly, in a very moving passage, Jerome declares that the most wonderful sign of all was Jesus' expelling the great multitude of money-changers from the Temple (21.15–16).

Jesus' Fearlessness in the Garden of Gethsemane

A recurrent theme in Jerome's commentary is his insistence that Jesus was fearless in the face of persecution and death.[154] Jerome deals with this subject especially in connection with Mt 26.37, where it is reported that in the Garden of Gethsemane Jesus "began to be grieved and distressed." Jerome plays down the apparent, obvious meaning, namely, that Christ in his human nature truly feared his imminent suffering and experienced grave and personal emotional distress on the eve of his Passion. Jesus' agony seems clearly manifested when he prays: "Father, let this cup pass from me" (Mt 26.39). Jerome emphati-

---

153. *In Ps.* 150.1 (CCL, 11.2191); cited by H. de Lubac, *Medieval Exegesis,* 1.258.

154. Cf. 14.13; 22.1–3; 26.1–2, 37, 39, 42, 45, 46, 53–55.

cally argues that Jesus was sorrowful and distressed not for himself, but out of his mercy and on account of the fate that would befall Judas, the apostles, the Jewish people, and pitiful Jerusalem as a result of his suffering and death. He was saddened for the same reason that Jonah was grieved at the withering of the gourd,[155] that is, not for his own sake but because he could foresee the grim fate of others.[156]

The scene of Jesus in agony in the Garden of Gethsemane posed serious interpretive problems for early Christian exegesis, beginning with Origen. It is known that Celsus exaggerated this episode in the Garden of Gethsemane and turned it into a reproach against Jesus.[157] Moreover, Porphyry had cited this passage to maintain that Jesus could not have been of a divine nature; and Julian the Apostate, whose work against the Christians is mentioned by Jerome in 1.16 and 9.9, had criticized Jesus as one who was a "miserable individual incapable of easily supporting his burden, and had need of comforting by an angel [cf. Lk 22.43] though he was supposed a god."[158] It is also possible that Arius and Eunomius had appealed to Jesus' distress in Gethsemane to prove that Jesus did not share in God's divine nature. For in 26.37 Jerome specifically attributes the interpretation to which he is opposed to "heretics."[159]

155. Cf. 26.37 (Jon 4.8).

156. Jerome's interpretation here is based on Hilary; see M. Weedman, *The Trinitarian Theology of Hilary of Poitiers* (Leiden: Brill, 2007), 39–40. It gave rise to a lively and edifying debate in 1499 between John Colet and Erasmus of Rotterdam over the nature of Christ's distress in the Garden of Gethsemane. Colet defended Jerome's interpretation, while Erasmus rejected it as far-fetched. See Desiderius Erasmus, *Epp.* 108 and 109 (published separately as *Disputatiuncula de Taedio, Pavore, Tristicia Iesu* (LB V, 1265–90); *The Distress of Jesus*, in Desiderius Erasmus, *Spiritualia and Pastoralia*, ed. J. O'Malley, CWE 70 (Toronto: University of Toronto Press, 1998), 1–67.

157. Cf. *Contra Celsum* 2.24–25.

158. Fragments from *Contra Galilaeos*, cited in W. Malley, *Hellenism and Christianity: The Conflict between Hellenic and Christian Wisdom in the* Contra Galilaeos *of Julian the Apostate and the* Contra Julianum *of St. Cyril of Alexandria* (Rome: Università gregoriana editrice, 1978), 185.

159. This conjecture seems to be confirmed at least for Eunomius by R. Vaggione, *Eunomius of Cyzicus and the Nicene Revolution*, 107. See the quotation above.

According to R. Layton, Origen had endeavored to harmonize the biblical language found here with Stoic theories of the emotions according to which the very existence of grief was a vice.[160] Origen allegedly found it impossible to believe that Christ should exhibit any such weakness that according to Stoic theory marked a flaw in the disposition of a wise man. Thus, Layton argues, Origen scrutinized the terminology of the narrative in search of evidence to prove that the Savior's mental state cannot be reprehended.[161] Jerome follows Origen in claiming that Jesus experienced "pre-passion" but not real "passion." The former refers to the beginning of agitation, which is not yet morally wrong because voluntary assent is lacking. The latter would be considered evil and wrong in the moral sense. While it seems true that Origen endeavored to defend Jesus against the charge of vice, Layton's analysis seems to ascribe too much concern on Origen's part for reconciling Christ with Stoicism.

Doubtless these pagan and heretical attacks on Jesus' character and nature help account for Jerome's strained and unconvincing position that Jesus was fearless and intrepid in the face of his coming death. Jerome states that it was not for his own sake that Jesus uttered the words, "Father, let this cup pass from me," but out of affection for those who were perishing (26.37). Jerome's interpretation of the words: "My soul is sorrowful *unto death*" (Mt 26.38) seems far-fetched, namely, that Jesus would be sad *until* the apostles had been delivered from sin by his redeeming death. It is scarcely to be doubted that Jerome is correct in recognizing that there is no question of cowardice or panic on the part of Jesus. But generally, Jerome's interpretation of the scene in Gethsemane seems forced. Surely the various reproaches that had been leveled against Jesus by pagans and heretics make Jerome's somewhat defensive explanations more understandable.

160. Cf. R. Layton, "From 'Holy Passion' to Sinful Emotion: Jerome and the Doctrine of *Propassio*," in P. M. Blowers, et al., eds., *Dominico Eloquio—In Lordly Eloquence: Essays on Patristic Exegesis in Honor of Robert Louis Wilken* (Grand Rapids: Eerdmans, 2002), 280–93.; idem, *Didymus the Blind and his Circle in Late-Antique Alexandria* (Urbana: University of Illinois Press, 2004).

161. Cf. Origen, *In Matth. comm. series*, 92 (GCS 38.205–6), cited and discussed by R. Layton, *Didymus the Blind and his Circle in Late-Antique Alexandria*, 121–22.

Primacy of Peter

The sheer number of passages in which Jerome mentions and discusses Peter suggests that he assigned a sort of primacy to him among the apostles.[162] He describes him as the "first among the first" (14.28). Jerome finds Peter to be a man of intensely burning faith and full of affection for Jesus (14.28; 26.33). He is the one on whom Christ will build his Church (16.22–23); he did not remain in the darkness of denial (26.74). Yet on repeated occasions Jerome dismisses the interpretation of Hilary and others who had minimized Peter's faults (16.22–23; 26.72).

8. Influence and Printed Editions

Jerome's *Commentary on Matthew* became a standard work in the Latin West. In his influential book *Institutiones*, Cassiodorus (490–583) mentioned the "diligent care" with which Jerome explained Matthew's Gospel.[163] The Venerable Bede (d. 735) cites Jerome's work frequently in his exegetical writings on the Gospels. Druthmar (d. 880) utilizes Jerome as a model exegete, as do Rabanus Maurus (d. 856), Paschasius Radbertus (d. 865), and scores of other medieval theologians, not least of all Bonaventure and Thomas Aquinas in the *Catena Aurea*. Doubtless one of the peaks of the Catholic veneration of St. Jerome was reached in the works of Erasmus of Rotterdam (d. 1536), whose scholarship was modeled on the multi-lingual Jerome's. Both his *Annotations* and *Paraphrase on Matthew* are infused with insights drawn from Jerome's exegesis. Erasmus's first printed edition of Jerome's complete writings in nine folio volumes was edited at the Froben Press in Basel in 1516.[164] It contains the first biography of the Saint that uses well-grounded critical principles.

The first complete edition of Jerome's letters and some of his other works were published in Rome in 1468 by Sweynheym and Pannartz.[165] Erasmus's edition of 1516–20 was followed by

---

162. Cf. 4.10; 7.25; 10.2; 14.28, 31; 16.17, 18, 22–23; 17.1; 26.33, 34, 51, 58, 72.

163. PL 70: 1119.

164. Cf. CWE 61, *The Edition of St. Jerome.*

165. For most of this information about the printed editions, I have fol-

the edition of Marianus Victorius (Rome, 1564–72), that of Tribbechovius (Leipzig, 1684), the Benedictine edition by Martianay (Paris, 1693–1706), and that of Vallarsi (Verona, 1734–42). Vallarsi's second edition (Venice, 1766–72) was reprinted in PL 22–30. The *Commentary on Matthew* appears in PL 26: 15–218. My translation is based on the CCSL critical text, edited by D. Hurst and M. Adriaen, although I have consulted Bonnard's SC edition extensively and profited a great deal from both his French translation and the copious footnotes. For scriptural passages, I have tried to follow the wording of the RSV as closely as the Latin permits.

lowed J. Scourfield, *Consoling Heliodorus: A Commentary on Jerome, Letter 60* (Oxford, 1993), 37.

COMMENTARY ON MATTHEW

PREFACE

HAT THERE WERE MANY who wrote gospels, both Luke the evangelist testifies, when he says: "Since indeed many have tried to tell a story of the things that have been completed among us, just as they themselves who from the beginning saw the word and ministered to him have handed down to us,"[1] and the literary monuments that endure unto the present time show, monuments which, published by various authors, have been the beginning of various heresies—for example, the gospels according to the Egyptians[2] and Thomas[3] and Matthias[4] and Bartholomew.[5] There is also a Gos-

---

1. Lk 1.1–2.

2. The *Gospel according to the Egyptians* is mentioned by Origen, *Hom. 1 in Lk.*, as one of the heretical gospels. It probably originated in the mid-second century and was a product of pantheistic Gnosticism. It was in special use among the Encratites and had a strong ascetical thrust. Clement of Alexandria, *Strom.* 3.9, reports that it contains a conversation between Jesus and Salome in which Christ declares to her: "I have come to destroy the works of the female." ANF 2.392. In another exchange, Salome asks: "How long shall Death reign?" and receives the answer: "So long as ye women give birth." She replies: "Then I have done well that I bare not." Fragments from this gospel are preserved in *2 Clement* 5, and it is referred to by Hippolytus and Epiphanius. See W. Schneemelcher, "The Gospel of the Egyptians," in Hennecke-Schneemelcher, *NTA* 1, 166–78.

3. The *Gospel according to Thomas* was the apocryphal gospel that received widespread acceptance in various Gnostic circles. It was known to Hippolytus, *Ref.* 5.7.20, and Origen, *Hom. 1 in Lk.*, and a redacted form of it was believed to have influenced the founder of Manicheism. See Quasten, *Patrology* 1.123. It seems to have been written in the second half of the second century and depends directly on the canonical Gospels. The tendency of this collection of "secret words of the living Jesus" is plainly gnostic, and its sayings fit perfectly into the Gnostic mythology described by Irenaeus (see, e.g., Saying 50). The complete text of this gospel was discovered in 1945 in the Coptic Gnostic library near Nag Hammadi. See Hennecke-Schneemelcher, *NTA* 1, 278–307.

4. The *Gospel according to Matthias* is also mentioned by Origen, *Hom. 1 in Lk.* It contained apocryphal discourses received by Matthias in secret instruction from Jesus and commended severe ascetic principles. Fragments are preserved by Clement of Alexandria, *Strom.* 2.9; 3.4; 7.13. See Hennecke-Schneemelcher, *NTA* 1, 308–13.

5. Very little is known of this gospel. Some simply identify it with the *Gospel*

51

pel of the Twelve Apostles,[6] and of Basilides[7] and of Apelles,[8] and of others whom it would be too long to list. For the present it is only necessary to say that certain men have arisen who without the Spirit[9] and without the grace of God "tried to tell a story"[10] rather than to compose historical truth. The following prophetic utterance can be justly applied to them: "Woe to those who prophesy from their own heart, who walk after their own spirit, who say: 'Thus saith the Lord,' but the Lord has not sent them."[11] The Savior also speaks of them in the Gospel of John: "All who came before me were thieves and robbers."[12] [Notice that the Lord says]: "who came," not "who were sent." For he himself says: "They came but I did not send them."[13] For with those who *come* there is arrogant presumption; with those who have been *sent* there is obedient service. But the Church, which has been founded upon the rock by the word of the Lord,[14] which the king has led into his chamber,[15] and to which he has

---

according to the Hebrews, based on the tradition recorded in Eusebius, *HE* 5.10 (cf. Jerome, *Vir. ill.* 36), that St. Bartholomew carried with him into India the Gospel of St. Matthew written in Hebrew characters. But neither Eusebius nor Jerome know of such an identification. See Hennecke-Schneemelcher, *NTA* 1, 484–86.

6. Origen mentions a *Gospel of the Twelve* in *Hom. 1 in Lk.* In *Contr. Pelag.* 3.1.2, Jerome seems to identify this gospel with both the *Gospel according to the Hebrews* and the gospel used by the Nazarenes. He writes: "In the Gospel according to the Hebrews, which is written in the Chaldee and Syrian language, but in Hebrew characters, and is used by the Nazarenes to this day (I mean the Gospel according to the Apostles or, as is generally maintained, the Gospel according to Matthew, a copy of which is in the library at Caesarea) . . ." NPNF2, 6.472. See below on Mt 6.11; 23.35. Hennecke-Schneemelcher, *NTA* 1, 278–307, reject Jerome's identification.

7. Basilides was a Gnostic who taught in Egypt in the first half of the second century. Origen, *Hom. 1 in Lk.*, reports that Basilides "dared to write a gospel and give it his own name." It is quite probable that Basilides, like Marcion, subjected this gospel to revision and alterations favorable to his preconceived dogmatic aims. See Hennecke-Schneemelcher, *NTA* 1, 346–48.

8. Apelles was a heretic of the second century, a disciple of Marcion, who broke with his master on certain issues; cf. Eusebius, *HE* 5.13. Origen reports of him *(Epist. ad amicos in Alex.,* in Rufinus, *Apol. pro Orig.)* that he, like Marcion, had subjected the Gospels and Paul to a process of purification. See Hennecke-Schneemelcher, *NTA* 1, 349–50.

9. Cf. Jude 19.
10. Cf. Lk 1.1.
11. Ezek 13.3.
12. Jn 10.8.
13. Jer 14.14; 23.21.
14. Cf. Mt 16.18.
15. Cf. Song 1.3; 2.4.

extended his hand through the opening[16] of the hidden descent,[17] [is] like a gazelle and like the fawn of deer.[18] Like the Paradise from which four rivers flow,[19] she [the Church] has four corners and rings[20] through which, as the Ark of the Covenant and the guardian of the Law of the Lord, she is conveyed by inflexible wooden poles.[21]

(2) The first of all is Matthew, the tax collector, who is also named Levi,[22] who published a Gospel in Judea in the Hebrew language, chiefly for the sake of those from the Jews who had believed in Jesus and who were by no means observing the shadow of the Law, since the truth of the Gospel had succeeded it.[23] Mark is the second, the interpreter of the apostle Peter and the first bishop of the Alexandrian church, who indeed did not himself see the Lord and Savior, but he narrated the things which he had heard his master preaching, in accordance with the reliability of the events rather than their sequence.[24] The third is Luke, the physician, a Syrian by birth from Antioch whose praise is in his Gospel, who also himself, a disciple of the apostle Paul,[25] composed his book in the regions of Achaia and Boeotia, tracing out certain matters more deeply, and as he himself admits in the preface, describing things that had been heard rather than seen.[26] The last is John the apostle and evangelist, whom Jesus loved very much. While reclining upon the Lord's breast,[27] he drank in the purest springs of doctrines. He alone deserved to hear from the cross: "Behold your mother."[28]

---

16. Cf. Song 5.4.

17. The doctrine of the "hidden descent" refers to the Incarnation of Christ. Its original source is Ignatius, *Ephes.* 19.1, and it proved fascinating to the Church Fathers. The idea was that the Incarnation was at first hidden from Joseph (cf. Mt 1.19), and it remained hidden from the devil (cf. 1 Cor 2.7–8).

18. Cf. Song 2.9; 8.14.   19. Cf. Gn 2.10.

20. Cf. Ex 25.10–12.   21. Cf. Ex 25.10–12.

22. Cf. Lk 5.27.

23. Cf. Col 2.17 and also Eusebius, *HE* 3.39 and especially 6.25.4, where Eusebius cites Origen. Elsewhere Jerome speaks of the authorship of Matthew in *Vir. ill.* 3.

24. Cf. Eusebius, *HE* 2.15; 3.39; 6.14.

25. Cf. 2 Cor 8.18; cf. Eusebius, *HE* 6.25.6.

26. Cf. Lk 1.1–4. See Eusebius (citing Origen), *HE* 6.25.6.

27. Cf. Jn 13.23; 21.25.

28. Cf. Jn 19.27.

When he was in Asia, even then the seeds of the heretics were already sprouting, of Cerinthus,[29] of Ebion,[30] and of the others who deny that Christ came in the flesh.[31] John himself in his epistle calls them antichrists,[32] and the apostle Paul frequently smites them.[33] At that time John was compelled by nearly all the bishops of Asia and delegations from many churches to write more deeply concerning the divinity of the Savior and to break through, so to speak, unto the very Word of God, through a boldness that was not so much audacious as blessed. This is the source of the church's historical tradition[34] that when he was compelled by the brothers to write, he answered that he would do so if a universal fast were proclaimed and everyone would pray to the Lord.[35] When this had been carried out and he had been abundantly filled with revelation, he poured forth that

29. On Cerinthus, the Syrian Gnostic, see Eusebius, *HE* 3.28; 4.14; 8.25. Eusebius depicts him as a chiliast who presented the coming earthly kingdom of Christ as a time of sensuous indulgence. Irenaeus, *Adv. haer.* 1.26, presents Cerinthus as a Gnostic theologian, educated in the wisdom of the Egyptians, who taught that Jesus was born naturally of Joseph and Mary. The idea that John wrote against Cerinthus can already be found in Irenaeus, *Adv. haer.* 3.2.1.

30. Jerome appears to be following the mistaken late tradition of an historical Ebion. Cf. 12.2, where he mentions that Paul was rejected by the Ebionites. According to Irenaeus, *Adv. haer.* 1.26.2, the Ebionites were a Judaizing heresy that used only Matthew's Gospel, repudiated Paul as an apostate from the Law, rejected the virgin birth of Christ, and insisted that the Law of Moses (including circumcision) had to be kept in order to achieve salvation. See also Eusebius, *HE* 3.27. They probably were named from the Hebrew word for "poor" (*ebion*), because of their physical poverty or their attachment to the beatitude: "Blessed are the poor" (though Eusebius says that their name arose "because of the poor and mean opinions they held about Christ"). Later heresiologists (Tertullian, *De praescriptione* 33; Epiphanius, *Haer.* 30.17; Rufinus's Origen, *ComRom* 3.11.2) adopted the apparently mistaken view that the sect was founded by a heretic named Ebion.

31. Cf. 1 Jn 4.2–3.

32. Cf. 2 Jn 7.

33. Cf. Rom 1.3; 2 Cor 5.16; Col 2.4; 2 Thes 2.4–12; 1 and 2 Tm; Eusebius, *HE* 3.28.

34. Cf. Eusebius, *HE* 3.24.11; 6.14.7; Irenaeus, *Adv. haer.* 3.1.1.

35. Jerome's immediate source is Eusebius, but the Muratorian Canon also reports that John ordered a three-day communal fast (cf. Est 4.16) to learn God's will, and that during that night it was revealed to the apostle Andrew that John was to write and publish everything under his name but with the approval of all. A. Wikenhauser, *New Testament Introduction* (New York: Herder & Herder, 1963), 284, is probably correct in saying that this story is legendary, since it contradicts the historical evidence by placing the composition of the fourth Gospel in a period when the twelve apostles were still alive.

heaven-sent prologue: "In the beginning was the Word and the Word was with God and the Word was God. He was in the beginning with God."[36]

(3) The book of Ezekiel also proves that these four Gospels had been predicted much earlier.[37] Its first vision is described as follows: "And in the midst there was a likeness of four animals. Their countenances were the face of a man and the face of a lion and the face of a calf and the face of an eagle."[38] The first face of a man signifies Matthew, who began his narrative as though about a man: "The book of the generation of Jesus Christ the son of David, the son of Abraham."[39] The second [face signifies] Mark in whom the voice of a lion roaring in the wilderness is heard: "A voice of one shouting in the desert: Prepare the way of the Lord, make his paths straight."[40] The third [is the face] of the calf which prefigures that the evangelist Luke began with Zachariah the priest.[41] The fourth [face signifies] John the evangelist who, having taken up eagle's wings[42] and hastening toward higher matters, discusses the Word of God.[43] The other things which follow [in Ezekiel's vision] promote the same sense: their legs were straight and their feet winged, and wherever the Spirit went, they too would go and not return; and their backs were full of eyes, and sparks and torches were moving to and fro in the middle, and there was a wheel in a wheel, and in each there were four faces.[44] This also explains the words

---

36. Cf. Jn 1.1–2.

37. As early as Irenaeus, *Adv. haer.* 3.11.8 (ANF 1.428), the creatures in Ezekiel's vision (Ezek 1.10; cf. Rv 4.7) were applied to the four evangelists; however, with the exception of identifying the Calf with Luke's Gospel, there was no agreement among the Fathers concerning the referents. Irenaeus understood the Lion, Calf, Man, and Eagle to refer to John, Luke, Matthew, and Mark, respectively. For Augustine (*Harmony of the Four Gospels* 1.9) they represent Matthew, Luke, Mark, and John, respectively. Jerome has them refer to Mark, Luke, Matthew, and John.

38. Cf. Ezek 1.5, 10. Cf. Homily 75(I) on the Beginning of the Gospel of St. Mark (1.1–12) in *The Homilies of St. Jerome,* vol. 2 (FOTC 57, 121); *Commentary on Ezekiel* 1.5–6.

39. Mt 1.1.

40. Mk 1.3.

41. Lk 1.5. The allusion is evidently to the priestly animal sacrifices. Cf. Lv 3–4.

42. Cf. Is 40.31.   43. Cf. Jn 1.1.

44. Cf. Ezek 1.4–19; 10.1–17.

found in the Apocalypse of John. After the description of the twenty-four elders who worship the Lamb of God while holding the harps and bowls, it introduces lightning and thunder and the seven spirits moving to and fro and the sea of glass and the four living creatures full of eyes.[45] Then it says: "The first living creature was like a lion and the second was like a calf and the third was like a man and the fourth was like a flying eagle." And a little bit later it says: "They were full of eyes and never ceased day and night from saying: 'Holy, holy, holy, Lord God Almighty, who was and who is and who is to come.'"[46] By all of these things it is plainly shown that only the four Gospels ought to be received, and all the lamentations of the Apocrypha should be sung by heretics, who, in fact, are dead, rather than by living members of the Church.[47]

(4) I am quite amazed, my dear Eusebius, that you should suddenly want me to give you this backpack full of food for your journey, as it were, now that you are just about to sail to Rome. You want me to explain Matthew briefly, to touch upon it lightly with a few words, yet to open up its wider meaning. If you had remembered my answer, you would not have requested within a few days a matter that requires years. For in the first place it is difficult to read everyone who has written on the Gospels. Then it is still more difficult to apply a standard of judgment and excerpt what is best. I confess that very many years ago[48] I read Origen's twenty-five books on Matthew[49] and just as many of his homilies and a kind of verse-by-verse interpretation.[50] I have also read the commentary of Theophilus, bishop of the city of

45. Cf. Rv 4.7.
46. Cf. Rv 4.4–6.
47. Cf. Jude 12; Jas 2.17, 26.
48. Jerome seems to be distancing himself from Origen due to the recent controversies over Origenism. It seems unlikely that Jerome had only read Origen's work "very many years ago" and not more recently, since his own work reproduces Origen's verbatim throughout.
49. Origen composed these at Caesarea in 246. Eight books (10–17) survive, which cover his comments on Mt 13.36–22.33. We also possess an anonymous Latin translation of the commentary that runs from Mt 16.13–27.63. The remains have been edited in the GCS by Klosterman: *Origenes Werke*, 10–12, GCS 40, 38, 41 (Berlin, 1935–1955). Books 10 and 11 were edited and translated by Girod (SC 162).
50. These have not survived.

Antioch;[51] also that of Hippolytus the martyr[52] and of Theodore of Heraclea[53] and of Apollinaris of Laodicea[54] and of Didymus of Alexandria.[55] Add to that the works of the Latins, Hilary,[56] Victorinus,[57] and Fortunatianus.[58] Had I simply excerpted a few things from these works, a commentary worthy of remembrance could have been written. But with Easter now imminent and the winds blowing, you are forcing me to dictate this work in two weeks, so that at one time the stenographers are taking notes, at another the sheets are to be written, at yet another corrections are being made, in order to complete it in the given time—and this especially when you are well aware that I have been so ill for the last three months that I am hardly now beginning to walk about, and could not possibly balance the immensity of the task against the brevity of time.

(5) Therefore, omitting the authority of the ancients, since

51. Theophilus became bishop of Antioch at the end of the second century. His apology for Christianity, *Ad Autolycum*, survives (ANF 2), but his commentary on Matthew is lost. See Jerome, *Vir. ill.* 25; *Ep.* 121.6.

52. Hippolytus, a disciple of St. Irenaeus, was a priest and martyr in Rome (d. 235). Except for this reference of Jerome, there is no knowledge of his commentary on Matthew.

53. Theodore was an anti-Nicene bishop of Heraclea in Thrace in the fourth century and died in 355. Cf. Jerome, *Vir. ill.* 90. J. Reuss edited some fragments that remain from his commentary on Matthew in *Matthäus-Kommentare aus der griechischen Kirche*, *TU* 61 (Berlin, 1957), 55–95.

54. Apollinaris, bishop of Laodicea, had been one of Jerome's teachers during his sojourn in Antioch in 378. See *Ep.* 84.3. His faulty understanding of the Incarnation, according to which Christ's human and divine natures were integrated into one, was later condemned by the Council of Ephesus (431) and Chalcedon (451). Fragments of Apollinaris's commentary on Matthew are found in Reuss (see previous note).

55. Didymus the Blind (313–398) was a celebrated exegete who taught in Alexandria and depended closely on Origen, both in exegesis and in doctrine. Jerome studied with him briefly in 386. Rufinus of Aquileia spent about eight years with him. Early on, Jerome admired Didymus so much that he translated his work *On the Holy Spirit*. Didymus's commentary on Matthew does not survive. See Jerome, *Vir. ill.* 109.

56. St. Hilary, bishop of Poitiers (315–68), was a great opponent of Arianism. His *Commentary on Matthew*, which is extant (PL 9: 917–1078; SC 254, 258), favors the allegorical method, which brings out the spiritual meaning behind the literal one. See Jerome, *Vir. ill.* 100.

57. St. Victorinus, bishop of Pettau in Pannonia, was martyred in 304 under Diocletian. See Jerome, *Vir. ill.* 74. Jerome refers to him also in the Prologue of his translation of Origen's *Homilies on Luke*.

58. Fortunatianus (d. 368) was bishop of Aquileia in the middle of the fourth

there is no opportunity for me to read or follow them, I have briefly composed an historical interpretation, which is the chief thing you requested. From time to time I have intermingled the flowers of the spiritual understanding, reserving a fully finished work for a future date.[59] Now if a longer life is granted to me, or if you fulfill your promises in returning, then I will endeavor to fill in what remains, or to put it better, I will place a very beautiful roof upon the foundations that have been laid and on these partially constructed walls.[60] Then you will know the difference between the presumptuous haste of dictating and the diligence of writing by lamplight through the long hours of the night. At least you know—and I would blush to summon you as a witness of my falsehood—that I dictated the present little work at such great speed that you would think that I was simply reading off someone else's work, rather than composing one myself. Please do not think that I have said this out of arrogant confidence in my natural talent, but rather I desire to prove to you how highly I regard you, since I would rather be at risk among the learned than deny you anything of what you are zealously requesting. This is why I ask that if the discourse is a bit unpolished and the speech is not given with the usual flow, please attribute this to haste rather than to ignorance.

(6) And when you arrive in Rome, give a copy to Principia,[61] Christ's virgin. She has asked me to write on the Song of Songs, but I was prevented from doing so by my protracted illness, and I have postponed the hope for the future. I bind you to the condition that if you withhold from her what I have written for you, she should lock up in her desk what remains to be written for her.[62]

century and was one of Athanasius's Western defenders. Jerome alludes to him in *Vir. ill.* 97. Some fragments of his works are found in CCSL 9, 365–70.

59. This promise was never fulfilled.

60. This image is found frequently in Jerome. Cf. *In Is.* 1.5 (PL 24: 154); *In Amos* 3.9.6 (PL 25: 1090 B).

61. Principia was a Roman lady who lived in virginity. A friend of Marcella, she was well known to Jerome. See Jerome's *Ep.* 127.8.

62. Jerome had written for Principia a commentary on the 45th Psalm (*Ep.* 65), in the close of which he says that she will hereafter understand not only that Psalm, but the whole of the Song of Songs. This seems to have led her to request from Jerome that he would write a commentary on the Song. It is uncertain whether he ever did this, though he did translate Origen's *Commentary on the Song of Songs.*

BOOK ONE (MATTHEW 1.1–10.42)

Chapter 1

HE BOOK OF THE genealogy of Jesus Christ (Mt 1.1). We read in Isaiah: "Who shall declare his genealogy?"[1] Let us not therefore think that the Gospel is contrary to the prophet, so that what the one said was impossible to utter, the other is beginning to declare. For Isaiah was speaking of the genealogy of his divinity, whereas Matthew has spoken about the Incarnation. But he began with fleshly matters, so that through the man we might begin to become acquainted with God.

1.1. *Son of David, son of Abraham.* The order is inverted, but it was changed out of necessity.[2] For if he had put Abraham first and David afterward, he would have had to repeat Abraham to compose the sequence of the genealogy. Therefore, omitting mention of the rest, he declared [him to be] the son of these [men], because the promise concerning the Christ was made only to them: to Abraham, when he said: "In your Seed, all the nations shall be blessed,[3] which is Christ";[4] to David, [in these words]: "I will place one from the fruit of your body upon your throne."[5]

1.3. *Judah begot Phares and Zara of Thamar.* In the Savior's genealogy it is remarkable that there is no mention of holy women, but only those whom Scripture reprehends, so that [we can understand that] he who had come for the sake of sinners, since he was born from sinful women, blots out the sins of everyone.

---

1. Is 53.8.
2. This same issue is addressed by Eusebius of Caesarea, *Quaestiones evangelicae* 5 (PG 22: 901B).
3. Gn 22.18
4. Gal 3.16.
5. Ps 132.11. Psalms are designated by modern numbering.

This is also why in what follows Ruth the Moabite and Bathsheba, the wife of Uriah, are recorded.

1.4. *Naasson begot Salmon.* This Salmon is the leader of the tribe of Judah, as we read in Numbers.[6]

1.8–9. *Joram begot Oziah, and Oziah begot Joatham.*[7] In the fourth book of Kings we read that Ochoziah was begotten from Joram, at whose death "Josabeth the daughter of king Joram, sister of Ochoziah," took Joash, the son of his brother, and rescued him from the slaughter which was being carried out by Athalia.[8] His son Amaziah succeeded him in the kingdom.[9] After him his son Azariah reigned, who is also called Oziah,[10] whom his son Joatham succeeded.[11] You see then that according to the witness of history, three kings intervened whom this Gospel has passed over, inasmuch as Joram did not beget Oziah but Ochoziah and the rest whom we have listed. But since the evangelist's purpose was to put down three groups of fourteen in different time periods,[12] and Joram had married into the family of the most impious Jezebel, therefore the memory of him is removed unto the third generation, lest she be recorded in the genealogy of the holy nativity.

1.12. *And after the deportation to Babylon, Jechoniah begot Salathiel.* If we want to place Jechoniah at the end of the middle group of fourteen, there will not be fourteen but only thirteen in the last group. Therefore, we should know that the Jechoniah mentioned first is the same person as Joiacim, but the Jechoniah mentioned second [that is, Joachin] is the son, not the father. The first of these names [Joiacim] is written with *c* and *m;* the second [Joachin] with *ch* and *n.*[13] Due to a fault of the copyists and to the passage of time, it was mixed up by the Greeks and Latins.

6. Nm 1.7. Jerome has made an error here. The text in Numbers speaks of Naasson, not Salmon.

7. Cf. Hilary, *In Matth.* 1.2.

8. Cf. 2 Kgs 11.2.

9. Cf. 2 Kgs 14.17.

10. Cf. 2 Kgs 15.1.

11. Cf. 2 Kgs 15.7.

12. The first is from Abraham to David; the second from Solomon to Joachim; the third from Joachin to Jesus.

13. Cf. Jerome's *Commentary on Daniel* 1 (PL 25: 495): "Let no one therefore imagine that the Jehoiakim in the beginning of Daniel is the same person as the

1.16. *And Jacob begot Joseph.* The emperor Julian[14] cites this passage to us as an example of a discrepancy among the evangelists: Why did the evangelist Matthew say that Joseph was the son of Jacob, and Luke named him the son of Heli?[15] He does not understand the usage of the Scriptures, that the one is his father according to nature, the other according to law. For we know the commandment given by God through Moses, that if a brother or close relative should die without children, another was to take his wife to raise up progeny for his brother or close relative.[16] On this matter, both the chronologer Africanus[17] and Eusebius of Caesarea have discussed the discrepancies in the Gospels more fully in their books.[18]

1.16. *He begot Joseph, the husband of Mary.* When you hear "husband," let no thought of marriage enter your mind, but remember the usage of the Scriptures, according to which betrothed women are called wives.

1.17. *And from the deportation to Babylon until the Christ fourteen*

---

one who is spelled Jehoiachin [Lat., *Joachin*] in the commencement of Ezekiel. For the latter has '-chin' as its final syllable, whereas the former has '-kim.' And it is for this reason that in the Gospel according to Matthew there seems to be a generation missing, because the second group of fourteen, extending to the time of Jehoiakim, ends with a son of Josiah, and the third group begins with Jehoiachin, son of Jehoiakim. Being ignorant of this factor, Porphyry formulated a slander against the Church which only revealed his own ignorance, as he tried to prove the evangelist Matthew guilty of error." Trans. Archer (1958), p. 19.

14. Julian the Apostate, the nephew of Constantine the Great, was emperor, 361–63. Raised Christian, he converted to paganism, restored Hellenic religion, and persecuted the Christians. He wrote a treatise against the Christians, whom he calls Galileans, which does not survive. But Cyril of Alexandria, who refuted it, cites long extracts from it in *Contra Julianum*. See Malley, *Hellenism and Christianity*.

15. Cf. Lk 3.23.

16. Cf. Dt 25.5.

17. Julius Africanus was a Christian writer of the first half of the third century. He had been an official under Septimius Severus. He exchanged letters with Origen on the subject of the authenticity of the story of Susanna in Daniel. In his letter to Aristides he dealt with the alleged discrepancy between Matthew and Luke on the subject of Christ's genealogy. Eusebius cites from this letter in *HE* 1.7, and introduces Africanus in *HE* 6.31.

18. Only a summary of Eusebius's work mentioned here survives. Cf. PG 22: 879–1006.

generations. Count from Jechoniah to Joseph and you will find thirteen generations. The fourteenth generation, however, shall be attributed to Christ himself.

1.18. *Now the generation of Christ was in this way.*[19] An attentive reader might pose this question: Since Joseph is not the father of the Lord and Savior,[20] how does the sequence of the genealogy descending to Joseph pertain to the Lord?[21] Our first response to this is that it is not the custom of Scripture to trace out the genealogies of women; secondly, Joseph and Mary came from the same tribe. This is why he was compelled by the law to take her, since she was a close relative.[22] Also, the fact that they are counted together [in the census] in Bethlehem[23] clearly shows that they were descended from a single stock.

1.18. *Since Mary his mother was betrothed.* Why is he conceived not from a simple virgin but from one betrothed? First, so that the origin of Mary would be shown through the genealogy of Joseph; second, to prevent her from being stoned by the Jews as an adulteress; third, so that when she fled to Egypt she might have solace. The martyr Ignatius[24] added even a fourth reason why he was conceived from a betrothed woman, saying that it was in order that his birth would be concealed from the devil, so long as he thought that the babe was not born of a virgin but of a wife.[25]

1.18. *Before they came together she was found to be with child from the Holy Spirit.*[26] She was found not by some other but by Joseph, who with the liberty, one might say, of a married man knew ev-

---

19. Cf. Ps. Theophilus of Antioch, *Comment. In IV Evang.*, ed. Otto, 279ff.

20. Cf. Jerome, *Adv. Helv.* 4.   21. Cf. Origen, *fragm.* 10.

22. Cf. Nm 36.8–9.   23. Cf. Lk 2.1–5.

24. Ignatius of Antioch (d. 110–130) wrote several letters en route to Rome, where he was martyred. Seven are extant. They were treasured in the early Church, and Origen, for example, had praised him in *Hom. 6 in Luc.* This may have been one cue for Jerome to cite him at this point. According to J. Lightfoot, *The Apostolic Fathers,* 2d ed., 5 vols. (part two, vol. 2, p. 76, n. 1), Jerome's knowledge of Ignatius was secondhand, not direct, and derived from Origen.

25. Ignatius, *To the Ephesians* 19.1. On this passage, see W. R. Schoedel, *Ignatius of Antioch: A Commentary on the Letters of Ignatius of Antioch* (Philadelphia: Fortress, 1985), 87.

26. Lit., "having in her womb" (*in utero habens*), which is a Hebraic way of describing pregnancy.

erything about his wife-to-be. It does not, however, follow from the words "before they came together" that they did come together afterwards; rather, the Scripture is simply pointing out what did not happen.

1.19. *But Joseph her husband, since he was just and was unwilling to disgrace her, wanted to put her away privately.* He who is joined to a prostitute "becomes one body with her."[27] There is also a precept in the law that not only the accused but also the confidants of evil deeds are guilty of sin.[28] If this is so, why is Joseph recorded to be just, when he is concealing the crime of his wife? This is a testimony to Mary that Joseph, knowing her chastity and perplexed by what had taken place, conceals in silence the mystery that he did not know about.

1.20. *"Joseph son of David, do not be afraid to take Mary as your wife."* We have already said above[29] that betrothed women are called wives. My book *Against Helvidius* shows this more fully. And with tender feeling, the angel speaks to him in a dream to approve the justice of his silence. At the same time one should note that Joseph is said to be a son of David, so that Mary too would be shown to be of the stock of David.

1.21. *"And you shall call his name Jesus; for he shall save his people."* Jesus in the Hebrew language means "Savior." The evangelist, then, has pointed to the etymology of his name, saying, in effect: "You shall call his name 'Savior,' because he shall save his people."

1.22–23. *Now all this came to pass that what was spoken by the Lord through the prophet might be fulfilled, saying: "Behold, the virgin shall have in her womb and shall give birth."*[30] In place of what the evangelist Matthew says: "She shall have in her womb," it was written in the prophet: "She shall receive in her womb." But because the prophet is predicting the future, he signifies what is going to happen and writes "she shall receive." The evangelist, because he is narrating the story not as a future event but as past, has changed "she shall receive" and has written "she shall have." For one who *has* is by no means going to *receive*.[31] We

---

27. 1 Cor 6.16.   28. Cf. Lv 5.1.

29. See on Mt 1.16.   30. Cf. Is 7.14.

31. Italics within the commentary here, as elsewhere, indicate that the emphasis has been added by the translator.

have a case of a similar sort in the Psalms: "Ascending on high, he took captivity captive, he received gifts among men."[32] In citing this testimony, the apostle did not say "received" but "gave," because the Psalm pointed to the future—to what Christ would receive—but the Epistle speaks of him who had already given what he had received.

1.24–25. *But arising from sleep, Joseph did as the angel of the Lord commanded him. He took her as his wife and he did not know her until she gave birth to her firstborn son.* Based upon this passage certain people most perversely surmise that Mary also had other sons. They claim that there could not be talk of a firstborn unless there are brothers, although it is the custom of the Holy Scriptures to call "firstborn" not one who is followed by brothers, but the first to be born. Read my above-mentioned book *Against Helvidius.*

Chapter 2

2.2. *"For we have seen his star in the east."* To the confusion of the Jews, in order that they might learn about the birth of Christ from the Gentiles, a star rises in the east. They had known that this would happen by the prediction of Balaam (whose successors they were).[33] Read the book of Numbers.[34] By the sign of the star the Magi are conducted to Judea, that the priests who had been questioned by the Magi concerning where the Christ was to be born might be without excuse concerning his advent.

2.5. *But they said to him: "In Bethlehem of Judea."* This [Judea] is an error of the copyists. For we think that it was first published by the evangelist as we read in the actual Hebrew:[35] Judah, not Judea.[36] For of other nations, what Bethlehem is there that re-

---

32. Ps 68.18; cf. Eph 4.8.   33. Cf. Origen, *fragm.* 24.
34. Cf. Nm 24.17.

35. Some think Jerome means here: "in the Hebrew gospel," i.e., in the *Gospel according to the Hebrews.* Cf. Hennecke-Schneemelcher, *NTA* 1, 141; A. Plummer, *An Exegetical Commentary on the Gospel According to Matthew,* 12.

36. The Hebrew text of Mi 5.2 has "O Bethlehem Ephrathah, who are little to be among the clans of Judah." Jerome thinks that a corruption of Matthew's text has occurred in which Judah was replaced by Judea. He has already treated this question in *Ep.* 57.8 to Pammachius.

quired here the use of the qualifying expression "of Judea"? But "of Judah" is written for this reason, because there is another Bethlehem in Galilee. Read the book of Joshua, son of Nave.[37] Finally, even in the very testimony which has been taken from the prophecy of Micah it is stated as follows: "And you Bethlehem, land of Judah."[38]

2.11. *And opening their treasures they offered him gifts of gold, frankincense, and myrrh.* Juvencus the priest[39] has comprehended the mysteries of the gifts most beautifully in a single brief verse:

> Gold, myrrh, and frankincense are the gifts they bring,
> To a man, to a God, and to a king.[40]

2.12. *And having received an answer in a dream that they must not return to Herod, they went back to their own country by another way.* Those who offered gifts to the Lord receive, in consequence, a response. Now the response (in Greek χρηματισθέντες) does not happen through an angel but through the Lord himself, that the special favor of Joseph's merits might be demonstrated. But they return by another way because they were not to be associated with the infidelity of the Jews.

2.13. *Behold, an angel of the Lord appeared to Joseph in a dream saying: "Arise and take the child and his mother, and flee to Egypt."* When he took the child and his mother to cross over to Egypt, he takes them at night and in the darkness; but when he returns to Judea, there is no mention of either night or darkness in the Gospel.

2.15. *In order that what was spoken by the Lord through the prophet might be fulfilled, saying: "Out of Egypt I have called my son."*[41] Let

---

37. Cf. Jos 19.15.

38. Mi 5.2. Jerome has not cited the OT text accurately here.

39. Juvencus was a Spanish Christian poet of the fourth century who flourished under Constantius. An admirer of Virgil, he wrote a hexameter life of the Lord Jesus based on the Gospels. This was the first effort to tell the Gospel story in metrical form. See Jerome's *Vir. ill.* 84. Irenaeus, *Adv. haer.* 3.9.2, links the myrrh with Christ's humanity/mortality, gold with Christ's kingship, and frankincense with his deity.

40. Juvencus, *Evang. Lib.* I, 250–251 (CSEL 24,16); cf. Virg., *Aen.* 2.49.

41. Cf. Hos 11.1.

those who deny the authenticity of the Hebrew volumes[42] answer where one may read this passage in the Septuagint.[43] When they fail to find it, we shall tell them that it is written in the prophet Hosea, as also the copies which we have recently published can attest.[44] We can confirm this passage even otherwise for the sake of the contentious, though the apostle Paul says that he and the church of Christ simply do not have this custom [of contention].[45] We bring forth a testimony from Numbers, with Balaam speaking: "God called him out of Egypt, his glory was like that of a unicorn."[46]

2.17–18. *Then was fulfilled what was spoken through Jeremiah the prophet, saying: "A voice was heard in Rama, weeping and much wailing, Rachel weeping for her children, and she was unwilling to be consoled, because they are not."*[47] Benjamin was born of Rachel, but there is no Bethlehem in his tribe. The question is raised, therefore, how Rachel could weep for the children of Judah, that is, of Bethlehem, as though they were her own.[48] We shall briefly answer that she was buried near Bethlehem in Ephratha (it received the name of the mother from the place of internment of the remains of her precious body); or because the two tribes of Judah and Benjamin bordered each other and Herod had commanded that the boys be killed not only in Bethlehem but in all its surrounding regions. We understand through the event at Bethlehem that many also from Benjamin were slaughtered. "She weeps for her sons and does not receive consolation" may be understood in two ways: either that she considered them to be dead forever, or that she did not want to console herself about those she knew would live. As for the words: "in

---

42. *Graeca veritas* and *hebraica veritas* are standard expressions for the original Greek and Hebrew texts as the reliable texts. See Jerome's preface to the Pentateuch.

43. Lit., "in seventy translators" (*in LXX . . . interpretibus*). The Septuagint (LXX) was the Greek translation of the Hebrew Bible made by Alexandrian Jews in the third century B.C. According to tradition, seventy translators were involved.

44. He is referring to his translations of the OT. Jerome also discusses this text in *Ep.* 57.7 to Pammachius.

45. Cf. 1 Cor 11.16.   46. Nm 23.22.

47. Jer 31.15; cf. Gn 35.18.   48. Cf. Origen, *fragm.* 34.

Rama," we are not to think that this is the name of the place near Gabaa. Rather, Rama is translated "on high," so that the meaning is: A voice has been heard on high, that is, it has gone forth far and wide.

2.20. *"Those who were seeking the life of the child are dead."* Based upon this passage we understand that not only Herod but also the priests and scribes had plotted the Lord's murder at that time.

2.21. *Arising, he took the child and its mother.* He did not say: "He took his own son and his own wife," but "the child and its mother." For he was a foster-father and not a husband.

2.22. *But hearing that Archelaus was reigning in Judea in place of Herod his own father.* Many, owing to their ignorance of history, fall into the error of thinking that this Herod is the same one by whom the Lord is mocked in his Passion[49] and who is now reported to be dead. In fact, that Herod, who later became friends with Pilate,[50] is the son of this Herod, the brother of Archelaus. Tiberius Caesar banished this very man [Archelaus] to Lyons, which is a city in Gaul, and he made his brother Herod the successor of his kingdom. Read the history of Josephus.[51]

2.23. *And he went and settled in a city which is called Nazareth, in order that what was spoken through the prophets might be fulfilled: "For he shall be called a Nazarene."* If he had recorded an exact citation from the Scriptures, he never would have said: "what has been spoken through the prophets," but simply: "what has been spoken through the prophet." But now, by saying "prophets" in the plural, he is showing that he has not taken the words, but rather the sense, from the Scriptures. "Nazarene" is translated "holy."[52] All Scripture relates that the Lord was to be holy. We can also explain this in another way, that according to the Hebrew truth, it is written in Isaiah even in the same words: "A shoot shall arise from the root of Jesse, and a Nazarene shall ascend from the root."[53]

---

49. Cf. Lk 23.11.　　　50. Cf. Lk 23.12.

51. According to Josephus (*AJ* 17.13.2), Archelaus was relegated to Vienna (in Gaul) and not to Lyons, as Jerome says.

52. Cf. Origen, *fragm.* 36.　　　53. Is 11.1.

Chapter 3

3.2. *"Do penance, for the kingdom of heaven has come near."* First, John the Baptist proclaims the kingdom of heaven, so that the Lord's precursor might be honored with this privilege.

3.3 *"For this is he who was spoken of through Isaiah the prophet, who said: 'A voice of one crying in the desert: Prepare the way of the Lord, make his paths straight.'"* He was preparing the souls of believers in which the Lord would walk. Thus the pure one would walk upon very pure ways, and say: "I shall dwell in them and I shall walk about and I shall be their God, and they shall be my people."[54] Porphyry[55] compares that passage to the beginning of the evangelist Mark, in which it is written: "The beginning of the Gospel of Jesus Christ, the Son of God; just as it is written in the prophet Isaiah: 'Behold, I am sending my messenger before your face, who will prepare your way, a voice of one crying in the desert: Prepare the way of the Lord, make his paths straight.'"[56] For since the testimony is woven together from Malachi and Isaiah,[57] he asks how we can think the citation has been taken from Isaiah alone. Men of the Church[58] have responded to him in great detail.[59] My opinion is either that the name of Isaiah was added by a mistake of the copyists, which we can prove has happened even in other passages, or at least that one unit has been created out of diverse scriptural testimonies. Read the thirteenth Psalm and you shall discover this same thing.[60]

---

54. Lv 26.12; 2 Cor 6.16.

55. Porphyry (232–305), a disciple of Plotinus, was a prestigious Neoplatonic philosopher and historical critic, who in 268 wrote in fifteen books a ferocious attack, entitled *Against the Christians,* in which he tried to point out the contradictions in the Christian Scriptures.

56. Mk 1.1–2. Cf. Jerome's Homily 75(I) on the beginning of the Gospel of St. Mark (1.1–12) in FOTC 57, 122.

57. Cf. Mal 3.1; Is 40.3.

58. Origen uses the term "man of the Church" (ἐϰϰλησιαστιϰὸς ἀνήϱ), as opposed to a follower of heretics, in *Hom. in Lk.* 16.6.

59. Porphyry's work was refuted by Methodius of Olympus, Apollinaris of Laodicea, and more thoroughly by Eusebius of Caesarea (*Preparation of the Gospel, Demonstration of the Gospel,* and another work that is lost).

60. Jerome seems to be referring to the way in which Paul, in Rom 3.10–12, cites Ps 14.3 at the head of a unit that comprises a string of other OT texts.

3.4. But John himself had clothing made of camels' hair and a leather girdle about his loins. It says he had [clothing made] "of hair," not of wool. The former is an indication of austere dress, the latter of luxury and softness. The leather girdle, too, with which Elijah was girded[61] is a σύμβολον [symbol] of mortification. What comes next:

3.4. His food was locusts and wild honey agrees well with his solitary abode. Thus he was satisfying not the [desire for the] delights of foods but the necessity of [our] human flesh.

3.9. "God is able to raise up sons for Abraham from these stones." He calls the pagans stones on account of their hardness of heart. Read Ezekiel, who says: "I shall remove from you the heart of stone, and I shall give a heart of flesh."[62] Hardness is shown by stone, and tenderness by flesh. Or it may simply indicate the power of God, that he who made everything out of nothing[63] can also produce a people from the hardest rocks.

3.10. "Behold, the axe has been placed at the root of the trees." The proclamation of the word of the Gospel, which is a sharp double-edged sword,[64] is called an axe according to Jeremiah the prophet. He compares the word of the Lord with an axe that can cut rock.[65]

3.11. "Whose sandals I am not worthy to carry." In another Gospel he says, "Whose sandal strap I am not worthy to loose."[66] In the one passage his humility is shown, in the other the mystery that Christ is the Bridegroom,[67] and John is not deserving to loose the strap of the Bridegroom, lest, according to the law of Moses and the example of Ruth, his house be called "the house of the un-sandaled."[68]

---

61. Cf. 2 Kgs 1.8.   62. Ezek 36.26.
63. Cf. 2 Mc 7.28.   64. Cf. Rv 1.16; cf. Heb 4.12.
65. Cf. Jer 46.22.   66. Lk 3.16.

67. The mystery, designated as such by Paul in Eph 5.32, is that Christ is the spouse of the Church and that he fulfills this role figuratively in the OT (Song of Songs, Hosea, Ezekiel, Isaiah).

68. Cf. Dt 25.10; Ru 4.8–11. Jerome is referring to the law of levirate marriage. If brothers dwell together and one of them dies without leaving behind sons, the wife will take her deceased husband's brother for a husband. If he refuses, she will remove his sandal and spit in his face, and his house will be called "the house of the un-sandaled."

3.11. *"He will baptize you in the Holy Spirit and fire."* This may mean that the Holy Spirit is a fire, as the Acts of the Apostles teaches, when he descended and sat as a fire upon the tongues of the believers,[69] and the word of the Lord was fulfilled, saying: "I have come to cast fire upon the earth and how I wish that it would burn."[70] Or it could mean that presently we are baptized with the Spirit, and in the future with fire. The apostle is also in agreement with this meaning: "The fire shall test the quality of each one's work."[71]

3.13. *Then Jesus came from Galilee to the Jordan to John that he might be baptized by him.* The Savior accepted baptism from John for three reasons: first, in order that, since he had been born man, he might fulfill all the justice and humility of the Law; second, so that by his own baptism he might give approval to John's baptism; third, so that by sanctifying the waters of the Jordan by the descent of the dove, he might show forth the coming of the Holy Spirit in the [baptismal] bath of believers.

3.15. *"Let it be so now."* "Now" was beautifully spoken. He wanted to show that Christ had to be baptized in water, but John had to be baptized by Christ in the Spirit. Or, here is another interpretation: "Let it be so now." That is, I, who have assumed the form of a slave, must fulfill also the humility of a slave.[72] But know this: you must be baptized by my baptism on the day of judgment. "Let it be so now," says the Lord. I have even another baptism by which I am to be baptized.[73] You baptize me in water, in order that I might baptize you for my sake in your blood.

3.15. *"For thus it is fitting for us to fulfill all justice."* He did not add justice "of the Law" or "of nature," so that we might understand both [forms of justice]. And if God accepted baptism from a man, no one should disdain receiving it from a fellow slave.

3.16. *The heavens were opened for him, and he saw the Spirit descending as a dove coming upon him,* etc. The mystery of the Trin-

69. Cf. Acts 2.3. In his haste Jerome's memory seems to have slipped. In Acts, the Holy Spirit does not descend on the tongues of believers, but in the form of tongues of fire.

70. Lk 12.49.   71. 1 Cor 3.13.
72. Cf. Phil 2.7.   73. Cf. Lk 12.50.

ity is shown in the baptism.[74] The Lord is baptized, the Spirit descends in the form of a dove, the voice of the Father is heard offering testimony to the Son. Now the heavens are opened not by an unbolting of the elements, but [they are opened] to the spiritual eyes, with which even Ezekiel at the beginning of his book records that they were opened.[75] A dove, too, sat upon the head of Jesus to prevent anyone from thinking that the Father's voice was addressing John and not the Lord.

Chapter 4

4.1. *Then he was led into the desert by the Spirit.* It is scarcely to be doubted that he was led by the Holy Spirit. For these words follow:

4.1. *To be tempted by the devil.* He is not led unwillingly, or as a captive, but with the intention of doing battle.

4.2. *And when he had fasted forty days and forty nights, afterward he was hungry.* In that number forty, a mystery is being shown to us. Both Moses, on Mount Sinai, and Elijah, near Mount Horeb, fasted by this number.[76] The body is permitted to hunger so that an opportunity might be granted to the devil to tempt him.

4.3. *"Tell these stones to become bread."* To one who is hungry, it is fittingly said: "Tell these stones to become bread." But you, O devil, are caught in a dilemma. If, at his command, stones can become bread, then you are tempting him in vain, who is in possession of such great power. But if, on the other hand, he cannot do it, then it is in vain that you suspect him to be the Son of God: "If you are the Son of God, tell these stones to become bread."

4.4. *He responded and said: "It is written: 'Man does not live by bread alone, but by every word that proceeds from the mouth of God.'"* The testimony has been taken from Deuteronomy.[77] Now the reason the Lord responds in this way was that he had resolved to conquer the devil by humility, not by force. At the same time it should be observed that if the Lord had not begun to fast,

---

74. Cf. Origen, *fragm.* 58.
76. Cf. Ex 24.18; 1 Kgs 19.8.
75. Cf. Ezek 1.1.
77. Cf. Dt 8.3.

there would have been no occasion for the devil to tempt him. This agrees with the following: "Son, when you come to the service of God, prepare your soul for temptation."[78] But even the very response of the Savior shows that he who was tempted was a man: "Man does not live by bread alone, but by every word that proceeds from the mouth of God." So then, if one does not feed on the Word of God, he does not live.

4.5. *Then the devil took him into the holy city.* The "taking" that is spoken of here did not come about because of [any] helplessness on the Lord's part, but from the arrogance of the enemy, who regards the willingness of the Savior as compulsion. From this passage the meaning of another passage is revealed, where it is written: "They went away into the holy city and appeared to many."[79]

4.5. *He stood him on the pinnacle of the temple,* so that he might also tempt with empty fame the one whom he had tempted with hunger.

4.6. *"If you are the Son of God, throw yourself down."* In all the temptations the devil carries on like this, in order to find out whether he is the Son of God. But the Lord tempers his response in such a way so as to leave him in doubt.

4.6. *"Throw yourself down."* This is the voice of the devil, by which he is always desiring the downfall of everyone. "Throw yourself," he says. This shows that he can persuade, but he cannot cast down.

4.6. *"He has commanded his angels concerning you, that they should take you up in their hands, lest perchance you strike your foot against a stone."* We read this in the ninetieth Psalm.[80] But there the prophecy is not about Christ but about a holy man. The devil therefore interprets the Scriptures badly.[81] At least, if he had known that it was truly written about the Savior, he should have also said what follows in the same Psalm against himself: "You shall tread upon the asp and the basilisk, and you shall trample on the lion and the dragon."[82] He speaks about the help of

---

78. Sir 2.1.   79. Mt 27.53.
80. Ps 91.11. Cf. Origen, *fragm.* 65.
81. Cf. Homily 20 on Ps 90 (91), FOTC 48, 161.
82. Ps 91.13.

angels, as if to a weakling, but like a shifty imposter he is silent about his own trampling.

4.7. *Jesus said to him: "Again it is written: 'You shall not tempt the Lord your God.'"* He breaks the false arrows of the devil drawn from the Scriptures upon the true shields of the Scriptures. Also to be noted is that he brought forth only the necessary citations from Deuteronomy, in order to make known the mysteries of the second law.[83]

4.8. *Again the devil took him to a very high mountain and showed him all the kingdoms of the world and their glory.* The glory of the world which is going to pass away with the world[84] is shown on a mountain and in loftiness (*supercilio*). But the Lord descends to the humble places and to the fields, in order to overcome the devil by humility. Further, the devil hastens to lead him to the mountains so that others as well might fall through those [mountains] through which he himself had fallen. This agrees with the words of the apostle: "lest having become puffed up he may fall into the judgment of the devil."[85]

4.9. *"All these things I shall give you, if you will fall down and worship me."* Arrogant and proud, he says this, too, out of boasting. It is not that the devil has the entire world in his power, so that he can give away all its kingdoms, since we know that very many holy men have been made kings by God. He says, "if you will fall down and worship me." Therefore, he who is going to worship the devil has previously fallen.

4.10. *Then Jesus said to him: "Go, Satan; it is written: 'You shall worship the Lord your God and you shall serve him alone.'"* It is not as the majority think, that Satan and the apostle Peter are condemned with the same judgment. For it is said to Peter: "Go behind me, Satan";[86] that is to say, follow me, you who are opposed to my will. But here he hears: "Go, Satan," and "behind" is not said to him. Thus one should understand: Go into the eternal fire which is prepared for you and your angels.[87]

4.9–10. *"You shall worship the Lord your God."* When the devil

83. Jerome is playing on the etymology of the word Deuteronomy (δεύτερος νόμος), i.e., "second law."

84. 1 Cor 7.31.   85. 1 Tm 3.6.
86. Mt 16.33.   87. Mt 25.41.

says to the Savior: *If you will fall down and worship me,* he hears the contrary, that he himself ought rather to worship him, his own Lord and God.

4.11. *Then the devil left him, and angels came and were ministering to him.* Temptation precedes so that victory may follow. The angels minister so that the worth of the victor might be proven.

4.15. *"Land of Zabulon and land of Nephthalim,"* and the rest. These were the first to hear the Lord preaching, so that where the first captivity of Israel by the Assyrians had been, there the proclamation of the Redeemer might arise.

4.17. *From that time Jesus began to preach and to say: "Do penance, for the kingdom of heaven will come near."*[88] When John was handed over, straight away Jesus begins to preach.[89] The consequence of the Law ceasing is that the Gospel arises. But if the Savior preaches the same things that John the Baptist had previously said, he shows that he is the Son of the same God whose prophet [John] is.

4.19. *"Come after me, and I shall make you become fishers of men."* These were the first ones to be called to follow the Lord. They are illiterate[90] fishermen and are sent to preach, lest it be thought that the faith of believers comes from eloquence and learning rather than from the power of God.[91]

4.24. *And he cured both lunatics and paralytics.* He is not speaking of those who were truly lunatics, but of those who were thought to be lunatics due to the deception of demons. By observing lunary seasons, demons long to defame the creation in order that blasphemies redound to the Creator.[92]

Chapter 5

5.1. *And seeing the crowds, he went up on a mountain, and when he had sat down, his disciples came to him.* The Lord goes up to the mountains to draw the crowds toward deeper matters with

---

88. The CCSL text has the future tense here. The SC changes this to the perfect.

89. Cf. Origen, *fragm.* 74.

90. Cf. Acts 4.13.

91. Cf. 1 Cor 2.4–5.

92. See below on Mt 17.15–16.

himself,[93] but the crowds are not capable of ascending. The disciples follow and he speaks to them, not standing, but sitting and drawn in. For they were unable to understand him shining in his majesty. Some of the more simple brothers think, in accordance with the letter, that it was on the Mount of Olives that he taught the Beatitudes and the other things which follow. This is hardly the case. For from what precedes and what follows, the location is shown to be in Galilee. In my opinion it is either Tabor or some other high mountain. After all, after he finished his words, it immediately follows: "Now when he had entered Capernaum."[94]

5.3. *"Blessed are the poor in spirit."* This is what we read elsewhere: "And he will save the humble in spirit."[95] But lest anyone think that the Lord is preaching that kind of poverty that is sometimes borne by necessity, he has added "in spirit," that you might understand humility, not indigence. "Blessed are the poor in spirit," who on account of the Holy Spirit are poor voluntarily. This is also why the Savior speaks through Isaiah concerning those who are poor in this way: "The Lord has anointed me; for this reason he sent me to evangelize the poor."[96]

5.4. *"Blessed are the meek, for they shall possess the land."* He does not mean the land of Judea or the land of this world, nor the accursed land that brings forth thorns and thistles.[97] For the cruelest warrior can possess that land. Rather, he means the land that the Psalmist desires: "I believe that I shall see the good things of the Lord in the land of the living."[98] One who possesses land in this way and who triumphs after the victory is further described in the forty-fourth Psalm: "Set out and proceed prosperously, and reign because of truth and meekness and justice."[99] For here below people possess land not through meekness, but through arrogance.

5.5. *"Blessed are those who mourn, for they shall be consoled."* The mourning recorded here is not the mourning of those who have died in accordance with the common law of nature, but

93. Cf. Jn 12.32.
94. Mt 8.5.
95. Ps 34.18.
96. Is 61.1.
97. Cf. Gn 3.18; Heb 6.8.
98. Ps 27.13. Cf. Origen, *fragm.* 82.
99. Ps 45.4.

the mourning over those who have died in their sins and vices. Thus did Samuel weep for Saul, because he made the Lord regret that he had anointed him king over Israel.[100] Thus did the apostle Paul claim to weep and mourn for those who did not do penance after committing fornication and uncleanness.[101]

5.6. *"Blessed are those who hunger and thirst for justice."* It does not suffice for us to want justice, if we do not experience a hunger for justice. Thus from this example we should understand that we are never sufficiently just, but it is always necessary to hunger for works of justice.

5.7. *"Blessed are the merciful."* Mercy is understood not only in almsgiving but in every sin of a brother. For we are to carry the burdens of one another.[102]

5.8. *"Blessed are the pure in heart, for they shall see God."* He is not referring to those who have no consciousness of sin. A pure man is conspicuous for his pure heart; the temple of God cannot be polluted.[103]

5.9. *"Blessed are the peacemakers."* This refers to those who make peace, first in their own heart, then among dissenting brothers.[104] For what use is it when others are pacified through you, if within your own heart there are wars of vices going on?

5.10. *"Blessed are those who suffer persecution for the sake of justice."* He has expressly added: "for the sake of justice." For many suffer persecution on account of their sins, and they are not just. At the same time observe that the eighth beatitude of the true circumcision[105] is terminated with martyrdom.[106]

5.11. *"Blessed are you when they revile you and persecute you and falsely say all manner of evil against you."* This kind of reviling is to be despised and produces blessedness, because it is brought forth from the lying mouth of a reviler. This is also why he has expressly defined what this blessed reviling consists in, when

---

100. Cf. 1 Sm 15.11.
101. Cf. 2 Cor 12.21.
102. Cf. Gal 6.2.
103. Cf. 1 Cor 3.16–17.
104. Cf. Homily 41 on Ps 119 (120) in FOTC 48, 315.
105. Cf. Rom 2.29; Phil 3.3. see below on Mt 9.18.
106. The number eight is symbolic of perfection and relates to circumcision, since the circumcision of infants took place on the eighth day. Cf. Lk 2.21. It relates to martyrdom, since martyrdom unites the Christian perfectly with Christ.

he says: "falsely saying all manner of reviling against you on account of me." So then, when Christ is its cause, reviling should be wished for.

5.12. *"Rejoice and exult."* I do not know who among us can fulfill these words, that when our reputation is torn to pieces by abusive speech, we should exult in the Lord. He who pursues empty fame cannot fulfill this. Therefore, we ought to rejoice and exult, so that a reward may be prepared for us in heaven. We read it elegantly written in a certain book: "Do not seek glory, and you will not grieve when you are without glory."[107]

5.13. *"You are the salt of the earth."* The apostles are called salt because through them the entire human race is seasoned.

5.13. *"But if the salt loses its strength, by what shall it be salted?"* If a teacher errs, by what other teacher shall he be corrected?

5.13. *"It is no longer of any use except that it be thrown out and trampled by men."* The example has been taken from agriculture. For salt is necessary as a condiment on foods and for drying meat. It has no other use. Of course, we read in the Scriptures that enraged conquerors sowed certain cities with salt, so that no sprout would arise in them.[108] So then, let teachers and bishops beware and see that "the mighty endure torments mightily."[109] There is no remedy for them, but the downfall of the great leads to Tartarus.[110]

5.14–15. *"You are the light of the world. A city set on a mountain cannot be hidden, nor do they light a lamp and place it under the measure,"* and the rest. He is teaching about courage in preaching. He wants to keep the apostles from hiding out of fear, like lamps placed under a measure. Rather, with complete freedom, they must let themselves be known, so that what they have heard in the rooms they should proclaim on the housetops.[111]

5.17. *"Do not think that I have come to destroy the law or the prophets; I have not come to destroy but to fulfill."* This means either that he fulfilled what was prophesied about himself through others, or that by his own preaching he has fulfilled the things that previously had been rough and imperfect, owing to the weakness

---

107. Sir 9.16?   108. Cf. Jgs 9.45.
109. Wis 6.7.   110. 2 Pt 2.4.
111. Mt 10.27.

of the hearers, removing wrath and the law of retaliation,[112] excluding even the lust hidden in one's heart.[113]

5.18. *"Until heaven and earth pass away."* A new heaven and a new earth are promised to us, which the Lord God is going to make. Therefore, if new things must be created, it is consistent that the old things are going to pass away.[114] But as for what follows:

5.18. *"Not one jot or tittle shall pass away from the law until all things are done,"* by a figure of the letter it is shown that even the things that are thought to be least in the law are full of spiritual mysteries, and that all things are recapitulated in the gospel. Who then possesses the erudition and learning to demonstrate how even the various sacrifices, which seem superstitious, are daily fulfilled in victims?[115]

5.19. *"Whoever destroys one of the least of these commands and so teaches men shall be called least in the kingdom of heaven; but whoever does them and teaches them shall be called great in the kingdom of heaven."* This section is rooted in the preceding testimony in which he had said: "Not one jot or one tittle shall pass away from the law until all things are done." Therefore, he is taunting the Pharisees who despised God's commands and were establishing their own traditions. He means that their teaching[116] among the people is of no benefit to them, if they destroy even a little bit from what was commanded in the law. We can also understand it in another way, that the learning of a teacher, even if he is guilty of a small sin, demotes him from the greatest position. Nor is it advantageous to teach a justice that the smallest fault destroys.[117] Perfect blessedness is to fulfill in deed what you teach in word.

5.22. *"Everyone who is angry with his brother."* In some codices the words are added: "without reason." But in the authentic texts the judgment is definite and anger is completely taken away, since the Scripture says: "Whoever is angry with his broth-

---

112. Cf. Mt 5.21–22.
113. Cf. Mt 5.27–28.
114. Cf. 2 Cor 5.17.
115. Cf. Rom 12.1.
116. *Doctrina.* This seems to refer to oral instruction, as opposed to tradition.
117. Cf. Ezek 18.26.

er." For if we are commanded to turn the other cheek to the one who strikes us,[118] and to love our enemies,[119] and to pray for those who persecute us,[120] every pretext for anger is removed. Therefore, the words "without reason" should be erased. For "man's anger does not work the justice of God."[121]

5.22. *"Whoever says to his brother, 'Raca.'"* Strictly speaking, this is a Hebrew word. For *raca* is said for κενός, that is, "void" or "empty." We can express this by the popular insult "brainless." If we are going to render an account for an idle word,[122] how much more are we going to render an account for insulting speech? Also, it is significantly added: "Whoever says to his *brother*, 'Raca.'" For no one is our brother except one who has the same father with us. Since then he likewise believes in God and knows Christ, the wisdom of God,[123] by what account can he be branded with an epithet of foolishness?

5.22. *"But whoever says: 'You fool,' shall be liable to Gehenna."* Ἀπὸ κοινοῦ [From its commonality with] what precedes, one may supply: "Whoever says *to his brother*, 'You fool,' shall be liable to Gehenna." For whoever says, "You fool," to one who equally believes in God, is impious in respect to religion.

5.23. *"If therefore you are offering your gift at the altar and there remember that your brother has something against you."* He did not say, If you have something against your brother, but if "your brother has something against you." Thus a greater responsibility to reconcile is imposed on you.[124] So then, as long as we are unable to placate him, I do not know whether it is consistent that we offer our gifts to God.

5.25–26. *"Be in agreement with your adversary quickly, while you are with him on the way, lest perchance the adversary hand you over to the judge, and the judge hand you over to the officer, and you should be thrown into prison. Amen I tell you: You shall not come out from there until you pay back the last penny."* In place of what we have in the Latin codices as "in agreement," in the Greek texts it is written as εὐνοῶν. This is translated as "benevolent" or "kind."

---

118. Cf. Mt 5.39.   119. Cf. Mt 5.44.
120. Cf. Mt 5.39; Lk 6.27–29.   121. Jas 1.20.
122. Cf. Mt 12.36.   123. Cf. 1 Cor 1.24, 30.
124. Cf. Homily 41 on Ps 119 (120) in FOTC 48, 312; *Ep.* 82.2; *Ep.* 13.

From what precedes and from what follows, the clear meaning is that so long as we are running down the road of this world, our Lord and Savior exhorts us to peace and to concord. This accords with the words of the apostle: "If it is possible, so far as it depends on you, have peace with all men."[125] For also in the preceding section he had said: "If you are offering your gift at the altar and there remember that your brother has something against you."[126] Having finished this, he immediately adds: "Be" benevolent or kind "with your adversary," etc. And in what follows he commands: "Love your enemies, do good to those who hate you, and pray for your persecutors."[127] Though this understanding is clear and consistent, very many[128] think it was spoken about the flesh and the soul, or about the soul and the spirit. This interpretation simply does not stand up. For how will flesh be thrown into prison, if it fails to be in agreement with the soul, seeing that both the soul and the flesh are to be equally shut away? Nor could the flesh do anything except what the mind commands. Or how could the Holy Spirit who dwells within us[129] hand over to the judge either the flesh or the spirit, which are at war,[130] when he himself is the Judge? Others[131] interpret the adversary as the devil in accordance with the epistle of Peter who says: "Our adversary the devil goes around like a roaring lion."[132] They understand the Savior to be commanding that, while it is in our power, we should be benevolent towards the devil, who is an enemy and avenger. We should not make him endure punishments for our sake; for though he himself supplies the incentives of the vices even to those of us who sin voluntarily, if we shall be in agreement with him who is suggesting the vices, then he will have to be tormented for us too. They

---

125. Rom 12.18.   126. Mt 5.23.

127. Mt 5.44.

128. Jerome may be referring to Origen's interpretation, that after death God will divide the souls from the bodies of the disobedient, and assign their soul to prison with unbelievers. See Origen, *ComRom* 2.9 (M893) = FOTC 103, p. 133, n. 250. See also Hilary, *In Matt.* 4.19 (938C).

129. Cf. 2 Tm 1.14.

130. Cf. Gal 5.17; Rom 7.23.

131. Cf. Origen, *fragm.* 102; Ambrose, *In Lucam* 7.

132. 1 Pt 5.8.

say that each of the saints is benevolent toward his own adversary, if he does not make him endure torments for the saint. Certain ones[133] explain it with an even more forced interpretation, referring the words to baptism, that each one enters into a pact with the devil and says: I renounce you, devil, and your pomp and your vices and your world which has been set under evil. If, then, we preserve the pact, we are being benevolent and in agreement with our adversary and by no means will we be shut up in prison. But in truth, to the extent that we have transgressed in those things that we had promised to the devil, we will be handed over to the judge and to the officer and we will be cast into prison and we shall not come out from it until we pay back the last penny [*quadrans*]. The *quadrans* is a kind of coin which is worth two cents [*minuta*]. This explains why in one Gospel that poor widow woman is said to have put a *quadrans* into the treasury, in another [Gospel it says] two cents.[134] It is not that the Gospels disagree but that one *quadrans* has the worth of two cents.[135] What he is saying, then, is this: You will not come out from prison until you pay in full for even the least sins.

5.28. *"Whoever looks upon a woman to lust after her has already committed adultery with her in his heart."* There is a difference between πάθος and προπάθεια, that is to say, between passion and pre-passion. Passion is regarded as a vice, but pre-passion (though it may have blame in its commencement), is not reputed as a sin.[136] Therefore, "whoever looks upon a woman," and

133. It is not clear to whom Jerome is referring here.

134. Cf. Mk 12.42; Lk 21.2.

135. As Simonetti, *Matthew 1a* (ACC), 107, indicates, Jerome's clarification is pointless. "In citing from memory, Jerome has forgotten that whereas Luke 21:2 has only 'two mites,' Mark 12:42 has 'two mites, which make a farthing.'"

136. For a discussion of this distinction and its reputed sources in Stoicism, see R. A. Layton, "From 'Holy Passion' to Sinful Emotion: Jerome and the Doctrine of *Propassio*." "Pre-passion" is frequently employed to designate the agonies of Christ before the Passion. See below on Mt 26.37 and Simonetti's comment cited there. There its meaning is "temptation." In *Ep.* 79 to Savina, Jerome translates προπάθεια as "antepassio"; cf. NPNF2, 6:167: "It is difficult, nay more it is impossible, to escape the beginnings of those internal motions which the Greeks with much significance call προπάθειαι, that is 'predispositions to passion.'"

his spirit becomes stimulated, has been struck by pre-passion; but if he consents and makes an affection out of the thought, then it has passed from pre-passion to passion, as is written in David: "They passed into the feeling of the heart."[137] To such a one, the will to sin is not absent, but only the opportunity. Whoever then "looks upon a woman to lust," that is, if he looks in order to lust, so that he is disposed to act, that one rightly is said to have "committed adultery with her in his heart."

5.29. *"But if your right eye is an occasion of sin to you,"* etc. Since he had spoken above about lust for a woman, he has now rightly named as the eye the thought and feeling that is flying about in different directions. By the right [hand] and by the other parts of the body are indicated the beginnings of the will and of feeling, so that what we conceive with the mind, we would fulfill in deed. We must beware, then, that what is best in us should not quickly slip into vice. For if the right eye and right hand are occasions for sin, how much more the things which are on the left in us. If the spirit slips, how much more the body, which is more prone toward sins. Here is another interpretation: By the right eye and right hand is shown affection for brothers, wife, children, neighbors, and close relatives.[138] If we see them as a hindrance to us in contemplating the true light, we ought to cut off such parts, lest, while we want to gain others, we ourselves may perish forever.[139] This is why it is said of the high priest whose

137. Ps 73.7.   138. Cf. Lk 18.29–30.

139. Cf. 1 Cor 9.22, 27; Rom 14.15. J. P. O'Connell, *The Eschatology of Saint Jerome,* 173–75, cites this passage along with six others (*In Ezechielem* 16.52 [2x]; *In Jeremiam* 17.2–4; *In Isaiam* 62.10–12; *In Ecclesiasten* 4.9–12; *In Matt.* 25.46) as evidence that suggests that for Jerome once professing the Christian faith is no assurance of avoiding eternal punishment and of finally entering heaven. On the basis of his words in *In Isaiam* 66.24 and *Dial. Adv. Pelag.* 1.28, however, Jerome has been accused of advocating "mercyism," i.e., the doctrine that all believing Christians will eventually be delivered from punishment. O'Connell, 175, thinks it probable that Jerome was a mercyist (as opposed to an Origenist, who asserted that all rational creatures, including the devil and his angels, will be restored). O'Connell admits, however, that the above seven passages, especially *In Matt.* 25.46, create tension for those (like himself) who question Jerome's orthodoxy on this question. Yet the present writer disagrees with O'Connell's statement that in the present passage (5.30) Jerome has in view the sin of the loss of faith. Jerome may be opposing Jovinian here.

spirit was consecrated to the worship of God: "For mother and father and sons, he will not be defiled."[140] This means that he will not know any affection except for him to whose worship he has been consecrated.

5.31–32. *"It was said: 'Whoever puts away his wife, let him give her a written notice of dismissal';*[141] *but I say to you, that everyone who puts away his wife,"* etc.[142] In a later section[143] the Savior explains this passage more fully, where he says that Moses commanded a notice of dismissal to be given on account of the hardness of heart of husbands. Moses was not conceding divorce, but taking away murder. For it is permitted as a far better thing that a deplorable discord should take place than that blood be shed through hatred.

5.34. *"But I tell you not to swear at all, neither by heaven,"* etc. The Jews always had this rotten habit of swearing by the elements, as the prophetic words frequently accuse them.[144] The one who swears venerates and esteems that by which he swears. In the Law there is a command that we should not swear except by the Lord our God.[145] The Jews, by swearing by angels and by the city of Jerusalem and by the Temple and the elements, were venerating creatures and fleshly things with the honor and obedience due to God. Finally, consider that the Savior here has not prohibited swearing by God, but by heaven and earth and Jerusalem and by your own head. This had been conceded by the Law, as it were to children, so that in what manner they were offering victims to God so as to avoid offering them to idols, thus also they were permitted to swear to God. It is not that they were right in doing this, but that it was better to exhibit it to God than to demons. But the gospel truth does not admit swearing, since entirely faithful words have replaced swearing on oath.

5.38–39. *"You have heard that it was said: 'An eye for an eye, a tooth for a tooth'; but I tell you not to resist evil."* The one who says: "An eye for an eye," does not want to remove the other's eye

---

140. Lv 21.11.
141. Cf. Dt 24.1.
142. Jerome explains this passage at length in *Ep.* 55.4 to Amandus.
143. Cf. Mt 19.8.   144. Cf. Is 65.16.
145. Cf. Dt 6.13; 10.20.

so much as to preserve both.[146] By removing reciprocation, our Lord is cutting off the commencement of sins. In the Law there is retribution; in the Gospel, grace; in the Law faults are corrected; in the Gospel the beginnings of sins are removed.

5.39–40. *"If someone strikes you on your right cheek, offer him the other also; and he who wants to go to court with you and take away your tunic, let him take your cloak as well."* A man of the Church[147] is described as an imitator of him who says: "Learn from me, for I am meek and humble in heart."[148] And he proved his own promise when he was slapped: "If I spoke evil, expose it; but if well, why do you strike me?"[149] David said something similar in the Psalm: "If I have rendered evil to those repaying me."[150] And Jeremiah says in the Lamentations: "It is good for a man to sit in his youth. Let him give his cheek to the one who strikes him, let him be filled with reproaches."[151] This contradicts those who think there is one God of the Law, another of the Gospel, for gentleness is taught under both. According to the mystical understanding, when our right [cheek] has been struck, we are commanded to offer not the left, but the "other," that is, another right cheek.[152] For a just man does not have a left.[153] If a heretic strikes us in a disputation and wants to wound right doctrine (*dextrum dogma*),[154] another testimony from the Scriptures should be opposed to him. And we should continuously offer successive right [cheeks] to the one who strikes, until the enemy's wrath wears down.

5.42. *"Give to him who asks of you, and do not turn away the one who wants to borrow from you."* If we understand this as having

---

146. In Jerome's view this law did not have vengeance as its goal but the prevention of violence. The two eyes described here are that of the victim and that of the one to be punished.

147. See above on Mt 3.3.   148. Mt 11.29.

149. Jn 18.23.   150. Ps 7.4.

151. Lam 3.27–30.

152. Cf. Homily 20 on Ps 90 (91) in FOTC 48, 161; *On Ezekiel* 41.23–26; *On Ecclesiastes* 10.

153. In many texts in the writings of the Church Fathers, "left" (Lat., *sinistra*) tends to symbolize what is evil and ill-favored. See Origen, *ComRom* 3.8.5 (FOTC 103, 220).

154. For *dextrum dogma*, see Origen, *fragm.* 108.

been said solely about alms, then it cannot apply to the majority of the poor. Moreover, if the rich were to give at all times, they would be incapable of giving always. Therefore, after having spoken to the apostles, that is, to the teachers, about the virtue of giving alms, he gives them the command that those who have received freely are to give freely.[155] This kind of money never runs out, but it is multiplied in proportion to the amount given. And though an adjacent field may harden [in a drought], the spring water never dries up.

5.44. *"But I say to you: Love your enemies, do good to those who hate you."* Many who measure God's commands according to their own feebleness, rather than by the strength of the saints, think that the things that have been commanded here are impossible. They say that in view of our strength, it is sufficient not to hate one's enemies; but to be commanded to love them, well, this goes beyond what is experienced by human nature. It needs to be known, therefore, that Christ does not command impossibilities, but perfection.[156] This is what David practiced with respect to Saul and Absalom.[157] Stephen too, the martyr, prayed for his enemies who were stoning him.[158] Moreover, Paul desires to be accursed on behalf of his own persecutors.[159] And Jesus both taught and practiced this when he said: "Father, forgive them; for they know not what they do."[160]

5.45. *"So that you may be sons of your Father who is in heaven."* If one becomes a son of God by keeping God's commands, then he is not a son by nature but by his own choice.

---

155. Cf. Mt 10.8.

156. Cf. Mt 5.48. Cf. the *Roman Catechism* (The Catechism of the Council of Trent), trans. J. A. McHugh and C. J. Callan (Rockford: Tan Books, 1982), part 3, p. 360: "The pastor should also teach that the Commandments of God are not difficult, . . . But should anyone plead human infirmity to excuse himself for not loving God, it should be explained that He who demands our love pours into our hearts by the Holy Ghost the fervor of His love."

157. Cf. 1 Sm 24.9; 26.5; 2 Sm 18.33. Notice that Jerome invokes OT and NT saints to illustrate Christ's perfection. This shows his understanding of the unity of the Bible's message.

158. Cf. Acts 7.59.   159. Cf. Rom 9.3.

160. Lk 23.34.

Chapter 6

6.2. *"Therefore, when you give alms, do not sound a trumpet ahead of you as the hypocrites do in the synagogues and streets, in order that they may be honored by men."* The one who sounds a trumpet while giving alms is a hypocrite, the one who prays in the synagogues and at street corners in order to be seen by men is a hypocrite, the one who disfigures his face when he fasts so that he might show the emptiness of his belly in his face, he too is a hypocrite. We gather from all of this that hypocrites are people who do things in order to be glorified by men. It seems to me that even the one who says to his brother: "Let me remove the speck from your eye,"[161] is doing this for the sake of glory, that he might be seen to be just. This is why the Lord says to him: "Hypocrite, first remove the plank from your own eye."[162] Only then is the virtue of observation accepted by God, if it is done for God's sake. And so, it is not virtue, but the motive of virtue, that has a reward with God. And if you turn aside a little from the right (*recta*) path, it does not matter whether you go to the right (*dextram*) or to the left (*sinistram*), since you have lost the true road.

6.3. *"But when you give alms, do not let your left hand know what your right hand is doing."* Not only in giving alms, but in doing any good works whatsoever, the left hand should not know. For if that one knows, immediately the right work (*dextra opera*) is co-defiled.[163]

6.5. *"Amen I tell you: They have received their reward,"* not God's reward but their own; for they have been praised by the men for whose sake they have practiced the virtues.[164]

6.6. *"But when you pray, go into your room and shut the door and pray to your Father in secret."* At the literal level, he is teaching the understanding hearer to flee from vain glory when praying. But it seems to me that there is more to this command. We should pray to the Lord with the thoughts of our heart shut in and with our lips compressed. This is what we read that Hannah (Anna)

---

161. Mt 7.4.
162. Mt 7.5.
163. Cf. Origen, *fragm.* 115.
164. Cf. Origen, *fragm.* 113.

did in the book of Kings. It says: "Only her lips alone were moving, but her voice was not heard."[165]

6.7. *"But when praying do not speak much, as the pagans do."* If a pagan speaks much in prayer,[166] then the one who is a Christian ought to say little. For "God is a hearer not of words but of the heart."[167]

6.8. *"For your Father knows what you need before you ask."* A heresy has arisen based upon this passage and also a perverse doctrine of philosophers, who say: If God knows what we should pray for and is aware of what we need even before we ask for it, then we are speaking in vain to the one who knows. One can respond briefly to these people by saying that [in prayer] we are not narrators but askers. For it is one thing to narrate to one who is ignorant; it is something else to make a request from one who knows. In the former there is the giving of information; in the latter there is obedience. In the former we faithfully inform; in the latter we pitifully implore.

6.9. *"Our Father who art in heaven."* By saying "Father," they confess themselves to be sons.

6.9. *"Hallowed be thy name,"* not in you but in us. For if on account of sinners the name of God is blasphemed among the Gentiles,[168] then, on the contrary, it is hallowed on account of the just.

6.10. *"Thy kingdom come."* He is either asking for the kingdom of the entire world in a general sense, that the devil would cease to reign in the world, or he is asking that God would reign in each one, and that sin would not reign in man's mortal body.[169] At the same time the following should be noted: that it pertains to one with great confidence and a pure conscience to ask for the kingdom of God without fearing the judgment.[170]

6.10. *"Thy will be done on earth as it is in heaven,"* so that in the

165. 1 Sm 1.13.
166. Verbosity in prayer was a commonplace in pagan worship. Cf. Seneca, *Ep.* 31.5; Martial 7.60.3.
167. Wis 1.6.
168. Rom 2.24.
169. Cf. Rom 6.12.
170. Cf. 1 Jn 3.21; 4.17–18.

same manner that the angels serve you blamelessly in heaven, thus might men serve you on earth.[171] Let those men blush who, on the basis of this statement, fabricate the idea that daily there are falls from heaven.[172] For what good to us is this comparison with heaven, if there is sin even in heaven?[173]

6.11. *"Give us today our supersubstantial bread."* What we have expressed by "supersubstantial" is rendered in Greek by ἐπιούσιον. The LXX interpreters very frequently translated this word by περιούσιον. We have therefore examined the Hebrew and have found that wherever they had rendered περιούσιον, in Hebrew it is the word *sogolla*. Symmachus[174] translated this word with ἐξαίρετον, that is, "select" or "outstanding," though in one passage it is translated "peculiar." So then, when we ask God to give us peculiar or select [or outstanding] bread, we are asking him who says: "I am the bread that has come down from heaven."[175] In the Gospel which is called "according to the Hebrews,"[176] I have found, instead of "supersubstantial" bread, *maar*, which means "tomorrow's."[177] Thus the sense is: "give us

171. Cf. Homily 58 on Ps 148 in FOTC 48, 419.

172. This is apparently directed against Origen who in *Peri Archon* proposed the theory that for every new human conception, another fall of a pre-existent soul has occurred. Prior to its earthly life the soul resided in heaven. God plants it in a human body as a punishment but with the view of setting it on the path to restoration by means of its bodily life.

173. Cf. Homily 88 in FOTC 57, 223.

174. Symmachus was the second-century Jewish translator of the Hebrew Bible into Greek, whose version occupied the fourth column of Origen's *Hexapla*. Eusebius, *HE* 6.16ff., states that he was an Ebionite, but Epiphanius says he was a Samaritan who became a Jewish proselyte.

175. Jn 6.51.

176. Jerome believed that the *Gospel according to the Hebrews* was essentially the same as the *Gospel according to the Nazarenes* and the *Gospel according to the Apostles*. Eusebius, *HE* 3.25, says that it was placed among the Recognized Books by some. Eusebius himself placed it among the Disputed Books. It owes the high honor in which it was once held to the fact that it was believed by the majority of Christians in the fourth century to be the Aramaic version of St. Matthew's Gospel, referred to by Papias (cf. Eusebius, *HE* 3.39; 6.25; Irenaeus, *Adv. haer.* 3.1.1; Epiphanius, *Haer.* 28.5; 29.9; 30.3, 13, 14). But it was known to have been altered by the Nazarenes and Ebionites, i.e., by the Judaizing Christians who made use of it.

177. For a discussion of this reading, see Hennecke-Schneemelcher, *NTA* 1, p. 142.

today our" tomorrow's, that is, future, "bread."[178] We can understand supersubstantial bread in another way as well: That which is over (*super*) all substances also surpasses all creatures. Others[179] think of it literally, in accordance with the apostle's words when he says, "Having food and clothes, we are content with these."[180] Thus, saints should care only about the present day's food, for which reason it is also commanded in what follows: "Do not think about tomorrow."[181]

6.13. *"Amen."* This is the seal of the Lord's Prayer. Aquila[182] translates it "faithfully." We can say: "truly."[183]

6.14. *"For if you forgive men their sins."* [Consider] what is written: "I have said, you are gods and you are all sons of the Most High, but you shall die like men and you shall fall as one of the rulers."[184] This is said to those who, on account of their sins, have deserved to go from being gods to men. Rightly also, then, those whose sins are forgiven are called men.

6.16. *"For they banish* (exterminant) *their faces in order to appear to men to be fasting."* The word *exterminant,* which is common in the Church's Scriptures, by a fault of the translators, signifies something far different from what is commonly understood. For exiles are banished who are sent beyond the borders *(extra terminos).* Therefore, in place of this word, we ought always to use *demoliuntur* [they disfigure]. For a hypocrite disfigures his face in order to feign sadness, and though his heart may be rejoicing, he wears a look of sorrow on his face.

6.17. *"But you, when you fast, anoint your head and wash your face."* He is speaking in accordance with a custom of the province of Palestine. There, people customarily anoint their heads

---

178. Cf. Homily 47 on Ps 135 (136) in FOTC 48, 355.

179. Cf. Cyprian, *De orat. dominica,* 19; Gregory of Nyssa, *De orat. dominica, orat.* 4.

180. 1 Tm 6.8.

181. Mt 6.34.

182. Aquila was a second-century Jew who published a slavishly literal Greek translation of the Hebrew OT that was intended to replace the LXX that was in use by the Christians. He was a native of Sinope in Pontus and lived under Emperor Hadrian. Jerome and Origen admitted the fidelity of his translation to the Hebrew. Aquila's text occupied the third column of Origen's *Hexapla.*

183. Cf. Jerome, *Ep.* 26.4.

184. Ps 82.6–7.

on feast days. And so, he is commanding that when we fast, we should show ourselves to be joyful and festive. On the other hand, many who read the words of the Psalmist: "Let not the oil of a sinner anoint my head,"[185] want there to be a good kind of oil, of which it is said elsewhere: "God, your God anointed you with the oil of exultation above your fellows."[186] And so, he is commanding that when practicing the virtues we should anoint the principal faculty of our heart with spiritual oil.

6.21. *"Where your treasure is, there is also your heart."* This should be understood not only of money, but of all passions. The god of a glutton is his belly.[187] Therefore, where his heart is set is precisely where also his treasure is found. Banquets are the treasure of the luxurious, partying of the lascivious, lust of a lover. "Each one is conquered by that to which he is enslaved."[188]

6.22. *"If your eye is single, your whole body will be lighted."* Those with sore eyes customarily see numerous lamps. A single and pure eye looks at simple and pure things. All this transfers to the senses. For just as the body, if there are no eyes, is totally in darkness, so if the soul loses its principal splendor, all the senses die with it in an obscure darkness.

6.23. *"If, then, the light that is in you is darkness, how great will be that darkness?"* If the senses, which are a light for the soul, are obscured by a fault, in what darkness do you think the obscurity itself is enveloped?

6.24. *"You cannot serve God and mammon."* In the Syriac language, riches are called *mammon*.[189] "You cannot serve God and mammon."[190] Let the greedy hear this, let him hear that the one who is enrolled by the name of Christian cannot serve Christ and riches at the same time.[191] And yet, he did not say: he who has riches, but: he who serves riches. For he who is a slave of riches guards his riches, like a slave; but the one who has shaken off the yoke of slavery distributes them, like a master.

---

185. Ps 141.5.

186. Ps 45.7.

187. Phil 3.19.

188. 2 Pt 2.19.

189. Cf. Homily 16 on Ps 83 (84), in FOTC 48, 119.; *Ep*. 121.6, 22.31.

190. Cf. Origen, *fragm*. 129.

191. This passage is reminiscent of Jerome's dream, recorded in *Ep*. 22.30, when Christ denounced him for being a Ciceronian and not a Christian, saying: "For where your treasure is, there shall your heart be also."

6.25. *"Do not be anxious for your life,*[192] *what you should eat, nor for your body, what you should wear."* In several manuscripts it is added: "nor what you should drink." Therefore, we should be entirely free from concern for what nature has bestowed upon all, and what is common to domestic animals, wild beasts, and human beings. But we are commanded not to be anxious about what we consume, because we prepare bread for ourselves by the sweat of our face.[193] Labor must be spent, but anxiety is taken away. As for the words: "Do not be anxious for your life, what you should eat, nor for your body, what you should wear," we should understand this of carnal food and clothing. On the other hand, we should always be anxiously concerned about spiritual food and clothing.

6.25. *"Is not life more than food and the body more than clothing?"* What he is saying is this: He who provided the greater things will most certainly provide the lesser things as well.

6.26. *"Look at the birds of heaven; they do not sow nor reap nor gather into barns, but your heavenly Father feeds them. Are you not more than they?"* The apostle commands us not to be wiser than is fitting.[194] That testimony should also be preserved in the present section. For there are some[195] who, wanting to go beyond the limits of the fathers[196] and fly on high,[197] are submerged in the lowest places. They claim that the birds of heaven refer to the angels and the other powers in service to God. Without a care of their own, they are fed by the providence of God. If this is so, as they want it to be understood, why [does Jesus go on] to speak to men in what follows: "Are you not more than they"? Therefore, it should be understood simply, that if the birds are without care and troubles, as they are fed by the providence of God, birds that are here today and will not exist tomorrow, birds whose life is mortal, and when they have ceased to exist, shall not always be in existence, how much more should men be directed by the choice of God, men to whom eternity is promised.

---

192. Or "soul" (*anima*).   193. Gn 3.19.
194. Rom 12.3.
195. This is probably directed against Origen's interpretations.
196. Cf. Prv 22.28.
197. Cf. Is 40.31.

6.27–28. *"Which of you can add to his stature one cubit? And why are you anxious about clothes?"* Just as by the comparison with birds he demonstrated that life is more than food, so from the things that follow he is showing that the body is more than clothes. He says:

6.28. *"Consider the lilies of the field, how they grow,"* etc. And indeed, what silk, what royal purple, what weaver's embroidery can be compared with flowers? What is so red as a rose? What gleams as white as a lily? No purple dye surpasses the purple of the violet. This is a judgment more of the eyes than of words.

6.34. *"Do not be anxious about tomorrow."*[198] So then, he has conceded that those whom he forbids giving thought about the future ought to be solicitous about the present. This is why the apostle says: "Laboring day and night with our hands that we should not be a burden to any of you."[199] In the Scriptures "tomorrow" refers to the time to come. Jacob says: "My justice shall answer for me tomorrow."[200] And in the apparition of Samuel, the woman with the pythonical spirit[201] says to Saul: "Tomorrow you will be with me."[202]

6.34. *"Sufficient for the day is its own evil."* When he says "evil" here, he does not mean the opposite of virtue, but the toil and affliction and anguish of the world. This is the kind of evil with which Sara afflicted Hagar her maidservant; significantly it is said in Greek as: ἐκάκωσεν αὐτήν.[203] Therefore, thinking about the present time suffices for us. Let us relinquish concern about the future, which is uncertain.

Chapter 7

7.1. *"Do not judge that you not be judged."* If he prohibits judging, how is it consistent that Paul judges the fornicator in Corinth, and Peter convicts Ananias and Sapphira of lying?[204]

---

198. Jerome has already commented on this verse for the priest Amandus, who had requested an interpretation of it. Cf. *Ep.* 55.1 (NPNF2, 6.109).

199. 1 Thes 2.9. 200. Gn 30.33.

201. Cf. Acts 16.16. 202. 1 Sm 28.19.

203. Cf. Gn 16.6 LXX. 204. Cf. 1 Cor 5.3–4; Acts 5.1–10.

But from what follows he shows what he has prohibited. He says: *for in what manner you judge, so shall it be judged concerning you.* Thus he has not prohibited judging, but taught it.

7.3. *"But why do you look at the speck in your brother's eye, and the plank in your own eye you do not see?"* etc. He is speaking about those who, though they themselves are held to be guilty of mortal sin, do not concede lesser sins in the brothers. Straining out a gnat, they swallow a camel.[205] Rightly, therefore, with their pretense of justice, they are called hypocrites, as we said above.[206] With a plank in their own eye, they spot the speck in their brother's eye.

7.6. *"Do not give what is holy to dogs."* What is holy is the bread of sons.[207] We ought not take the bread of sons and give it to dogs.

7.6. *"Do not cast your pearls before swine."* A swine does not receive adornment, since it returns to wallowing in the mud.[208] And according to the Proverbs of Solomon: "If it has a golden ring, it is found to be filthier."[209] Some[210] want these dogs to be understood as those who after [coming to] faith in Christ turn back to the vomit of their sins.[211] They interpret the swine as those who have not yet believed the Gospel and are wallowing in the mud of unbelief and in vices. It is not appropriate, then, quickly to entrust the pearl of the Gospel to men of that sort. For they may trample it, and then turn and start tearing you to pieces.

7.7. *"Ask and it shall be given to you, seek and you shall find, knock and it shall be opened to you."* He who had above forbade asking for carnal things shows what we ought to seek. If it is given to the one who asks, and the one who seeks finds, and it will be opened to the one who knocks, then to whom it is not given and who does not find and to whom it will not be opened, it appears that he has not asked well, sought well, and knocked well. And so, let us knock on the door of Christ,[212] concerning which it is said: "This is the gate of the Lord, the just shall enter

---

205. Cf. Mt 23.24.
207. Cf. Mt 15.26.
209. Prv 11.22.
211. Cf. 2 Pt 2.22; Prv 26.11.

206. See on Mt 6.2; 6.16.
208. 2 Pt 2.22.
210. Who?
212. Cf. Jn 10.7.

through it."[213] When we have thus entered, may the hidden and secret treasures in Christ Jesus, in whom is all knowledge,[214] be opened to us.

7.11. *"If, then, you though you are evil know to give good things to your sons."* One should note that he has called the apostles "evil." It is possible, however, that under the persona of the apostles he is condemning the entire human race, whose heart from infancy is set toward evil in comparison with the divine mercy. Read Genesis.[215] It is not surprising that men of this age are called evil, since even the apostle Paul records: "Redeeming the time, since the days are evil."[216]

7.13. *"Enter through the narrow gate; how wide is the gate and broad the road[217] which leads to destruction, and many are they who enter through it; how narrow the gate and constricted the way that leads to life, and few are they who find it."* The broad road refers to the pleasures of the world that men seek; the narrow road is the one that is opened by means of labors and fasting.[218] The apostle had taken this road, and he exhorts Timothy to take it as well.[219] At the same time consider how distinctly he has spoken about both roads. Many walk down the broad one; few find the narrow one. We do not seek the broad road, nor is it necessary to discover it. It offers itself of its own accord, and is the way of those who are astray. But neither do all find the narrow road, nor do those who find it immediately take it. Indeed, many who have found the way[220] of truth are taken captive by the pleasures of the world and turn back from the middle of the road.

7.15. *"Beware of false prophets who come to you in sheep's clothing, but inside they are ravenous wolves."* To be sure, this can be understood about all who promise one thing by their dress and speech, but who demonstrate something else by their deeds.[221] But it should be understood particularly of the heretics. By their continence, chastity, and fasting, they appear to be wearing, as it were, a kind of garment of piety, but inwardly they have poison-

---

213. Ps 118.20.
214. Cf. Col 2.3.
215. Cf. Gn 8.21.
216. Eph 5.16.
217. Or "way" (*via*).
218. Cf. 2 Cor 6.5; 11.27.
219. Cf. 1 Tm 5.21; 2 Tm 2.1–10.
220. Or "road" (*via*).
221. Cf. Origen, *fragm.* 145.

ous hearts, and they deceive the hearts of the simpler brothers. By the fruits of their soul, then, by which they entice innocence to its destruction, they are compared with ravenous wolves.[222]

7.18. *"A good tree cannot produce evil fruit, nor can an evil tree produce good fruit."* Let us ask a question of the heretics, who claim that there are two mutually opposed natures [of souls].[223] If in accordance with their understanding, a good tree can never produce evil fruit, how is it that Moses, who was a good tree, sinned at the water of contradiction?[224] How is it that David killed Uriah and lay with Bathsheba?[225] Peter too, at the Lord's Passion, denied him, saying: "I do not know the man."[226] Or with what consistency did Jethro, the father-in-law of Moses, an evil tree who assuredly did not even believe in the God of Israel, give good counsel to Moses?[227] Moreover, Achior said something useful to Holofernes.[228] Also, the apostle approved what the comic-poet had spoken well: "Bad company corrupts good morals."[229] And when the heretics find nothing to say in response, we will add as well the fact that Judas, who at one time was a good tree, produced evil fruit when he betrayed the Savior.[230] And Paul, who was an evil tree at the time when he was persecuting Christ's Church, produced good fruit later when he was transformed

---

222. Origen speaks of the excellent life of some heretics in *Homilies on Ezekiel*, 7.3. (These sermons were translated by Jerome himself). Elsewhere, Origen speaks of the Encratites, who are reported to abstain from types of food and drink that they believed were opposed to chastity. Cf. Origen, *ComRm* 10.1 (M1250) (FOTC 104, 254). On the other hand, Epiphanius (*Haer.* 67) says that the Encratites abstain from certain foods not for the sake of continence or piety, but from fear and for appearance's sake. Epiphanius also notes that the Ebionites once took pride in virginity. Cf. *Haer.* 30.2.6. Jerome seems to be following Epiphanius's more cynical attitude toward these groups.

223. Here Jerome is thinking chiefly of Gnostic heretics such as Marcion, Valentinus, Basilides, and Manicheus, who taught that salvation and damnation were determined by the nature one receives at birth, and that no conduct in this life could alter one's destiny. Cf. Origen, *fragm.* 147; *Peri Archōn* 2.9.5; Jerome, *Ep.* 133.9 to Ctesiphon; *In Is.* 1.1, 16, 57; *Adv. Jov.* 2.3.

224. Cf. Dt 32.51.   225. Cf. 2 Sm 11.27.
226. Cf. Mt 26.72.   227. Cf. Ex 18.19.
228. Jdt 5.5.
229. Menander, *Thais;* cited by Paul in 1 Cor 15.33.
230. Cf. Jn 13.2.

from a persecutor into a vessel of election.[231] Therefore, a good tree does not produce evil fruit, as long as it continues in the pursuit of goodness, and an evil tree abides in the fruits of sins, as long as it is not converted to repentance. For no one who remains in what he was, begins what he has not yet begun to be.

7.21. *"Not everyone who says to me: 'Lord, Lord,' shall enter into the kingdom of heaven, but he who does the will of my Father who is in heaven."* Just as he had said above,[232] that those who were not wearing the garment of a good life must not be received on account of the wickedness of their dogmas, so now he asserts the converse, in order to prevent the faith from being accommodated to those who, though they may be strong with the soundness of faith, live basely and by their evil works destroy the soundness of their doctrine. For both are necessary to God's servants, so that the works are proven by words, and one's words are proven by one's works. But [the following words] might seem contrary to this statement: "No one can say: 'Lord Jesus,' except by the Holy Spirit."[233] But it is a usage of the Scriptures to understand what is said for what is done. Thus immediately in what follows, Jesus proves that they are refuted who claim the knowledge of the Lord without works. For they hear from the Savior: "Depart from me, workers of iniquity, I do not know you."[234] And the apostle says in the same sense: "They profess to know God, but by their deeds they deny him."[235]

7.22–23. *"Many shall say to me on that day: 'Lord, Lord, did we not prophesy in your name and in your name drive out demons and in your name do many miracles?' And then I shall confess to them: 'I never knew you; depart from me, you who are working iniquity.'"* To prophesy and to do miracles and to expel demons sometimes does not come from the merit of him who works them, but either the invocation of the name of Christ does it, or it is granted on account of the condemnation of those who invoke his name or for the benefit of those who see and hear them.[236] Thus, even though

---

231. Cf. Phil 3.6; Acts 9.15.   232. Cf. Mt 7.15.

233. 1 Cor 12.3. Cf. Origen, *fragm.* 150.

234. Lk 13.27.   235. Ti 1.16.

236. A difficult passage. Jerome appears to say that prophecy, miracle-working, and exorcism can be granted to martyrs, that is, those who are condemned for invoking Christ's name, or for the purpose of the conversion of onlookers.

men may be seeing those who are doing the signs, nevertheless they should glorify God, at whose invocation such great miracles are being done. For Saul and Balaam and Caiaphas prophesied without knowing what they were saying.[237] Pharaoh and Nebuchadnezzar know the future by means of dreams.[238] And in the Acts of the Apostles the sons of Sceva appeared to expel demons.[239] It is also narrated that the apostle Judas, with the heart of a traitor, did many signs along with the other apostles.[240]

7.23. *"Then I shall confess to them."* He has expressly said: "I shall confess," because, for a long time previous to this, he had avoided saying: I have not known you. The Lord does not know those who perish.[241] But observe this as well: Why would he have added: "I have never known you," if, as some say,[242] all men have always lived among rational creatures?

7.23. *"Depart from me, you who are working iniquity."* He did not say: You who have worked iniquity, lest he should seem to take away repentance, but "you who are working," that is, you who up to the present hour, though the time of judgment has come, although you do not have the possibility to sin, nevertheless you still have an affection for it.

7.25. *"And the rain came down and the rivers came and the winds blew."* This rain that tries to undermine the house is the devil. The rivers are all the antichrists, who think contrary to Christ. The winds are the spiritual wickedness in the heavenly places.[243]

7.25. *"And it did not fall; for it had been founded on the rock."* Upon this rock the Lord founded the Church; from this rock

---

237. 1 Sm 10.6–12; Nm 24.17; Jn 11.50–51.

238. Cf. Gn 41.17–36; Dn 2.29–46.   239. Cf. Acts 19.14–16.

240. Lk 9.6.

241. Cf. Origen, *ComRom* 7.7.5 (M1123): "But of the others [those who perish], however, God is said not only not to foreknow, but not even *know* them." FOTC 104, 85.

242. He probably means Origen, who had speculatively proposed that human souls are angels (rational creatures) that became embodied as a result of their antecedent falling away. According to this hypothesis, at the first moment of their embodied existence, men have guilt. Jerome seems to mean that Christ could not say to these men, "I never knew you," if he had known them previous to their embodied life. For a citation of Origen's conjectural theories, see Jerome, *Ep.* 124.3 to Avitus.

243. Cf. Eph 6.12; Origen, *fragm.* 151.

also the apostle Peter was allotted his name.[244] The tracks of the serpent are not found upon a rock of this sort.[245] The prophet also speaks confidently about this rock: "He has established my feet upon the rock,"[246] and in another place: "The rock is a refuge for" hares, or "badgers."[247] For a timid animal finds refuge in the crevices of a rock, and its rough and completely armored hide protects it from javelins by such a covering. This is also why it is said to Moses, at the time when he had fled from Egypt and was a little hare of the Lord: "Stand in the crevice of the rock, and you will see my back parts."[248]

7.26. *"He who built his house on sand."* The foundation that the apostle, as the builder, laid is our one Lord Jesus Christ.[249] Upon this foundation, stable and firm, and founded by its own robust mass, the church of Christ is being built. But upon sand, which is fluid and can neither be joined together nor collected into one union, all the words of the heretics are built unto this end, that they might collapse.

7.29. *But he was teaching them as one having authority, and not as the scribes.* The scribes were teaching the people what was written in Moses and the prophets; but Jesus, as the God and Lord of Moses himself, by the freedom of his own intention, was either adding to the Law what it seemed to be lacking, or he modified it as he preached to the people. This is what we read above as well: "It was said to the ancients; but I say to you."[250]

Chapter 8

8.1–2. *When he had come down from the mountain, great crowds followed him. And behold, a leper came and was worshiping him.* When the Lord comes down from the mountain, the crowds run to him, because they had been incapable of ascending to the higher things. And first a leper runs up to him. For because of his leprosy he was not yet able to hear the Savior's many

244. Cf. Mt 16.18.
246. Ps 40.2.
248. Ex 33.22–23.
250. Mt 5.21–22.

245. Cf. Prv 30.19.
247. Ps 104.18.
249. Cf. 1 Cor 3.10.

words on the mountain. It should be noted that he was the first one who was individually cured. The second was the centurion's servant;[251] the third was the mother-in-law of Peter, who was suffering with a fever in Capernaum.[252] In the fourth place he cured those who were brought to him troubled by a demon, whose spirits he expelled with a word, when he also cured all who were sick.[253]

8.2. *And behold, a leper came and was worshiping him, saying.* It is appropriate that after his preaching and teaching, an opportunity for a sign presents itself. In this way the words he has just spoken are confirmed among his hearers by means of miraculous powers.

8.2. *"Lord, if you are willing, you can cleanse me."* He who is requesting the [Lord's] willingness is not in doubt about the [Lord's] power.

8.3. *And stretching forth his hand, Jesus touched him, saying: "I am willing, be cleansed."* When the Lord stretches forth his hand, immediately the leprosy flees. At the same time consider how humble and without ostentation was his response. The leper had said: "If you are willing." The Lord responded: "I am willing." The leper had previously said: "You can cleanse me." The Lord adds to this and says: "Be cleansed." It is not, then, as the majority of the Latins think, that these phrases should be joined and read: I am willing to cleanse. Rather, they should be read separately, so that he first says, "I am willing," and then he gives the command: "Be cleansed."

8.4. *And Jesus said to him: "See to it that you tell no one."* And in fact, why was it necessary to boast with his words over something that he was revealing with his body?

8.4. *"But go, show yourself to the priest and offer the gift which Moses prescribes as a testimony to them."* He sends him to the priest for several reasons. First, for humility's sake, that he might be seen to defer to the priests. For there was a precept in the Law that those who had been cleansed of leprosy were to offer gifts to

251. Lit., "boy" (*puer*). Cf. Mt 8.13.
252. Cf. Mt 8.15.
253. Cf. Mt 8.16. For a continuation of Jerome's enumeration of the miraculous signs, see below on Mt 8.23.

the priests.[254] Second, so that those who saw that the leper had been cleansed might either believe in the Savior, or not believe. If they believed, they would be saved; if they refused to believe, they would be without excuse. A concurrent reason is so that he would not seem to be breaking the Law. This was a charge with which they were very frequently accusing him.[255]

8.5–7. *A centurion came to him asking and saying: "Lord, my servant is lying at home paralyzed and badly tormented." And Jesus said to him: "I shall come and heal him,"* etc. We should not accuse the Lord of presumption, because he promises that he will go at once and heal [the boy]. For he saw the centurion's faith, humility, and wisdom: faith in that he as a Gentile believed that a leper[256] could be healed by the Savior; humility because he judged himself unworthy to have the Lord come under his roof; wisdom because beneath the covering of the body he saw the concealed divinity. He recognized not what would be profitable for himself, which was something that was seen even by unbelievers, but what was lying hidden within. From this wisdom he says this as well:

8.9. *"Behold, though I am a man, I say to this one: 'Go,' and he goes,"* etc. He wants to show that the Lord too can fulfill what he wants, not so much by coming in person, as by the ministries of angels.[257]

8.10. *Now when Jesus heard this, he was amazed.* He was amazed because he saw that the centurion comprehended his majesty. For the bodily infirmities, or rather the opposing powers that had produced the weakness, powers to which man is often subjected, had to be expelled. This was done both by the Lord's word and by the ministries of angels.

8.10. *"Amen I say to you: I have not found such great faith in Israel."* He is speaking of those who were present at the time, not about all the patriarchs and prophets of the past, unless per-

254. Cf. Lv 14.2–32.
255. Cf. Mt 12.2; 15.2.
256. Jerome's memory has slipped, since the narrative concerns a paralytic, not a leper. Many manuscripts make the correction as does Jerome himself at 8.23.
257. Cf. Origen, *fragm.* 156.

haps, in the centurion, the faith of the Gentiles is placed ahead of Israel's faith.

8.11. *"Many shall come from the east and the west and shall recline with Abraham and Isaac and Jacob in the kingdom of heaven."* Because the God of Abraham, the Creator of heaven, is the Father of Christ, therefore Abraham too is in the kingdom of heaven. The nations that have believed in Christ, who is the Son of the Creator, will recline with him. And in like manner that sense is fulfilled concerning which we spoke above,[258] that in the faith of the centurion the special favor for the Gentiles originates. For the people who will believe from the east and the west are commemorated in that man's readiness to believe.

8.12. *"But the sons of the kingdom."* By "sons of the kingdom" he is signifying the Jews in whom God previously reigned.

8.12. *"They will be thrown out into the outer darkness."* Darkness is always inner, not outer. But because the one who is cast out by the Lord has abandoned the light, it is named outer darkness.

8.12. *"There will be weeping and gnashing of teeth."* If there is weeping of the eyes, and if the gnashing of teeth demonstrates the existence of bones, it is then a true resurrection of bodies and of the same members that had died.[259]

8.14–15. *When Jesus had come to the home of Peter, he saw his mother-in-law lying sick with a fever. He touched her hand, and the fever left her, and she got up and was ministering to them.* The woman's hand is touched. When her works are healed, the infirmity of her sins takes flight. Human nature is such that after a fever bodies are rather worn out, and when the healing begins, the body still feels the ill effects of the illness. But a healing conferred by the Lord renders the body whole at once. It is not enough that she was healed, but in order that the ἐπίτασις[260] of her strength might be indicated, it is added: "and she got up and was minis-

---

258. Cf. Mt 8.10.

259. This is possibly directed against a spiritualized understanding of the resurrection body, which was one of the issues during the Origenist controversies.

260. "Intensity, augmentation." This word comes from ἐπιτείνω, "to stretch over or tighten," and is used of musical strings. It is used metaphorically by Plato in the sense of "to increase in intensity, to augment."

tering to them." That hand that had been touched and healed was ministering.

8.16. *But when evening came, they brought to him many who had demons, and he was expelling the spirits with a word, and he was curing all who were ill.* All are cured, not in the morning, not at midday, but in the evening, when the sun is about to set, when the grain of wheat dies in the earth, so that it may bear much fruit.[261]

8.19–20. *And a scribe approached and said to him: "Teacher, I shall follow you wherever you go." And Jesus said to him: "Foxes have holes and the birds of heaven have nests, but the Son of man has nowhere to recline his head."* If this scribe of the Law, who knew only the dying letter,[262] had said: "*Lord,* I shall follow you wherever you go," he would not have been rebuffed by the Lord. But because he regarded him as a teacher, one among many, and because he was a man of letters (which is expressed more clearly in Greek by γραμματεύς)[263] and not a spiritual hearer, therefore he has no place where Jesus can recline his head. But it is also shown to us why the scribe was repudiated, because when he saw the greatness of the signs, he wanted to follow the Savior in order to acquire a profit from the miraculous works. He was longing for the same thing that Simon Magus had also wanted to purchase from Peter.[264] Such faith, then, is rightly condemned by the pronouncement of the Lord. It is said to him: Why do you desire to follow me for the sake of riches and worldly gain, when I am one of such great poverty that I do not even have a little shelter, and I do not even use my roof?

8.21. *But another of his disciples said to him: "Lord, permit me first to go and bury my father."* What similarity is there between the scribe and the disciple? The former calls him teacher, the latter confesses him Lord. The latter, for the sake of an occasion of piety, desires to go and bury his father. The former, who is seeking not a teacher but profit from the teacher, promises that he is going to follow him anywhere.

8.22. *Jesus said to him: "Follow me and let the dead bury their own*

261. Cf. Jn 12.25.
262. Cf. 2 Cor 3.6.
263. The Greek word for "letter" is γράμμα.
264. Cf. Acts 8.19.

dead. "Whoever does not believe is dead. But if the dead buries the dead, we should not have concern for the dead, but for the living, lest, while we are being solicitous concerning the dead, we too may be called dead.[265]

8.23. *And when he was getting into the boat, his disciples followed him,* and the rest. He did the fifth sign[266] when, while getting into the boat from Capernaum, he commanded the winds and the sea.[267] The sixth was when, in the region of Gerasenes, he gave authority to the demons to enter the swine.[268] The seventh was when, upon entering his own city, he cured the second paralytic on the mat.[269] For the first paralytic was the centurion's servant.[270]

8.24–25. *But he was sleeping. And they came and woke him up saying: "Lord save us."* We read of a type of this sign in Jonah, when, while the others are in danger, he himself is safe and sleeping.[271] He is awakened, and he delivers those who wake him by a command and also by the mystery of his own suffering.[272]

8.26. *Then he got up and rebuked the winds and the sea.* From this passage we understand that all created things perceive the Creator. For those to whom the rebuke and the command are given perceive the one giving the command. This accords with the majesty of the Creator, but not with the error of the heretics, who think that all things have souls.[273] Things which are insensible to us are sensible to him.

265. According to J. P. O'Connell, *The Eschatology of St. Jerome,* 1, Jerome interprets the "dead" here to mean those who are in a state of sin and to whom the office of burying the dead is to be left. Cf. *In Is.* 26.19; *In Dan.* 13.22; *In Jer.* 9.21.

266. See above on Mt 8.1–2.   267. Cf. Mt 8.26.

268. Cf. Mt 8.32.   269. Cf. Mt 9.2–8.

270. Cf. Mt 8.6. In 8.5–7 Jerome had called the centurion's servant a leper.

271. Cf. Jon 1.5.

272. Jonah sacrificed himself to save the mariners: "Take me up and throw me into the sea; then the sea will quiet down for you"; Jon 1.12. Since Jesus in Mt 12.39 had made a link between himself and Jonah, Jerome found here a type of Christ. In *Ep.* 53.8 to Paulinus of Nola, he writes: "Jonah, fairest of doves, whose shipwreck shows in a figure the passion of the Lord, recalls the world to penitence, and while he preaches to Nineveh, announces salvation to all the heathen." NPNF2, 6.100.

273. This is probably a reference to the Manicheans. See below on 8.31.

8.27. *Then the men were amazed and said: "What sort of man is this that even the winds and the sea obey him?"* It is not the disciples but the sailors and the others who were in the boat who were amazed. But if someone is contentious and wants those who were amazed to be the disciples, we shall respond that they are rightly called men, for they did not yet know the power of the Savior.[274]

8.29. *"What is there between us and you, Son of God? Have you come here to torment us before the time?"* This is not a voluntary confession for which a reward for confessing follows.[275] Rather, it is an extortion of necessity which compels the unwilling, just as if runaway slaves should see their master after a long time. They beg for nothing else except to be spared the lash. In this way also the demons, upon seeing that the Lord was suddenly living on earth, believed that he had come to judge them. The presence of the Savior is torment for demons. Some people[276] ridiculously think that the demons know the Son of God[277] but the devil is ignorant of him, because they are less evil than he whose servants they are. But since all the knowledge of disciples should be referred to the teacher, so also should the demons, as well as the devil, be understood as suspecting, rather than knowing, that he is the Son of God. "For no one knows the Father except the Son and to whom the Son wants to reveal him."[278]

8.31. *"If you expel us, send us into the herd of pigs." And he said to them: "Go."* When he said, "Go," it is not that the Savior was conceding to the demons what they were requesting, but that an opportunity for salvation to men was being offered through the destruction of the pigs. For when those shepherds see this, they immediately announce it to the city. Let Manicheus[279] blush.

---

274. The same interpretation is found at Mt 16.15, where Jerome makes a distinction between "men," who think of Christ as a human being, and the "apostles," who are not to be called "men," but "gods," because they confess him to be God.

275. Cf. Rom 10.10.

276. Possibly, Origen in a text no longer extant.

277. Cf. Jas 2.19.   278. Cf. Mt 11.27.

279. The most striking point of contact with Buddhist influence is in Manicheus's doctrine of metempsychosis, i.e., the transference of human souls into the bodies of animals. This is apparently the point Jerome is attacking here.

For if the souls of men and beasts are of the same substance and from the same creator, how is it that for the sake of one man's salvation two thousand pigs are drowned?[280]

8.34. *And behold, the whole city went out to meet Jesus, and when they saw him they asked him to move on from their borders.* Those who ask him to move on from their borders do this not out of pride (as some think)[281] but out of humility. They judge themselves unworthy of the presence of the Lord, just as Peter did also at the catch of the fish, when he fell down at the knees of the Savior and said: "Depart from me, Lord, for I am a sinful man."[282]

Chapter 9

9.1–2. *And he came to his own city. And behold, they brought to him a paralytic lying on a mat. Now when Jesus saw their faith, he said to the paralytic: "Take courage, son, your sins are forgiven you,"* and the rest. By "his city" we should understand no other than Nazareth. This is why he was called a Nazarene.[283] Now, as we said above,[284] they carried to him a second paralytic lying on a mat, because he was not strong enough to enter. "But when Jesus saw the faith," not of him who was being carried, but of those who were carrying him, he said to the paralytic: "Take courage, son, your sins are forgiven you." Oh, what wonderful humility! He calls him "son," this despised cripple, weakened in all his joints, whom the priests did not consider worthy to touch. Surely, then, he calls him "son" because his sins are forgiven him. According to a tropology,[285] sometimes a soul lying in its body, with all the strength of its members weakened, is brought to be cured by the perfect doctor, the Lord. If it is healed by his mer-

---

280. Cf. Homily 76 in FOTC 57, 142.

281. Cf. Origen, *fragm.* 171. Actually Origen's interpretation is probably more justifiable than Jerome's here.

282. Lk 5.8.   283. Cf. Mt 2.23.

284. Cf. Mt 8.23.

285. Tropology refers to a deeper and more figurative interpretation. Simonetti, *Matthew 1a* (ACC), 173, observes: "The term *tropologia* originally meant an allegorical interpretation in general. From the late fourth century, however, it came to mean specifically a moral allegory, as in this example from Jerome."

cy, it receives such great strength that it would immediately carry its mat.[286]

9.3. *And behold, some of the scribes said among themselves: "This man is blaspheming."* We read that God says in the prophet: "I am he who blots out your iniquities."[287] Consequently, then, the scribes, since they were thinking that he was a man and they understood the words of God, accuse him of blasphemy. But the Lord, seeing their thoughts, shows himself to be God, who can recognize what is hidden in the heart. In a way he speaks by his silence and says: By the same majesty and power with which I perceive your thoughts, I can also forgive men their sins. Understand for yourselves what the paralytic attained.

9.5. *"What is easier to say: 'Your sins are forgiven you,' or to say: 'Rise and walk'?"* The difference between saying and doing is great. Only he who forgave them could have known whether the paralytic's sins had been forgiven. But the words: "rise and walk" are something that both he who got up as well as those who saw him rise could prove to be true. There is then a bodily miracle that proves the truth of the spiritual miracle. Yet the same power is needed to forgive the faults both of the body and of the soul. It is also given to us to understand that most bodily weaknesses happen on account of sins. This is perhaps why the sins are forgiven first, so that when the causes of the weakness have been taken away, wholeness might be re-established.

9.6. *"Take up your mat and go to your home."* The paralyzed soul, if it gets up, if it recovers its former strength, carries its own mat on which it was lying before it had been weakened. It carries it to the home of its own virtues.[288]

9.9. *And when Jesus passed on from there, he saw a man by the name of Matthew sitting at the tax-collector's place, and he said to him: "Follow me." And he arose and followed him.* Out of respect and honor, the other evangelists were unwilling to call him by the common

286. Above on Mt 8.14–15, Jerome offered a similar interpretation, that a healing conferred by the Lord renders the body whole at once. Here the immediate carrying of the mat points again to the "intensity" of power that the Lord's healing bestows.

287. Is 43.25.

288. See on Mt 9.1–2.

name of Matthew.[289] Instead, they called him Levi.[290] In fact, he went by two names. But Matthew identifies himself as Matthew and as a tax-collector. He wants to show to his readers that no one should despair of salvation if he is converted to better things. For he himself suddenly changed from tax-collector into apostle. This accords with what is commanded by Solomon: "A just man is his own accuser at the beginning of a speech";[291] and in another place: "Tell your sins that you may be justified."[292] Porphyry[293] and the emperor Julian denounced in this passage both the lack of skill of a historical fabricator and the folly of those who on the spot followed the Savior, as though they irrationally followed any man who calls. They say this in spite of the fact that very great powers and signs had preceded the call. Nor is there any doubt that the apostles had seen these things before they believed. Surely, the very splendor and majesty of his hidden divinity, which was even shining forth in his human face, was capable from the first glance of drawing those who looked toward it. For if in a magnetic stone and in amber such force is said to exist that rings and cylinders and rods can be joined together,[294] how much more was the Lord of all creatures able to draw to himself those whom he wanted.[295]

9.10. *And it came to pass as he was reclining in a house, behold, many tax collectors and sinners came and were reclining with Jesus,* and the rest.[296] They had seen that a tax collector had found room for repentance, having converted from sins to better things. For this reason they too do not despair of salvation. But they do not come to Jesus while continuing in their former vices, as the Pharisees and scribes are murmuring. On the contrary, they

289. Cf. Origen, *fragm.* 173.
290. Cf. Mk 2.14; Lk 5.27. For the same observation, see Jerome, *Comm. in Is.* 9.37; Chrysostom, *Hom. in Matth.* 30.
291. Prv 18.17.
292. Is 43.26.
293. Cf. Porphyry, *Adv. Christianos, fragm.* 6. Jerome cites Porphyry's work seven times in his commentary.
294. For the magnet's power of attraction, see Plato, *Ion* 533d–e; for a similar discussion of amber, cf. Pliny, *HN* 48.
295. Cf. Jn 12.32; 11.27.
296. Jerome has already commented on this verse for Damasus (*Ep.* 21.2).

have done penance, as the following words of the Lord indicate, saying:

9.13. *"'I want mercy and not sacrifice.' I have not come to call the just but sinners."* The Lord went to the banquets of sinners, in order to have an opportunity to teach and in order to offer spiritual food to those who had invited him. After all, when he is described as going frequently to the banquets, nothing else is related except what he did and taught there. Thus both the humility of the Lord in going to sinners and the power of his teaching in the conversion of the repentant are demonstrated. Then it continues that he brought forth a testimony from the prophet: "I want mercy and not sacrifice";[297] and [he added]: "I have not come to call the just but sinners." These statements confront the scribes and Pharisees, who were reckoning themselves to be just and were refusing fellowship with sinners and tax collectors.

9.14. *Then the disciples of John approached him saying: "Why do we and the Pharisees often fast, but your disciples do not fast?"* The question is arrogant and filled with pharisaical superciliousness. At the least (to say nothing else), their boasting about fasting is reprehensible. The disciples of John could not fail to be without blame, since they were calumniating him whom they knew had been foretold by the voice of their teacher. Moreover, they had joined up with the Pharisees, whom they knew John had condemned with the words: "Brood of vipers, who warned you to flee from the coming wrath?"[298]

9.15. *Jesus said to them: "Can the sons of the bridegroom mourn while the bridegroom is with them? But the days will come when the bridegroom will be taken away from them, and then they will fast."* Christ is the Bridegroom, the Church is the bride.[299] From this holy and spiritual marriage, the apostles were created, who cannot mourn as long as they see the bride in the chamber[300] and know that the Bridegroom is with the bride. But when the wedding is past and the time of the Passion and Resurrection comes, then the sons of the Bridegroom will fast. On account of

297. Hos 6.6.   298. Mt 3.7.
299. Cf. Is 62.4; 2 Cor 11.2; Eph 5.32.
300. Cf. Song 8.2.

this statement, some think that fasts should be commenced after the forty days of the Passion.[301] Yet the day of Pentecost and the coming of the Holy Spirit invite us at once to festivity. Based on this pretext, Montanus,[302] Prisca, and Maximilla even make a forty-day fast after Pentecost, because [they say] when the bridegroom is taken away, the sons of the bridegroom ought to fast. But the custom of the Church comes to the Passion of the Lord and the Resurrection by means of the humbling of the flesh. Thus by the fasting of the body we are prepared for spiritual feasting. But according to the rules of tropology,[303] one should know that as long as the bridegroom is with us and we are rejoicing, we can neither fast nor mourn; but when he withdraws from us and flies away on account of our sins, at that time a fast must be proclaimed, at that time mourning must be taken up.

9.16–17. *"No one puts a patch of unshrunk cloth on an old garment; for it takes away its fullness from the garment, and the tear becomes worse. Nor do they put new wine into old wineskins; otherwise, the wineskins will burst, and the wine will be poured out, and the wineskins will perish; but they put new wine into new wineskins, and both are preserved."* What he is saying is this: Until someone has been reborn[304] and, having laid aside the old man, has put on the new man through my Passion,[305] he cannot endure the more severe fasts and the precepts of continence. For through the ex-

---

301. Jerome is referring to the Ascension of Christ, which according to Luke occurred forty days after the Passion. Cf. Acts 1.3.

302. Montanus, a native of Ardabau, a village in Phrygia, in the late second century (155–160) originated a schism that took its name from him (Montanism) and spread far and wide. It even won Tertullian for an adherent in 207. Montanus claimed to be a prophet and a mouthpiece of the Holy Spirit. Prisca and Maximilla were two of his female disciples who outdid him in prophesying. Both had been previously married and left their husbands. The sect initiated new fasts after Pentecost, to which Jerome alludes here. In his *Ep.* 55.3 to Marcella, Jerome summarizes the teachings of the Montanists and says that they keep three Lents in the year, as opposed to Catholics, who have one. "I do not mean, of course, that it is unlawful to fast at other times through the year—always excepting Pentecost [i.e., from Easter to Pentecost Sunday]—only that while in Lent it is a duty of obligation, at other seasons it is a matter of choice." NPNF2, 6.56.

303. See n. 285 on Mt 9.1–2.   304. Cf. Jn 3.3.

305. Cf. Col 3.9–10; Rom 6.6.

cessive austerity he would lose even the faith that he now seems to have. He recorded two examples, that of a garment and that of old and new wineskins. We should understand the old as referring to the scribes and the Pharisees. The cloth of the new garment and the new wine should be understood as the Gospel precepts which the Jews cannot endure, lest a greater tear is made. Even the Galatians were desiring to do something similar, when they wanted to intermingle precepts of the Law with the Gospel and "put new wine into old wineskins." But the apostle says to them: "O foolish Galatians, who has bewitched you from obeying the truth?"[306] Therefore, the words of the Gospel ought to be poured by the apostles, rather than by the scribes and Pharisees, who were corrupted by the traditions of the elders and were not able to keep the sincerity of the precepts of Christ.[307] For the purity of a virginal soul[308] and of one that has not been previously polluted by any contact with vice is one thing; but the defilements of those who have lain in lust with a multitude are something else.

9.18–19. *Behold, a ruler approached and was worshiping him, saying: "My daughter has just now died, but come, place your hand upon her, and she will live." And Jesus arose and followed him, and so did his disciples.* This is the eighth sign,[309] in which a ruler asks that his daughter be raised. He is unwilling to be excluded from the mystery of true circumcision.[310] But a woman flowing with blood enters by stealth, and is healed in the eighth place.[311] Thus the ruler's daughter, who was excluded from this number, comes to the ninth. This accords with what is said in the Psalms: "Ethiopia will hasten [to stretch forth] her hand to God";[312] and "when the fullness of the Gentiles enters in, then all Israel will be saved."[313]

---

306. Gal 3.1.   307. Cf. 2 Cor 11.3.

308. Cf. 2 Cor 11.2.   309. See above on Mt 5.10.

310. Cf. Rom 2.29. Since circumcision took place on the eighth day (cf. Lk 2.21), and since Paul had taught that true circumcision takes place in baptism (cf. Col 2.11–12), the Fathers viewed the number eight as containing a Christological mystery. Cf. Origen, *ComRom* 4.2.4 (M967) (FOTC 103, 248).

311. See above on Mt 8.23.   312. Ps 68.31 LXX.

313. Rom 11.25–26.

9.20. *Behold, a woman who was suffering from a flowing of blood for twelve years came up behind him and touched the fringe of his garment.* In the Gospel according to Luke it is written that the ruler's daughter was twelve years old.[314] Note, then, that it was at that time, when the nation of the Jews believed, that this woman, that is, the people of the Gentiles, began to get sick. For vice is not shown except in comparison with virtues. Now this woman flowing with blood does not approach the Lord in a home, nor in a city, because according to the Law she was excluded from cities. Instead she approaches on the road, as the Lord is walking along, so that the one woman is cured while he is going to someone else. This is why even the apostles say: "It was indeed necessary that the word be preached to you, but because you have judged yourselves unworthy of salvation, we are going over to the Gentiles."[315]

9.21. *For she was saying to herself: "If I only touch the fringe of his garment, I will be saved."* According to the Law, one who touches a menstruous woman or one flowing with blood is unclean.[316] Therefore, it is she who touches the Lord, that she may likewise be cured from the blemish of blood.

9.22. *"Take heart, daughter, your faith has saved you."* You are a "daughter" because "your faith has saved you." He did not say: Your faith will save you, but "has saved"; for you have already been saved by what you have believed.

9.23. *And when Jesus went into the ruler's house, and saw the flute players and the crowd making a din.* Up to today a girl lies dead in the ruler's house, and those who seem to be teachers are the flute-players playing a funeral song. And the crowd of Jews is a crowd not of believers, but of those making a din.

9.24. *"The girl is not dead but sleeps,"* because all things are alive to God.[317]

9.25. *And when the crowd had been put out, he entered and took her*

---

314. Cf. Lk 8.42. Simonetti, *Matthew 1a* (ACC), 183, explains: "The hemorrhaging woman, symbolic of the Gentiles, had been ill for twelve years, the age of the ruler's dying daughter—symbolic of the Jews. When the Jews began to believe in God, the pagans became spiritually ill."

315. Acts 13.46.   316. Cf. Lv 15.19.

317. Cf. Lk 20.38.

hand. For they were not worthy to see the mystery of one who was to rise again, since they were deriding with unworthy insults the one who was going to raise her.

9.25. *And he took her hand and the girl arose.* Unless the hands of the Jews, which are full of blood,[318] should first be cleansed,[319] their dead synagogue does not rise.[320]

9.27–28. *And while Jesus was passing on from there, two blind men followed him, crying out and saying: "Have pity on us, son of David!" And when he came home, the blind men approached him.* The Lord Jesus passes by the ruler's house and proceeds to his own home, as we read above: "Getting into a boat, he crossed over and came to his own city."[321] Two blind men cried out, saying: "Have pity on us, son of David." And yet, they are not cured on the road, not in passing, as they were thinking, but after he came to his own home. They approach him and enter. First he talks to them about their faith, so that in this way they may receive the light of the true faith. To the first sign of the ruler's daughter, which we explained above,[322] and to that of the hemorrhaging woman, this one is consequently joined. What death and disability demonstrated there, here blindness demonstrates. For both peoples were blind to the Lord as he was passing through this world and desiring to return to his own home. They will not receive the original light, unless they confess and say: "Have pity on us, son of David." And when Jesus asks: "Do you believe that I can do this?" they need to respond to him: "Yes, Lord." In another evangelist a single blind man is recorded, with torn clothes and sitting in Jericho. He is hindered by the apostles from crying out, but he receives healing by his impudence.[323] Since that passage properly pertains to the people of the Gentiles, it should be explained in its own book.

9.27. *"Son of David, have pity on us!"* Let Marcion and Manich-

318. Cf. Is 1.15.   319. Cf. Is 1.16.
320. Cf. Is 26.14, 19.   321. Mt 9.1.
322. See on Mt 9.18–19.

323. Cf. Mk 10.50–52. Jerome apparently misremembers some of the details of the pericope in Mark. It is not said that the blind man had torn clothes, but that he threw off his cloak. Moreover, it is not said that the disciples hindered him, but that "many rebuked him."

eus and the other heretics who mangle the Old Testament hear this. Let them learn that the Savior is called the son of David. For if he was not born in the flesh, how could he be called a son of David?

9.30–31. *And Jesus sternly warned them, saying: "See that no one knows." But they went out and spread his fame abroad in that whole land.* The Lord had commanded this on account of his humility. He was fleeing from the glory of boasting, but they are unable to be silent about the kind deed on account of the memory of the favor. Note therefore that there is some legitimacy in their being opposed to each other. These blind men are healed in the tenth place.[324]

9.32–33. *But when they had gone out, behold, they brought to him a man having a mute demon, and when the demon was expelled, the mute man spoke.* The eleventh [miracle] is the mute man who receives a tongue for speaking.[325] Now what the Greek language expresses by κωφός is more common in ordinary language and is understood as deaf rather than mute. But in the Scriptures it is customary to say κωφός indifferently of either a mute or a deaf person. Now spiritually, just as the blind men receive light, so also the tongue of the mute is opened for speaking, that it might confess him whom it was formerly denying.

9.33–34. *And the crowds were amazed, saying: "Never has the like been seen in Israel." But the Pharisees were saying: "By the ruler of the demons, he expels demons."* The crowd confesses the works of God and says: "Never has the like been seen in Israel." In the crowd [we observe] the confession of the nations. But the Pharisees, because they were not able to deny the miracle, speak evil of the works and say: "By the ruler of the demons, he expels demons." By their calumny they demonstrate the unbelief of the Jews until the present day.

9.35. *And Jesus was going about all the cities and villages, teaching in their synagogues and preaching the Gospel of the Kingdom and curing every kind of disease and infirmity.* You see that he preached the Gospel equally in the country and in cities and in villages,

---

324. See above on Mt 8.1–2; 8.23; 9.18–19.
325. See ibid.; also on 9.30–31.

that is, to both the great and the small. Thus he did not consider the power of the noble but the salvation of believers. "He was going about the cities." This was the task that his Father had commanded for him. It was for this that he hungered, that he might save unbelievers by his teaching. Now he was teaching the Gospel of the Kingdom in the synagogues and villages. After preaching and teaching he would cure every kind of disease and infirmity, so that his works might persuade those whom his words had not persuaded.[326] It is properly said of the Lord: "curing every kind of disease and infirmity"; for indeed nothing is impossible for him.[327]

9.36. *But seeing the crowds, he was moved with compassion for those who were harassed and helpless, like sheep without a shepherd.* The harassment of a flock, whether of sheep or of crowds, is the fault of the shepherds and the sin of the teachers. This is why it says in what follows:

9.37. *"The harvest indeed is great, but the workers are few."* The great harvest signifies the multitude of peoples; the few workers indicate the lack of teachers. He commands that they ask the Lord of the harvest to send out workers into his harvest. These are the workers of whom the Psalmist speaks: "Those who sow in tears will reap in joy. While going, they were going and weeping, carrying their seed, but in coming back, they will come in exultation, carrying their sheaves."[328] Let me speak more plainly: the great harvest is the whole crowd of believers; the few workers are the apostles and their imitators who are sent to the harvest.[329]

Chapter 10

10.1. *And having summoned his twelve disciples, he gave them power over unclean spirits, that they might cast them out, and to cure every kind of disease and infirmity.* The kind and clement Lord and Teacher[330] does not jealously refuse to give his miraculous powers to his servants and disciples.[331] On the contrary, just as he

---

326. See above on Mt 8.2.
328. Ps 126.5–6.
330. Cf. Jn 13.14.

327. Cf. Lk 1.37; 18.27; Mk 10.27.
329. Cf. Origen, *fragm.* 189.
331. Cf. Origen, *fragm.* 193.

had cured every kind of disease and infirmity,[332] so too he gave to his apostles the power to cure every kind of disease and infirmity. But there is great difference between having and bestowing, between giving and receiving. Whatever he does, he does with the authority of the Lord; but when they do anything, they confess their own weakness and the power of the Lord, saying: "In the name of Jesus, rise and walk."[333] One should note that the power of working miraculous signs is conceded to the apostles in the twelfth place.[334]

10.2. *Now these are the names of the twelve apostles.* The list of apostles is recorded, so that those who beyond these are going to be false apostles may be excluded.

10.2. *First, Simon who is called Peter, and Andrew his brother.* It belonged to him who searches into the secrets of the heart to distribute the order of the apostles and the merit of each one. Simon is the first to be recorded. He was surnamed Peter to distinguish him from another Simon who is called the Cananean, from the village of Cana of Galilee, where the Lord turned water into wine.[335] He also names James [the son] of Zebedee, because there follows also another James, [the son] of Alphaeus. He is grouping teams and pairs of apostles. He joins Peter and Andrew, brothers not so much in the flesh as in the spirit; James and John, who followed the true Father, after leaving behind their physical father;[336] Philip and Bartholomew, Thomas too and Matthew the tax-collector. In the linking of names, the other evangelists put Matthew first and Thomas afterward,[337] nor do they attribute to him the name of tax-collector. They wanted to avoid affronting the evangelist by recording his former manner of life. That man indeed refers to himself as a tax-collector, as we said above,[338] and places himself after Thomas, so that "where sin abounded, grace might superabound."[339]

10.4. *Simon the Cananean.* He is the one who is described

---

332. Cf. Mt 9.35. 333. Cf. Acts 3.6.

334. Jerome's point seems to focus on the number twelve, which is the number of apostles. See on Mt 8.1–2; 8.23; 9.18–19; 9.30–31; 9.32–33.

335. Cf. Jn 2.8. 336. Cf. Mt 4.22.

337. Cf. Mk 3.18; Lk 6.15. 338. Cf. Mt 9.9.

339. Cf. Rom 5.20.

by another evangelist as "the zealot."[340] In fact, Cana means "zeal."[341] Ecclesiastical history hands down the tradition that Thaddeus was sent to Edessa to Abgar, the king of Osroene.[342] He is called Judas son of James by the evangelist Luke,[343] and elsewhere is named Lebbaeus,[344] which means "little heart." One must believe that he had three names, just as Simon was named Peter, and the sons of Zebedee were called Boanerges, from the strength and greatness of their faith.[345] Judas took the name "Iscariot," either from the village in which he was raised, or from the tribe of Issachar[346] so that he was born with a kind of prophecy of his own condemnation. For Issachar translates as "wages," that the betrayer's wages might be signified.[347]

10.5–6. *"Do not go into the way of the Gentiles and do not enter the cities of the Samaritans, but go rather to the lost sheep of the house of Israel."* This passage is not contrary to the command that is given later: "Go, teach all nations, baptizing them in the name of the Father and of the Son and of the Holy Spirit."[348] For the former was commanded before the Resurrection, but the latter was said after the Resurrection. And it was necessary first to announce the advent of Christ to the Jews, lest they have a just excuse, claiming that they had rejected the Lord because he sent the apostles to the Gentiles and Samaritans. But according to a tropology,[349] it is commanded to us who are registered with the name of Christ, that we should not go into the way of the Gentiles and the error of the heretics, so that from those from

340. Cf. Lk 6.15.

341. The Hebrew *qannâ* refers to ardor in defending a cause.

342. Cf. Eusebius, *HE* 1.13. Osroene was a province in northwest Mesopotamia. Its capital was Edessa. It is Eusebius who reports the legendary visit of Thaddeus with Abgar.

343. Cf. Lk 6.16; Acts 1.14.

344. Lebbaeus is testified in some Greek manuscripts of Mt 10.3. See B. Metzger, *A Textual Commentary on the Greek New Testament* (Stuttgart: United Bible Societies, 1971; corrected ed., 1975), 26.

345. Cf. Mk 3.17. Boanerges means "sons of thunder."

346. Cf. Gn 49.14–15.

347. Cf. Mt 26.15. See Homily 35 on Ps 108 (109) in FOTC 48, 260.

348. Mt 28.19.

349. See above on Mt 9.1–2.

whom our religion is separated, our life may also be separated.

10.7–8. *"Now as you go, preach, saying that the kingdom of heaven is at hand; cure the sick, raise the dead, cleanse the lepers, cast out demons; freely you have received, freely give."* Lest it turn out that no one believe these rustic men, unschooled and illiterate,[350] and lacking the charm of eloquence, who are promising the kingdom of heaven, he gives them power: "Cure the sick, cleanse the lepers, cast out demons." Thus the greatness of the signs will prove the greatness of the promises. And because spiritual gifts are always demeaned if wages intervene, he adds a condemnation of avarice: "Freely you have received, freely give." I, your Teacher and Lord,[351] gave this to you free of charge, and you are to give free of charge, lest the grace of the Gospel be corrupted.[352]

10.9–10. *"Do not possess gold or silver or money in your belts, no wallet for the journey, nor two tunics, nor sandals, nor a staff in your hand; for the worker is worthy of his food."* This command is consistent with what he had previously said to the evangelizers of the truth: "Freely you have received, freely give."[353] For if they preach in such a way that they do not accept pay, the possession of gold and silver coins is superfluous. For if they had gold and silver, they would seem to be preaching not for the sake of human salvation but rather for the sake of gain. "Nor copper in your sacks."[354] He who decapitates wealth practically cuts off what is necessary for life. Thus the apostles, the teachers of the true religion, who were instructing that all things are governed by providence, show that they themselves take no thought for tomorrow.[355] "No wallet for the journey." By this precept he convicts the philosophers who are commonly called "Bactroperitae,"[356] because, as despisers of the world, they considered all things as nothing and took the pantry along with them. "Nor two tunics." It seems to me that by "two tunics" he is pointing to two sets of clothes. He does not mean that in the frozen regions and

---

350. Cf. Acts 4.13.   351. Cf. Jn 13.13.

352. Cf. 1 Cor 9.12.   353. Mt 10.8.

354. Cf. Mk 6.8; Lk 10.4.   355. Cf. Mt 6.34.

356. "Bactroperitae" = "experts carrying a staff." This is a nickname for Cynic philosophers. Cf. Horace, *Satires* 1.3.134; Martial 4.53.

glacial snow of Scythia[357] a person ought to be content with a single tunic. Rather, by tunic we should understand clothing. We should have one set of clothes and should not keep another set for ourselves out of fear for the future. "Nor sandals." Even Plato commands that the two extremities of the body are not to be covered nor should they be accustomed to the softness of cap and shoes.[358] For when these are tough, the other parts are tougher. "Nor staff." Since we have the Lord's help,[359] why should we seek the aid of a staff?[360] He had sent the apostles to preach when they were stripped,[361] so to speak, and unencumbered, so that the condition of the teachers seemed to be hard. Now he has tempered the severity of the command with the following judgment, saying: "The worker is worthy of his food." Receive, he says, only as much as is necessary for yourselves by way of food and clothing. For this reason the apostle also repeats this: "Having food and clothes, we are content with these";[362] and in another passage: "But let the one who is instructed share in every good thing with him who instructs."[363] Thus as the disciples reap spiritual things, they make their teachers sharers in their own material things.[364] This is done not out of greed but out of necessity. We have said these things at the level of historical interpretation.[365] But there is a lesson at the level of the anagogical interpretation.[366] He says that it is not permitted to teachers to possess gold, silver, and money in their belts. Now we often read "gold" for "thought," "silver" for "speech," and "copper" for "voice." It is not permitted to us to receive these things from others. Rather, they should be possessed as things given from the Lord. Nor is it permitted to take up the disciplines of perverted teaching from the heretics and philosophers; nor

---

357. The rigors of the country of the Scythians are a common theme in Latin poetry. Cf. Ovid, *Pont.*; Tertullian, *Adv. Marc.*, Bk 1 pref.

358. Cf. Plato, *Tim.* 74b–75a; *Laws* 12, 2, 942d–e.

359. Cf. Ps 121.2.   360. Cf. Ps 23.4.

361. Cf. Jn 21.7.   362. 1 Tm 6.8.

363. Gal 6.6.   364. Cf. Rom 15.27.

365. *Haec historice diximus.*

366. *Anagōgē* refers to the spiritual meaning of the text that usually transcends the literal level of interpretation. It is synonymous with tropology and aims at applying the text to the life of the Church and the soul of the believer.

to be weighed down by a secular paycheck, nor to be double-minded.[367] Moreover, our feet should not be bound with deadly chains, but should be bare as we walk on holy ground.[368] Nor should we have a staff that turns into a snake,[369] nor should we lean on any fleshly aid, since a rod and staff of that sort is like a reed which, if you press it a little bit, breaks and pierces the hand of the one leaning on it.[370]

10.11. *"In whatever city or village you enter, inquire who in it is worthy, and remain there until you leave."* Paul says with respect to the ordination of a bishop and deacon: "Now it is also necessary that they have a good testimony among those who are outside."[371] Upon entering a new city, the apostles were unable to know what the people would be like. Therefore, a host is to be selected by his reputation among the people and by the judgment of the neighbors. This way the dignity of the proclamation will not be disfigured by the ill repute of the one receiving it. Although they are to preach to everyone, one host is chosen. He does not give a benefit to him who is going to stay among them, but he receives one. For he says this: "who in it is worthy." Thus the host knows that he is receiving a favor rather than giving one.

10.12–13. *"As you enter the house, greet it, and if the house becomes worthy, your peace will come upon it; but if it does not become worthy, your peace will return to you."* In a concealed way he has expressed a greeting of the Hebrew and Syriac languages. For what is said in Greek by χαῖρε and in Latin by *ave* is said in Hebrew and Syriac speech as *shalom lach* or *shalama lach*, that is, "peace be with you." He is commanding the following: When you enter a house, you should call down peace upon the host, and as far as it depends on you,[372] settle the wars of discord. But if opposition arises, you will have a reward from the peace offered, and they will possess the war that they wanted to have.

10.14. *"And whoever does not receive you or listen to your words, when you go forth outside the house or city, shake the dust from your feet."* Dust is shaken from the feet in testimony of their labor,

367. Cf. Jas 1.8.
369. Cf. Ex 4.2–3.
371. 1 Tm 3.7.

368. Cf. Ex 3.5.
370. Cf. Is 36.6; 2 Kgs 18.21.
372. Cf. Rom 12.18.

since they entered the city and the apostolic preaching reached them. Or dust is shaken off so that from those who spurned the Gospel, they take nothing, not even the necessary livelihood.

10.15. *"Amen I say to you: It will be more tolerable for the land of Sodom and Gomorrah*[373] *in the day of judgment than for that city."* It will be more tolerable for the land of Sodom and Gomorrah than for that city which does not receive the Gospel. The reason it will be more tolerable for them is that it was not preached to Sodom and Gomorrah, whereas it was preached to this city, and yet it did not receive the Gospel. If this is so, then there are different punishments among sinners.

10.16. *"Behold, I am sending you like sheep in the midst of wolves."* He is calling the scribes and Pharisees, who were the clergy of the Jews, wolves.

10.16. *"Therefore, be as wise as serpents and as simple as doves."* The reason he says this is because by wisdom they can avoid plots, and by simplicity they can avoid doing evil.[374] The cunning of a serpent is placed as an example because by using its whole body it hides its head and protects that part in which its life resides.[375] In the same way, we should guard our head, who is Christ,[376] by risking our bodies. The simplicity of doves is manifested in the outward form of the Holy Spirit.[377] This is why the apostle says: "Be children in respect to evil."[378]

10.19, 17, 18. *"But when they hand you over, do not think about how or what you are to say."* Above he had said: *"For they will hand you over to councils, and they will flog you in their synagogues, and you will be led even unto governors and rulers on account of me."*[379] When therefore we are led for the sake of Christ unto judges, we ought to offer only our willingness on Christ's behalf. But Christ himself, who dwells in us,[380] will speak on his own behalf, and the grace of the Holy Spirit will be accorded in the response.

10.21. *"But brother will hand over brother to death; and father, his*

---

373. Lit., "land of the Sodomites and Gomorreans" (*terra Sodomorum et Gomorraeorum*), here and in the following sentence.

374. Cf. Origen, *fragm.* 202.

375. Cf. Homily 50 on Ps 139 (140) in FOTC 48, 364.

376. Cf. Eph 1.22; Col 1.18.   377. Cf. Mt 3.16; Lk 3.22.

378. 1 Cor 14.20.   379. Mt 10.17–18.

380. Cf. Eph 3.17.

son; and sons will rise up against parents." We frequently see this happening during persecutions, nor is there any reliable affection between those whose faith is different.

10.22. "*He who has persevered to the end will be saved.*" For virtue consists not in having begun, but in having completed.

10.23. "*But when they persecute you in one city, flee to another. Amen I say to you: You will not complete the cities of Israel until the Son of man comes.*" This should be referred to that time when the apostles were being sent to preach. Strictly to them was it said: "Do not go in the way of the Gentiles and do not enter into the cities of the Samaritans."[381] They were not to fear persecution, but they should avoid it. In fact, we see that at the beginning the believers did this. When they had been dispersed into all Judea by a persecution that arose in Jerusalem, the occasion of tribulation became the seedbed for the Gospel.[382] Now spiritually we can say: When we are persecuted in one city, that is, in one book or testimony of the Scriptures, we should flee to other cities, that is, to other books. However contentious the persecutor becomes, the protection of the Savior will arrive before victory is conceded to the adversaries.

10.25. "*If they have called the master of the house Beelzebub, how much more those of his household.*" Beelzebub is an idol of Ekron, which in the Book of Kings is called the idol of the mouse.[383] *Beel* refers either to Bel or Baal, and *zebub* means "mouse." Therefore, with the designation of this most filthy idol, whose name means "mouse," they were naming the prince of demons. The name is derived from the uncleanness which drives out the sweetness of oil.[384]

10.26. "*For there is nothing hidden that will not be revealed, and nothing secret that will not be known.*" How is it that the vices of many are not known in the present age?[385] This is written, however, about the future time, when God will judge the secrets of men,[386] will illumine the hidden places of darkness, and will manifest the counsels of hearts.[387] And the sense is: Do not fear

---

381. Mt 10.5.
382. Cf. Acts 8.1.
383. Cf. 1 Kgs 1.2.
384. Cf. Eccl 10.1.
385. Cf. Origen, *fragm.* 206.
386. Cf. Rom 2.16.
387. Cf. 1 Cor 4.5.

the savageness of persecutors and the ferocity of those who blaspheme. For the day of judgment will come, on which both your virtue and their wickedness will be manifested.

10.27. *"What I tell you in the darkness, speak in the light, and what you hear in the ear, preach from the housetops."* What you have heard in a mystery, proclaim very openly; what you have learned secretly, speak publicly; what I have instructed you in the little locale of Judea, speak boldly in all cities and in the whole world.

10.28. *"Do not fear those who kill the body, but cannot kill the soul."* If those who kill the body are not able to kill the soul, then the soul is invisible and incorporeal, I mean in comparison with[388] the denser substance of our body. Or at least at that time when the former body receives [the soul] back,[389] it will be punished and will feel torments, so that it is punished along with that with which it sinned.

10.28. *"Fear him who can destroy soul and body in Gehenna."* The term Gehenna is not found in the ancient books, but is first recorded by the Savior.[390] Let us then seek what may be the occasion for this word. We read more than once that the idol Baal was near Jerusalem, at the roots of Mount Moriah in which Siloa flowed.[391] This valley and little plain of a field was well-watered, covered with foliage, and filled with pleasures. There was a sacred grove in it that was dedicated to the idol. But the people of Israel had fallen into such great madness that they deserted the precincts of the Temple and were sacrificing victims there. Pleasure had overcome the rigor of religion, and they were burning, or rather "initiating," their sons to the demon. The place itself was called Gehennon, that is, the valley of the sons of Hennon. The books of Kings, Chronicles, and Jeremiah write in great detail about this.[392] God threatens that he is going to fill this place with the bodies of the dead, with the result that it will by no

---

388. Lat., *secundum.*   389. Cf. 2 Cor 4.10.

390. He means that this term is not applied to hell in the OT and that Christ was the first to use it in that sense. Jerome speaks of the origin of this new name for hell elsewhere in *Liber de situ et nominibus* (PL 23: 901B); *In Jer.* 7.30–31 (PL 24: 735). For a discussion of these passages, see J. P. O'Connell, *The Eschatology of Saint Jerome,* 139–40.

391. Cf. 1 Kgs 16.31.

392. Cf. 2 Kgs 23.4–20; 2 Chr 28.21–25; Jer 7.32; 19.6.

means be called Topheth and Baal, but will be called Polyandrion, that is, the mound of the dead. Therefore, the future punishments and the eternal penalties with which sinners are to be tormented are denoted by the name of this place. Now we read very fully in Job that there are two Gehennas, one of excessive fire and one of excessive cold.[393]

10.29–31. *"Are not two sparrows sold for a penny? And not one of them falls to the ground without your Father. But even the hairs of your head are numbered. Therefore, do not fear; you are worth more than many sparrows. "* The Lord's words are rooted in each other. What is said later depends upon what precedes. Prudent reader, always beware of a superstitious interpretation. Do not accommodate the Scriptures to your meaning, but link your meaning to the Scriptures and understand what follows. Above he had said: "Do not fear those who kill the body, but cannot kill the soul."[394] Now he speaks of the consequence of these words: "Are not two sparrows sold for a penny? And not one of them falls to the ground without your Father." Thus the meaning is: If common and insignificant animals do not die apart from their Creator, God, and there is a providence in all things, and among these things the things that are going to perish do not perish without the will of God, then you who are eternal should not fear that you live without the providence of God.[395] This sense has also been spoken above: "Look at the birds of the sky, since they do not sow or reap or gather into their own barns, and your heavenly Father feeds them; are not you worth more than these?"[396] And then: "Consider the lilies of the field, how they grow," etc. "But if God so clothes the grass of the field, which is here today and tomorrow is thrown into the furnace, how much more [will he clothe] you of little faith?"[397]

Some[398] force the passage about the two sparrows to refer to the soul and the body. They also interpret as the senses the five sparrows (according to Luke)[399] which are sold for two pennies.

---

393. Cf. Jb 24.19.
394. Mt 10.28.
395. Cf. Origen, *fragm.* 211, 212.
396. Mt 6.26.
397. Mt 6.30.
398. Cf. Ambrose, *In Luc.* 7; Hilary, *In Matth.* 10.18–19.
399. Cf. Lk 12.6.

But how that interpretation can be made to fit into the general context of the words of the Gospels is no small difficulty: "But even all the hairs of your head are numbered; therefore, do not fear; you are better than many sparrows." The sense expressed by our explanation above is clearer: that they should not fear those who can kill the body and cannot kill the soul. For if even insignificant animals do not die without the knowledge of God, how much more man, who is supported with apostolic dignity? But what he says:

"But even the hairs of your head are numbered," shows the immense providence of God toward men. These words indicate unspeakable affection, because nothing about us escapes God's notice. Not even trivial and careless words escape his knowledge.[400] Those who deny the resurrection of the flesh mock the ecclesiastical interpretation in this passage, as though we are saying that we and all our hairs will rise again, that is, the hairs that have been counted and cut off by the barber. But the Savior did not say: "But even all your hairs" are going to be saved, but "are numbered." Where there is [talk of] a number, the knowledge of the number is being shown, not the preservation of the same number.

10.34. *Do not think that I have come to send peace on the earth: I have not come to send peace but a sword.* Above he had said: "What I say to you in the darkness, speak in the light, and what you hear in the ear, preach on the housetops."[401] Now he adds what is to follow after the preaching. The whole world is divided against itself over faith in Christ. Each household has both unbelievers and believers. The reason that the good war has been sent is so that the evil peace might be shattered. It is written in Genesis that God did something similar to this against rebellious men. They had been roused from the east and were striving to construct a tower by which they wanted to reach the heights of heaven. Then God divided their languages.[402] This is why David prays in the Psalm: "Lord, disperse the nations that want wars."[403]

10.35–36. *For I have come to divide a man against his father*

---

400. Cf. Mt 12.36.
402. Cf. Gn 11.8.

401. Mt 10.27.
403. Ps 68.30.

and a daughter against her mother and a daughter-in-law against her mother-in-law. A man's enemies will be the members of his household. " This passage is written in the prophet Micah in nearly the same words.[404] One should also note that whenever a testimony is recorded from the Old Testament,[405] it agrees, whether only the meaning, or also the words.

10.37. *"He who loves father or mother more than me is not worthy of me,"* etc. He had previously said: "I have not come to send peace but a sword,"[406] and [I have come] to divide men against father and mother and mother-in-law. Now, lest anyone put piety before religion, he adds something, saying: "He who loves father or mother more than me." In the Song of Songs we read: "Order love in me."[407] This order is necessary in all our affections. After God, love your father, love your mother, love your children. But if the necessity comes that love for parents and children are pitted against the love of God, and if it is impossible for both to be preserved, then hatred for one's own is piety toward God. So then, he has not prohibited loving father or mother, but has expressly added: "He who loves father or mother more than me."[408]

10.38. *"And he who does not take up his cross and follow me is not worthy of me."* In another Gospel it is written: He who does not take up his cross *daily.*[409] We must not think that a one-time ardor of faith can suffice. The cross must always be carried, so that we might always show that we love Christ.

10.40. *"He who receives you, receives me; and he who receives me, receives him who sent me."* The order is very beautiful. He sends them out to preach; he teaches them that dangers are not to be feared; he subordinates affection to religious duty. Above he had taken away gold and had removed copper from their belts.[410] The condition of the evangelists is hard. Where then do they get the necessities for their living expenses? He tempers the austerity of the commands with the hope of promises, saying: "He who receives you, receives me, and he who receives

404. Cf. Mi 7.6.
406. Mt 10.34.
408. Cf. Origen, *fragm.* 216.
410. Cf. Mt 10.9.

405. Lat., *de veteri instrumento.*
407. Song 2.4.
409. Cf. Lk 9.23.

me, receives him who sent me," so that every believer will consider that by receiving the apostles he is receiving Christ.

10.41. *"He who receives a prophet in the name of a prophet, will
receive a prophet's reward,"* etc. He who receives a prophet as a
prophet, and who understands that he is speaking about the future, will receive a prophet's reward. Therefore, the Jews, since
they understand prophets in a fleshly manner, will not receive
the reward of prophets. Here is another interpretation: In every profession [of faith], there are weeds mixed in with the
wheat.[411] He had previously said: "He who receives you, receives
me, and he who receives me, receives him who sent me."[412] He
had challenged the disciples to receive teachers. A concealed
reply of the believers could have been: Should we then receive
even false prophets and Judas the traitor, and supply their cost
of living? The Lord, attending to this matter earlier, says that it
is not the persons who are to be received, but the offices; and
those who receive them will not lose their reward, even if the
one who is received is unworthy.

10.42. *"And whoever gives a drink to one of these least ones, even a
cup of cold water, in the name of a disciple, amen I say to you, he shall
not lose his reward."* We read in the prophet David: "excuses for
excusing their sins."[413] Many offer just pretexts, as it were, as an
excuse for their sins. They want to appear to be sinning by necessity, when in fact they are willfully delinquent. The Lord, who
is the searcher of the heart and soul, looks intently at the future
thoughts in each.[414] He had said: "He who receives you, receives
me."[415] But many false prophets and false preachers were able to
impede this command. He has also cured this stumbling-block,
saying: "He who receives a just man in the name of a just man,
will receive a just man's reward."[416] Again, someone else could
plead and say: I am hindered by my poverty, my lack keeps me
back, so that I cannot be hospitable. And he gets rid of this excuse with the very light command, that we should supply a cup
of cold water from our whole heart. He says: "of *cold* water," not
of hot water, lest in the word "hot" people plead the pretext of

411. Cf. Mt 13.25.   412. Mt 10.40.
413. Ps 140.4 LXX.   414. Cf. Ps 7.10.
415. Mt 10.40.   416. Mt 10.41.

poverty and lack of firewood. The apostle, as we said earlier,[417] commands something similar to the Galatians: "Let the one who is instructed share with him who instructs him in all good things."[418] He is exhorting disciples to refresh their teachers. People could have pleaded poverty as an excuse and evaded the command, even before he set it forth. This is why he resolves this imminent objection and says: "Be not deceived, God is not mocked; for what a man has sown, these things also shall he reap."[419] The meaning is: In vain do you plead lack of resources, when there is consciousness of something else. You can fail to live up to my exhortation, but know that only to the extent that you have sown will you also reap.[420]

417. Cf. on Mt 10.9–10.
418. Gal 6.6. Earlier (under Mt 10.9–10), he cites the text in the singular ("in every good thing") rather than the plural as here.
419. Gal 6.7.
420. Cf. 2 Cor 9.6.

BOOK TWO (MATTHEW 11.2–16.12)

Chapter 11

BUT WHEN JOHN HEARD *in prison of the works of Christ, he sent two of his disciples to say to him: "Are you he who is to come, or do we wait for another?"* (11.2–3) He asks, but not as one who is ignorant of the answer. For he had pointed him out to others who did not know about him when he said: "Behold the Lamb of God, behold him who takes away the sins of the world."[1] Also, he had heard the voice of the Father, thundering: "This is my beloved Son in whom I am well pleased."[2] Rather, it is just as when the Savior asks where Lazarus has been laid. He did this so that those who pointed out the location of the tomb would at least be thus prepared for faith and see the dead man rising.[3] Thus, when John was about to be killed by Herod, he sends his disciples to Christ, so that on this occasion, when they see the signs and miracles, they may believe in him and, with their teacher asking, learn for themselves. An earlier question also demonstrated, however, that the disciples of John were puffed up against the Lord. They had caustic feelings toward him that sprang from resentment and envy. The evangelist reports: "Then the disciples of John approached him, saying: 'Why do we and the Pharisees often fast, but your disciples do not fast?'"[4] And in another passage it says: "Teacher, the one for whom you offered testimony at the Jordan, behold, his disciples are baptizing, and more are coming to him."[5] It is as though they had said: This is a rarity, the crowd is flocking to him.

11.3. *Are you he who is to come, or do we wait for another?* It does not say: are you he who has come, but: "are you he who is to

1. Jn 1.29.
3. Cf. Jn 11.34.
5. Jn 3.26.

2. Mt 3.17.
4. Mt 9.14.

come?" The meaning is: Command me, since I am about to descend to the lower world, whether I should announce you even in the lower world, whom I announced in the upper world.[6] Or does it not befit the Son of God that he should taste death?[7] Are you going to send another to carry out these mysteries?[8]

11.4–5. *Jesus responded and said to them: "Go, report back to John what things you have heard and seen: the blind see, the lame walk, the lepers are cleansed, the deaf hear, the dead rise."*[9] Through his disciples John had asked: "Are you he who is to come or do we wait for another?" Christ points out the signs, not as a means of responding to the things which he had been asked, but as a stumbling block to the messengers. Go, he says, and tell John the signs which you see, the blind seeing, the lame walking, etc., and what is not less than these: *the poor are being evangelized.*[10] This refers either to the poor in spirit,[11] or at least to the poor in respect to wealth. Thus there is to be no distinction between the noble and the ignoble, between the rich and the needy, in the proclamation of the Gospel. These things prove the rigor of the teacher and they prove the truth of the preacher, since with him everyone is equal who can be saved. But what he says:

11.6. *"And blessed is he who is not scandalized in me,"* is an attack on the messengers, as will be demonstrated in what follows.

11.7–8. *Then as they went away, Jesus began to speak to the crowds about John: "Why did you go out into the desert? To see a reed shaken by the wind? But why did you go out? To see a man dressed in fine clothes?"* etc. If the earlier judgment, that is, his words: "Blessed is he who is not scandalized in me,"[12] had been brought forth

---

6. J. P. O'Connell, *The Eschatology of Saint Jerome*, 134, cites this text along with a host of others in Jerome's writings to conclude that there is abundant testimony in Jerome's writings that suggests that Christ's coming effected a change in the status of the souls of the good. O'Connell adds, however, that in none of these passages does Jerome indicate any such change in the status of the wicked. In fact, Jerome fails to speak of such a change at times when we would expect him to mention it, if he believed that such a change had occurred.

7. Cf. Heb 2.9.

8. Cf. Origen, *fragm.* 220; Jerome, *Ep.* 121.1; D. Scheerin, "St. John the Baptist in the Lower World," *VC* 30 (1976): 1–22.

9. Cf. Is 29.18; 35.5.

10. 11.5. Cf. Is 61.1.

11. Cf. Mt 5.3.

12. Mt 11.6.

against John, as many think, how is it that now John is preached with such great praises? Rather, it was because the crowd standing around was not aware of the mystery of [John's] question. They thought that John was in doubt about the Christ, whom he himself had pointed out. Therefore, in order that they might understand that John had asked not for himself but for his disciples, he says: "Why did you go out into the desert?" Surely it was not to see a man who is borne about by every wind[13] like a reed, and that wavers with a fickleness of mind concerning the one whom he had previously predicted? Or perhaps you think that John is compelled by the goads of envy against me and that his preaching is a pursuit of empty fame, so that he seeks a profit from it? Why should he desire riches? That he might have abundant feasts? But his food is locusts and wild honey.[14] Or why should he desire to be clothed in fine clothing? Camel's hair is his covering.[15] Food and clothing of that sort are received for lodging in a prison, and the proclamation of the truth has such a habitation. But those who are flatterers and pursue profit and seek wealth and abound in pleasures and wear fine clothing, are in kings' homes. From this he shows that a rigid life and austere preaching ought to avoid the courts of rulers and turn away from the palaces of luxurious men.

11.9. *"But why did you go out? To see a prophet? Yes, I tell you, and more than a prophet."* John is greater than the other prophets in that the one whom they had predicted as coming, he pointed out with his finger as having come, when he said: "Behold the Lamb of God, behold him who takes away the sins of the world."[16] And because in addition to the privilege of being his prophet there also came to the Baptist the reward of baptizing his own Lord, he then adds an αὔξησιν [increase] of merits, producing the testimony from Malachi in which even the angel[17] is predicted.[18] Now here we should not think that John is called an "angel" as one who participates in their nature, but

13. Cf. Eph 4.14.   14. Cf. Mt 3.4.
15. Cf. Mt 3.4.   16. Jn 1.29.
    17. Lat., *angelus.* Cf. Homily 16 on Ps 83 (84), in FOTC 48, 125; *Against the Luciferians* 7; *Against Jovinian* 2.27.
    18. Cf. Mal 3.1.

by the dignity of his office, namely, that of messenger.[19] For he brought the message that the Lord was coming.

11.11. *"Amen I tell you: There has not arisen among those born of women one greater than John the Baptist."* He says, "among those born of women." So then, John is put ahead of those men who have been born of women and who come from intercourse with a man. But he is not put ahead of him who was born of the Virgin and the Holy Spirit.[20] Although in his words: "There has not arisen among those born of women one greater than John," he has not put John ahead of the other prophets and patriarchs and all men, but he has equated the others with John. For it does not immediately follow that if the others are not greater than he is, he is greater than the others. Rather, he is equal with the other saints.

11.11. *"But he who is least in the kingdom of heaven is greater than he."* Many[21] want this to be understood of the Savior, that he who is least in age is greater in dignity. But we should understand it simply, that every saint who is already with God is greater than one who is still in the battle.[22] For it is one thing to possess the crown of victory, something else to be still contending in the line of battle.[23] Some[24] want to understand that the lowest angel serving the Lord in heaven is better even than the leading men who live on earth.

11.12. *"From the days of John the Baptist until now the kingdom of heaven suffers violence."* If as we said above John first announced repentance to the people, saying: "Do penance, for the kingdom of heaven has come near,"[25] it is consistent that from the days of that man, "the kingdom of heaven suffers violence, and

---

19. This is probably directed against Origen, who did not distinguish the nature of angels from that of human souls.

20. Cf. Mt 1.18.

21. Cf. John Chrysostom, *In Matth., Hom.* 37(38).2.

22. This thought is also found in *Ep.* 39.6; 75.1.

23. Cf. J. P. O'Connell, *The Eschatology of Saint Jerome,* 91: "The happiness that the saints enjoy between death and the general judgment is a reward for their life on earth." Cf. Jerome, *Ep.* 23.3.

24. Cf. John Chrysostom, *In Matth., Hom.* 37(38).3. Jerome speaks of this explanation in his *Ep.* 121.

25. Mt 3.2.

violent men have been laying waste to it." For there is great violence involved when we who have been born on the earth seek
to possess a heavenly home through virtue, which we have not
retained through nature.[26]

11.13. *"For all the prophets and the law prophesied until John."* It
is not that he is excluding the prophets after John (for we read
in the Acts of the Apostles that both Agabus and the four virgin daughters of Philip had prophesied).[27] Rather, he means
that whatever the Law and the prophets prophesied, which we
read in written form, was predicted about the Lord. Therefore,
when it is said: "All the prophets and the Law prophesied until
John," the time of Christ is shown. Thus John showed that the
one whom they said was coming had come.[28]

11.14–15. *"If you are willing to receive it, he is Elijah who was to
come. He who has ears to hear, let him hear."* The words: "If you are
willing to receive it, he is Elijah," are mystical and are in need of
an interpretation. The following words of the Lord demonstrate
this, when he says: "He who has ears to hear, let him hear." For
if the meaning were plain and the thought manifest, why was it
necessary that we be prepared in advance for the understanding of it? John, then, is called Elijah. This is not in accordance
with the foolish philosophers and certain heretics who introduce μετεμψύχωσιν,[29] but, according to another testimony of
the Gospel, he came in the spirit and power of Elijah.[30] He had
the same grace or measure of the Holy Spirit.[31] But also the austerity of life and the rigor of mind of Elijah and John are the
same. The one lived in the desert, so did the other; the one was
girded with a leather belt, the other had a similar girding; the
one was compelled to flee because he rebuked King Ahab and
Jezebel for impiety;[32] the other had his head cut off because he
rebuked the illicit marriage of Herod and Herodias.[33] There are

---

26. Cf. Jerome's *Ep.* 121; Homily 71 on Ps 93 (94) in FOTC 57, 105.

27. Cf. Acts 11.28; 21.9.

28. Cf. Origen, *fragm.* 229.

29. Metempsychosis. This is the belief of the heretic Basilides, that souls pass
into new bodies after death, i.e., the doctrine of reincarnation.

30. Cf. Lk 1.17.   31. Cf. Rom 12.3.

32. Cf. 1 Kgs 19.3.   33. Cf. Mt 14.3–11.

those[34] who think that John is called Elijah because, as at the second advent of the Savior according to Malachi,[35] Elijah will precede and announce the coming Judge, so did John at the first advent, and because both are messengers, either of the first advent of the Lord or of the second.

11.16–19. *"Now to what shall I compare this generation? It is like children sitting in the market place, who call out to their companions and say: 'We played for you, and you did not dance; we sang dirges for you, and you did not mourn.' For John came neither eating nor drinking, and they say: 'He has a demon.' The Son of man came eating and drinking, and they say: 'Behold a gluttonous man and a wine-drinker, a friend of tax-collectors and sinners.' Yet wisdom is justified by her children."* The generation of the Jews is compared with children sitting in the market place and with those calling out and saying to their companions: "We played for you, and you did not dance; we sang dirges, and you did not mourn." For the Scripture says: "To what will I liken this generation? It is like children sitting in the market place," etc. So then, an unrestrained and sweeping use of allegorical interpretation is not allowed to us. Rather, whatever we are going to say about the children has to be referred to the comparison with that generation. The children who sit in the market place are those concerning whom Isaiah speaks: "Behold, I and my children whom God gave me."[36] And in the eighteenth Psalm it says: "The testimony of God is sure, offering wisdom to little children."[37] Elsewhere it is written: "From the mouth of babes and sucklings you have perfected praise."[38] These children, then, sat in the market place, or, as it says more expressively in Greek, ἐν ἀγορᾷ, where there are many things for sale. And, because the people of the Jews were unwilling to listen, not only did they speak to them, but they called out with loud voices: "We played for you, and you did not dance." That is to say: we challenged you to do good works to our song and to dance to our flute, just as David danced be-

---

34. The opinion Jerome here attributes to others, that Elijah will come again into this world, he himself adopts as his own at 17.11. Cf. *Ep.* 121.1. For a discussion of these texts, see J. P. O'Connell, *The Eschatology of Saint Jerome,* 21–22.

35. Cf. Mal 4.5.   36. Is 8.18.

37. Ps 19.7.   38. Ps 8.2.

fore the ark of the Lord,[39] but you were unwilling. "We played a dirge" and challenged you to penance, but you were not even willing to do this. You spurned both proclamations, the one of encouragement leading to the virtues, the other of penance after sins. It is not surprising that you despised both paths to salvation, seeing that you equally scorned both fasting and sufficiency. If fasting pleases you, why was John displeasing? If sufficiency pleases you, why was the Son of Man displeasing? You have declared the one to be demon-possessed, the other a glutton and a drunkard.[40] Therefore, because you were unwilling to receive either discipline, "wisdom"—that is, the dispensation and doctrine of God—"is justified by her children." And it is I who am the power of God and the wisdom of God.[41] I have been approved as one who has acted justly by the apostles, my children, to whom the Father revealed things that he had hidden from those who are wise and prudent among themselves.[42] In some Gospels it reads: "Wisdom is justified by her works."[43] Indeed, wisdom does not seek the testimony of words but of deeds.

11.20. *Then he began to reproach the cities in which most of his miracles had been done, because they had not done penance.* A reproach of the cities of Chorazin and Bethsaida and Capernaum is expanded upon from the heading of this section. The reason he reproached them was that they did not do penance after miracles had been done and after very many signs.

11.21–22. *"Woe to you, Chorazin; woe to you, Bethsaida; for if in Tyre and Sidon had been done the miracles which were done in you, they would have done penance long ago in sackcloth and ashes. But I say to you: It will be more tolerable for Tyre and Sidon on the day of judgment than for you."* The Savior laments for Chorazin and Bethsaida, cities of Galilee, because after such great signs and miracles they did not do penance. To them he prefers Tyre and Sidon, cities that were surrendered to idolatry and vice. Now the reason they are preferred is because Tyre and Sidon only trampled upon natural law, but these, after transgressing natural and written law, even slighted the signs that were done among them.

---

39. 2 Sm 6.14.   40. Cf. Lk 7.33–34.
41. Cf. 1 Cor 1.24.   42. Cf. Mt 11.25; Rom 12.16.
43. Lk 7.35.

Let us ask where it is written that the Lord did signs in Chorazin and Bethsaida. We read above: "He was going about all the cities and villages, curing every disease," etc.[44] One must reckon, then, that among the other cities and villages, the Lord also did signs in Chorazin and Bethsaida.

11.23. *"And you, Capernaum, will you be exalted up to heaven? You will descend into the nether world."* In another copy we have found: "And you Capernaum, *you who have been exalted up to heaven,* you will descend to the nether world."[45] There is a twofold understanding: either you will descend to the nether world because with supreme arrogance you resisted my preaching, or, since by my hospitality and my signs and miracles you have been exalted up to heaven, having had such a great privilege, you will be struck with greater punishments, because you were unwilling to believe even in these.

11.23. *"For if the miracles had been done among the inhabitants of Sodom that were done in you, perhaps they would have remained up to this day."* A wise reader may inquire and say: If Tyre and Sidon and Sodom were capable of doing penance in response to the preaching of the Savior and to the miracles of the signs, then they are not to blame for the fact that they did not become believers. Rather, there is a fault of silence on the part of the one who was unwilling to preach to those who would do penance.[46] The response to this is easy and candid: that we are ignorant of the judgments of God and do not know the mysteries of each of his dispensations. The Lord had resolved not to go beyond the borders of Judea, lest he give to the Pharisees and priests a just pretext for persecution. This is also the reason he commanded the apostles before the Passion: "Do not go in the way of the Gentiles and do not enter into the cities of the Samaritans."[47] Therefore, Chorazin and Bethsaida are condemned because they were unwilling to believe in the Lord, who was present among them. Tyre and Sidon are justified because they believed his apostles.[48] You should not inquire about the timing, when

44. Mt 9.35.
45. This is a variant reading of the parallel passage in Lk 10.15.
46. Cf. Ezek 3.18.   47. Mt 10.5.
48. For the activity of Jesus and his apostles in and around Tyre and Sidon, cf. Mk 3.8; Mt 15.21; Acts 21.3; 27.3.

you are beholding the salvation of believers. In Capernaum, however, whose name means "very beautiful village,"[49] unbelieving Jerusalem is condemned, to whom Ezekiel says: "Sodom has been justified above you."[50]

11.25. *At that time Jesus answered and said: "I confess to you, Father, Lord of heaven and earth."* Confession does not always signify penance but also thanksgiving, as we read very often in the Psalms. Let those who revile the Savior as not born but created hear this.[51] He calls God his own Father, but he also calls him the Lord of heaven and earth. For if he himself is a creature, and a creature can call its own Creator its Father, it was foolish not to call him both his own Lord and Father, and similarly the Lord and Father of heaven and earth.

11.25. *"Because you have hidden these things from the wise and prudent and you have revealed them to little children."* He gives thanks and exults in the Father because he disclosed the mysteries of his advent to the apostles, things which the scribes and Pharisees ignored. They are the ones who seem wise to themselves and prudent in their own sight. "Wisdom is justified by her children."[52]

11.26. *"Yes, Father, for thus was it pleasing before you."* He speaks to the Father with tender feeling,[53] that the benefit begun in the apostles might be completed.

11.27. *"All things have been delivered to me by my Father."* Understand in a mystical way that the Father delivers and the Son receives. Otherwise, if we want to understand according to our frailty, we would say that since he who has received has begun to have, then he who gave will begin not to have. But the "all things" that have been delivered to himself should not be understood of heaven and earth and the elements and the other

49. Elsewhere, Jerome gives a different etymology for Capernaum: *De interpr. nom. hebr.* 64, "field or village of consolation"; Homily 76 (FOTC 57, 138): "field of consolation or most beautiful land." His current etymology is not in agreement with Origen's; see *In Matth.*, 13.

50. Ezek 16.52.

51. This is directed against the Arians.

52. Mt 11.19.

53. For another use of this phrase, see below on Mt 26.25.

things which he himself made and established. Rather, it should be understood of those who have access to the Father through the Son. Formerly they were rebels, but afterward they began to understand God.

11.27. *"And no one knows the Son except the Father, nor does anyone know the Father except the Son and him to whom the Son wills to reveal."* Let Eunomius blush. He boasts to have for himself as much knowledge of the Father and the Son as they have among themselves. But if he becomes contentious and consoles his own insanity by the words that follow: "and him to whom the Son wills to reveal," [let him realize that] it is one thing to know what he knows by the equality of nature, but it is something else to know this by the status of one who reveals.

11.28. *"Come to me, all who labor and are burdened, and I will refresh you."* The prophet Zechariah also testifies that the burdens of sin are heavy.[54] He says that iniquity sits upon a leaden weight.[55] And the psalmist laments: "My iniquities have weighed down upon me."[56] Or at the least he is inviting those who were oppressed by the very heavy yoke of the Law to the grace of the Gospel.

11.30. *"For my yoke is easy and my burden light."* How is the Gospel lighter than the Law, when in the Law murder is condemned,[57] [but] in the Gospel, anger?[58] By what account is the grace of the Gospel easier, when in the Law adultery is punished,[59] [but] in the Gospel, lust?[60] In the Law there are many precepts which the apostle teaches cannot be fulfilled perfectly.[61] In the Law works are demanded in which he who does them will live;[62] in the Gospel willingness is sought which, even if it does not have the effectual achievement, nevertheless does not lose its reward. The Gospel commands things that we are able to do, for example, that we should not lust. This lies within our choice. Though the Law does not punish the willingness, it does punish the effectual achievement: "Thou shalt not commit adultery." Imagine some

54. Cf. Origen, *fragm.* 245.
56. Ps 38.4.
58. Cf. Mt 5.23.
60. Cf. Mt 5.28.
62. Cf. Lv 18.5; Prv 4.4; 7.2.

55. Cf. Zec 5.7.
57. Cf. Ex 20.13.
59. Cf. Ex 20.15.
61. Cf. Rom 7.14–23; Acts 15.10.

virgin who was treated like a prostitute during a persecution. Under the Gospel she is received as a virgin, since she does not sin willingly; under the Law she would be repudiated as one who had been corrupted.

Chapter 12

12.1. *At that time Jesus went through the standing grain on the Sabbath; and his disciples, being hungry, began to pluck ears of grain and to eat.* As we also read in another evangelist,[63] on account of excessive importunity they did not even have the chance to eat, and therefore as men they were hungry. Now the fact that they rub the ears of grain in their hands and relieve their hunger is an indication of the more austere life of those who seek simple food and not prepared meals.

12.2. *But when the Pharisees saw this, they said to him: "Behold, your disciples are doing what is not lawful for them to do on the Sabbath."* Note that the apostles of the Savior are the first to destroy the letter of the Sabbath. This contradicts the Ebionites,[64] who, though they receive the other apostles, repudiate Paul as a transgressor of the Law.

12.3–4. *But he said to them: "Have you not read what David did when he hungered and those who were with him, how he entered into the house of God and ate the bread of proposition, which was not lawful for him to eat nor for those who were with him, but only for priests?"* To refute the false accusation of the Pharisees he calls to mind ancient history. When David was fleeing from Saul, he came to Nob, and when he had been received by Ahimelek the priest, he asked for food.[65] Since he did not have ordinary bread, he gave him consecrated bread, which was not lawful to eat but only for priests and Levites. He only asked whether the young men were undefiled by women. And when David answered: "since yesterday and the day before," Ahimelek did not hesitate to give the bread, thinking that it is better to deliver the men from the danger of starvation than to offer sacrifice to God. For the prophet

---

63. Cf. Mk 2.23; Lk 6.1.   64. See above, Preface (2), n. 30.
65. Cf. 1 Sm 21.1–6.

says: "I want mercy and not sacrifice."[66] Indeed, the salvation of men is an appeasing sacrifice to God. Therefore, the Lord objects and says: If David is holy and the priest Ahimelek is not reprehended by you, both of whom transgressed the command of the Law with an acceptable excuse, and hunger is the reason, why do you not approve the same hunger in the apostles, which you approve in the others? Yet there is a great difference in the fact that the apostles rub ears of grain in their hands on the Sabbath, whereas David's men ate the bread of Levites, and the days of the New Moon yielded to the solemnity of the Sabbath. It was during these days that David fled from the royal palace when he had been asked for at the feast.[67] Observe that neither David nor the young men with him received the bread of proposition until they had responded that they were undefiled by women.

12.5. *"Or have you not read in the Law that on the Sabbath days the priests in the Temple violate the Sabbath and are guiltless?"* You unjustly attack my disciples, he says, because when passing through the standing grain they crushed ears of corn. They did this when compelled by the necessity of hunger. Yet you yourselves violate the Sabbath when sacrificing victims in the Temple, slaughtering bulls, burning holocausts in fire on a pile of wood, and, according to the evidence of another Gospel, circumcising little children on the Sabbath.[68] Thus while you long to keep the other laws, you destroy the Sabbath. But the laws of God are never contrary to one another. Jesus shows prudence in that, when his disciples could have been convicted of transgression, he says that they have followed the examples of David and Ahimelek; but against those who had made the false charge, he reports a real transgression of the Sabbath, which lacked the excuse of necessity.

12.6. *"But I say to you that one greater than the Temple is here."* In this passage "here" *(hic)*[69] should be read as an adverb, not a pronoun: for the place that holds the Lord of the Temple is greater than the Temple.

---

66. Hos 6.6.   67. Cf. 1 Sm 20.14, 24, 27.
68. Cf. Jn 7.22–23.
69. *Hic* is both a pronoun meaning "this" and an adverb meaning "here."

12.7. *"But if you knew what this means: 'I want mercy and not sacrifice,' you would never have condemned the innocent."* Above[70] we have explained what this means: "I want mercy and not sacrifice." Now what follows: "you would never have condemned the innocent," should be understood of the apostles. The meaning is: If you approve the mercy of Ahimelek when he revived David, who was in danger of starvation, and his young men, why do you condemn my disciples who have done nothing of the sort?

12.9–10. *And when he passed on from there, he went into their synagogue. And behold, there was a man who had a withered hand.* This man who is cured in the synagogue is the thirteenth [miracle].[71] It should be noted that his hand became withered not on the journey and outside, but in the meeting place of the Jews.[72]

12.10. *And they were questioning him, saying: "Is it lawful to cure on the Sabbath?" in order to accuse him.* He had excused the breaking of the Sabbath that the Pharisees were charging against his disciples with a plausible example. Therefore, they want to accuse him falsely and to ask whether it is lawful to cure on Sabbath days. Thus, if he does not cure him, they will accuse him of cruelty or powerlessness; if he does cure him, they will accuse him of a transgression.

12.11–12. *But he said to them: "What man will there be among you who, if he has a single sheep and it falls into a pit on the Sabbath, will not take hold of it and lift it out? How much better is a man than a sheep! And so, it is lawful to do good on the Sabbath."* Thus he resolved the question that had been raised by condemning the avarice of those who asked it. He says, if you hasten to rescue a sheep and any other animal that falls into a pit on the Sabbath, not out of consideration for the animal, but out of your avarice, how much more should I deliver a human being, who is much better than a sheep?

12.13. *Then he said to the man: "Stretch forth your hand." And he stretched it forth, and it was restored to soundness, [to being] just like the other.* In the Gospel that the Nazarenes[73] and Ebionites[74] use,

70. Cf. commentary on Mt 12.3–4.
71. See on Mt 8.1–2; 8.23; 9.18–19; 9.30–31; 9.32–33; 10.1.
72. See below on Mt 12.13. Cf. Origen, *fragm.* 249.
73. See Jerome's Preface, n. 6.
74. See Jerome's Preface, n. 30.

which we recently translated into Greek from the Hebrew language, and which many call the authentic Gospel of Matthew,[75] this man who has the withered hand is described as a stonemason.[76] He prays for help with words of this sort: "I was a stonemason, seeking a livelihood with my hands; I plead with you, Jesus, that you restore soundness to me, that I might not have to beg for my food in base fashion." Until the coming of the Savior, there was a withered hand in the synagogue of the Jews. The works of God were not being done in it. But after he came to earth, the right hand was given back in the apostles, who believed, and it was restored to its former work.

12.14. *But the Pharisees went out and took counsel against him, how they might destroy him.* Envy is the cause of their plots against the Lord. For what had he done that would provoke the Pharisees to murder him? Naturally, that the man had stretched forth his hand. For what Pharisee did not stretch forth his hand on the Sabbath day, while carrying food, offering a cup and the other things which are necessary for nourishment? If, then, it is no crime to stretch forth a hand and lift up food or drink on the Sabbath, why do they convict another of what they themselves are also convicted of doing, especially since that stonemason[77] carried no such thing, but stretched forth only his hand at the Lord's command?

12.15. *But, knowing this, Jesus withdrew from there.* Knowing their plots, that they wanted to destroy their own Savior, he withdrew from there, so that he might remove from the Pharisees the opportunity for impiety against himself.

12.18. *"Behold my servant*[78] *whom I have chosen, my beloved,"* etc. This is spoken under the Father's persona by Isaiah the prophet: "I will put my Spirit upon him."[79] The Spirit is put not upon the Word of God and upon the Only-begotten who proceeded from the bosom of the Father,[80] but upon him of whom it is said: "Behold my servant."

75. This is apparently based on the tradition of Papias, recorded in Eusebius, *HE* 3.39, that Matthew originally wrote his Gospel in Hebrew (Aramaic). See Preface (1), n. 6.

76. See Hennecke-Schneemelcher, *NTA* 1, 147–48.

77. See above on Mt 12.13.   78. Lat., *puer*, i.e., "boy," "child."

79. Is 42.1.   80. Cf. Jn 1.1, 18; 8.42.

12.19. *"Nor will anyone hear his voice in the streets."* For "broad and spacious is the road that leads to destruction, and many enter through it."[81] Who are the "many"? Those who do not hear the voice of the Savior, since they are not on the narrow road, but are on the spacious one.

12.20. *"A bruised reed he will not break, and a smoldering wick he will not put out."* A person breaks a bruised reed who does not reach out his hand to the sinner, nor carry the burden of his brother.[82] And one who despises the tiny spark of faith in little children puts out the smoldering wick. Christ did neither of these things. For he had come for this purpose, to save what was lost.[83]

12.22. *Then there was brought to him a blind and mute man having a demon, and he cured him so that he spoke and saw.* Three signs were accomplished simultaneously in a single man: a blind man sees, a mute speaks, a man possessed by a demon is delivered. This was done at that time physically, to be sure, but even on a daily basis it is fulfilled in the life of believers. Thus when the demon has been expelled, first they look at the light of faith, then they open their previously silent mouths to the praises of God.

12.25. *But Jesus, knowing their thoughts, said to them: "Every kingdom divided against itself will be brought to desolation."* The crowds were amazed and confessed that he who was doing such great signs was the son of David; but the Pharisees were attributing the works of God to the prince of demons. The Lord responds not to their words but to their thoughts, so that they would be thus compelled to believe in the power of him who could see the secrets of their heart.[84]

12.26. *"If Satan casts out Satan, he is divided against himself; how then shall his kingdom stand?"* A kingdom and city cannot continue when it is divided against itself, but as little things increase by means of concord, so by discord the greatest things will be dissipated.[85] If then Satan fights against himself and a demon is inimical to demons, the end of the world would have already

---

81. Mt 7.13. Cf. Origen, *fragm.* 258.
82. Cf. Gal 6.2.
83. Cf. Mt 18.11; Lk 19.10. Cf. Origen, *fragm.* 262.
84. Cf. Mt 9.3.
85. This line is borrowed from Sallust, *Jug.* 10.6.

come, nor would there be room in it for adversarial powers. For war among them means peace for men. But if you think, O scribes and Pharisees, that the withdrawal of demons means obedience to their prince, so that they delude ignorant men by a fraudulent pretense, what can you say about the physical healings that the Lord has accomplished? It is another matter if you also assign to demons the diseases of the members and the extraordinary signs of spiritual miracles.[86]

12.27. *"If I cast out demons by Beelzebub, by whom do your sons cast them out? Therefore, they shall be your judges."* By "sons of the Jews" he is signifying by a customary expression either the exorcists of that nation or the apostles who were born of that stock.[87] If he means the exorcists who were casting out demons at the invocation of God, he is forcing them by means of a clever question to confess that the work is of the Holy Spirit. He is saying: If the casting out of demons by your sons is attributed to God, not to demons, why would the same work done by me not have the same cause as well? Therefore, "they shall be your judges," not with the authority [to judge] but in comparison.[88] For while they attribute the casting out of demons to God, you attribute it to Beelzebub, the prince of demons. But if this has been said about the apostles, which is also the way we ought to interpret it, the meaning is that they will be judges of them, because they will sit on the twelve thrones, judging the twelve tribes of Israel.[89]

12.28. *"But if I cast out demons by the Spirit of God, then the kingdom of God has come upon you."* In Luke we read this passage written as follows: "But if I cast out demons by the finger of God."[90] This is the finger that even the magicians confess, who were doing the signs against Moses and Aaron, saying: "This is the finger of God."[91] By means of it the stone tablets were written on Mount Sinai.[92] If, then, the Son is the hand and arm of God,

---

86. In 385, Jerome discussed this passage in *Ep.* 42.1 to Marcella: "If it is the devil's object to injure God's creation, how can he wish to cure the sick and to expel himself from the bodies possessed by him?" NPNF2, 6.56.

87. Cf. Homily 76 in FOTC 57, 143.

88. See below on Mt 12.41.

90. Lk 11.20.

92. Cf. Dt 9.10.

89. Mt 19.28; Lk 22.30.

91. Ex 8.19.

and the Holy Spirit is his finger, then there is one substance of the Father and of the Son and of the Holy Spirit. Do not let the inequality of the members cause you to stumble, since the unity of the body builds up. "The kingdom of God has come upon you." [By these words] he is either signifying himself, of whom it is written in another passage: "The kingdom of God is within you,"[93] and "In your midst stands one whom you do not know";[94] or, at the least, he means that kingdom that both John and the Lord himself had announced, when they said: "Do penance, for the kingdom of heaven has come near."[95] There is also a third kingdom, that of Holy Scripture, which is taken away from the Jews and is handed over to a nation producing its fruits.[96]

12.29. *"Or how can anyone enter the house of a strong man and plunder his goods unless he first binds the strong man? And then he will plunder his house."* We must not be secure; our adversary is acknowledged to be strong, even by the words of his vanquisher. His house is the world, which has been set under evil.[97] This is not from the status of a creator, but from the magnitude of his guilt. We were once his goods. The strong man was bound and packed off to Tartarus,[98] having been crushed under the Lord's foot.[99] And when the tyrant's residence had been plundered, captivity was led captive.[100]

12.30. *"He who is not with me is against me, and he who does not gather with me scatters."* Let no one think that this is said about the heretics and schismatics. Granted, it could be understood in this way by extension. But from what follows and from the context of the words, it refers to the devil. For the works of the Savior cannot be compared with the works of Beelzebub. The latter desires to hold the souls of men captive; the Lord wants them to be liberated. The one preaches idols; the other, the knowledge of the one God. The one drags people to the vices; the other calls them back to the virtues. How, then, can there be concord between them, since their works are opposed?

12.32. *"Whoever speaks a word against the Son of man, it will be*

---

93. Lk 17.21.
95. Cf. Mt 3.2; 4.17.
97. Cf.1 Jn 5.19.
99. Cf. Rom 16.20.

94. Jn 1.26.
96. Cf. Mt 21.43.
98. Cf. 2 Pt 2.4.
100. Cf. Ps 68.18; Eph 4.8.

forgiven him; but he who speaks against the Holy Spirit, it will not be forgiven him, neither in this age nor in the future age."[101] Now how is it that certain of our own receive back bishops and priests into their [former] rank, after these men have committed blasphemy against the Holy Spirit, when the Savior says that every sin and blasphemy is forgiven men, but as for those who commit blasphemy against the Holy Spirit, this is not forgiven them, neither in the present time nor in the future? Perhaps we should take up the following citation from the evangelist Mark. He expressed the grounds for such great anger more manifestly when he said: "Because they were saying: 'He has an unclean spirit.'"[102] Therefore, whoever attributes the works of the Savior to Beelzebub, the prince of demons, and says that the Son of God has an unclean spirit, to this one the blasphemy will not be forgiven at any time. Or this passage is to be understood in this way: He who speaks a word against the Son of man, having been scandalized at my flesh,[103] thinks that I am merely a man. He thinks that I am the son of a carpenter, that I have James, Joseph, and Judas as brothers,[104] and that I am a glutton and winedrinker.[105] Such a blasphemous opinion, although it is not free from blame, nevertheless can obtain a pardon for the error, owing to the lowly condition of the body. But he who clearly understands the works of God, since he cannot deny the miraculous power, yet is goaded on by envy and raises false charges against these things and says that the Christ and the Word of God, and also the works of the Holy Spirit, are Beelzebub, he will not be forgiven, neither in the present age nor in the future.

12.33. *"Either make a tree good and its fruit good, or make a tree evil and its fruit evil. For by its fruit, a tree is known."* He binds them by means of a syllogism, which the Greeks call ἄφυκτον. We can call it "inescapable." He shuts in from both directions those whom he interrogates and he presses them on both horns. If, he says, the devil is evil, then he cannot do good works. But if the deeds that you see are good, it follows that it is not the devil

---

101. This text is interpreted by Jerome against the rigorism of the Novatianists in *Ep.* 42 to Marcella. For Novatian, see below on Mt 13.21.

102. Mk 3.30.   103. Cf. Mt 11.6.

104. Cf. Mt 13.55; Mk 6.3; Lk 4.16.   105. Cf. Mt 11.19.

who is doing them. For it is not possible for good to arise from evil, or evil from good. But in what follows:

12.34. *"Brood of vipers, how can you speak good things, when you are evil?"* He shows that it is they who are the evil tree. They are producing in abundance the fruits of blasphemy, and have the devil's kind of seed.[106]

12.35. *"A good man brings forth good things from a good treasure, and an evil man brings forth evil things from an evil treasure."* Either he is showing from what sort of treasure the Jews who are blaspheming the Lord are bringing forth their blasphemies; or his judgment here is rooted in the earlier question,[107] that just as a good man cannot bring forth evil things, nor can an evil man bring forth good things, so Christ cannot do evil works, and the devil cannot do good works.

12.36. *"I tell you that every idle word that men have spoken, they will render an account for it on the day of judgment."* This, too, is rooted in what precedes. The meaning is: If the idle word that does not edify the hearers is not without danger to the one who speaks it, and if each person will render an account on the day of judgment for his words, how much more are you going to render an account for your false charges! You are speaking evil of the works of the Holy Spirit. You are saying that I cast out demons by Beelzebub, the prince of demons. An idle word is one that is spoken without benefit to both the speaker and the hearer, for example, when we speak about frivolous things to the neglect of serious matters, or when we tell old wives' tales.[108] But as for the one who repeats scurrilous things and makes people's mouths drop open with loud laughter, and who brings forth anything disgraceful, he will be indicted not for an idle word, but for a criminal one.

12.38. *Then some of the scribes and Pharisees answered him, saying: "We want to see a sign from you."*[109] They demand a sign, as if the signs that they had seen did not exist. Now in another evan-

---

106. Jn 8.44.

107. I.e., Mt 12.34: "How can you speak good things, when you are evil?"

108. Cf. *Ep.* 121.10 to Algasia, where Jerome treats Jewish traditions about tales of old women. There the reference is clearly to pagan mythological fables.

109. Mt 12.38.

gelist, what they ask for is explained in more detail: "We want to see from you a sign from heaven."[110] Either in the manner of Elijah, they were desiring fire to come from on high,[111] or in imitation of Samuel, they longed for thunder to roar, lightning to flash, and rain to pour down in the summer time.[112] As if they would not be able to bring false accusations against these things as well and say that they happened from hidden and varied disturbances of the air! But as for you who falsely accuse things that you see with your eyes, hold in your hands, and understand by its benefit, what will you do in response to these things that come from heaven? Assuredly you will respond that even the magicians in Egypt did many signs from heaven.[113]

12.39–40. *He said to them: "A perverse and adulterous generation."* "Adulterous" is an excellent way to characterize that generation, since it had divorced its husband and, according to Ezekiel, united itself with many lovers.[114]

12.39–40. *"[It] seeks a sign, and a sign will not be given to it except the sign of the prophet Jonah. For just as Jonah was three days and three nights in the belly of the whale, so shall the Son of man be three days and three nights in the heart of the earth."* We have treated this passage more fully in the commentary on the prophet Jonah.[115] Therefore, we refer the diligent reader to that passage. For now, let us be content with saying briefly that by using a synecdoche (συνεκδοχικῶς), the whole can be understood from the part.[116] It is not that the Lord spent the whole of three days and three nights in the nether world. Rather, the three days and three nights refer to part of the day of preparation, part of the Lord's day, and the whole of the Sabbath day.

12.41. *"The men of Nineveh will rise in the judgment with this generation and will condemn it."* He does not mean that they will have

---

110. Mk 8.11.

111. Cf. 1 Kgs 18.38 and 2 Kgs 1.9–14.

112. Cf. 1 Sm 12.18.

113. Cf. Ex 7.12, 22.

114. Cf. Ezek 16.26.

115. Cf. Jerome, *In Jon.* 2.2 (PL 25: 1131B–D).

116. Cf. Homily 36 on Ps 109 (110) and Homily 58 on Ps 148 in FOTC 48, 274 and 421; *Commentary on Isaiah* 14.2.

the authority to render the verdict, but that they will be compared and used as an example.[117]

12.41. *"And behold, here there is one greater than Jonah."* You should understand "here" as an adverb in this passage, not a pronoun.[118] The sense is: Jonah (according to the LXX)[119] preached for only three days,[120] whereas I have preached for such a long time. Jonah preached to the unbelieving nation of the Assyrians, but I am preaching to Jews, the people of God. Jonah preached to wanderers, but I am preaching to fellow citizens. Jonah spoke with simple words and did no signs, whereas I have done such great signs and sustain the false charge of Beelzebub. In this sense, then, is one greater than Jonah here; that is, he is among you for the present.

12.42. *"The queen of the south will rise in the judgment with this generation and will condemn it, because she came from the ends of the earth to hear the wisdom of Solomon."* The queen of the south will condemn the people of the Jews in the same manner as the men of Nineveh will condemn unbelieving Israel. Now, the queen of Sheba is she of whom we read in the book of Kings and in the Chronicles.[121] With very great hardships, she abandoned her own nation and empire and came to Judea to hear the wisdom of Solomon, and she conferred upon him many gifts. Now in Nineveh and in the queen of Sheba, the hidden faith of the Gentiles is put ahead of that of Israel.[122]

12.43, 45. *"But when an unclean spirit has gone out of a man, it roams through dry places seeking rest, and it does not find it,"* etc. Some[123] think that this passage has been spoken about the heretics, that the unclean spirit that formerly dwelt in them when they were pagans is cast out upon their confession of the true

---

117. The same explanation is found above under Mt 12.27.

118. The same observation is found above on Mt 12.6.

119. Lit., "seventy translators" (*LXX interpretes*).

120. Cf. Jon 3.3–4. Jerome may be confused. Both the Greek and Hebrew texts speak of Nineveh being a great city, "three days' journey in breadth" (Jon 3.3). But there is a textual difference on Jon 3.4. The Hebrew says: "Yet forty days, and Nineveh will be overthrown," whereas the LXX reads: "Yet three days, . . ."

121. Cf. 1 Kgs 10.1–7; 2 Chr 9.1–9.   122. Cf. Mt 8.10.

123. Who?

faith. But later, when they have transferred themselves to a heresy and set their house in order with feigned virtues, then the devil returns to them, accompanied by seven other evil spirits. He dwells in them, and their last state becomes worse than the first. To be sure, the heretics are in a much worse state than the pagans, since in the latter there is the hope of faith, in the former a battle of discord. Though this interpretation holds forth a certain plausibility and the luster of learning, I do not know whether it contains the truth. For the parable and lesson concluded with the words: "So shall it be with this evil generation."[124] This compels me to refer the parable not to the heretics and to just any men, but to the people of the Jews. Thus the context of the passage does not have general and haphazard application. It does not vacillate in different directions, nor is it confused in the manner in which fools speak. On the contrary, it is coherent on its own terms and is related to both what precedes and what follows. An unclean spirit went out of the Jews when they received the Law. It roamed through dry places, seeking rest for itself. That is to say, when it had been expelled from the Jews, it roamed through the deserted places of the Gentiles. Though they would later on believe in the Lord, at the time the unclean spirit found no place among the nations. Then it said:

12.44. *"I will return to my former house from which I went forth."* That is to say, I am going [back] to the Jews, whom I had previously left.[125]

12.44. *"And when it comes, it finds the house vacant and swept clean."* For the Temple of the Jews was vacant. It did not have Christ as a guest, who says: "Rise, let us go from here."[126] And in another place he says: "Your house will be left to you deserted."[127] Since, therefore, they did not have the protection of God and his angels, and since they adorned themselves with superfluous observances of the Law and with the traditions of the Pharisees, the devil returns to his own former habitation. And with seven accompanying demons, he takes up residence in his former house. Thus the last state of that people becomes worse than the

124. Mt 12.45.   125. Or "divorced" (*dimiseram*).
126. Jn 14.31.   127. Lk 13.35.

first.[128] For as they blaspheme Christ Jesus in their synagogues, it is clear that they are now possessed by a greater number of demons than they had been possessed with in Egypt, before the knowledge of the Law. Indeed, it is one thing not to believe in one who is coming, but it is something else not to receive him who has come.[129] Now as for the number seven that is added to the devil, this should be understood either because of the Sabbath, or because of the number of the Holy Spirit. Thus just as in Isaiah the seven spirits of the virtues are described as having descended upon the shoot from the root of Jesse and upon the flower who rises from the root,[130] so, on the contrary, the number of the vices is consecrated to the devil.

12.46–47. *While he was still speaking to the crowds, behold, his mother and his brothers were standing outside, seeking to speak with him. But someone said to him: "Behold, your mother and your brothers are standing outside, seeking you."* The Lord was occupied in the work of the word, in teaching the people, in the duty of preaching. His mother and brothers come and stand outside and desire to speak with him. Then someone announces to the Savior that his mother and brothers are standing outside seeking him. It seems to me that the one who announces this does not simply happen to announce it by chance, but he is plotting against him, to see whether Jesus will prefer [his own] flesh and blood to spiritual activity. This is why the Lord refused to go out. It is not that he was denying his mother and brothers, but he wanted to respond to the one who was plotting:

12.49. *Stretching forth his hand toward his disciples, he said: "Behold my mother and my brothers."* They are my mother who daily give birth to me in the souls of believers.[131] They are my brothers who do the works of my Father.[132] He has not denied his mother, then, in the sense that Marcion and Manicheus think, as one who was thought to have been born of a phantom. Rather, he preferred the apostles to his relatives, that we too, in terms of degree of affection, might prefer the spirit to the flesh. "Behold, your mother and your brothers are standing outside, seek-

---

128. Cf. Mt 12.45; 2 Pt 2.20.   129. Cf. Jn 1.11.

130. Cf. Is 11.1–5.   131. Cf. Gal 4.19.

132. Cf. Jn 8.41; 9.3; 9.4; 10.37; 14.12.

ing you." Some surmise that the brothers of the Lord are sons of Joseph by another wife.[133] They follow apocryphal nonsense, fabricating some little woman named Escha.[134] But as the book that we have written against Helvidius shows, we understand the brothers of the Lord to be not sons of Joseph, but first cousins of the Savior. They are children of the Mary who was the Lord's aunt, who is said to be the mother of James the less and of Joses and Jude.[135] We read in another passage of the Gospel that they are called brothers of the Lord.[136] Now all of Scripture demonstrates that first cousins are called brothers.[137] Let us also speak in another manner. The Savior is speaking to the crowds. The inner meaning is that he is instructing the nations. His mother and brothers, that is, the synagogue and people of the Jews, are standing outside. They desire to enter, and they become unworthy of his words. Whenever they ask and seek and send a messenger, they receive the response that they have free choice. They can enter, if they are willing to believe; but they cannot enter unless they ask the others.

Chapter 13

13.1–2. *On that day Jesus went out of the house and was sitting near the sea. Great crowds were gathered unto him.* The people were

133. Origen reports this as the view of "some" in *In Matth.* 10.17. He says it was based on a tradition found in the apocryphal *Gospel of Peter* and the apocryphal *Book of James* (*The Protevangelium of James;* see ANF 8.363). Origen says that he admires the way these interpreters wish to preserve the honor of Mary's virginity to the end, so that her body never knew intercourse. Origen also seems to accept the opinion that the brothers of the Lord were children from Joseph's previous marriage. He mentions it several times in his writings; cf. *Fragm. In Joh.* 31 (GCS 4, 506).

134. The *Protevangelium of James,* a work that is referred to by Origen (see previous note) and that has been attacked not only by Jerome but also by later Popes, contains the story about Jesus having stepbrothers. Eastern Greek Fathers highly valued this work; see Hennecke-Schneemelcher, *NTA* 1, 373–74. In this passage, however, the *Protevangelium of James* does not seem to be Jerome's immediate target because it does not mention anyone named Escha.

135. Cf. Mt 27.56; Lk 24.10; Mk 15.47.

136. Cf. Mt 13.55; Mk 6.3.   137. Cf., e.g., Gn 13.8.

not able to enter the house of Jesus nor to be there where the apostles were listening to the mysteries. Therefore, the compassionate and merciful Lord[138] goes out from his own house and sits near the sea of this world, so that the crowds may gather to him and listen at the shore to the things that they did not deserve to hear when they were inside.

13.2. *So that he got into a boat, and sat down. And the whole crowd stood on the shore.* Jesus is in the midst of the waves and is being pounded back and forth by the sea. He is secure in his own majesty and causes his boat to approach the land. The people, on the other hand, who were not in any danger, nor surrounded by temptations that they were unable to bear,[139] stand on the shore with their feet planted in order to listen to the things that are said.

13.3. *And he spoke many things to them in parables, saying.* The crowd is not of a single opinion; rather, there are different intentions in each person. This is why he speaks to them in many parables, that they may receive the different teachings in accordance with their various motivations. Also to be noted is that he spoke many things, but not all things, to them in parables. For if he had spoken everything in parables, the people would have gone away without profit. Thus he intermingles clear things with obscure things, so that by means of the things that they do understand, they might be challenged to the knowledge of those things which they do not understand.

13.3. *"Behold, the sower went out to sow."* He was inside, he was staying at home, and he was speaking mysteries to the disciples. So then, he who sows the word of God went out from his house to sow among the crowds. Now this sower who sows signifies the Son of God the Father, who sows the word among the people. And at the same time observe that this is the first parable that is given with its own interpretation. We need to be very cautious whenever the Lord explains his words. When he is questioned by his disciples and then explains the inner meaning, we must not wish to understand anything more or less than what he has explained.

138. Cf. Ps 103.8; 145.8.
139. Cf. 1 Cor 10.13.

1 3.4–5. *"Some fell along the path, and the birds came and ate it up. Other seeds fell upon rocky ground where they did not have much earth, "* etc. Valentinus used this parable to prove his own heresy.[140] He introduced the [doctrine of the] three natures: spiritual, soulish, and earthly, though here there are four: one near the road, another on rocky ground, a third on ground full of thorns, a fourth on good earth. We postpone his [Jesus'] interpretation for a little bit, since we want to listen to what is said to the disciples in secret:

1 3.9. *"He who has ears to hear, let him hear."* We are challenged to understand the things said, as often as we are admonished by his words.

1 3.10. *And his disciples approached and said to him.* One should ask how the disciples could approach him, seeing that Jesus is sitting in a boat. Perhaps it is given to be understood that they had climbed into the boat long before this. While standing there with him, they asked for an interpretation of the parable.

1 3.12. *"He who has, it will be given to him, and he will abound, but he who does not have, even what he has shall be taken away from him."* To those who have, more is given. From those who do not have, even what they seem[141] to have is taken away. This does not seem to be an equitable judgment. And yet, it is given to the apostles who have faith in Christ, even if they are somewhat deficient in the virtues, whereas from the Jews who did not believe in the Son of God, it is taken away, even if they possess something by the good of nature. For they are unable to understand anything wisely who do not have the head of wisdom.

1 3.13–14. *"Therefore, I speak to them in parables, because seeing they do not see, and hearing they do not hear."* He is saying this about those who are standing on the shore and are separated from Jesus. Because of the noise of the waves, they do not hear clearly what is being said. "In them is fulfilled the prophecy of Isaiah: 'By hearing you will hear and will not understand, and seeing you will see and you will not see.'"[142] These things were proph-

---

140. The literary source is unknown.

141. Cf. Lk 8.18. Jerome has blended the wording of Luke with that of Matthew.

142. Mt 13.14; Is 6.9.

esied about the crowds that stand on the shore and do not deserve to hear the words of God. Let us then approach Jesus with the disciples. Let us ask him for an explanation of the parable, lest with the crowds we seem to have ears and eyes to no purpose.

13.15. *"For the heart of this people has been hardened, and with ears they have heard with difficulty, and they have closed their eyes,"* etc. He gives the reasons why "seeing they do not see" and "hearing they do not hear," because, he says, "the heart of this people has been hardened, and with" their "ears they have heard with difficulty."[143] And lest perhaps we should think that the hardness of heart and the difficulty of the ears are by nature and not voluntary, he attaches the blame to their choice and says: "They have closed their eyes lest at any time they might see with their eyes and hear with their ears and understand in their heart and be converted, and I would heal them."[144] They do hear, then, in parables and in a riddle,[145] these people who with closed eyes are unwilling to discern the truth.

13.16. *"But blessed are your eyes because they see and your ears because they hear."* If we had not read above that the hearers were challenged to understand, when the Savior said: "He who has ears to hear, let him hear,"[146] we would have thought that now the eyes and ears which receive the blessing are to be understood as the fleshly eyes. But instead, they seem to me to be those blessed eyes that can recognize the mysteries of Christ and that Jesus commanded to be lifted up on high to see the white fields.[147] And the ears referred to here are those blessed ears of which Isaiah speaks: "The Lord has assigned an ear to me."[148]

13.17. *"Indeed, amen I say to you, that many prophets and just men longed to see what you see, and they did not see, and to hear what you hear, and they have not heard."* This passage seems contrary to what is said elsewhere: "Abraham longed to see my day, and he saw and rejoiced."[149] He, however, did not say: *all* the prophets and

143. Is 6.9. Cf. Origen, *fragm.* 286.   144. Is 6.10.
145. Cf. Prv 1.6.   146. Mt 13.9.
147. Cf. Jn 4.35.
148. Is 50.4 LXX. Cf. Origen, *fragm.* 287.
149. Jn 8.56.

just men longed to see what you see, but *many*. Among many it can happen that some see,[150] others do not see, although even in this the interpretation is perilous. For we seem to be making some sort of distinction between the merits of the saints. Therefore, Abraham saw in a riddle;[151] he saw in appearance, but you possess the presence; you have your Lord, and you can question him at will and eat with him.[152]

13.19. *"Everyone who hears the word of the kingdom and does not understand."* By saying this first, he exhorts us to hear more diligently what is said.

13.19. *"The evil one comes and snatches away what has been sown in his heart."* The evil one snatches away the good seed. And understand at the same time that it was sown in the heart, and the diversity of ground refers to the souls of believers.

13.21. *"But when trouble and persecution come on account of the word, immediately he falls away."* Attend to what is said: "Immediately he falls away." Therefore, there is some distinction between the one who is compelled to deny Christ amidst many troubles and punishments, and the one who immediately falls away and is ruined at the first persecution.[153]

13.22. *"But that which is sown[154] among the thorns, this is he who hears the word, and the care of this age and the deceitfulness of riches chokes the word and it is made fruitless."* It seems to me that the following words that were literally spoken to Adam: "You will eat your bread among thorns and thistles,"[155] are a mystical signification of what we read here. That is, whoever devotes himself to the pleasures of the age and to the cares of this world devours the heavenly bread and the true food that is among thorns. And he has elegantly added: "the deceitfulness of riches chokes the word." For riches are alluring. They promise one thing, but they achieve something else. The possession of them is a slippery

---

150. Cf. Gn 32.30.   151. Cf. 1 Cor 13.12.

152. Cf. Rv 3.20.

153. This is apparently directed against Novatian, founder of the sect of the Novatianists, who denied the possibility of a second repentance after an act of apostasy. Cf. Jerome's *Ep.* 42 to Marcella.

154. Lit., "he who was sown" (*qui . . . seminatus est*).

155. Gn 3.18.

thing, while they are borne about here and there by the one without any stable footing. Either they abandon those who have them, or they choke those who do not. This is why the Lord claims that it is with difficulty that the rich enter the kingdom of heaven.[156] For their riches choke the word of God and soften the rigor of their virtues.

13.23. *"But that which is sown in the good earth is the one who hears the word and understands and bears fruit."* Just as there were three diverse types in the bad earth: that along the path and that on rocky places and that on thorny places, so there is a threefold diversity in the good earth: fruit of one hundredfold, sixtyfold, and thirtyfold.[157] Now both in the one and in the other, it is not the substance that is changed, but the will. And both in the unbelievers and in the believers, it is the heart that receives the seed. "The evil one comes," he says, "and snatches away what was sown in his heart."[158] And in both the second and the third cases: "This is he," he says, "who hears the word." Also, in the explanation of the good earth, there is this: "he who hears the word." So then, first we must hear, then we must understand, and after understanding we must render the fruits of the instruction and produce either one hundredfold fruit, or sixtyfold, or thirtyfold. We have spoken about these things in more detail in the book *Against Jovinian*,[159] and now we touch on it briefly. We attribute the one hundredfold fruit to the virgins, the sixtyfold to widows and the continent, the thirtyfold to holy matrimony. For "let marriage be honorable and the marriage bed undefiled."[160] Certain of our people[161] refer the hundredfold fruit to the martyrs; but if so, the holy partnerships of marriage are excluded from the good fruit.

13.24–25. *He set before them another parable, saying: "The kingdom of heaven is like a man who sowed good seed in his field; but while the men were sleeping, his enemy came and sowed over it weeds in the midst of the wheat,"* etc. This second parable is not immediately accompanied by its own interpretation, but it is explained after

---

156. Cf. Mt 19.23.   157. Cf. Origen, *fragm.* 296.
158. Mt 13.19.
159. Cf. *Adv. Jov.* 1.3 (PL 23: 223B–224A) and *Ep.* 49 to Pammachius.
160. Heb 13.4.   161. Who?

other parables come in between. For it is proposed here, then Jesus goes home after dismissing the crowds. Then his disciples come to him, "asking: 'Explain to us the parable of the weeds of the field,'" etc.[162] For we must not out of a premature desire for understanding seek knowledge of it before it is explained by the Lord.

13.31. *He set before them another parable, saying.* The Lord was sitting in the boat, while the crowd was standing on the shore. They were listening at a distance, the disciples closer up. He sets before them yet another parable, as though he is a wealthy master of a household, refreshing his guests with various foods, so that each would receive the various forms of nourishment according to the nature of his own stomach.[163] This is also why in the previous parable he did not say "the other" but "another." For if he had first said "the other," we could not expect a third. He prefaced "another" so that more could follow.

13.31–32. *"The kingdom of heaven is like a grain of mustard seed, which a man took and sowed in his field. This indeed is the least of all seeds, but when it grows up it is larger than all the garden plants and becomes a tree, so that birds of the sky come and dwell in its branches."* May it not be annoying to the reader if we set forth all the parables. For the things that are obscure need to be explained more fully, lest through excessive brevity the sense becomes covered up rather than exposed. The kingdom of heaven is the preaching of the Gospel and the knowledge of the Scriptures, which leads to life and about which it is said to the Jews: "The kingdom of God will be taken away from you and given to a nation bearing its fruits."[164] This sort of "kingdom, therefore, is like a grain of mustard seed, which a man took and sowed in his field." The man who sows in his field is understood by the majority to be the Savior, because he sows in the souls of believers. By others it is understood that he himself sows into his own field, that is, into his very self and into his heart. Who is it that sows except the mind and heart, which upon receiving the grain of preaching and nurturing the seed sown with the moisture of faith causes it to sprout in the field of his heart? The preaching of the Gos-

---

162. Mt 13.36.   163. Cf. 1 Cor 3.2.
164. Mt 21.43.

pel is the least of all instruction. Indeed, in the initial teaching, it does not have the conviction of truth. It preaches a God who is a man, a Christ who died, and the scandal of the cross. Compare teaching of this sort with the doctrines of the philosophers, with their books, and with the splendor of their eloquence and the composition of their words. Then you will see how much less than the other seeds is the sowing of the Gospel. But when those seeds grow, they demonstrate no bite, no vigor, no vitality. They are entirely flaccid and droopy. They sprout forth into garden plants and herbs which quickly wither and fall. But this preaching, which seemed trivial at the beginning, when it has been sown, either into the soul of the believer or into the whole world, does not rise up into a garden plant, but it grows into a tree, so that the birds of the sky, which we ought to understand either as the souls of believers or their resolutions submitted to the service of God, come and dwell in its branches. I think the branches of the Gospel-tree which grows from the grain of mustard seed are the diverse kinds of dogmas in which each of the above-mentioned birds finds rest. Let us as well use the wings of a dove,[165] so that by flying on high we might be able to dwell in the branches of this tree and make little nests of doctrines for ourselves. Let us flee from earthly things and hasten toward heavenly things.[166] When they read that the grain of mustard seed is the least of all the seeds, and also the following that is said by the apostles in the Gospels: "Lord, increase our faith,"[167] and the Savior replies to them: "Amen I say to you: If you have faith as the grain of a mustard seed, you would say to this mountain, 'Move from this place,' and it would move,"[168] many[169] think either that the apostles are asking for a small faith, or that the Lord has doubts about the smallness of their faith. Yet the apostle Paul judges a faith that is compared with a grain of mustard seed to be the greatest. For what does he say? "If I have all faith so that I may move mountains, but do not have love, it profits me nothing."[170] Therefore, what the Lord has said can happen with a faith that is compared with the grain

---

165. Ps 55.6.
167. Lk 17.5.
169. Who?

166. Col 3.2.
168. Lk 17.6.
170. 1 Cor 13.2.

of a mustard seed, the apostle teaches can happen with all faith.

13.33. *He told them another parable: "The kingdom of heaven is like leaven, which a woman took and buried in three measures of flour until the whole thing was leavened."* Human stomachs are different. Some are attracted to bitter foods, others to sweet; some to austere kinds of food, others to milder kinds. And so, the Lord sets forth diverse parables, as we have already said above,[171] so that according to the varieties of wounds, there might also be different kinds of medicine. This woman who took the leaven and buried it in three measures of flour until the whole thing might be leavened seems to me to refer either to the apostolic preaching or to the Church, which has been gathered from various nations. She takes the leaven, that is, the knowledge and understanding of the Scriptures, and she buries it in three measures of flour so that the spirit, soul, and body,[172] having been gathered into one, might not have discord among themselves, but would agree with two and three and would obtain from the Father whatever they ask for.[173] This passage is also explained in another way. We read in Plato, and it is a common dogma among the philosophers, that there are three passions in the human soul: τὸ λογιστικόν, which we can translate "rational," τὸ θυμικόν, which we call "full of anger" or "irascible," and τὸ ἐπιθυμητικόν, which we call "desirous."[174] That philosopher thinks that our rational part resides in the brain, anger in the gall bladder, and desire in the liver. And therefore, if we take the Gospel-leaven of the Holy Scriptures, which has been mentioned above, the three passions of the human soul are gathered into one. Thus by means of reason we possess prudence, by anger we have hatred of the vices, and by desire we have the longing for the virtues. And all this takes place through the doctrine of the Gospel, which Mother Church has presented to us. I should also tell a third interpretation of certain people,[175] so that the curious reader might be able to pick out from the many

---

171. Cf. Mt 13.3; 13.31.
172. Cf. 1 Thes 5.23. Cf. Origen, *fragm.* 302.
173. Cf. Mt 18.19.
174. Cf. Plato, *Rep.* 1.4, 439d–440e.
175. Who?

the one that pleases him. These interpreters say that the woman is the Church, which has mixed the faith of a man into three measures of wheat by means of belief in the Father, in the Son, and in the Holy Spirit. And since the Church has been fermented into one, this leads us not to a threefold God, but to the knowledge of the one divinity. They interpret the three measures of wheat this way: while there is not a different nature in each [person of the Trinity], they tend toward a unity of substance. This is a godly interpretation to be sure, but a doubtful understanding of a parable and an enigmatic saying[176] can never advance the authority of dogmas. Now a *satum* (measure) is a kind of measure in use in the province of Palestine. It holds one and a half pecks.[177] Other things are said about this parable as well, but there is no time now to say everything that could be said about every detail.

13.34. *Jesus spoke all these things to the crowds in parables, and without parables he did not speak to them.* It was not to the disciples but to the crowds that he spoke in parables. Even down to today the crowds hear in parables, while disciples question the Savior at home.

13.35. *In order that what was spoken through the prophet might be fulfilled, saying: "I shall open my mouth in parables; I will utter things hidden since the foundation of the world."* This testimony is taken from the seventy-seventh Psalm.[178] I have read in several manuscripts, and a diligent reader would perhaps be able to find it, that in place of this passage that we have recorded and that the vulgate edition has as: "in order that what was spoken through the prophet might be fulfilled, saying," in those manuscripts it is written as: "through Isaiah the prophet, saying." Because the text is not at all found in Isaiah, I think it was later removed by prudent men. In my judgment, it was originally published as follows: "[in order that what was written] through Asaph the prophet, saying."[179] For the seventy-seventh Psalm, from which this testimony was taken, is ascribed to Asaph the prophet in

---

176. Cf. Prv 1.6.
177. A peck is one-sixth of a bushel.
178. Ps 78.2.
179. Cf. Homily 11 in FOTC 48, 81.

the title.[180] And it seems that, because the first copyist did not understand "Asaph," he thought that it was a mistake of a copyist, and he changed the name to Isaiah, whose name was more familiar. And so one should be aware that in the Psalms and hymns and canticles of God, not only David but also other men whose names are prefixed deserve to be called prophets. This applies to men like Asaph,[181] Idithon,[182] Aeman the Ezrahite,[183] Aetham,[184] the sons of Korah,[185] and the rest whom Scripture mentions. And in everything that is said under the persona of the Lord: "I will open my mouth in parables; I will utter things hidden since the foundation of the world," one should attentively consider and discover that the departure of Israel from Egypt is being described and all the signs are being narrated that are contained in the history of Exodus.[186] From this we understand that all the things that are written should be interpreted as parables, so to speak. Not only does the obvious meaning of the letter ring out, but hidden mysteries are found there.[187] For this in effect is what the Savior promises when he says that he is going to open his mouth and speak in parables and utter things that have been hidden since the foundation of the world.

13.36. *Then he dismissed the crowds and went into the house. And his disciples came to him saying: "Explain to us the parable of the weeds of the field."* Jesus dismisses the crowds and returns home in order that the disciples may approach him and question him in secret about things that the people were neither deserving nor able to hear. "Explain to us the parable of the weeds."

13.37. *Responding, he said: "He who sows the good seed is the Son of man."*[188] He has clearly explained that the field is the world, the sower is the Son of man, the good seed is the sons of the kingdom, the weeds are the sons of the evil one,[189] the sower of the weeds is the devil, the harvest is the consummation of

---

180. Cf. Ps 78.1.

181. Cf. Ps 78.1; 79.1; *et passim.*

182. Cf. Ps 77.1

183. Cf. Ps 88.1.

184. Cf. Ps 89.1

185. Cf. Ps 85.1; 87.1.

186. Cf. Ps 78.11–13.

187. Jerome means that the stories recounted in Ps 78 (77 LXX) should be interpreted as spiritual allegories referring to Christ and the Church.

188. Cf. Origen, *In Matt.* 10.2.

189. Lit., "of the worst one" (*pessimi*).

the age, the harvesters are angels. The weeds refer to all stumbling blocks, and the just are reputed as sons of the kingdom. Therefore, as I have said above,[190] we need to accommodate the faith to these things that have been explained by the Lord. But as for the things about which he is silent and that he leaves to our interpretation, these should be touched upon briefly. Understand the men who are asleep as the teachers of the churches. Understand the servants of the householder as none other than the angels who daily see the face of the Father.[191] Now, as for the devil, he is called "an enemy *man*" because he ceased being a god. In the ninth Psalm it is written of him: "Rise up, O Lord, let not the *man* prevail."[192] In light of this, those who are put in charge in the Church must not fall asleep. Otherwise, while they are showing such negligence, the enemy man will introduce the sowing of weeds, that is, the dogmas of the heretics. Now he leaves room for repentance in the words: "Lest perhaps while gathering the weeds you may at the same time uproot also the grain."[193] Here we are admonished not to cut off a brother quickly. For it can happen that the one who today has been seduced by a harmful doctrine, tomorrow may come to his senses and begin to defend the truth. Now the words that follow: "Leave both to grow until the harvest,"[194] seem to contradict the command: "Remove the evil from your midst,"[195] and the command that we are by no means to have fellowship with those who are called brothers and are adulterers and fornicators.[196] For if uprooting is prohibited and patience is to be preserved until the harvest, how is it that certain ones must be expelled from our midst? There is a remarkable likeness between wheat and the weed that we call darnel. As long as it is a plant and its stem does not come to ear, it is just about impossible, or at least extremely difficult, to discern any distinction between them. Therefore, the Lord is warning us in advance that we must not quickly make a judgment when the matter is doubtful. Rath-

---

190. Cf. 13.3; 13.24.
192. Ps 9.19.
194. Mt 13.30. Cf. Origen, *fragm.* 299.
195. Dt 13.5; 17.7; cf. 1 Cor 5.13.
196. 1 Cor 5.11.

191. Cf. Mt 18.10.
193. Mt 13.29.

er, we should reserve the conclusion to God the Judge, so that when the day of judgment comes, he may cast out from the assembly of the saints not the mere suspicion of sin, but manifest guilt. Now, he has said that the bundles of weeds are handed over to the fires and the wheat is gathered into barns.[197] This makes plain that the heretics, and those who are hypocrites in the faith, are to be burned in the fires of Gehenna. The saints, on the other hand, who are called wheat, are taken into the barns, that is, into heavenly mansions.[198]

13.43. *"Then the just will shine like the sun in the kingdom of their Father."* In the present age the light of the saints shines before men.[199] After the consummation of the world, however, the just themselves "will shine like the sun in the kingdom of their Father."

13.44. *"The kingdom of heaven is like a treasure hidden in a field, which the man who finds, hides; and in his joy he goes and sells everything that he has, and he buys that field."*[200] We have been delayed by the numerous obscurities of the parables. Now we must depart from a verse-by-verse interpretation so that it may seem that we have passed from one kind of interpretation to another. This treasure, "in which there are hidden all the treasures of wisdom and knowledge,"[201] is either the Word of God, who is seen to be hidden in the flesh of Christ,[202] or it is the Holy Scriptures, in which the knowledge of the Savior is stored away. When anyone finds him hidden in them, he should despise all the gains of this world[203] in order to be able to possess the one he has found. Now the following words: "which when the man found, he hid it," do not mean that he is acting out of ill will. Rather, he does this as one who is fearfully guarding something and unwilling to lose it. Thus he hides in his heart the one whom he has preferred to this former wealth.

13.45–46. *"Again the kingdom of heaven is like a businessman seeking good pearls. When he found a pearl of very great price, he went off and sold all that he had and bought it."*[204] With different words,

---

197. Mt 13.30.
198. Cf. Jn 14.2.
199. Cf. Mt 5.16.
200. Cf. Origen, *In Matth.* 10.5.
201. Cf. Col 2.3.
202. Cf. Jn 1.1, 14.
203. Cf. Phil 3.7.
204. Cf. Origen, *In Matth.* 10.8.

this is the same thing that is said above.[205] The good pearls that the salesman[206] seeks are the Law and the prophets. Listen, Marcion; listen, Manicheus; the good pearls are the Law and the prophets and the knowledge of the Old Testament,[207] but the one pearl of very great price is the knowledge of the Savior and the concealed mystery of his Passion and Resurrection. When the businessman finds it, he acts as the apostle Paul does. He despises as offscourings and refuse all the mysteries of the Law and the prophets and the former observances in which he had lived blamelessly, that he might gain Christ.[208] It is not the case that the finding of the new pearl means that the old pearls are condemned. Rather, it means that in comparison with it, every other gem is rather cheap.

13.47–49. *"Again, the kingdom of heaven is like a net cast into the sea that gathered in fish of every kind. When it was filled they hauled it out, and, sitting down on the beach, they gathered the good fish into their vessels, but they cast out the bad ones. So shall it be at the consummation of the age,"* etc. The prophecy of Jeremiah has been fulfilled that says: "Behold, I am sending many fishermen to you."[209] For after Peter and Andrew, [and] James and John, the sons of Zebedee, heard the words: "Follow me, and I will make you fishers of men,"[210] they wove for themselves out of the Old and New Testaments a net of Gospel-doctrines.[211] They cast it into the sea of this world, and it stretches out in the midst of the waves until the present day, capturing anything that falls into it from the salty and bitter waters. That is to say, it catches both good and bad men, both the best fish and the worse. But when the consummation and end of the world comes, as he explains more clearly below, at that time the net will be drawn to shore. Then a true judgment for separating the fish will be demonstrated, and, as though in some very quiet harbor, the good will be

205. Cf. Mt 13.44.

206. I follow the SC editors who read *institor* (salesman), rather than *institutor* (arranger), as the CCSL edition has.

207. *Veteris instrumenti.* The point here is that Christ is found hidden and prophesied in the OT, something Marcion denied.

208. Cf. Phil 3.8. Cf. Origen, *In Matth.* 10.9.

209. Cf. Jer 16.16.   210. Mt 4.19.

211. Cf. Origen, *In Matth.* 10.13.

cast into the vessels of the heavenly mansions,[212] but the flame of Gehenna will take the bad to be baked and dried.

13.51. *"Have you understood all these things?" They said to him: "Yes."*[213] These words are especially addressed to the apostles. It is said to them: "Have you understood these things?" He wants them not merely to hear, as the people do, but to understand, as those who are going to be teachers.

13.52. *Therefore, every scribe taught in the kingdom of heaven is like a householder who brings forth from his treasury new things and old.* The apostles, as the scribes and secretaries of the Savior, impressed his words and commands on the fleshly tablets of their heart.[214] They had been instructed in the mysteries of the heavenly kingdoms. They were powerful in the wealth of the householder, and from the treasury of their doctrines they cast out new things and old. Thus whatever they proclaimed in the Gospel, they proved by means of the words of the Law and the prophets. This is why the bride says in the Song of Songs: "I have saved for you new things with the old, my brother."[215]

13.53–54. *And it came about when Jesus had finished these parables, that he passed on from there, and coming to his own land, he was teaching them in their synagogue.* After the parables, which he spoke to the people and which only the apostles understand, he passed on to his own country that he might teach more openly there.

13.54. *"Where does this man's wisdom come from and the miraculous powers?"* The folly of the Nazarenes is amazing.[216] They wonder where wisdom draws its wisdom and where miraculous power draws its miraculous powers. But their error is obvious: they were surmising that he was the carpenter's son.

13.55. *"Is not this the carpenter's son? Is not his mother called Mary*

212. Cf. Jn 14.2. 213. Mt 13.51.
214. Cf. 2 Cor 3.3.

215. Song 7.13. Notice that the biblical text uses the word "brother" (*fratruelis*) to describe the relation of a kinsman. See below on 13.55–56.

216. Cf. Origen, *fragm.* 312. In this section Jerome seems to imply that the Nazarenes rejected the Virgin Birth. But in 404 (*Ep.* 112.13) he writes that they believed in the Virgin Birth and in Christ's Passion and Resurrection, in spite of their being both Christian and Jewish. This contradiction regarding such a central point suggests that Jerome's actual knowledge of them was meager.

and his brothers James and Joseph, Simon and Judas? And are not his sisters all among us?" The error of the Jews is our salvation and the condemnation of the heretics. For so much so did they discern Jesus Christ as a man that they thought him to be the son of a carpenter: "Is not this the carpenter's son?" Since they are in error about the father, are you surprised if they err about the brothers? This passage has been explained more fully in the little book mentioned above against Helvidius.[217]

13.57. *But Jesus said to them: "A prophet is not without honor except in his own country and in his own house."* It is practically second nature for citizens always to envy fellow-citizens.[218] For they do not consider the present works of the man but they recall his tender infancy. As though they themselves had not reached a mature age by the same stages of growth!

13.58. *And because of their unbelief, he did not do many miracles there.* It is not that he was unable to do many miracles, even for these unbelievers, but he wanted to avoid condemning the unbelieving citizens by doing many. Now it can also be understood in another way. Jesus is despised at home and in his own country, that is, among the people of the Jews. Therefore, he did few signs there lest they should become totally inexcusable. But daily through the apostles he does greater signs among the Gentiles, not so much in the healing of bodies as in the salvation of souls.

Chapter 14

14.1–2. *At that time Herod the tetrarch heard about the fame of Jesus, and he said to his servants: "This is John the Baptist; he has risen from the dead, and that is why miraculous powers are at work in him."* Some ecclesiastical interpreters seek the reasons why Herod was suspicious enough to think that John had been resurrected from the dead, and that is why miraculous powers are at work in him. As though we need to give a reason for the error of an

---

217. Cf. *Adv. Helvidium* (PL 23: 188A, 196C); see above on 12.49.

218. This is perhaps a personal memory, since Jerome was badly received in his own country. Cf. *Ep.* 7.5 to Chromatius.

outsider! Or as if the sect of μετεμψύχωσις needs a pretext for their doctrine from these words! Surely, at the time when John was beheaded, the Lord was thirty years old, but the doctrine of μετεμψύχωσις says that souls are inserted into different bodies after many cycles of years.[219]

14.3–4. *But Herod had seized John and bound him and put him in prison on account of Herodias, his brother's wife. For John had been saying to him: "It is not permitted for you to have her."* Ancient history[220] narrates that Philip, the son of Herod the Great under whom the Lord fled to Egypt,[221] was the brother of this Herod, under whom Christ suffered.[222] Philip married Herodias, the daughter of the king of Phetrai. Afterward, however, when certain pretenses had arisen against his son-in-law, his father-in-law took his own daughter and, to the grief of her former husband, joined her in marriage to his enemy Herod. Now who this Philip is, the evangelist Luke teaches more fully: "In the fifteenth year of the reign of Tiberius Caesar, while Pontius Pilate was procurator of Judea, and Herod tetrarch of Galilee, and Philip his brother tetrarch of the district of Iturea and Trachonitis."[223] Therefore, John the Baptist, who had come in the spirit and power of Elijah,[224] accused Herod and Herodias with the same authority with which Elijah had rebuked Ahab and Jezebel.[225] John told him that they had committed an unlawful marriage and that it was not permitted, while the real brother is alive, to marry his wife. John preferred to put himself in danger before the king, rather than to forget about God's commands on account of flattery.

14.5. *And wanting to kill him, he feared the people, because they re-*

---

219. Cf. Origen, *In Matth.* 10.20; however, Origen uses the term μετενσωμάτωσις rather than μετεμψύχωσις. Origen did make some questionable speculations on this doctrine early on. See J. Lienhard, "Origen's Speculation on John the Baptist," in *Origeniana Quinta,* ed. R. Daly (Leuven: Leuven University Press, 1992), 449–53. Lienhard argues that Origen's views of John the Baptist developed during his lifetime, from his speculative and ambiguous early writings to more ecclesiastically orthodox views in his late writings.

220. Cf. Josephus, *AJ* 18.5.1–2.   221. Cf. Mt 2.14.
222. Cf. Lk 23.7ff.   223. Lk 3.1.
224. Cf. Lk 1.17.   225. 1 Kgs 21.18–24.

garded him as a prophet. He did indeed fear a sedition of the people on account of John. He knew that very large crowds had been baptized by him in the Jordan.[226] But he was overcome by love for his wife, on account of whose passion he had even disregarded the commands of God.

14.6. *But on Herod's birthday, the daughter of Herodias danced in the midst of the banquet, and she pleased Herod.* We have found that no other people observed their birthdays except Herod and Pharoah.[227] Thus there was a single feast day for those whose impiety was on the same level.

14.7. *When he promised with an oath to give her whatever she might ask of him.* I do not excuse Herod by saying that he committed murder reluctantly and against his will on account of the oath. For he perhaps took the oath in order to create the conditions for this future occasion. Otherwise, if he claims to have done it on account of the oath, what if she had demanded the death of his father or mother? Would he have done it or not? Therefore, what he would have repudiated in their case, he should have condemned in the case of the prophet.

14.8. *"Give to me,"* she said, *"here on a platter the head of John the Baptist."* Herodias fears that Herod might come to his senses at some time or become friends with his brother Philip. She fears that the illicit marriage might end in divorce. So she advises her daughter immediately at the very feast to ask for John's head as a worthy price in blood for the worthy work she had done by dancing.

14.9. *And the king was very grieved.* It is customary in the Scriptures for the historian to tell the opinion of many just as it was believed by everyone at the time. Thus, just as Joseph is called the father of Jesus, even by Mary herself,[228] so also Herod is now said to have been very grieved, because this is what his guests thought. For he was hiding his true thoughts. This cunning fabricator of murder was feigning sadness in his countenance, while he had joy in his heart.

14.9. *But on account of the oath and those who were reclining to-*

---

226. Cf. Mt 3.5–6.
227. Cf. Gn 40.20; Origen, *In Matth.* 10.22; Homily 8.3 on Leviticus.
228. Cf. Lk 2.48.

gether, he commanded it to be given. He excuses a criminal act by appealing to his oath. Thus under the pretext of piety, he becomes impious. But in what he has added: "and on account of those who were reclining together," he intends for all to be accomplices of his crime, as the bloody dish is carried into the luxurious and impure banquet.

14.11. *And his head was brought on a platter and given to the girl, and she carried it to her mother.* In Roman history[229] we read about the Roman general Flaminius, who consented to a prostitute who was reclining nearby, who claimed that she had never seen a man decapitated. So, some man who was guilty of a capital crime was cut in two at the banquet. He [Flaminius] was driven out of the Senate by the censors,[230] because he mixed the dishes with blood. For the pleasure of another, he offered up a man to death, however guilty, so that lust and murder were equally mixed together. How much more criminal are Herod, Herodias, and the girl who danced for the price of blood. She demands the head of the prophet, that she might hold his tongue under her power, the tongue that had condemned an illicit marriage. This was carried out literally. But down to the present day we discern in the head of the prophet John the fact that the Jews destroyed Christ, who is the head of the prophets.[231]

14.12. *And his disciples came and took his body and buried it, and they went and told Jesus.* Josephus reports that John was decapitated in a certain town in Arabia.[232] We can understand what follows: "His disciples came and took the body," as referring to disciples both of John himself and of the Savior. "And they went and told Jesus."

14.13. *When Jesus heard this, he withdrew from there in a boat to a desert place apart.* They announce the death of the Baptist to the Savior. When he hears about it, he withdraws to a desert place.

---

229. Cf. Livy 39.43.

230. I follow the change in punctuation suggested by the SC editors. CCSL reads that the man guilty of the capital crime was cut in two by the censors. If the latter is indeed the correct reading, then this is another mistake on Jerome's part that is attributable to his hasty composition.

231. Cf. Origen, *In Matth.* 10.22, and Mt 14.13 below.

232. Cf. Josephus, *AJ* 18.5.2.

He did this not because, as some think, he feared death, but to spare his enemies from adding one murder to another, or in order to postpone his own death to the day of Passover, on which, for the sake of a sacred mystery, a lamb is sacrificed and the doorposts of believers are sprinkled with blood.[233] Or he withdrew in order to offer to us an example of avoiding the rashness of those who hand themselves in of their own accord.[234] For not everyone perseveres with the same constancy in the tortures to which they offer themselves to be tortured. This is why in another passage he gives the command: "When they persecute you in one city, flee to another."[235] It was also nicely stated by the evangelist: "He withdrew to a desert place," not "he fled." In other words, Jesus was avoiding his persecutors; he did not fear them.[236] Here is another interpretation:[237] After the head of the prophet was cut off by the Jews and by the king of the Jews, prophecy among them lost its tongue and voice. Then Jesus passed over to the desert place of the Church, which had not previously had a husband.[238]

14.13. *And when the crowds heard, they followed him on foot from the cities.* It is possible that it was for another reason that he withdrew to a desert place when he heard about the killing of John: he wanted to test the faith of believers. After all, "the crowds followed him on foot," not on beasts of burden, not in different kinds of vehicles, but by the effort of their own feet. Thus they showed the burning zeal of their heart. If we want to unfold the rational grounds for each word, we would exceed the brevity of the work we have proposed. It should be said in passing, however, that after the Lord came into the desert, very great crowds followed him. For before he came among the lonely places of the Gentiles, he was worshiped by only one people.

---

233. Cf. Ex 12.6–7; 1 Cor 5.7; 1 Pt 1.2. Origen, *In Matth.* 10.23.

234. For the same teaching about avoiding rash acts of self-betrayal during persecution, see Eusebius, *HE* 4.15.8.

235. Mt 12.23.

236. Jerome stresses the bravery of Christ in the face of his own suffering throughout this commentary. See below on Mt 26.2.

237. Cf. Origen, *In Matth.* 10.23.

238. Cf. Is 54.1; Gal 4.27.

14.14. *And going out, he saw a great crowd.* In the words of the Gospels, the Spirit is always joined to the letter. Things that seem frigid at first glance will warm up if you touch them. The Lord was in a desert place. Crowds followed him, having left their cities, that is, their former ways of life and the varieties of doctrines.[239] But Jesus "goes out." This represents the fact that the crowds had the will to go, to be sure, but they lacked the strength to arrive. Therefore, the Savior "goes out" from his own place and travels to meet them. This is exactly what happens to the repentant son in another parable.[240] And when he sees the crowd, he has compassion on them and heals their diseases.[241] Thus the fullness of their faith attains its reward at once.

14.15. *But when evening came, his disciples came to him, saying,* etc. Everything here is full of mysteries. He withdraws from Judea, he comes to a desert place, crowds follow him, having left their cities, Jesus goes out to them, he has compassion on the crowd, he heals their diseases, and he does this not in the morning, not in the advancing day, not at noon, but in the evening,[242] when the sun of justice has set.[243]

14.16. *But Jesus said to them: "They do not need to go away; you give them something to eat."*[244] They do not need to seek different kinds of foods and to buy unknown bread for themselves, when they have the heavenly Bread[245] with them. "You give them something to eat." He invites the apostles to the breaking of the bread, that the greatness of the sign may become more widely known to those who testify that they do not have any.

14.17. *They replied to him: "We have here only five loaves and two fish."* In another evangelist we read: "There is a boy here who has five loaves."[246] It seems to me that the boy signifies Moses.[247] Now we interpret the two fish either as the [two] Testaments, or because an even number refers to the Law. Therefore, before

---

239. Cf. Origen, *In Matth.* 10.23.   240. Cf. Lk 15.20.
241. Cf. Mt 9.35–36.
242. Cf. the spiritual exegesis found at Mt 8.16.
243. Cf. Mal 4.2.   244. Mt 14.16.
245. Cf. Jn 6.32.   246. Jn 6.9.
247. The number five represents Moses, the author of the five books of the Pentateuch. The word "Pentateuch" means "five books."

the Savior's Passion and before the lightning flash of the Gospel, the apostles had only five loaves and two little fish, which were living in the salty waters and in the bitter waves.

14.18. *He said to them: "Bring them here to me."* Listen, Marcion; listen, Manicheus; Jesus commands five loaves and two little fish to be brought to him that he might sanctify and multiply them.[248]

14.19. *And when he had commanded the crowd to recline on the grass.* The literal meaning is plain, but let us open up the mysteries of the spiritual interpretation. They are commanded to recline on the grass. According to another evangelist,[249] they recline on the earth in groups of fifties[250] and hundreds. Thus after they trampled on their flesh and all its flowers,[251] that is, on the pleasures of the world, as if they were placing dry grass under themselves, then by means of the repentance that is signified in the number fifty, they ascend to the perfect summit that is signified in the number one hundred.[252]

14.19. *He took the five loaves and two fish, looked up to heaven, blessed and broke the loaves, and gave them to his disciples.* He looks up to heaven to show that eyes ought to be directed there. He took the five loaves and two little fish in his hands, broke them, and gave them to the disciples. It is when the Lord breaks the food that the seedbed of food is produced. For if they had been whole and not torn apart into bits or divided into an abundant crop, they would not have been able to feed the crowds, both children and women and a great multitude. Therefore, the Law is broken with the prophets, and it is torn up into bits, and its

248. Jerome's point seems to be that Jesus, unlike Marcion and Manicheus, did not reject or disparage the (five) books of Moses that are represented in the boy's five loaves. Rather, he received them, declared them holy, and even multiplied them by increasing the demand of the Law in some cases, e.g., on the question of divorce. See on Mt 19.8. Cf. Irenaeus, *Adv. haer.* 4.13.

249. Cf. Mk 6.40.

250. Fifty symbolizes repentance, in reference to the Hebrew jubilee year, which recurred every fifty years and during which all debts were forgiven. Cf. Lv 25.10–17.

251. Cf. Is 40.6–8.

252. Cf. Origen, *In Matth.* 11.3. One hundred is a number symbolizing perfection.

mysteries are set forth in public, so that what was not providing nourishment when whole and while abiding in its original state, can nourish the multitude of the nations when it is divided into parts.

14.19. *And he gave the loaves to the disciples, and the disciples gave them to the crowds.* The crowds receive nourishment from the Lord through the apostles.

14.20. *And they took the remains, twelve baskets full of fragments.* Each of the apostles fills his own basket from the remains of the Savior. Thus he has a source from which he can later supply food to the Gentiles, or he shows from the remains that it was true bread[253] that was later multiplied. At the same time, try to explain how in a desert and in such a vast solitude only five loaves and two little fish are found, yet twelve baskets are found with such ease.

14.21. *Now the number of those who ate was five thousand men, without counting the women and small children.* The multitude of five thousand men who ate corresponds with the number of five loaves. For it had not yet reached the number seven that the four thousand[254] eat, as the narrative of another passage states.[255] This latter number corresponds with the number of Gospels. But five thousand men eat, who had grown into the perfect man[256] and who were following him of whom Zechariah says: "Behold the man, his name is Rising."[257] But women and children, the fragile sex and the lesser age, are unworthy of the number. This is also why in the Book of Numbers as often as priests and Levites and armies or groups of soldiers are recorded, slaves, women, children, and the ignoble crowd are passed over without a number.[258]

14.22. *And he compelled his disciples to get into the boat and to go ahead of him across the sea, until he dismissed the crowds.* He ordered the disciples to cross the sea and he compelled them to get into the boat. By these words it is shown that they withdrew from the Lord unwillingly, since for love for their teacher they do not

---

253. Cf. Jn 6.32.   254. Cf. Mk 8.9.
255. Cf. Mk 8.5.   256. Cf. Eph 4.13.
257. Zec 6.12. Cf. Origen, *In Matth.* 11.3.
258. Cf. Nm 1; 3.18. See Origen, *Hom* 1 *In Num.*

want to be separated from him even for a moment of time.[259]

14.23. *And when he had dismissed the crowd, he went up on a mountain alone to pray.* If the disciples Peter, James, and John, who had seen the glory of the transfigured one,[260] had been with him, perhaps they would have gone up on the mountain with him, but the crowd cannot follow to the heights. He can only teach them near the sea on the shore and feed them in the desert. Now it says that he went up alone to pray. You should refer this not to him who, from five loaves, satisfied five thousand men, not counting the women and children, but to him who, when he heard about the death of John, withdrew to a lonely place. It is not that we separate the person of the Lord, but that his works have been divided between his deity and his humanity.[261]

14.24. *But the boat was being buffeted by the waves in the midst of the sea.* It was right that the apostles departed from the Lord against their will and reluctantly. They did not want to suffer a shipwreck in his absence. Finally, while the Lord was delaying at the top of the mountain, at once a contrary wind arises and disturbs the sea. The apostles are in danger, and a shipwreck continues to be imminent, until Jesus comes.

14.25. *But at the fourth watch of the night, he came to them, walking upon the sea.* Guard duties and military watches are divided into intervals of three hours. So then, when he says that the Lord came to them at the fourth watch of the night, he is showing that they were in danger through the whole night. Then, at the end of the night and at the consummation of the world, he will bring help to them.[262]

14.26. *And when they saw him walking upon the sea, they were alarmed and said: "It is a ghost!"* If, in accordance with Marcion and Manicheus, our Lord was not born of a virgin, but appeared as an imaginary representation, how is it that the apostles are now *afraid* that they are seeing a ghost?

14.26. *And they cried out for fear.*[263] A confused outcry and uncertain voice is a sign of great fear.

14.27. *And immediately Jesus spoke to them, saying: "Have cour-*

259. Cf. Origen, *In Matth.* 11.5.   260. Cf. Mt 17.1–8.
261. Lit., "between the God and the man" (*inter Deum hominemque*).
262. Cf. Mt 28.20.   263. Mt 14.26.

age; I am. " In the first place, this brings a remedy for what was the cause [of their fear]. He commands those who are afraid, saying: "Have courage," do not fear. In the words that follow: "I am," he is not adding who he is. For they could either have understood him from his voice, which was familiar to them and which was speaking through the misty darkness of the night; or they could have recalled that he was the one who they knew had spoken to Moses: "You are to tell this to the sons of Israel: He who is has sent me to you."[264]

14.28. *But Peter responded and said: "Lord, if it is you, command me to come to you on the water."* In all passages Peter is found to be a man of an intensely burning faith. When the disciples are asked who men were saying Jesus is, Peter confesses him to be the Son of God.[265] When the Savior wills to go to his Passion, Peter is unwilling that he whom a little earlier he had confessed to be the Son of God should die.[266] I grant that Peter was in error on this matter, but the error was not in the affection he had. Peter goes up on the mountain with the Savior, as first among the first.[267] And in the Passion, Peter alone follows.[268] With bitter tears he immediately washed away the sin of denial into which he had fallen due to sudden fear.[269] After the Passion, when they were fishing at Lake Genesareth, while the Lord was standing on the shore, the others were taking their time in sailing back. But Peter brooks no delay. He wraps himself with his garment and at once plunges headfirst into the waves.[270] Therefore, with the same ardor of faith that he always has, now too, while the others are silent, he believes that by the will of his Master, he can do what Jesus was able to do by nature. "Command me to come to you on the water." You give the command, and on the spot the water will grow solid, the body will become light, which in its own right is heavy.

14.29. *And getting out of the boat, Peter walked on the water.* Let those who think that the body of the Lord was not a true body[271] because it went softly like air over the soft water answer how it

---

264. Ex 3.14.
266. Cf. Mt 16.22.
268. Cf. Mt 26.58.
270. Cf. Jn 21.7.

265. Cf. Mt 16.13–16.
267. Cf. Mt 17.1.
269. Cf. Mt 26.75.
271. This refers to the docetists.

was that Peter walked. Surely they are not going to deny that Peter was a true man.

14.30. *But when he saw the strong wind, he was afraid, and, beginning to sink, he shouted out, saying: "Lord, save me!"* The faith of his heart was burning, but human weakness dragged him into the depths. Therefore, he is abandoned for a little while in temptation, that his faith might increase and he might understand that he has been saved not by the easiness of a request but by the Lord's power.

14.31. *And Jesus at once stretched forth his hand and took hold of him and said to him: "You of little faith, why did you doubt?"* Because the apostle Peter had grown a little afraid, Jesus said to him, "You of little faith, why did you doubt?" Now we have spoken above about Peter's faith and ardor of mind.[272] It was he who had courageously asked the Savior, saying, "Lord, if it is you, command me to come to you on the water."[273] If this is so, what will Jesus say to us, who do not even have the smallest particle of this little faith?

14.33. *Those who were in the boat came and worshiped him, saying: "Truly you are the Son of God."* At a single sign when the tranquility of the sea is restored, which normally happens after occasional heavy storms, the sailors and passengers confess that he is truly the Son of God; and yet in the Church Arius proclaims him to be a creature!

14.34. *And when they had crossed over, they came to the land of Genesareth.* If we knew what Genesareth corresponds to in our language,[274] we would understand how it is that Jesus, through the figure of the apostles and the boat, leads the Church across to the shore, a Church delivered from the shipwreck of persecutions, and how he has it find rest in a most tranquil harbor.

14.35. *And when the men of that place recognized him, they sent into the whole of that region.* They recognized him by report, not by face, or possibly he was known even by face to some, on account of the great signs that he did among the people. And consider what great faith there was among the people of the land

---

272. Cf. 14.28.   273. Ibid.

274. This is taken verbatim from Origen, *In Matth.* 11.6, who also declared his lack of certainty about the meaning of the Hebrew word.

of Genesareth. They are not content merely with the salvation of those present, but they send to other cities in a circuit that all might run to the doctor.

14.35–36. *And they brought to him all the sick, and they were entreating him to let them touch the tassel of his garment, and whosoever touched him were saved.* Those who are sick should touch not the body of Jesus nor his whole garment but the end of his tassel. Whoever touches it will be healed. Interpret the tassel of his garment as the least command. Whoever transgresses it "shall be called least in the kingdom of heaven."[275] Or it may mean his assumption of a body by means of which we come to the Word of God, and later we enjoy the majesty of that Word.

Chapter 15

15.2. *"Why do your disciples transgress the tradition of the elders?"* The foolishness of the Pharisees and scribes is remarkable. They accuse the Son of God of not keeping the traditions and commands of men.

15.2. *"For they do not wash their hands when they eat bread."* The hands, that is, the works, not of the body but of the soul, must be washed, that the Word of God may come into them.[276]

15.3. *But he responded and said to them: "And why do you transgress the commandment of God on the basis of your tradition?"* He refutes the false charge with a true answer. Since you, he says, because of human tradition neglect the Lord's commandments, why do you believe that my disciples are to be accused because they do not give much weight to the prescriptions of the elders that they may keep the statutes of God?

15.4–6. *"For God said: 'Honor your father and mother,' and 'Let him who curses his father or mother be put to death.'*[277] *But you say: 'Whoever says to his father or mother: Whatever from me would be a benefit to you is a gift,' he also has not honored*[278] *his father and mother."*

275. Mt 5.19.

276. Cf. Origen, *In Matth.* 11.8.

277. Lit., "die by death" (*morte moriatur*); cf. Ex 20.12; 21.15–17; Lv 20.9.

278. A variant reading is "shall not honor" (*honorabit*); see CCSL 77, 127, note on line 1415.

In the Scriptures, "honor" is understood to refer not so much to greetings and the duties that must be given, as to alms and the offering of gifts. The apostle says: "Honor widows who are truly widows."[279] Here "honor" is understood as a gift. And in another passage he says: "Priests, especially those who labor in the word and teaching of God, are to be honored with double honor."[280] By this command, we are ordered not to muzzle the mouth of an ox treading the grain, and we are told that a worker should be worthy of his wage.[281] In consideration of the parents' frailty, age, or poverty, the Lord had commanded that the sons should "honor" their parents, namely, by ministering to them the necessities of life. But the scribes and Pharisees wanted to subvert this most provident law of God in order to introduce impiety under the name of piety.[282] They taught wicked sons that if anyone wanted to make a vow to God, who is their true Father, of the things that were to be offered to their parents, then the Lord's offering should be placed ahead of the gifts to the parents. Or at least, when these parents saw that these things had been dedicated to God, they would be done-in by their need, declining [these things] from fear of incurring the charge of sacrilege. Thus it was that under the pretext of God and Temple, the children's offering would yield a profit to the priests. For the Pharisees this very base tradition came by another occasion. Many who had borrowed money from others were unwilling to pay back what they owed and would establish ties to the priests, so that the money that was demanded might serve the ministries of the Temple and their uses. Now briefly, [this passage] can also have this sense: "The gift which is from me would be a benefit to you." He is saying: You compel sons to tell their parents: Whatever gift I was going to offer to God I am wasting on your food, and it is a benefit to you, O father and mother. The result of this is that those who are afraid to take what they see has been given to God wish to lead an impoverished life, rather than to feed off things that have been dedicated.

279. 1 Tm 5.3.
280. 1 Tm 5.17.
281. Cf. Dt 25.4; 1 Cor 9.9, 23; Lk 10.7; 1 Tm 5.18.
282. Cf. Origen, *In Matth.* 11.9.

15.11. *"It is not what enters the mouth that defiles* (communicat) *a man, but what proceeds from the mouth, this defiles a man."* The verb *communicat* is unique to the Scriptures and is not used in public speech. The people of the Jews, boasting that they are God's portion,[283] call the food that all men use "common," for example, swine flesh, oysters, hare, animals that do not have a split hoof or chew the cud, and among the fish, those without scales.[284] This is why in the Acts of the Apostles it is written: "What God has sanctified, you should not call common."[285] It is called common, then, instead of unclean, because it lies open to other men and, as it were, is not from the portion of God. "It is not what enters into the mouth that defiles (*coinquinat*) a man, but what proceeds from the mouth, this defiles (*coinquinat*) a man." An intelligent reader may object and say: If what enters into the mouth does not defile a man, why do we not eat things sacrificed to idols? And the apostle writes: "You cannot drink the cup of the Lord and the cup of demons."[286] One should know, therefore, that these foods, and indeed all of God's creatures, are clean in and of themselves, but the invocation of idols and demons makes them unclean.

15.12. *Then his disciples came and said to him: "Do you know that when the Pharisees heard these words, they were scandalized?"* By one statement, all the superstition of Judaic observances was struck down, of those who think that their religion consists in the receiving and abominating of foods. And because "scandal" is frequently used in the Church's Scriptures, we should briefly speak about what it signifies. We can express *scolon* and *scandalum* as "little obstacle" or "falling and striking against the foot." So then, when we read: "Whoever 'scandalizes' any of the least of these,"[287] we understand this: the one who by word or deed gives to anyone an occasion for falling.

15.13. *But he answered and said: "Every plant that my heavenly Father has not planted will be uprooted."* Even things that seem clear in the Scriptures give rise to a mass of problems.[288] "Ev-

---

283. Cf. Dt 32.9.
284. Cf. Lv 11.1–13.
285. Acts 10.15.
286. 1 Cor 10.21.
287. Mt 18.6; Mk 9.42; Lk 17.2.
288. Lit., "are filled with questions" (*plena sunt quaestionibus*).

ery plant," he says, "that my heavenly Father has not planted will be uprooted." Well then, will even that plant be uprooted about which the apostle says: "I planted, Apollos watered"?[289] But the problem is resolved because of what follows: "But God gave the growth."[290] And he himself says: "You are God's field, God's building";[291] and in another place he says: "We are God's co-workers."[292] But if we are co-workers, then while Paul plants and Apollos waters, God is planting and watering along with his workers. They misuse this passage who introduce diverse natures and say: If the plant that the Father has not planted will be uprooted, then the one that he did plant cannot be uprooted. But let them hear the following from Jeremiah: "I have planted you as a true vineyard; why did you turn into the bitterness of a foreign vine?"[293] God planted it indeed, and no one can uproot his plant. But because that plant depends on the willingness of its own choice, no other can uproot it unless it grants assent.

15.14. *"Leave them; they are blind guides of the blind."* This is what the apostle had commanded: "After the first and second admonition, avoid the heretical man, knowing that such a one is perverted and self-condemned."[294] In this sense, the Savior also commands that bad teachers should be left to their own choice. He knows that it is difficult for them to be able to be drawn to the truth. They are blind, and they draw blind people into error.

15.15–16. *But Peter answered and said to him: "Explain this parable to us." And he said: "Are you also still without understanding?"* What had been said openly and was accessible for hearing, the apostle Peter thinks was spoken as a parable. In a matter that is manifest, he is seeking a mystical understanding. And he is reproached by the Lord for having thought that what he spoke clearly was said parabolically. The lesson from this is that a hearer is at fault who wants to understand either obscure things plainly or things that have been said plainly as obscure matters.[295]

---

289. 1 Cor 3.6.
290. 1 Cor 3.7.
291. 1 Cor 3.9.
292. 1 Cor 3.9, cf. 3 Jn 8.
293. Jer 2.21.
294. Ti 3.10–11.

295. This is an important statement of Jerome's exegetical method. Irenaeus, *Adv. haer.* 2.27.1, emphasizes the same point, namely, that ambiguous expressions should not determine the explanation of parables.

15.17. *"Do you not understand that everything that enters into the mouth goes into the belly and is cast out into the drain?"* Among the heretics and the perverse-minded,[296] all passages in the Gospels are filled with scandals. From this little statement, some of them find material for unjust criticisms. They say that the Lord was ignorant of physiology and thought that all food goes into the belly and is then dispersed into the drain, whereas in reality food that is taken in is immediately spread through the limbs and veins and marrow and nerves. They say further that the reason why many people who experience continuous vomiting after dinners and breakfasts due to stomach ailments immediately vomit what they have ingested, and yet they remain fat, is because at the first contact, the liquefied food and drink spreads through the members. But men of this sort reveal their own ignorance, while trying to reprehend the ignorance of others. For although a liquid is tenuous and food is fluid, when it is digested and spread into the veins and limbs, it will disperse below through hidden passages of the body, which the Greeks call πόροι [pores], and it goes into the drain.

15.19. *"For out of the heart come evil thoughts, murders, adulteries, fornications,"* etc. "Out of the heart," he says, "come evil thoughts." Therefore, the master faculty of the soul is not in the brain, as Plato claims, but according to Christ it is in the heart.[297] Also, on the basis of this statement, we can expose the error of those who think that thoughts are inspired by the devil and do not arise from one's own will.[298] The devil can be a helper and an inciter of evil thoughts, but he cannot be their author. Yet he always lies in wait and kindles small sparks in our thoughts with his own tinder. We should not imagine that he searches the secrets of the heart as well,[299] but from the gestures and demeanor of our body, he

296. Cf. Ti 3.10–11. This is probably directed against Porphyry. Cf. Porphyry, *Adv. Christianos, fragm.* 56.

297. *Animae principale* refers to the master or governing part of the soul, what the Stoics call ἡγεμονικόν. Plato describes this as the rational part of the soul (*Pol.* 4.439c–d) and locates it in the brain and in the head, which is the most divine part of us and master of all the other parts (*Tim.* 44d). Cf. Jerome, *Ep.* 64 to Fabiola.

298. He may have Hilary in mind. See below on Mt 16.23.

299. Cf. Rom 8.27; 1 Cor 2.10.

guesses what is going on inside of us, for example, if he sees us repeatedly looking at a lovely woman. Then he understands that our heart has been wounded by the dart of love.

15.21. *And having gone out from there, Jesus withdrew to the district of Tyre and Sidon.* He leaves his false accusers, the scribes and Pharisees, and goes to the district of Tyre and Sidon in order to cure the residents of Tyre and Sidon. But a Canaanite woman leaves her native land and cries out to procure healing for her daughter. Observe that this Canaanite daughter is healed in the fifteenth place.[300]

15.22. *"Have pity on me, Lord, son of David, my daughter is badly vexed by a demon."*[301] She knew to call him "son of David" because she had already come forth from her land and had left the error of the Tyrians and Sidonians by a change of place and of faith. "My daughter is badly vexed by a demon." I believe that the daughter of the Church refers to the souls of believers, which were badly vexed by a demon. They did not know the Creator and were worshiping stone.[302]

15.23. *He answered her not a word.* [His silence was] due not to some sort of pharisaical arrogance or superciliousness of the scribes, but that he might not seem to be opposed to his own statement by which he had commanded: "Do not go into the way of the Gentiles and do not enter into the cities of the Samaritans."[303] For he was unwilling to give an occasion to his false accusers, and he was reserving the perfected salvation of the Gentiles for the time of his Passion and Resurrection.

15.23. *And his disciples came and were asking him, saying: "Dismiss her, because she is calling out after us."* Even at that time the disciples did not know the mysteries of the Lord. They were either moved by compassion to make this request for the Canaanite woman (whom another evangelist calls a Syrophoenician),[304] or they were longing to be free from her importunity, since she was calling out repeatedly, not as if for a kind physician, but for a harsh one.

---

300. But what happened to number fourteen? Though Jerome did not identify it as such, it was probably the blind and mute man of Mt 12.22.

301. Cf. Origen, *In Matth.* 11.16.

302. Cf. Mt 15.25.   303. Mt 10.5.

304. Cf. Mk 7.26.

15.24. *"I was not sent except to the lost sheep of the house of Israel."* He is not saying that he was not also sent to the Gentiles, but that he was sent first to Israel. In that way the transference to the Gentiles would be just, since Israel did not receive the Gospel.[305] He has expressly said: "to the lost sheep of the house of Israel." Thus, on the basis of this passage, we can also understand the one wandering sheep of another parable.[306]

15.25. *But she came and worshiped him, saying.* In the person of the Canaanite woman, we should admire the faith, patience, and humility of the Church: faith, by which she believed that her daughter could be healed; patience, by which she perseveres in prayer, after having been so often scorned; humility, by which she compares herself not with dogs but with puppies. Now, pagans are called dogs on account of their idolatry.[307] They have surrendered themselves to the eating of blood, and by the bodies of the dead are carried off into madness. Note that this Canaanite woman with persistence first calls him son of David, then Lord, and finally she worships him as God.

15.27. *But she said: "Yes, Lord, for even the puppies eat from the crumbs that fall from the table of their masters."* I know, she says, that I do not deserve the sons' bread. I am incapable of taking whole food or of sitting at the table with the Father. But I am content with what is left over for the puppies, so that by the humility of crumbs I might come to the greatness of the whole loaf. Oh, what a marvelous transformation of things! Israel was once a son, and we were the dogs. The arrangement of the titles is changed due to the difference in faith. Of Israel it is later said: "Many dogs have surrounded me";[308] and: "Beware of the dogs, beware of the evil workers, beware of the mutilation."[309] But with the Syrophoenician woman and with the woman who flowed with blood, we have heard: "Great is your faith; let it be done to you according to your faith";[310] and: "Daughter, your faith has saved you."[311]

15.29–30. *And when Jesus had passed on from there, he came near the Sea of Galilee, and going up on a mountain, he sat down there.*

---

305. Cf. Jn 1.11; Acts 13.46.
307. Cf. Rv 22.15.
309. Phil 3.2.
311. Mt 9.29.

306. Cf. Lk 15.4.
308. Ps 22.16.
310. Mt 15.28.

And great crowds came to him, having with them the mute, the lame, the blind, the crippled, and many others, and they set them down at his feet. In this passage where the Latin translator rendered "crippled," in Greek it is written κυλλούς. This is the term used not of a general debilitation but of a particular weakness. Thus, in the same manner that one who is lame in one foot is called "lame," so one is called κυλλός who has one crippled hand. We [Latins] do not have the equivalent of this word. This is why in what follows the evangelist explained the healings of the other cripples, but he was silent about these. For what follows?

15.30–31. *And he cured them, so that the crowds were amazed, seeing the mute speaking, the lame walking, the blind seeing; and they praised the God of Israel.* Concerning the κυλλούς, and only concerning this term, he was silent, because he had no antithetical term. But let us consider this: when the daughter of the Canaanean woman has been healed, Jesus returns to Judea and to the Sea of Galilee. He goes up on a mountain, and, just as a bird challenges its tender fledglings to fly,[312] so he sits down there, and the crowds run to him, leading or carrying with them those who were oppressed by various infirmities. After he healed them, he gave them food, and, when this was done, he got into a boat and came into the district of Magedan.[313]

15.29–30. *And going up on the mountain he sat there, and the crowds came to him.* Observe that many lame and blind are led to the mountain to be cured there by the Lord.

15.32. *But Jesus called together his disciples and said: "I have compassion on the crowd because they have now remained with me for three days and they do not have anything to eat. I do not want to send them away fasting, lest they faint on the way."* He wants to feed those whom he has cured. First, he takes away their infirmities; then he offers food to those who have been healed. He also calls his disciples together and tells what he is going to do. Either he wants to offer them the example of a teacher sharing his plans with his inferiors and disciples; or his aim is that from the discussion they might understand the greatness of the miraculous sign, when they answer that they have no bread in the desert.

312. Cf. Dt 32.11.
313. Cf. Mt 15.39.

He says: "I have compassion on the crowd because they have now remained with me for three days." He has compassion on the crowd because in the number of the three days, they were believing in the Father, the Son, and the Holy Spirit. "And they do not have anything to eat." The crowd is always hungry and without food, unless it be satisfied by the Lord. "And I do not want to send them away fasting, lest they faint on the way." After the experience of having suffered great infirmities, they were hungry and were awaiting the coming food with patience.[314] Jesus does not want to send them away fasting, lest they faint on the way. Therefore, he is in danger who hastens to reach the desired mansion[315] without heavenly bread. This is also why an angel says to Elijah: "Rise and eat, because you are going to walk a long way."[316]

15.33–34. *And the disciples said to him: "But in a desert, where are we to get enough loaves to satisfy such a great crowd?" And Jesus said to them: "How many loaves do you have?" But they said: "Seven, and a few little fish,"* etc. We have already spoken above[317] about this miraculous sign, and it is superfluous to repeat the same things. Let us linger only on the discrepancies. Above we read: "Now when evening came, the disciples came to him saying: 'This is a deserted place,'" etc.[318] But here it says that when he had called his disciples together, the Lord himself says: "I have compassion on the crowd, because they have now remained with me for three days." In the former passage, there were five loaves and two fish,[319] here there are seven loaves and a few small fish. There they recline on grass,[320] here upon the ground. There those who eat are five thousand, which corresponds to the number of the loaves that they consume; here there are four thousand. There twelve baskets are filled with the remains of the fragments, here there are seven small baskets. In the sign above, then, since the five senses were present and near at hand, it is not the Lord himself who directs attention to them, but the dis-

---

314. Cf. Rom 8.25.   315. Cf. Jn 14.2.
316. 1 Kgs 19.7.   317. Cf. Mt 14.16–21.
318. Mt 14.15. Cf. Origen, *In Matth.* 11.19.
319. Cf. Mt 14.17.
320. Cf. Mt 14.19.

ciples; and they direct attention [to them] in the evening because night is near and the sun is already setting.[321] But here
the Lord himself brings up the matter. He says that he has compassion, and he sets forth the reasons for his compassion: "Because they have now remained with me for three days," and he
does not want to send them away fasting, lest they faint on the
way. Those who are nourished from the seven loaves, that is,
from a consecrated and perfect number, are not five thousand
but four thousand. The number four is always recorded with
praise. A quadrangular stone does not move. It is not unstable,
and on this account even the Gospels are consecrated by the
same number.[322]

Chapter 16

16.2–3. *But he answered and said to them: "When evening comes,
you say: 'It will be fair, for the sky is red'; and in the morning: 'Today
there will be a storm, for the sky is red and threatening.' You know, then,
how to judge the appearance of the sky, but you are unable to judge the
signs of the times."* This is not found in the majority of manuscripts,[323] and the sense is clear, that from the arrangement and
constancy of the elements, both fair and rainy days can be fore-
cast. But the scribes and Pharisees, who seemed to be teachers
of the Law, were unable to understand the advent of the Savior
from the predictions of the prophets.

16.4–5. *And he left them and went away, and when his disciples
crossed the sea, they had forgotten to take bread.* When he left the
scribes and Pharisees, to whom he had said: "An evil and adulterous generation seeks a sign, and a sign shall not be given to it
except the sign of Jonah,"[324] he rightly went across the sea, and

---

321. Cf. Mt 14.15.   322. See Preface (1–3).

323. Verses 2 (from "when evening comes") and 3 are not found in part of
the manuscript tradition. Most scholars regard the passage as a later insertion
from a source similar to Lk 12.54–56. On the other hand, other scholars (like
Scrivener and LeGrange) argue that the verses were omitted by copyists in cli-
mates such as Egypt where red sky in the morning does not announce rain. See
Metzger, *Textual Commentary,* 41.

324. Mt 16.4.

the people of the Gentiles followed him. But the meaning of the sign of Jonah has already been given above.[325]

16.6. *"Beware of the leaven of the Pharisees and Sadducees."* He who is wary of the leaven of the Pharisees and the Sadducees does not observe the precepts of the Law and of the letter. He neglects human traditions in order to do God's command.[326]

16.8–12. *"You of little faith, why are you thinking among yourselves that you have no bread? Do you not yet understand or remember the five loaves and the five thousand men and how many baskets you took up?"* etc. On the occasion of an instruction by which the Savior had commanded, saying: "Beware of the leaven of the Pharisees and the Sadducees,"[327] he teaches them the significance of the five and seven loaves, and of the five thousand and four thousand men, who were fed in the desert. Thus, although the greatness of the signs is clear, yet something else may be shown by the spiritual understanding. For if the leaven of the Pharisees and the Sadducees signifies not physical bread, but perverse traditions and heretical dogmas, why may not the food on which the people of God are nourished signify true and sound doctrine?[328] Someone may ask and say: How is it that they had no bread? For they had gotten into the boat immediately after the seven little baskets were filled. Then they came to the region of Magedan,[329] and while sailing there they hear that they must beware of the leaven of the Pharisees and the Sadducees. But the Scripture testifies that they had forgotten to take it with them. This is the leaven of which the apostle also speaks: "A little leaven ruins the whole lump."[330] Marcion, Valentinus, and all the heretics had leaven of this sort. By all means it must be avoided. Leaven has this power, that if it is mixed with flour, that which seemed small grows greater and draws all the dough[331] to its fla-

---

325. Cf. Mt 12.39–40.   326. Cf. Mt 15.3.

327. Mt 16.6.

328. This text shows how Jerome's allegorical exegesis is rooted not only in Pauline thought (1 Cor 10.6, etc.) but also in the words of Jesus.

329. Cf. Mt 15.37, 39.

330. 1 Cor 5.6.

331. Jerome uses the same Punic Latin word for dough (*consparsio*) that is used by Tertullian, *Adv. Marc.* 4.24.

vor. In the same way, then, heretical teaching, if it casts a little spark[332] into your breast, in a little while rises up as a huge flame and draws to itself[333] the possession of the entire man. Finally, it follows: "Then they understood that he did not tell them to beware of the leaven of bread, but of the teaching of the Pharisees and the Sadducees."[334]

332. For this phrase, see above on Mt 12.20; 15.19.
333. Cf. Jn 12.32.
334. Mt 16.4.

BOOK THREE (MATTHEW 16.13–22.40)

OW WHEN JESUS CAME into the region of Caesarea Philippi (16.13). This Philip is the brother of the Herod of whom we spoke above.[1] He was the tetrarch of the regions of Iturea and Trachonitis.[2] He named this region Caesarea Philippi in honor of Tiberius Caesar. Today it is called Paneas.[3] It is in the province of Phoenicia. Philip did this in imitation of his father Herod, who in honor of Caesar Augustus had given the name of Caesarea to the village previously named Tower of Strato,[4] and who on the other side of the Jordan had also built Libias, which was named after his daughter.[5] Caesarea Philippi

1. Cf. Mt 2.17–18, 20, 22; Mt 11.2–3, 14–15; Mt 14.1–4, 6–11.

2. Cf. Lk 3.1.

3. Paneas is now called Banias. The original name came from the fact that the village was dedicated to the god Pan. Jerome made contradictory statements about this town, sometimes distinguishing it from Dan (*Onomasticon* 77), and sometimes identifying the two places (*Comm. in Ezek.* 27.19, PL 25: 258), *Comm. in Amos* (PL 25: 1084). According to J. F. Wilson, *Caesarea Philippi: Banias, the Lost City of Pan* (London: I. B. Tauris, 2004), Jerome received his information about the town not firsthand but from Eusebius, Jewish rabbis, and Josephus, *AJ* 18.2.1; cf. also *BJ* 2.167–68.

4. This second Caesarea first appears as a Phoenician city apparently built by Strato, a king of Sidon, in the fourth century B.C. Cf. Josephus, *AJ* 13.15.4. It was the official residence of the Roman procurator.

5. The SC editors think that Jerome has erred by attributing the foundation of Libias to Philip. But they seem to have misread Jerome's text, since the *qui* that forms the subject of the second clause, *qui . . . ex nomine filiae eius Libiadem, trans Iordanem exstruxit*, refers to Herod, not to Philip. But Jerome has erred when he identifies the name of this village with that of the daughter of the emperor. Rather, it is the name of the emperor's wife. According to Josephus, *AJ* 18.11.1 and *BJ* 2.9.1, Philip named ancient Bethsaida Julias "from the name of the daughter of the emperor [Augustus]"; his brother Herod Antipas named the ancient Betharan in Perea beyond the Jordan Julias from the name of the wife of the emperor. Only this latter village is customarily designated under the name Livias. One can

is located where the Jordan has its source in Lebanon. Its two springs are there, one named *Jor* and another *Dan*. These have been combined in the name Jordan.[6]

16.13. *And he asked his disciples, saying: "Who do men say that the Son of man is?"* He did not say, "Who do men say that *I* am," but "the Son of man." He wanted to avoid the appearance of asking about himself in a boasting fashion.[7] And note that wherever "Son of man" is written in the Old Testament, the Hebrew has "son of Adam." And that which we read in the Psalm: "sons of men, how long will you have a heavy heart?"[8] is said in Hebrew as "sons of Adam." It is well that the Savior asks: "Who do men say that the Son of man is?" For those who speak about the Son of man are men; but those who understand his deity are not men but are called gods.[9]

16.14. *But they said: "Some say John the Baptist; others say Elijah; and others Jeremiah or one of the prophets."* I marvel that certain interpreters[10] inquire about the causes of each of these errors. They compose very lengthy disputations about why some were thinking that our Lord Jesus Christ was John, others Elijah, but others Jeremiah or one of the prophets. Yet they could have erred about Elijah and Jeremiah in the same manner in which Herod had erred about John when he said: "John whom I beheaded has himself risen from the dead, and miraculous powers are at work in him."[11]

16.15–16. *"But you, who do you say that I am?" Simon Peter answered: "You are the Christ, the Son of the living God."* Wise reader, notice from what follows and from the context of the words that the apostles are by no means called men, but gods.[12] For though he had said: "Who do men say that the Son of man is?" he has

---

explain the double name that it bears thus by the fact that the empress Livia received the official name of Julia in the will of Augustus in 14 A.D.

6. Although Jerome's explanation is no longer accepted today, there is no agreement about the actual etymology of the Jordan.

7. Mk 8.27 and Lk 9.18 have: "Who do men say that *I* am?"

8. Ps 4.2.

9. Cf. Jn 10.34; Ps 82.6. See Homily 71 on Ps 93 (94) in FOTC 57, 103.

10. Cf. Origen, *In Matth.* 12.9. A similar anonymous criticism of Origen is found under Mt 14.1–2.

11. Cf. Mk 6.16.   12. Cf. Jn 10.34.

added: "But you, who do you say that I am?" For the former, since they are thinking human things, are men, but you who are gods, who do you consider me to be? Representing[13] all the apostles, Peter professes: "You are the Christ, the Son of the living God." He calls him a living God in comparison with those gods that are thought to be gods but are dead. This refers to Saturn, Jove, Ceres, Liberus, Hercules, and the rest of the portents of the idols.

16.17. *Jesus answered and said to him: "Blessed are you, Simon Bar-Jona, for flesh and blood has not revealed this to you, but my Father who is in heaven."* For the apostle's testimony concerning himself, Jesus repays in turn. Peter had said: "You are the Christ, the Son of the living God."[14] A true confession received its reward: "Blessed are you, Simon Bar-Jona." Why? Because flesh and blood has not revealed it to you, but the Father has revealed it. What flesh and blood was not able to reveal, the grace of the Holy Spirit has revealed. Therefore, because of his confession, a name is allotted to him that has been revealed by the Holy Spirit, whose son he is to be called. For indeed, in our language Bar-Jona sounds like "son of the dove."[15] Others[16] take it more simply, that Simon, that is, Peter, is the son of John in accordance with the question found in another passage: "Simon, son of John, do you love me?" He answered: "Lord, you know."[17] They think there has been a corruption through the fault of the copyists, so that in place of Bar-Johanna, that is, "son of John," it was written Bar-Jona, with one syllable having been deleted. Now Johanna is translated "grace of the Lord."[18] Both names can be interpreted mystically. Thus "dove" signifies the Holy Spirit, and "grace of God" signifies a spiritual gift. Moreover, compare his words: "For flesh and blood has not revealed it to you," with the apostolic narrative in which it says: "I did not immediately take counsel with flesh and blood."[19] In that passage [Paul] is signi-

13. Or "under the persona" (*ex persona*).
14. Mt 16.16.
15. Jerome is referring to the descent of the Holy Spirit in the form of a dove. Cf. Mt 4.16. For the etymology, see Jerome, *De interpr. hebr. nom.*, p. 60, line 22.
16. Who?   17. Jn 21.16.
18. Cf. Jerome, *De interpr. hebr. nom.*, p. 65, lines 1–2.
19. Gal 1.16.

fying the Jews by the term "flesh and blood." Thus here too, by another interpretation, it is shown that Christ was revealed to him as the Son of God, not through the teaching of the Pharisees, but by the grace of God.

16.18. *"And I say to you."* What do his words mean: "And I say to you"? [They mean this:] Since you have said to me: "You are the Christ, the Son of the living God," "I also say to you," not with empty words that have no effect, but "I say to you" because with me to have spoken is to have done.

16.18. *"For you are Peter, and upon this rock I will build my Church."* He himself gave light to the apostles that they might be called the light of the world,[20] and the other designations that were allotted from the Lord. In the same way, to Simon,[21] who believed in Christ the rock [*petra*], was granted the name of Peter [*Petrus*]. And in accordance with the metaphor of rock [*petra*], it is rightly said to him: "I will build my Church" upon you.

16.18. *"And the gates of hell*[22] *shall not prevail against it."* I think the gates of hell are vices and sins, or at least the doctrines of the heretics through which men are enticed and led to Tartarus.[23] Consequently, let no one think that this is being said about death, that is, that the apostles were not subjected to the condition of death, whose martyrdoms one may see shining forth.[24]

16.19. *"And I will give to you the keys of the kingdom of heaven, and whatever you bind on earth will be bound also in heaven, and whatever you loose on earth will be loosed also in heaven."* The bishops and priests do not understand this passage. They assume for themselves some of the superciliousness of the Pharisees when they either condemn the innocent[25] or think that they can loose the guilty. Yet in the sight of God it is not the verdict of the priests but the life of the accused that is examined.[26] We read in Leviticus about lepers that they are commanded to show themselves

---

20. Cf. Mt 5.14.   21. Cf. 1 Cor 10.4.

22. Lit., "of the underworld" (*inferi*).

23. Cf. 2 Pt 2.2, 4. Cf. Origen, *In Matth.* 12.12.

24. This was the interpretation of A. von Harnack, who believed that the Lord's promise was a prophecy of Peter's immortality.

25. Cf. Mt 12.7.

26. Cf. Origen, *In Matth.* 12.14. Origen goes even further and says that a priest or bishop only effectively remits sins when he is holy like Peter.

to the priests and, if they have leprosy, then they are established as unclean by the priest. This does not mean that the priests make them leprous and unclean, but that they have knowledge of the leprous and the non-leprous, and they can discern who is clean and who is unclean.[27] Therefore, just as in that passage it is the priest who "makes" the leper unclean, so also here the priest or bishop binds or looses, not those who are innocent or guilty, but because of his own office. When he hears the various kinds of sins, he knows who should be bound, and who should be loosed.

16.20. *Then he commanded his disciples to tell no one that he was Jesus Christ.* Above, when he sent the disciples to preach,[28] he commanded them to proclaim his advent. Here he commands them not to tell that he is Jesus Christ. It seems to me that to preach Christ is one thing, but to preach Jesus Christ is something else.[29] For Christ is a common term of dignity, but Jesus is the Savior's proper name.[30] Now it is possible that he did not want himself to be preached before his Passion and Resurrection so that, after the mystery of the blood had been completed, he could say to the apostles more opportunely: "Go, teach all nations," etc.[31] And lest anyone think that this is merely our own interpretation and not the meaning of the Gospel, the words that follow set forth the reasons for the prohibition on preaching that took place at that time.

16.21. *From that time Jesus began to show his disciples that he must go to Jerusalem and suffer many things from the elders and scribes and chief priests and be put to death and on the third day rise again.* Now the sense is: After I have suffered these things, preach me at that time. For it is not beneficial to preach Christ publicly and to spread abroad among the people the majesty of him whom, in a little while, they are going to see scourged and crucified, and suffering many things from the elders and scribes and chief priests. And even now, Jesus suffers many things from those who all over again crucify for themselves the Son of God.[32] And though they may be thought to be elders in the Church and

---

27. Cf. Lv 14.2–4.
28. Cf. Mt 10.7.
29. Cf. Origen, *In Matth.* 12.16.
30. Cf. Origen, *In Matth.* 12.17.
31. Mt 28.19.
32. Cf. Heb 6.6.

chief priests, when they follow the simple letter, they put to death the Son of God, who is perceived entirely in the Spirit.

16.22–23. *And Peter took him aside and began to rebuke him, saying: "Far be it from you, Lord; this shall not happen to you." But he turned and said to Peter: "Go behind me, Satan; you are a stumbling-block to me, for you do not have in mind the things of God but the things of men."* We have often spoken[33] of the extreme zeal and very great love Peter had for the Lord and Savior. He had already made his confession in which he had said: "You are the Christ, the Son of the living God."[34] He had heard the Savior's reward: "Blessed are you, Simon Bar-Jona, for flesh and blood has not revealed it to you, but my Father who is in heaven."[35] After all this, suddenly he hears from the Lord that he must go to Jerusalem and suffer many things there from the elders and scribes and chief priests and be put to death and on the third day rise again. Peter does not want his own confession to be negated, nor does he think it possible that the Son of God be put to death. Therefore, out of his affection he takes him aside, or rather, he leads him off privately, lest he seem to be confronting his teacher in the presence of his fellow disciples. Then he begins to rebuke him with the affection of a lover, and he speaks his wish: "Far be it from you, Lord," or better, as it is found in the Greek: Ἵλεώς σοι κύριε, that is: "May you be favorably disposed, Lord; this shall not be." He means: That the Son of God is to be killed is something that cannot happen. My ears refuse to hear it. The Lord turned to him and said: "Go behind me, Satan; you are a stumbling-block to me." Satan is translated as "adversary" or "the opposer."[36] He is saying: Because you are speaking things opposed to my will, you ought to be called an adversary. Many[37] think that it is not Peter who is rebuked, but the adversarial spirit who suggested these things for the apostle to speak. But in my opinion it will never seem that an apostolic error and one coming from pious feeling was inspired by the devil.[38] "Go behind me, Satan," is told to the devil.[39] "Go behind," Peter hears. "Go

---

33. Cf. Mt 14.28, 31.
34. Mt 16.16.
35. Mt 16.17.
36. Cf. Origen, *In Matth.* 12.21.
37. Cf. Hilary, *In Matth.* 16.10 (PL 9: 1011B).
38. See above on Mt 15.19.
39. Cf. Origen, *In Matth.* 12.22.

behind me," that is, follow my thought, "for you are not think-ing the things of God but the things of men." It is my will and the Father's, whose will I have come to do,[40] that I die for the salvation of men. Because you are considering only your own will, you do not want the grain of wheat to fall to the ground so that it might bear much fruit.[41] The intelligent reader may in-quire how, after such a great blessing: "Blessed are you, Simon Bar-Jona,"[42] and, "You are Peter, and upon this rock I will build my Church, and the gates of hell will not prevail against it, and I will give you the keys of the kingdom of heaven,"[43] and what you bind or loose on earth will be bound or loosed in heaven,[44] he should now hear: "Go behind me, Satan; you are a stumbling-block to me." How did such a sudden conversion occur, that af-ter such great rewards he is now called Satan? But let the one who asks this consider that this blessing, favor, and authority, as well as the building of the Church upon him, was promised to Peter for the future. It is not given in the present. He says: "I *will* build my Church upon you, and the gates of hell *will* not prevail against it, and I *will* give to you the keys of the kingdom of heav-en." All these things concern the future. If he had given them to him at once, the error of a perverse confession would never have found room in him.

16.24. *Then Jesus said to his disciples: "If anyone wants to come after me, let him deny himself and take up his cross and follow me,"* etc. He who lays aside the old man with his works[45] denies him-self. He is one who says: "But I live no longer, but Christ lives in me."[46] And he who is crucified to the world takes up his own cross.[47] Now the one to whom the world has been crucified is following the crucified Lord.[48]

16.26. *"Or what shall a man give in exchange for his soul?"* For Israel the exchange is given of Egypt, Ethiopia, and Seba.[49] For a human soul the only repayment is what the Psalmist sings:

40. Cf. Jn 6.38.   41. Cf. Jn 12.24–25.
42. Mt 16.17.   43. Mt 16.18–19.
44. Cf. Mt 16.19.   45. Cf. Col 3.9–10.
46. Gal 2.20.   47. Cf. Gal 6.14.
48. Cf. Origen, *In Matth.* 12.24.
49. Cf. Is 43.3. Cf. Origen, *In Matth.* 12.28.

"What shall I repay to the Lord for all that he has paid back to me? I will take up the cup of salvation and call upon the name of the Lord."[50]

16.27. *"For the Son of man is going to come in the glory of his Father with his angels, and then he will render to everyone according to his conduct."* Peter was scandalized by the proclamation of the Lord's death and had been rebuked by a judgment of the Lord. The disciples were challenged to deny themselves and to take up their cross and to follow their Master with a spirit that is ready for death. Great was the terror of those who heard [these words], and it was a terror that could even inspire fear in others, since the leader of the apostles had been thoroughly terrified. For that reason these grievous words are succeeded by joyful news. Jesus says: "The Son of man is going to come in the glory of his Father with his angels." You are afraid of death, so hear about the glory of the triumphant one; you are afraid of the cross, so hear about the ministries of the angels. "And then," he says, "he will render to everyone according to his works." There is no distinction between Jew and pagan,[51] man and woman,[52] poor and rich. For it is not persons that he considers, but their works.[53]

16.28. *"Amen I say to you: There are some standing here who will not taste death until they see the Son of man coming in his kingdom."* He had willed to heal the terror of the apostles by the hope of the promises when he said: "The Son of man is going to come in the glory of his Father with his angels,"[54] and over and above this by the authority of a judge, it is added: "And he will render to everyone according to his works."[55] The silent reflection of the apostles could endure a scandal of this sort, [namely,] that you are now saying that killing and death are coming. But your

50. Cf. Ps 116.12–13.   51. Cf. Rom 10.12.
52. Cf. Gal 3.28.

53. J. P. O'Connell, *The Eschatology of St. Jerome*, 34, comments on this text: "The point Jerome is making when he insists on the presence of all classes before the tribunal of Christ is that no one can claim exemption on the grounds of his position, race, wealth, dignity, etc. For all men, by reason of the fact that they are men, will be brought to judgment. Whence, as Jerome points out, all men have reason to fear." Cf. *Ep.* 59.2; *In Ecclesiasten* 12.14.

54. Mt 16.27.   55. Ibid.

promise about coming in the glory of the Father with the ministries of angels and with the authority of a judge will be later and will be postponed for a long time. Seeing in advance that they could make such objections, then, the one who knows secrets compensates for their present fear with an immediate reward. For what does he say? "There are some standing here who will not taste death until they see the Son of man coming in his kingdom." Thus on account of your lack of faith, the manner in which he is going to come later will be shown in the present time.[56]

Chapter 17

17.1. *And after six days, Jesus took Peter, James, and John, his brother.* We have frequently talked about[57] how in certain passages of the Gospels, Peter, James, and John are separated from the others, and about what privileges they had beyond the other apostles.[58] Now it is asked how it can be that after *six* days he takes them and leads them "onto a high mountain by themselves." For Luke the evangelist records the number *eight*.[59] But the answer is easy: here only the days in between are recorded, whereas there the first and last days are added. For it does not say: After eight days Jesus took Peter, James, and John, but: on the eighth day.[60]

17.1. *And he led them onto a high mountain by themselves.* For the disciples to be led to the mountainous places is their portion in the kingdom. The reason they are led by themselves is because "many are called, few are chosen."[61]

---

56. Jerome's interpretation reflects the thought of 2 Pt 1.17–19, where the Transfiguration is viewed as a preview, not of the Resurrection, but of the second coming of Christ. See on 17.2.

57. See above on Mt 13.47–49; 14.23.

58. Cf. Homily 77 in FOTC 57, 149.

59. Cf. Lk 9.28.

60. Actually, the text in Luke 9.28 does not say "on the eighth day" but "about eight days after these words." The mistake is another sign of hasty composition. Cf. Homily 80 in FOTC 57, 161.

61. Mt 20.16; 22.14.

17.2. *And he was transfigured before them.* He appeared to the apostles in the form in which he will appear at the time of judgment. But as for what it says: "He was transfigured before them," let no one think that he lost his original form and appearance, or that he lost the reality of his body and took up either a spiritual or an airy body. On the contrary the evangelist shows how he was transformed when he says:

17.2. *And his face shone like the sun, and his clothing became white like snow.* When the splendor of the face is shown and the brilliance of the clothing is described, it is not that the substance is removed, but the glory is changed.[62] "His face shone like the sun." Surely, the Lord was transformed into that glory with which he is going to come later in his kingdom. The transformation added splendor; it did not make his face disappear. Let it be that his body became spiritual.[63] Were his garments also changed, which became so brilliant that another evangelist said: "Such as a fuller on earth is not able to make them"?[64] Well, what a fuller on earth cannot do has to be something bodily and tactile, not something spiritual and airy that deceives the eyes and is seen only as an imaginary representation.

17.3. *And behold, Moses and Elijah appeared to them, speaking with him.* When the scribes and Pharisees tested him and demanded signs from heaven, he was unwilling to give them.[65] Instead he silenced the perverse request with a prudent answer. Here, however, in order to increase the faith of the apostles, he gives a sign from heaven. Elijah comes down from heaven to the place where Jesus had ascended. Moreover, Moses rises up from the lower world.[66] This is exactly what Ahaz is commanded

---

62. Cf. *Adv. Jov.* 1.36; *In Is.* 58.14; *In Is. prol. In lib.* 17.

63. Cf. 1 Cor 15.44.   64. Mk 9.2.

65. Cf. Mt 12.38.

66. Jerome distinguishes the place occupied by Moses from that of Elijah: Moses is with the other OT saints in the underworld; Elijah is in heaven. Elsewhere Jerome speaks of Elijah and Enoch being in heaven and paradise. Cf. *In Amos* 9.2, 6; *Contra Jo. Hier.* 29; *In Zach.* 6.11. J. P. O'Connell, *The Eschatology of St. Jerome,* 21, says that Jerome does not seem to have answered the difficulty that arises from this of how heaven would be said to have been closed before Christ. Origen's answer to a related question about Elijah and Enoch in *ComRom* 2.5.4 (M1029) is that things that are said about all men shall not

through Isaiah, that he seek a sign for himself from on high or from below.[67] As for what they talked about when it says: "Moses and Elijah appeared to them, speaking with him," it is related in another Gospel that they announced to him what he was going to suffer in Jerusalem.[68] This passage points to the Law and the prophets,[69] which by repeated utterances announced both the Passion of the Lord and his Resurrection.

17.4. *Then Peter answered and said to Jesus: "Lord, it is good for us to be here."* Since he had gone up on the mountainous places, he does not want to descend to the earthly regions. He would rather remain forever in the lofty places.

17.4. *"If you want, I will make here three tabernacles, one for you, one for Moses, and one for Elijah."* You are astray, Peter, or as another evangelist testifies: You do not know what you are saying.[70] Do not seek three tabernacles, since there is one tabernacle of the Gospel in which the Law and the prophets are summed up.[71] But if you seek three tabernacles, by no means should you compare servants with their Master. But make three tabernacles, nay rather, make one for the Father and the Son and the Holy Spirit, so that there might be one tabernacle in your heart for those whose divinity is one.

17.5. *While he was still speaking, behold, a bright cloud overshadowed them and there was a voice from the cloud saying: "This is my beloved Son in whom I am well pleased; listen to him."* Because [Peter] had asked imprudently, he is not worthy of an answer from the Lord. Instead, the Father answers on behalf of the Son. Thus the word of the Lord is fulfilled: "I do not testify for myself, but the Father who sent me, he himself testifies for me."[72] But the cloud seems bright and shades them. Thus those who were seeking a physical tabernacle from branches or tents are covered by

---

immediately be deemed false if a dispensation of God has been made in the case of one or two men.

67. Cf. Is 7.11.   68. Cf. Lk 9.31.

69. Represented by Moses and Elijah, respectively.

70. Cf. Lk 9.33.

71. The term "sum up" or "recapitulate" is taken from Pauline usage (Eph 1.10): ἀνακεφαλαιώσασθαι, "to sum up under one head." Cf. Origen, *In Matth.* 12.40.

72. Jn 5.37; 8.18.

the shade of the bright cloud. Also, the Father's voice from heaven is heard speaking. It offers testimony to the Son and shows the truth to Peter, his error having been removed; nay rather, through Peter it teaches the truth to the rest of the apostles. It says: "This is my beloved Son." In other words, it is for this one that a tabernacle must be made, it is to this one that obedience must be given. "*This* is my Son," *they* are his servants. And Moses and Elijah themselves along with you ought to prepare a tabernacle for the Lord in the inner reaches of their heart.

17.6. *And on hearing it the disciples fell on their faces and were exceedingly afraid.* They are overcome by fear and panic for three reasons. First, they had recognized that they had erred; second, the bright cloud had covered them; and third, because they had heard the voice of God the Father speaking.[73] Human weakness is not patient in bearing the sight of greater glory. It shudders with its whole spirit and body and falls to the ground. In proportion to how much someone seeks what is more, to that degree it falls to what is lower, if it fails to recognize its own measure.

17.7. *And Jesus came near and touched them.* They were lying down and were unable to rise. So he comes near and gently touches them in order to banish their fear by his touch and to strengthen their weakened limbs.[74]

17.7. *And he said to them: "Arise and do not be afraid."* With a command he heals those whom he had healed with his hand. "Do not be afraid." First, fear is expelled so that afterward doctrine may be imparted.

17.8. *But when they had lifted up their eyes, they saw no one except Jesus alone.* There is a reason why, after they arose, they saw no one except Jesus alone. If Moses and Elijah had remained with the Lord, then the words of the Father about him might have seemed uncertain. For the Father had given a very powerful testimony about him. Therefore, they see Jesus standing there, after the cloud has been removed. Moses and Elijah have vanished, because after the shadow of the Law and the prophets departs, which had covered the apostles with its veil,[75] both are rediscovered in the Gospel.[76]

---

73. Cf. 2 Pt 1.17–18.
75. Cf. 2 Cor 4.14–16.

74. Cf. Heb 12.12.
76. Cf. Origen, *In Matth.* 12.43.

17.9. *And as they were coming down from the mountain, Jesus commanded them, saying: "Tell the vision to no one until the Son of man has risen from the dead."* A preview of the future kingdom and the glory of the triumphant one had been shown on the mountain. The reason he does not want this to be preached among the peoples is both that it would be impossible to believe, in light of the greatness of the event, and also that, after such great [manifestation of] glory, the cross that follows would create a stumbling block among ignorant minds.[77]

17.10. *And the disciples asked him, saying: "Why then do the scribes say that Elijah must come first?"* Unless we understand the reasons why the disciples question him about the name of Elijah, their question will seem extraordinarily foolish. For what does the question about the coming of Elijah have to do with the things that are written above? There was a tradition among the Pharisees, in accordance with the prophet Malachi, who was the last among the twelve,[78] that Elijah would come before the advent of the Savior. He would lead back the hearts of the fathers to their sons and the hearts of the sons to their fathers and would restore all things to their ancient state.[79] The disciples are thinking, then, that this glorious transformation is the one that they had seen on the mountain. Thus they say: If you have already come in glory, how is it that your precursor does not appear? They especially want to know this in light of the fact that they had seen Elijah depart. But when they add: "The scribes say that Elijah must come *first*," by saying *first,* they show that [they think that] unless Elijah comes, it is not the advent of the Savior in accordance with the Scriptures.[80]

17.11–12. *But he answered and said to them: "Elijah will indeed come and will restore all things; but I say to you that Elijah has already come,"* etc. He who will come in bodily reality at the Savior's second advent has now come through John in power and spirit.[81]

77. Cf. ibid.
78. I.e., the twelve minor prophets.
79. Cf. Mal 4.5–6; Sir 48.10.
80. Cf. Origen, *In Matth.* 13.1.
81. Cf. Lk 1.17; Cf. Origen, *In Matth.* 13.2. Notice that Jerome has now adopted the teaching that Elijah will come again at the Savior's second advent. At 11.14 he attributed this view to others.

"But they did not recognize him, and they did to him whatever they wanted." That is to say, they spurned and decapitated him.[82]

17.12. *"So also the Son of man will suffer from them."* The question is raised:[83] It was Herod and Herodias who killed John. How is it, then, that they are also the ones who are said to have crucified Jesus? For we read that Jesus was killed by the scribes and Pharisees.[84] Briefly, one may respond that the sect of the Pharisees also consented to the death of John, and that Herod united his own will to the killing of the Lord. For he is the one who, after mocking him and treating him with contempt, released him to Pilate to have him crucified.[85]

17.15–16. *"Lord, have pity on my son, for he is a lunatic and suffers severely. For often he falls into fire and frequently into water; and I brought him to your disciples, and they were unable to cure him."* Above[86] we have given the reason why a demon observes the course of the moon, seizes men, and strives to defame the Creator through the creatures. Now it seems to me that, according to tropology, a lunatic is one who from time to time falls into vice. He does not persist in what he has begun,[87] but he increases and decreases.[88] Now he is carried off into the fire with which the hearts of the adulterous are inflamed;[89] the next moment he falls into the water, which does not have the strength to extinguish love.[90] But what he says: "I brought him to your disciples, and they were unable to cure him," is an implicit accusation of the apostles. For the inability to cure is sometimes referred not to the weakness of those doing the curing, but to the faith of those who are to be cured. This is what the Lord says: "Let it be done to you according to your faith."[91]

17.17. *Jesus answered and said: "O unbelieving and perverse generation, how long will I be with you? How long will I put up with you?"* It is not that Jesus was overcome by frustration, that is, that the

---

82. Cf. Mt 14.10.

83. Cf. Origen, *In Matth*. 13.2.

84. Cf. Mt 16.21.

85. Cf. Lk 23.11.

86. Cf. Mt 4.24.

87. Cf. Sir 27.11–12.

88. Cf. Origen, *In Matth*. 13.1.

89. Cf. Hos 7.4; Origen, *In Matth*. 13.4.

90. Cf. Song 8.7.

91. Mt 9.29; Mk 5.34; 10.52.

gentle and meek one, who like a lamb before its shearer did not open his mouth,[92] erupted in words of rage. On the contrary, in the manner of a physician who sees a sick person acting contrary to his orders,[93] he says: How long shall I come to your house? How long shall I waste my energy and skill? For I command you to do one thing, and you do something else! It is really the case that he is angry not with the man but with the vice. And through this one man, he convicts the Jews of infidelity. This is why he adds at once: "Bring him here to me."

17.18. *And Jesus rebuked him, and the demon went out from him.* It was not the man who was suffering that had to be rebuked, but the demon. Or, it may be that he rebuked the boy, and the demon went out from him because the boy had been oppressed by the demon on account of his own sins.

17.19–20. *And they said: "Why could we not cast it out?" He said to them: "On account of your unbelief."* This is what he says in another passage: "Whatever you ask in my name, believing, you will receive."[94] Therefore, whenever we do not receive, it is not a question of the inability of the giver, but the fault lies with those who are praying.

17.20. *"If you have faith like a mustard seed, you will say to this mountain: 'Move from here,' and it will move."* Some[95] think that faith that is compared to a mustard seed is called small in order that the kingdom of heaven may be compared with a mustard seed. For the apostle says: "And if I have all faith so that I may remove mountains."[96] Faith is large, then, which is equated with a mustard seed.[97] The removal of a mountain signifies the removal not of the mountain that we see with the fleshly eyes, but of that one that had been removed by the Lord from the lunatic. For what does he say? "You will say to *this* mountain: 'Move from here,' and it will move." From this it is possible to refute the follies of those who claim that, since none of apostles and

92. Cf. Is 53.7.
93. Cf. Origen, *ComRom* 2.6.3 (FOTC 103,119).
94. Mt 21.22; Jn 14.14.
95. Cf. Origen, *In Matth.* 13.7.
96. 1 Cor 13.2; cf. Origen, *In Matth.* 13.7.
97. Cf. on Mt 13.31–32.

no believers have ever removed mountains, they did not even possess a little faith. For no great advantage comes from the removal of a mountain from one place to another, only the vain display that is sought in signs. But when that mountain is removed that is said by the prophet to corrupt the whole earth,[98] this brings very great advantage for everyone involved.

17.21. *"But this kind is not cast out except by prayer and fasting."* By showing us how a very wicked demon can be expelled, he instructs everyone for life.

17.22–23. *Now while they were together in Galilee, Jesus said to them: "The Son of man is to be betrayed into the hands of men, and they will kill him, and on the third day he will rise again." And they were exceedingly grieved.* He always mixes sadness in with the happy things, so that when the sad things come suddenly, they will not terrify the apostles, but will be endured by souls that have been prepared in advance. For if it saddens them that he is going to be killed, it ought to gladden them that it is said: He will be resurrected on the third day. Further, the fact that they are grieved, indeed exceedingly grieved, comes not from their lack of faith. For in any case they knew that Peter had been rebuked for having thought not the things of God but the things of men.[99] On the contrary, their grief comes from their love for their teacher. They cannot endure to hear anything evil or lowly about him.

17.24. *And when they came to Capernaum, those who were collecting the didrachma came to Peter, and said: "Does your Master not pay the didrachma?" And he said to them: "Yes."* After Caesar Augustus, Judea was made a tributary state, and everyone registered in the census was plundered for tax. This is why Joseph, with Mary his relative,[100] declared himself in Bethlehem. So here, tribute is once again demanded, since he had been raised in Nazareth, which is a village in Galilee adjacent to the city of Capernaum. And because of the greatness of the signs, those who exacted it do not dare to seek it from him directly, but they meet with his disciple. Or possibly, they are asking with malicious intent whether he pays tribute or whether he opposes the will of Cae-

---

98. Cf. Jer 51.25.
100. Cf. Lk 2.5.

99. Cf. Mt 16.23.

sar. This would agree with what we read in another passage: "Is it permitted to pay tribute to Caesar or not?"[101]

17.25. *And when he entered the house, Jesus anticipated him, saying.* Those who exacted the didrachma had met privately with Peter. Thus, after he entered the house, but before Peter could suggest anything, the Lord asks. He does not want the disciples to be scandalized at the demand for tribute, when they see that he knows what things had transpired in his absence.

17.25–26. *"How does it seem to you, Simon? The kings of the earth, from whom do they collect tribute or tax, from their own sons or from others?" And he said: "From others." Jesus said to him: "Then the sons are exempt."* Our Lord was the Son of a king, both according to the flesh and according to the spirit, both as one generated from the stock of David,[102] and as the Word of the Almighty Father.[103] Therefore, as a son of kings, he did not owe tribute, but he who had taken on the humility of flesh had to fulfill all justice.[104] But for the sake of us wretches, who are enrolled with the name of Christ and who do nothing worthy of such great majesty, he both endured the cross and paid the tribute for us. We do not pay tribute in return for his honor, and, as if we were the sons of a king, we are exempt from taxation.

17.27. *"Go to the sea and cast a hook and take the fish that comes up first. And when you open its mouth, you will find a stater. Take it and give it to them for me and you."* In this passage I do not know what I should admire first, the foreknowledge or the greatness of the Savior. He shows foreknowledge by knowing that the fish had a stater in its mouth and that it would be the first to be caught. He shows his greatness and power by the fact that at his word, a stater was immediately created in the mouth of the fish; and by speaking, he himself enacted what eventually happened. Now it seems to me that according to the mystical interpretation, this "first fish" that was captured represents what was in the depths of the sea and was lingering in the salty and bitter waves. Thus the first Adam was delivered through the second Adam.[105] And

---

101. Mk 12.14.
103. Cf. Jn 1.1, 14.
105. Cf. 1 Cor 15.45–49; Wis 10.1.

102. Cf. Rom 1.3.
104. Cf. Mt 3.15.

what was found in its mouth, that is, in its confession, was paid for Peter and for the Lord.[106] And it is beautifully said that a price is indeed given, but it is divided. For the price was paid for Peter, as for a sinner, but our Lord committed no sin, and no deceit was found in his mouth.[107] A stater is worth two didrachmas. Thus the likeness of flesh is shown,[108] seeing that both the Lord and his servant are delivered by the same price. But even the literal understanding edifies the hearer, namely, the point that the Lord was a man of such great poverty that he had no means of rendering the tribute for himself and the apostle. But if someone wants to object: But how is it that Judas carried money in a purse?[109] We will respond that [Judas] thought it a crime to convert for private use what was meant for the poor,[110] and likewise he set an example for us.[111]

Chapter 18

18.1. *At that hour the disciples came to Jesus, saying: "Who do you think is greatest in the kingdom of heaven?"* What I have often warned about should be observed here as well. Reasons need to be inquired into for each of the Lord's statements and deeds. What does this sudden question of the apostles mean to them, since it comes after the finding of the stater and the payment of the tribute? It says: "*At that hour* the disciples came to Jesus, saying: 'Who do you think is greatest in the kingdom of heaven?'" Here is my answer. They had seen that the same tribute was given for Peter and for the Lord. Because of the equality of price, they thought that Peter had been put ahead of all the apostles. For it was he who had been compared with the Lord in the payment of the tribute. Therefore, they ask who is the greatest in the kingdom of heaven. And when Jesus sees their thoughts and discerns the reasons for their error, he wants to heal their desire for glory by a competition for humility.

18.2. *And summoning a small child, Jesus set him in their midst.*

106. Cf. Origen, *fragm.* 373.   107. Cf. Is 53.9; 1 Pt 1.22.
108. Cf. Rom 8.3.   109. Cf. Jn 13.29.
110. Cf. Jn 12.6–7.   111. Cf. Jn 13.15.

He may have set a small child in their midst simply in order to make an inquiry about its age and to demonstrate an image of innocence;[112] or at least he did this to give them an example of humility, namely, that of himself, who had come not to be served but to serve.[113] Others[114] interpret the child as the Holy Spirit, whom he put into the hearts of the disciples that they might exchange their arrogance with humility.

18.3. *"Amen I say to you: Unless you are converted so that you become as little children, you will not enter into the kingdom of heaven."* The apostles are not being commanded to have the age of little children, but to possess their innocence by means of their own diligent effort, an innocence that children possess because of their years. Thus they become children not in respect to wisdom, but to malice.[115]

18.4. *"Therefore, whoever humbles himself as this little child, he is the greatest in the kingdom of heaven."* Just as this little child, whose example I offer to you, does not persist in wrath, does not remember injuries, is not enticed when it looks upon a beautiful woman, does not think one thing and say something else, so also you. For unless you have such innocence and purity of heart, you will not be able to enter the kingdom of heaven. Here is another interpretation: "Whoever humbles himself as this little child, he is greatest in the kingdom of heaven." That is to say, the one who imitates me and humbles himself through my example, so that he lowers himself as much as I have lowered myself when I "took the form of a servant,"[116] he will enter the kingdom of heaven.

18.5. *"And he who receives one such little child in my name receives me."* He who becomes the kind of person who imitates the humility and innocence of Christ, in him Christ is received. And he wisely added that they are not to be received on the basis of their own merit, but for the honor of their teacher. For otherwise, when this was made known to the apostles, they may have thought that they themselves had been honored.

18.6. *"But whoever scandalizes one of these little ones."* Note that

---

112. Cf. Hilary, *In Matth.* 18.1. 113. Cf. Mt 20.28.
114. Cf. Origen, *In Matth.* 13.18. 115. Cf. 1 Cor 14.20.
116. Cf. Phil 2.7.

the one who is scandalized is little. For the great do not receive stumbling blocks *(scandala)*.

18.6. *"It is better for him that a millstone be hung around his neck and he be drowned in the depths of the sea."* Although this could be a general judgment against all who scandalize anyone, yet in the context it can likewise be understood to be directed to the apostles. For when they asked about who was the greatest in the kingdom of heaven, they seemed to be competing for honor between themselves. Had they persisted in this vice, through their own stumbling block they could have caused the ruin of those whom they were calling to faith, when these others see apostles fighting about honor among themselves.[117] The words: "It is better that a millstone be hung around his neck" refer to a provincial custom among the Jews of old. This was the punishment for greater crimes: namely, people were drowned in the depths with a stone tied to them. Now the reason [he says] that it is better for him is because it is much better to receive a brief punishment for a crime than to be reserved for eternal torments.[118] "For the Lord will not avenge twice for the same thing."[119]

18.7. *"Woe to the world because of scandals. It is necessary that scandals come; nevertheless, woe to the man through whom scandal comes."* It is not that it is necessary that scandals come.[120] If this were the case, those who cause scandal would be without blame. Rather, he means that since it is necessary that there be scandals in this world, each one by his own fault is exposed to scandals. At the same time by this general judgment, he strikes down Judas, who had prepared his heart for the betrayal.

18.8–9. *"But if your hand or your foot is an occasion to sin for you,*[121] *cut it off and throw it from you,"* etc. To be sure, it is neces-

---

117. Cf. Rom 14.15, 20.   118. Cf. 2 Pt 2.9.

119. Cf. Na 1.9. The citation from Nahum is given according to the Old Latin version. In his *Commentary on Nahum* 1.9, Jerome uses both this form of the text and that found in the Vulgate: "There shall not rise a double affliction." This citation allows him to justify the severity of the chastisements of God in the OT: the flood, the destruction of Sodom and Gomorrah, etc. They are punished by God at the time in order to avoid eternal punishment.

120. Cf. Homily 35 on Ps 108 (109), in FOTC 48, 266; Homily 85, in FOTC 57, 196.

121. Lit., "scandalizes you" or "causes you to stumble" *(scandalizat te)*.

sary for scandals to come, but woe to that man who by his own fault brings into being through himself that which is necessary to be in the world. Therefore, every affection is cut off, all affinity is removed, lest by the pretext of piety each one is exposed to the scandals of believers. He is saying this. Suppose it is like this. Someone is attached to you like a hand, a foot, or an eye, who is useful, solicitous, and piercing in vision. Yet suppose this person causes a scandal for you, and, on account of the dissonance of morals, is dragging you down to hell. Well, it is better that you be deprived of the relationship with this person and these material advantages than, while you are seeking to gain friends and relatives,[122] you have a cause of destruction. And so, let not brother, wife, children, friends, or any affection that can exclude us from the kingdom of heaven be put before our love for the Lord.[123] Every believer knows what is harmful to himself and by what his heart can be stirred up and often tempted. It is better to lead a solitary life than on account of the necessities of the present life to lose eternal life.[124]

18.10. *"See to it that you do not despise one of these little ones. For I tell you that their angels always see the face of my Father who is in heaven."* Above he had said by [the metaphor of] hand and foot and eye that all relationships and connections that can cause scandal must be cut off. Consequently, he tempers the severity of this judgment with the command that he adds here: "See to it that you do not despise one of these little ones." Thus, he says, I command severity, that I might teach mildness commingled with it. For your part, do not despise them, but through [the achievement of] your salvation, seek their healing as well. But if you see them continuing in sins and serving the vices, it is better to be saved alone than to perish with many. "Because their angels in heaven always see the face of the Father." The worth of souls is so great that from birth each one has an angel assigned to him for his protection. This is why we read in the Apocalypse of John: To the angel of Ephesus,[125] of Thyatira,[126] and to the an-

122. Cf. Lk 16.9.

123. Cf. Lk 18.29. Cf. Origen, *In Matth.* 13.25.

124. This sounds very much like an autobiographical reflection. Cf. Jerome's *Ep.* 125.12 to Rusticus.

125. Cf. Rv 1.11; 2.1; 3.1.   126. Cf. Rv 2.18.

gel of Philadelphia,[127] and to the four angels of the rest of the churches, write these things. The apostle also commanded the heads of women to be covered in the churches on account of angels.[128]

18.12. *"How does it seem to you? If someone has a hundred sheep, and one of them goes astray, does he not leave the ninety-nine in the mountains and go in search of the one that has gone astray?"* It is natural that he exhorts mildness in those to whom he had previously said: "See to it that you do not despise one of these little ones." He adds the parable of the ninety-nine sheep left in the mountains and of the one stray that was unable to walk because of its great weakness. The good shepherd carried it back on his shoulders to the rest of the flock. Some[129] think that this shepherd is "he who while in the form of God did not think it robbery to be equal to God, but he emptied himself, taking the form of a slave, having become obedient to the Father, to the point of death, even death on a cross."[130] They think that the reason he came down to the earthly regions was to save the one little sheep that had perished, that is, the human race. But others[131] think that by the ninety-nine sheep the number of the just should be understood, and by the one little sheep we should understand the number of sinners. This accords with what he said in another passage: "I have not come to call the just but sinners; for the healthy do not need a physician, but those who are sick."[132] In the Gospel according to Luke, this parable is recorded along with two other parables, that of the ten drachmas and that of the two sons.[133]

18.14. *"Thus it is not the will of your Father who is in heaven that one of these little ones perish."* This applies to what was proposed higher up where he said: "See to it that you do not despise one of these little ones."[134] On the basis of those words, he teaches the parable that is set down here, that little ones should not be despised. Now in what he says: "It is not the will of your Father

---

127. Cf. Rv 3.7.   128. Cf. 1 Cor 11.19.

129. Cf. Hilary, *In Matth.* 18.6.   130. Phil 2.6–8.

131. This may be the interpretation of Didymus; cf. Ambrose, *In Luc.* 7.

132. Lk 5.32–33.   133. Cf. Lk 15.8–32.

134. Mt 18.10.

that one of these little ones perish," it is shown that whenever one of the little ones perishes, it was not by the Father's will that he perished.

18.15–17. *"But if your brother sins against you, go and correct him between you and him,"* etc. If our brother sins against us and injures us for any reason, we have the power, or rather the obligation, to forgive. For we are commanded to forgive debts for our debtors.[135] But if anyone sins against God, it no longer depends on our choice. For the Holy Scripture says: "If a man sins against a man, the priest will pray for him; but if he sins against God, who will pray for him?"[136] In contrast with this, we are mild about an injury to God, but annoyed to the point of hatred about insults to ourselves! Now our brother ought to be corrected privately. Otherwise, he may all at once lose his shame and modesty and continue in sin.[137] And if he in fact listens, we have gained his soul, and by the salvation of another we have achieved salvation for ourselves as well.[138] On the other hand, if he is unwilling to listen, a brother should be summoned. And if he does not listen to that one, even a third brother should be summoned. This is done either out of zeal for correcting him or for the purpose of meeting together with witnesses. Next, if he is unwilling to listen to them, then the matter must be told to many. In this way they formally renounce the one who could not be saved by shame, in the hope that he might be saved by their reproaches. Now when it is said: "Let him be to you as a pagan and a tax collector,"[139] it is shown that the one who has the name of believer but who does the works of unbelievers is more accursed than those who are openly Gentiles. For they are called "tax collectors" as a figure of speech *(tropologia)* referring to those who pursue worldly gain and collect taxes by means of business, fraud, theft, crimes, and perjury.

18.18. *"Amen I say to you: Whatever you bind on earth shall be bound also in heaven, and whatever you loose on earth shall be loosed also in heaven."* He had said: "But if he does not listen to the Church, let him be to you as a pagan and a tax collector."[140]

---

135. Cf. Mt 6.12.
137. Cf. Rom 6.1.
139. Mt 18.17.

136. 1 Sm 2.25.
138. Cf. Jas 5.20; 1 Tm 4.16.
140. Ibid.

Now the secret response or unspoken thought of this brother who despises [the Church] could be: Well, if you despise me, I also will despise you. If you condemn me, you too will be condemned by my sentence of judgment. Because of this possibility, Jesus gave authority to the apostles to ensure that those who are condemned by such measures may know that the human verdict is corroborated by a divine verdict, and whatever is bound on earth is equally bound in heaven.

18.19–20. *"Again I say to you that if two of you agree on earth about any matter, whatsoever they ask, it will be done for them by my Father who is in heaven. For where two or three are gathered in my name, there am I in their midst."* All the words above this exhort us to concord. Therefore, a reward is even promised that we might hasten toward peace more solicitously, since he says that he will be in the midst of the two or three. This accords with that [famous] example of the tyrant[141] who made prisoners of two men who were friends. One of them left his friend as a hostage in his place and went back to see his mother. By keeping the one man in prison while releasing the other, the tyrant wanted to test them. When the friend returned on the appointed day, the tyrant so admired the fidelity of both men that he begged them to enroll himself as the third partner in their friendship.[142] We can also interpret this spiritually, that where the spirit, soul, and body[143] agree and do not have a war of diverse wills between them, as the flesh lusts against the spirit and the spirit against the flesh,[144] concerning any matter that they ask, they will procure it from the Father. No one doubts that when the body wants to have the same things that the spirit wants, it is a request for good things.[145]

18.21–22. *Then Peter came to him and said: "Lord, how often shall*

141. In Greek and Roman history, the term "tyrant" did not necessarily reflect negatively on the moral character of the individual, but referred to rulers who came to power through abnormal means, rather than through the lawful political process. In the case of Dionysius, however, we are dealing with a tyrant in the modern sense of the word.

142. This story concerns the friendship of Damon and Phintias, who showed this affection for each other when they had been imprisoned and condemned to death by the tyrant Dionysius. Cf. Cicero, *De officiis* 3.45; *Tusc* 5.63. A variant of the story is recorded in Iamblichus, *Life of Pythagoras* 33.

143. Cf. 1 Thes 5.23.   144. Cf. Gal 5.17.

145. Cf. Origen, *In Matth.* 14.3.

my brother sin against me and I forgive him? Up to seven times?" etc. The Lord's words are rooted in each other like a triple rope that cannot be broken.[146] Above he had said: "See to it that you do not despise one of these little ones."[147] Then he added: "If your brother sins against you, go and correct him between you and him."[148] He also promised a reward saying: "If two of you agree on earth about any matter," they will procure what they have asked for,[149] and "I will be in their midst."[150] Challenged by these words, the apostle Peter asks how often he should forgive his brother who sins against him. He offers an opinion along with his question: "Up to seven times?" Jesus responded to him: "Not seven times, but seventy times seven," that is, four hundred ninety times. Thus the sinning brother cannot sin as many times in a day as Peter should forgive him.[151]

18.23. *"Therefore, the kingdom of heaven is likened to a man who is a king who wanted to settle accounts with his servants."* It is customary in Syria, and even more so in Palestine, to join parables to all of one's words. In this way, by comparisons and examples, hearers can grasp what cannot be grasped by simple commands. And so, he has given a command to Peter by means of this comparison to a king, a master, and a slave who owes ten thousand talents. The slave procures a pardon from his master when he asks for it, that he too might forgive his fellow servants when they sin in lesser amounts. For if that king and lord so easily forgave his slave who owed ten thousand talents, how much more ought slaves forgive lesser amounts to their fellow slaves? Let me try to make this clearer by an example: Suppose one of us commits adultery, murder, blasphemy, and greater crimes of ten thousand talents. Those who ask are forgiven, if they themselves forgive lesser amounts to those who sin. But if we refuse to be appeased for an insult that has been made, and if we have continual discord because of a word spoken too bitterly, does it not seem right that we should be led back to prison and that, based on the example of our conduct, no pardon should be granted to us for our great transgressions?

146. Cf. Eccl 4.12. 147. Mt 18.10.
148. Mt 18.15. 149. Mt 18.19.
150. Mt 18.20.
151. Cf. Homily 41 on Ps 119 (120) in FOTC 48, 313.

18.24. *"One was brought to him who owed ten thousand talents."* I know that some[152] interpret that man who owed ten thousand talents to be the devil. They think that the selling of his wife and children, as he persevered in malice, refers to his folly and evil thoughts. For just as wisdom is called the wife of a just man,[153] so folly is called the wife of the unjust and the sinner.[154] But how is it that the Lord forgives him ten thousand talents and he refused to forgive us, his fellow servants, one hundred denarii? This is no ecclesiastical interpretation, nor is it one that should be received by prudent men.

18.25. *"So also my heavenly Father will do to you, if each of you does not forgive your brother from your heart."* It is an alarming sentence of judgment, if God's verdict is changed and altered on the basis of our attitude of mind. If we do not forgive our brothers trivial things, God will not forgive us great things. And since anyone could say: "I have nothing against him; he himself knows it; he has God as his judge; it does not matter to me; whatever he wants to do, I pardon it"; he confirms his own verdict and undermines all pretense of a feigned peace by saying: "If each of you does not forgive your brother from your heart."

Chapter 19

19.3. *And the Pharisees came to him, testing him and saying: "Is it lawful for a man to divorce his wife for any cause?"* He had come from Galilee to Judea. That is why the sect of the Pharisees and scribes asks him whether it is lawful for a man to divorce his wife for any cause. They want to catch him between the horns of a dilemma, as the saying goes.[155] Whatever he responds will expose him to a quibble. If he says that a wife ought to be divorced for any cause and another can be married, this preacher of chastity will seem to be teaching contradictions. But if he responds that for no cause should she be divorced, he will be held guilty of

---

152. Cf. Origen, *In Matth.* 14.10.   153. Cf. Prv 4.5–9.

154. Cf. Prv 7.6–27.

155. For the expression "horns of a dilemma" (*cornuato syllogismo*), cf. Jerome's *Ep.* 69.2 to Oceanus.

blasphemy and as acting contrary to the doctrine of Moses, and, through Moses, to that of God. Therefore, the Lord tempers his response in such a way that he evades the trap. He cites Holy Scripture as testimony and opposes natural law and God's first sentence of judgment to the second judgment that was conceded not by the will of God but as a necessity for those who sin.

19.4. *"Have you not read that he who made them from the beginning made male and female?"* This is written at the beginning of Genesis.[156] Now by saying "male and female," he shows that second marriages should be avoided. For he does not say: male and *females*, which were demanded from the repudiation of the former ones, but "male and *female*," in order to link partnerships together by a single marriage.[157]

19.5. *"For this reason a man leaves father and mother and will cleave to his wife."* In a similar way,[158] he says: "he will cleave to his *wife*," not *wives*.

19.5. *"And the two will be in one flesh."* The reward of marriage is the making of one flesh out of two. Chastity, when united with the Spirit, makes one spirit.[159]

19.6. *"Therefore, what God has joined together let no man separate."* God has joined them together by making one flesh of the man and woman. Man cannot separate this flesh, only perhaps God alone. Man separates it when, out of the desire for a second wife, we divorce the first one. God separates the one he had also joined together when, by consent and on account of service to God, since the time is short, we have wives in such a way as though not having them.[160]

19.7. *They say to him: "Why then did Moses command a bill of divorce to be given and to divorce?"* They betray the calumny that they had been preparing. And surely the Lord had not brought forth his own opinion, but he had recalled ancient history and the commands of God.

---

156. Cf. Gn 1.27.

157. For a detailed treatment of celibacy, continence, and remarriage in the early Church, see F. Cochini, *The Apostolic Origins of Priestly Celibacy* (San Francisco: Ignatius, 1981).

158. See under Mt 19.4.   159. Cf. 1 Cor 6.16–17.

160. Cf. 1 Cor 7.5, 29.

19.8. *He said to them: "Moses permitted you to divorce your wives*[161] *in view of the hardness of your heart; but from the beginning it was not so."* What he means to say is this: Is God able to contradict himself? Does he first command one thing and then break his own judgment by a new command? One must not understand things in this way. Rather, when Moses saw that, on account of the desire for second marriages to women who were richer, younger, or prettier, the first wives were either killed or were leading an evil life, he preferred to grant the discord than to allow hatred and murder to continue. At the same time, consider what he did not say: "On account of hardness of your heart, *God* permitted you." Rather he says: "Moses." This is in agreement with the apostle, [who says] that it is a counsel of man, not a command of God.[162]

19.9. *"But I say to you that whoever divorces his wife, except on account of fornication, and marries another, commits adultery; and whoever marries a divorced woman commits adultery."* It is fornication alone that conquers the affection for one's wife. Indeed, the "one flesh" he has with his wife, he shares with another woman. By fornication she separates herself from her husband. She should not be held, lest she cause her husband to be cursed too, since the Scripture says: "He who holds an adulteress is foolish and impious."[163] Therefore, whenever there is fornication and suspicion of fornication, a wife is freely divorced. And since it could have happened that someone brought a false charge against an innocent person, and on account of the second marriage-union hurled a charge at the first wife, it is commanded to divorce the first wife in such a way that he has no second wife while the first one is living. For he says the following: If you divorce your wife not on account of lust, but on account of an injury, why after the experience of the first unhappy marriage do you admit yourself into the danger of a new one? And besides, it could have come to pass that according to the same law, the wife too would have given a bill of divorce to the husband. And so by the same precaution, it is commanded that she not receive a second husband. And since a prostitute and she who had once been an adulteress were not afraid of reproach, the second hus-

---

161. Cf. Dt 24.6.   162. Cf. 1 Cor 7.6.
163. Prv 18.22.

band is commanded that if he marries such a woman, he will be under the charge of adultery.

19.10. *The disciples said to him: "If the case between a man and wife is like this, it is not expedient to marry."* The burden of having wives is a heavy one, if, with the exception of the cause of fornication, it is not lawful to divorce them. What then? Should a woman be retained who is given to drinking, who is wrathful or of evil character, who is luxurious, gluttonous, unfaithful, a nag, and an evil speaker? Whether we want her or do not want her, she has to be endured. For when we were free, we voluntarily subjected ourselves to servitude. Therefore, the apostles, when they see that wives are a heavy yoke to bear, express the inclination of their heart and say: "If the case between a man and wife is like this, it is not expedient to marry."

19.11. *He said: "Not all receive these words, but those to whom it is given."* Let no one think that by these words he is introducing the doctrine of fate or chance and is saying that they are virgins to whom it is given by God, or whom some sort of chance led to this state. On the contrary, it is given to those who ask, who have willed it, who have expended effort to receive it. For to everyone who asks, it will be given; and the one who seeks will find; and to the one who knocks, it will be opened.[164]

19.12. *"For there are eunuchs who were born so from their mother's womb, and there are eunuchs who were made so by men, and there are eunuchs who have made themselves eunuchs*[165] *for the kingdom of heaven. He who can receive it, let him receive it."* There are three kinds of eunuchs, two fleshly and the third spiritual.[166] There are some who are born so from their mother's womb, others whom either captivity or womanish pleasures make them so. There is a third kind "who have made themselves eunuchs[167] for the kingdom of heaven" and who, though they could be men, become eunuchs for Christ. To these a reward is promised, but to the former types, for whom there is compulsion to chastity, not the will for it, nothing is owed at all. We can explain this in another way:

---

164. Cf. Mt 7.8; Lk 11.10.
165. Lit., "castrated themselves" (*se ipsos castraverunt*).
166. Cf. Origen, *In Matth.* 15.4. See also Jerome's *Ep.* 22.19 to Eustochium.
167. See n. 165 above.

There are eunuchs from their mother's womb who are of a rather frigid nature and not inclined to lust. There are others who become so by men: either philosophers make them so, or they are softened into females on account of the worship of idols, or they feign chastity out of a heretical conviction, in order that they might falsely claim the truth of religion.[168] But none of them attains to the kingdom of heaven, only those who have made themselves eunuchs for Christ. This is why he adds: "He who can receive it, let him receive it." Thus each one should consider his strength to see whether he can fulfill the precepts of virginity and chastity. For in itself chastity is alluring, and it entices anyone to itself. But our strength needs to be taken into consideration, so that "he who can receive it, let him receive it." The voice of the Lord is, as it were, exhorting and stirring up his soldiers to the prize of chastity: "He who can receive it, let him receive it." That is, he who can fight, let him fight, let him conquer, and let him triumph.

19.13. *Then little children were presented to him that he might lay hands on them and pray; but the disciples rebuked them.* It is not that they did not want the children to be blessed by the hand and voice of the Savior, but that, since they did not yet have the fullness of faith, they thought that he who was in the likeness of men[169] was exhausted by the importunity of those who were presenting them.

19.14. *"Let the little children come to me and do not hinder them; for of such is the kingdom of heaven."* He has expressly said: "of such," not "of these," in order to show that it is not the age but the conduct that is the supreme thing. To those who have an innocence and simplicity that is similar [to that of children], a reward is promised. The apostle, too, is consistent in the same opinion: "Brothers, do not be children in your minds, but be little children in respect to malice; but in your thinking you should be perfect."[170]

---

168. Epiphanius, *Panarion, Haer.* 67, said that the Encratites abstained from certain foods not for the sake of continence or piety, but from fear and for appearance' sake. He also noted that the Ebionites once took pride in virginity. Cf. *Panarion, Haer.* 30.2.6.

169. Cf. Phil 2.7.   170. 1 Cor 14.20.

19.16. *Behold, one came and said to him: "Good master, what good should I do to have eternal life?"* This man who is asking how to attain eternal life is young, rich, and haughty, and, according to another evangelist,[171] he does not ask with the expectation of a learner but as a tempter.

19.17. *"Why do you ask me about the good? One is good, God."* Since he had called the master good and had not confessed him to be God or the Son of God, he learns that, however holy a man is, in comparison with God he is not good, of whom it is said: "Confess to the Lord, for he is good."[172] But lest anyone think that because God is called good, the Son of God is excluded from goodness, let us read in another passage: "The good shepherd lays his life down for his sheep";[173] and in the prophet the Spirit is called good and the earth is called good.[174] Therefore, the Savior is not refusing a testimony of goodness, but he excludes the error of his being a teacher who is independent of God.

19.17–19. *"If you want to enter into life, keep the commands."* He *said to him: "Which ones?" But Jesus said: "You shall not murder, you shall not commit adultery,"* etc., *"and you shall love your neighbor as yourself."* We can prove that this young man is a tempter even from the fact that when the Lord says to him: "If you want to enter into life, keep the commands," he is dishonest and asks once again: What are these commands? It is as though he himself has not read them, or as though the Lord [Jesus] could command things contrary to God.

19.20. *The young man said to him: "I have kept all these things; what still do I lack?"* The young man is lying. For if he had fulfilled in deed what is recorded among the commandments: "You shall love your neighbor as yourself," why is it that when he later hears: "Go, sell what you have and give to the poor," he went away sad, since he had "many possessions"?

19.21. *Jesus said to him: "If you want to be perfect, go, sell what you have and give to the poor, and you will have treasure in heaven, and come, follow me."* It is in our power whether we want to be per-

---

171. Cf. Lk 10.25.   172. Ps 118.1.
173. Jn 10.11. Cf. Homily 53 on Ps 142 (143) in FOTC 48, 379.
174. Cf. Ps 143.10; Ezek 17.8.

fect. Yet whoever wants to be perfect ought to sell what he has and sell not merely a part of it, as Ananias and Sapphira did,[175] but sell everything. And when he has sold it he must give everything to the poor. In this way he prepares for himself a treasure in the kingdom of heaven. Nor is this sufficient for perfection, unless, after wealth has been despised, one follows the Savior. That is to say, when the evils have been forsaken, one must do good things. For a wallet is more easily despised than the will. Many who abandon wealth do not follow the Lord.[176] But he follows the Lord who is his imitator and walks in his footsteps. For "whoever claims to believe in Christ ought to walk just as he walked."[177]

19.22. *He went away sad, for he had many possessions.* This is the sadness that leads to death.[178] The cause of his sadness is also recorded, that he had many possessions. There are the thorns and thistles that choked the Lord's seed.[179]

19.23. *But Jesus said to his disciples: "Amen I say to you that it is difficult for a rich man to enter the kingdom of heaven."* But how did the rich men Abraham, Isaac, and Jacob[180] enter the kingdom of heaven? And in this Gospel, how is it that Matthew and Zacchaeus are commended by the Lord's testimony when they abandoned their wealth?[181] Well, one should consider that at the time when they entered, they had ceased being rich. Therefore, they will not enter as long as they are rich. And yet, since riches are despised with difficulty, he did not say: It is *impossible* for the rich to enter the kingdom of heaven, but it is *difficult.* Where difficulty is recorded, he is not alleging an impossibility, but pointing out a rarity.

19.24–26. *"And again I say to you: It is easier for a camel to pass through the eye of a needle than for a rich man to enter into the kingdom of heaven."* By this saying it is shown to be not difficult but

175. Cf. Acts 5.1–10.
176. As for example the philosopher Crates. See below at Mt 19.28.
177. 1 Jn 2.6.
178. Cf. 2 Cor 7.10. Cf. Origen, *In Matth.* 15.19.
179. Cf. Mt 13.22.
180. Cf. Gn 13.2; 26.13–14; 36.9.
181. Cf. Mt 9.9; Lk 19.8. Cf. Homily 16 on Ps 83 (84), in FOTC 48, 119; *Epp.* 79.4; 145.

impossible. For if, in the same way that a camel cannot pass through the eye of a needle, so a rich man cannot enter into the kingdom of heaven, then no rich man will be saved. But if we read Isaiah, how camels of Midian and Ephah come to Jerusalem with gifts and offerings,[182] and those that were previously bent and distorted by the depravity of vices entered the gates of Jerusalem, we will see how even these camels to which the rich are compared, when they have laid aside their heavy burden of sins and the crookedness of their whole body, they can enter through the narrow and strait road that leads to life.[183] Now when the disciples ask about this and marvel at the severity of these words, [they say]: "Who then will be saved?" His clemency has tempered the severity of the judgment by saying: "Things that are impossible with men are possible with God."

19.27. *Then Peter responded and said to him: "Behold, we have left everything and have followed you; what then will there be for us?"* This is great confidence. Peter was a fisherman; he was not a rich man. He sought his food by hand and skill, and yet he speaks confidently: "We have left everything." And because it is not sufficient merely "to leave," he adds what is perfect: "and we have followed you." We have done what you commanded; what reward then will you give to us?

19.28. *And Jesus said to them: "Amen I say to you that you who have followed me, in the regeneration when the Son of man sits on the throne of his majesty, you will sit on twelve thrones judging the twelve tribes of Israel."* He did not say: You who have left everything, for even Crates[184] the philosopher did this, and many others have despised wealth, but "you who have followed me." This is a thing proper to apostles and believers. "In the regeneration when the Son of man sits on the throne of his majesty," when they rise from the dead, incorrupt from corruption,[185] you too

---

182. Cf. Is 60.6.

183. Cf. Mt 7.14.

184. Crates of Thebes (ca. 368–285 B.C.) was a Cynic philosopher and poet who went to Athens as a young man, became a follower of Diogenes, and gave his wealth to the poor. The majority of copyists through ignorance have corrected Jerome's text to read "Socrates" instead of Crates. But Jerome is still following Origen, who also reports the example of Crates. Cf. Origen, *In Matth.* 15.15.

185. Cf. 1 Cor 15.52.

will sit on judges' thrones, condemning the twelve tribes of Israel. For they were unwilling to believe, while you have believed.

19.29–30. *"And every one who has left home or brothers or sisters or father or mother or wife or children or fields for my name's sake will receive a hundredfold and will possess eternal life. But many that are first shall be last and the last shall be first. "* This passage agrees with that judgment in which the Savior says: "I have not come to send peace but a sword; for I have come to separate a man from his father and a mother from her daughter and a daughter-in-law from her mother-in-law, and a man's enemies will be the members of his own household."[186] Therefore, those who for the sake of faith in Christ and the proclamation of the Gospel have despised all affections and wealth and the pleasures of the world, they "will receive a hundredfold and will possess eternal life." Using this sentence as a pretext, some introduce the "thousand years" after the resurrection. They claim that at that time a hundredfold of all the things that we have given up is going to be given back to us, as well as eternal life. They do not understand that if the promise applies to these other things, then moral disgrace would arise in connection with wives. Thus the one who gave up one wife for the Lord's sake would receive a hundred of them in the future.[187] The meaning, then, is this: He who has given up material things for the Savior's sake will receive spiritual things, which in comparison and worth will be just as if the number one hundred is compared with a small number. This is why the apostle, who had given up merely one house and small fields in a single province,[188] says: "As having nothing and possessing everything."[189]

Chapter 20

20.1–2. *"The kingdom of heaven is like a householder who went out early in the morning to hire workers for his vineyard. After agreeing with the workers for a denarius a day, he sent them into his vineyard. "* This parable or similitude of the kingdom of heaven is under-

---

186. Mt 10.34–36.
188. Source?

187. On chiliasm see Introduction.
189. 2 Cor 6.10.

stood from the things that have been said previously.[190] For before this the following is written: "Many that are first shall be last, and the last shall be first,"[191] where the Lord is describing not the timing but their faith. And he says that the householder went out early in the morning to hire workers for his vineyard. He established the wage of a denarius for the work. Then, when he went out at around the third hour, he saw others standing in the marketplace idle, and for these he had promised not a denarius, but "what is just." And at the sixth hour and at the ninth he did likewise. But at the eleventh hour he found others standing around who had been idle the entire day, and he sent them into his vineyard. But when evening came, he commanded his steward to begin to pay from the last, that is, beginning with the workers of the eleventh hour and proceeding to the workers of the first hour. And everyone equally was roused by ill will against the last ones, and they accused the householder of injustice, not because they had received less than what had been agreed on, but because they wanted to receive more than those on whom the clemency of the contractor had poured forth. It seems to me[192] that the workers of the first hour are Samuel, Jeremiah, and John the Baptist, who can say with the Psalmist: "From my mother's womb you are my God."[193] But the workers of the third hour are those who began to serve God from adolescence.[194] The ones of the sixth hour are those who took up Christ's yoke at a mature age.[195] Those of the ninth hour are the ones who are already declining with the feebleness of age. Finally, those of the eleventh hour are the ones who are extremely old. And yet, all equally receive the wage, though their labor varied. There are those who have explained this parable in a different way.[196] They want the meaning to be that at the first

190. Cf. Origen, *In Matth.* 15.28.

191. Mt 19.30.

192. Jerome's interpretation, which applies the hours of the parable to the ages of life, is traditional. Cf. Hilary, *In Ps.* 129 (PL 9: 724B); Origen, *In Matth.* 15.36.

193. Ps 22.10. Cf. 1 Sm 1.11, 28; Jer 1.5; Lk 1.15.

194. Cf. Origen, *In Matth.* 15.32; Hilary, *In Matth.* 20.6.

195. Cf. Mt 11.29.

196. Jerome's alternate interpretation, in which he applies the hours of the

hour Adam and the rest of the patriarchs until Noah were sent into the vineyard. At the third hour Noah is sent [and the others] down to Abraham and the circumcision given to him. The sixth hour goes from Abraham to Moses when the Law was given. At the ninth hour, Moses is sent, and the prophets. At the eleventh hour, the apostles are sent and the people of the Gentiles, and everyone is envious of them.[197] Because the evangelist John understands this very thing, after the eleventh hour had passed, when the sun had nearly set and it was toward evening, he says: "My little children, it is the last hour."[198] And at the same time, consider this: with regard to the workers of the eleventh hour, everyone equally accuses the householder of injustice. Yet they do not understand their own treatment to be unjust. For if the householder is unjust, he is not unjust toward one but toward all, since the worker of the third hour did not labor in such a way as the one who was sent into the vineyard at the first hour. Similarly, the worker of the sixth hour labored less than the worker of the third hour, and the worker of the ninth hour less than the worker of the sixth. And so, every calling is envious of the Gentiles behind them and is tormented by the grace of the Gospel. This is why the Savior concludes the parable by saying: "The first shall be last, and the last first." For the Jews have turned from the head into the tail, and we are changed from the tail into the head.[199]

20.13. *"Friend, I am doing you no wrong."* I have read in someone's book[200] that this friend who is rebuked by the householder, the worker of the first hour, is understood as the first-formed man[201] and those who believed at that time.

20.13. *"Did you not agree with me for a denarius?"* A denarius has the figure of the ruler on it. Therefore, you have received the wage that I had promised to you, that is, my image and like-

---

parable to the ages of the history of the world, is equally traditional. In his own *In Michaeam* 4 (PL 25: 1186B) he applies the eleventh hour to the coming of the Messiah, making use of the same text from John's First Epistle. Cf. Hilary, *In Matth.* 20.6 (PL 9: 1059C); Origen, *In Matth.* 15.32; and Jerome, *Ep.* 21.40–41 to Damasus.

197. Cf. Rom 10.19; 11.11, 14.   198. 1 Jn 2.8.
199. Cf. Dt 28.44.   200. Cf. Origen, *In Matth.* 15.35.
201. Cf. Wis 7.1; 10.1.

ness. Why do you seek more? And yet, it is not so much that you desire to receive more yourself, but that another should receive nothing, as though the merit of your reward is diminished by the participation of another.

20.14. *"Take what is yours and go."* Under the Law, a Jew is saved not by grace but by conduct. For "the one who does it will live in these things."[202] This is why it is said to him:

20.15–16. *"Or is your eye evil because I am good?"* The parable in Luke harmonizes with this, when the elder son is envious of the younger one and does not want him to be received as a penitent and accuses the father of injustice.[203] And that we might know that what we have said is the sense, the heading and the conclusion of this parable agree. "Thus," he says, "the last shall be first, and the first last; for many are called but few are chosen."[204]

20.17–19. *And as Jesus was going up to Jerusalem, he took his twelve disciples aside and said to them: "Behold, we are going up to Jerusalem, and the Son of man will be handed over to the rulers of the elders and to the scribes, and they will condemn him to death, and they will hand him over to the Gentiles to be mocked and scourged and crucified, and on the third day he will rise again."* He had said this very thing frequently to the disciples, but what they had heard was able to slip from their memory, since many things had been discussed in the meantime. Thus when he is about to go to Jerusalem, leading the apostles with him, he prepares them to be tested, lest when the persecution comes they be scandalized by the disgrace of the cross.

20.20–21. *Then the mother of the sons of Zebedee came to him with her sons, adoring and asking something from him. He said to her: "What do you want?" She said to him: "Say that these two sons of mine may sit, one at your right and one at your left, in your kingdom."* What is the source of the opinion about the kingdom that the mother of the sons of Zebedee has? For the Lord had said: "The Son of man will be handed over to the rulers of the priests[205] and to the

---

202. Cf. Rom 10.5; Lv 18.5.   203. Cf. Lk 15.28–30.

204. Jerome's eye seems to have skipped down to Mt 22.14, which he links with Mt 20.16.

205. "Rulers of the priests": *principibus sacerdotum*. Notice that the lemma in Mt 20.17–19 reads "rulers of the elders" (*principibus seniorum*).

scribes, and they will condemn him to death, and they will hand him over to the Gentiles to be mocked and scourged and crucified." Moreover, he had announced the disgrace of his Passion to the disciples when they were afraid.[206] Yet she demands the glory of the triumphant one? I think that it was for the following reason: after everything else, the Lord had said: "And on the third day he will rise again." Thus the woman thought that immediately after the Resurrection he would begin his reign, and what was promised for the second advent would be fulfilled at the first. And with a feminine eagerness she longs for the presence of what she has forgotten belongs to the future. Now what the Lord asks in response to this woman's request: "What do you want?" did not spring from ignorance, but it is said under the persona of him who was to be scourged and crucified. In a similar way he said to the hemorrhaging woman: "Who touched me?"[207] and with reference to Lazarus: "Where have you placed him?"[208] Even in the Old Testament [the Lord says]: "Adam, where are you?"[209] and: "I will go down and see whether they are acting in accord with the outcry against them which has come to me, or whether it be not so, that I might know."[210] But the mother of the sons of Zebedee asks this by a womanish error springing from a feeling of piety. She did not know what she was asking. It is not surprising that she is convicted of ignorance. For it was said of Peter, when he wanted to make the three tabernacles: "not knowing what he was saying."[211]

20.22. *And Jesus answered and said: "You do not know what you are asking."*[212] The mother asks, and the Lord speaks to the disciples, for he understands that her prayers come from the will of the sons.

20.22. *"Can you drink the cup that I am going to drink?"* In the Holy Scriptures we understand the cup to refer to the Passion:[213] "Father, if it is possible, let this cup pass from me";[214] and in the

206. Cf. Mk 10.32.
207. Lk 8.45.
208. Jn 11.34.
209. Gn 3.9.
210. Gn 18.21.
211. Mk 9.6; cf. Mt 17.4.
212. Plural in the Latin: *Nescitis quid petatis.*
213. Cf. Origen, *In Matth.* 16.6; Jerome, Homily 40 on Ps 115 (116B) in FOTC 48, 296.
214. Mt 26.39.

Psalm: "What shall I give back to the Lord for all that he has given to me? I will take up the cup of salvation and call upon the name of the Lord."[215] And immediately the Psalmist reports what this cup is: "Precious in the sight of the Lord is the death of his saints."[216]

20.23. *He said to them: "You will indeed drink my cup, but to sit at my right and at my left is not mine to give to you, but to those for whom it has been prepared by my Father."* People ask how the sons of Zebedee, namely, James and John, drank the cup of martyrdom, when the Scripture narrates that James alone of the apostles was beheaded by Herod,[217] but that John, on the other hand, ended his life by natural death.[218] But the ecclesiastical histories we read report that John too, for the sake of martyrdom, was put into a cauldron of boiling oil.[219] After that the athlete of Christ proceeded to take up the crown when he was immediately packed off to the island of Patmos.[220] Thus we see that his heart did not fall short of martyrdom, and that John drank the cup of the confession. The three youths in the fiery furnace also drank from this cup, even though their persecutor did not shed their blood.[221] Now, as for what he says: "to sit at my right and left is not mine to give to you, but to those for whom it has been prepared by my Father," this should be understood in the following manner: the kingdom of heaven does not belong to the one giving but the one receiving, "for there is no receiving of persons with God."[222] But whoever behaves in such a way that he becomes worthy of the kingdom of heaven[223] will receive what has been prepared,[224] not for particular persons but for a particular kind of life.[225] And so, if you merit to attain to the king-

215. Ps 116.12–13.

216. Ps 116.15.

217. Cf. Acts 12.2. Cf. Origen, *In Matth.* 16.6.

218. Cf. Jn 21.23.

219. Cf. Tertullian, *De praescript.* 36.3 (ANF 3.260).

220. Cf. Rv 1.9; Eusebius, *HE* 3.18.

221. Cf. Dn 3.23. Jerome's view seems to derive from Origen, *In Matth.* 16.6, for whom the martyrdom of John predicted by Christ is his exile to Patmos.

222. Acts 10.34.   223. Cf. 2 Thes 1.5.

224. Cf. Mt 25.34.

225. Cf. *In Sophoniam* 3.1; *Ep.* 79.1; *Contra Jo. Hier.* 44.

dom of heaven,[226] which my Father has prepared for the triumphant victors,[227] you too will receive it. Others[228] want this saying to refer to Moses and Elijah. A little earlier the disciples had seen them speaking with him on the mountain.[229] But this hardly seems right to me. For the reason he does not name those who are to sit down in the kingdom of heaven is to prevent the others from thinking that they have been excluded because of the few who had been named.

20.24. *And when the ten heard it, they were indignant at the two brothers.* The ten apostles are not indignant at the mother of the sons of Zebedee, nor do they refer the audacity of the request to the woman. Instead, they refer it to the sons, because in their ignorance of their own stature, they were inflamed by immoderate ambition. Even the Lord had said to them: "You[230] do not know what you are asking." Now this is what is additionally understood here, both from the Lord's response and from the indignation of the other apostles: It was the sons who had sent their mother to make this grandiose request.

20.25. *But Jesus called them to himself and said: "You know that the rulers of the Gentiles lord it over them,"* etc. The humble and meek Master neither convicts the two who made a request that sprang from immoderate ambition nor rebukes the remaining ten for their indignation and jealousy. Instead, he offers an example to teach them that the greatest is the one who becomes least, and he who is the slave of all is the one who becomes lord. In vain, therefore, had the two brothers sought things that were beyond their measure, and in vain do the others grieve over their desire to be greatest. For one comes to the summit of virtue not by power but by humility. Finally, he sets forth the example of himself, so that those who may think little of his words will be ashamed when they see his actions. He says:

20.28. *"Just as the Son of man did not come to be served but to serve."* Note what we have frequently said,[231] that he who serves is called the Son of man. "And to give his life as a redemption

---

226. Cf. Lk 20.35.   227. Cf. Rv 2.7, 17, 26; 3.5.
228. Cf. Hilary, *In Matth.* 20.10.   229. Cf. Mt 17.3.
230. This is plural in the Latin; see n. 212 above.
231. Cf. Mt 16.27, 28; 17.9, 22–23; 20.20–21.

for many." This took place when he took the form of a slave that he might pour out his blood for the world.[232] And he did not say "to give his life as a redemption" for all, but "for many," that is, for those who wanted to believe.

20.29–31. *And when they went out from Jericho, a great crowd followed him. And behold, two blind men sitting by the wayside heard that Jesus was passing by, and they cried out, saying: "Lord, have mercy on us, son of David." But the crowd rebuked them, that they should be quiet. But they cried out all the more saying: "Lord, have mercy on us, son of David."* There were many thieves in Jericho who went out and descended from Jerusalem and were accustomed to kill and wound. This is why the Lord went to Jericho with his disciples. He wanted to deliver those who had been wounded[233] and to draw a great crowd with him.[234] Finally, when he wanted to go out from Jericho, a great crowd followed him. If he had remained in Jerusalem and had not descended to the lowly places, the crowd would have sat in darkness[235] and in the shadow of death[236] until today. Now, [it also says] that the two blind men were by the wayside. He is calling those "blind" who were not yet able to say: "In your light we will see light."[237] He says: "by the wayside"[238] because while they seemed to have knowledge of the Law, they were ignorant of the Way[239] that is Christ.[240] Now very many[241] understand them to represent the Pharisees and Sadducees. Others[242] think that they stand for the two peoples, the one of the Old Testament and that of the New. For both were blind, the one by following written law, the other by following natural law without Christ. Since they were not able to see by themselves, they heard the Savior's proclamation and confessed him to be the son of David. On the other hand, if both blind men are referred to the people of the Jews, the words that follow: "the crowd was rebuking them," should be understood

---

232. Cf. Phil 2.7; 1 Jn 2.2. Cf. Origen, *In Matth.* 16.8.
233. Cf. Ps 107.13.   234. Cf. Jn 12.32.
235. Cf. Is 9.2.   236. Cf. Ps 107.14; Ps 23.4; Lk 1.79.
237. Ps 36.9. Cf. Origen, *In Matth.* 16.10.
238. Lat., *secus viam.*   239. Lat., *viam.*
240. Cf. Jn 14.6. Cf. Origen, *In Matth.* 16.10.
241. Who?   242. Who?

about the pagans, whom the apostle admonishes not to boast and vaunt themselves arrogantly over their root. For since they themselves were inserted from a wild olive tree into a good olive tree, due to the error of the first people, by no means should they be envious about the salvation of the first people.[243]

20.31. *"Have mercy on us, son of David."* Though rebuked by the crowds, they refuse to be silent, but they repeat their cry with greater frequency, that they might show their full desire for the true light.

20.32. *Jesus stopped and called them and said.* They were blind; they did not know where they were going; they were incapable of following the Savior. In Jericho there are many pitfalls, many cliffs and precipices that fall into bottomless depths. For that reason the Lord stops, so that they may be able to come. He orders them to be called and prevents the crowd from hindering them. He asks them, as though ignorant, about what they want, so that from the response of the blind men their weakness may be made manifest and his power will be recognized from the healing.

20.34. *But Jesus had pity on them and touched their eyes, and immediately they saw and followed him.* He touches their eyes. The Creator[244] supplies what nature had not given, or at least, what an infirmity had taken away, mercy freely gives. And at once "they saw and followed him." Those who previously sat shriveled up in Jericho, who knew only how to shout, afterward follow Jesus, not so much with their feet as with their virtues.

Chapter 21

21.1–3. *And when they had drawn near to Jerusalem and had come to Bethphage at the Mount of Olives, then Jesus sent two disciples, saying to them: "Go into the village that is opposite you, and at once you will find a donkey tied up and a colt with it. Untie them and bring them to me, and if anyone says anything to you, say that the Lord has need of them, and immediately he will let them go."* He departs

---

243. Cf. Rom 11.18.
244. Lat., *artifex.*

from Jericho, leading forth huge crowds. And after healing the blind men, he draws near to Jerusalem, having been enriched by great wares.[245] Having given salvation to those who believe, he desires to enter the city of peace and the place of the vision of God[246] and the citadel of the watchman.[247] "And when he had drawn near to Jerusalem and had come to Bethphage," that is, to the "house of jaws"[248]—a village of priests that bore a type of confession.[249] It was situated on the Mount of Olives, where there is the light of knowledge,[250] and where there is rest from labors and griefs—"he sent two of his disciples." The two disciples represent θεωρητικὴν καὶ πρακτικήν, that is, knowledge and works.[251] He orders them to enter the village, saying to them: "Go into the village that is opposite you." For it was opposed to the apostles,[252] nor did it want to take up the yoke of doctrines.[253] "And at once," he says, "you will find a donkey tied up and a colt with it. Untie them and bring them to me." The donkey had been tied by the many chains of sins. The colt too was frisky and impatient of bridle, along with its mother. According to the Gospel of Luke, it had many masters.[254] This means that it was not subject to one single error and doctrine but that many masters laid claim to an illicit authority for them-

245. Lat., *magnis ditatus mercibus.* Cf. Is 62.11: *ecce merces eius cum eo,* "Behold, his wares are with him." Cf. Origen, *In Matth.* 16.17.

246. "Vision of peace" was a popular etymology of the name Jerusalem. Cf. Philo, *On Dreams* 2.38.250; Clement, *Strom.* 1.5.29.4; Origen, *Hom. in Jos.* 21.2; *Hom. in Jer.* 9.2; *ComRom* 3.4.

247. Cf. *De interpr. hebr. nom.,* p. 50, line 9; p. 39, line 25.

248. Cf. *De interpr. hebr. nom.,* p. 60, line 24; Origen, *In Matth.* 16.17.

249. Cf. Homily 81 in FOTC 57, 170.

250. Olives were the source of the oil used in lamps. Cf. Ex 25.6; Origen, *In Matth.* 16.17.

251. The distinction between θεωρητικὸς and πρακτικὸς is Aristotelian. In Christian authors θεωρία covers the contemplative life, and πρᾶξις refers to conduct in conformity with the contemplated truths. The opposition between θεωρητική and πρακτική (sc. φιλοσοφία) is current in Origen and other Greek Fathers. Jerome translates these by *scientia* and *opera,* two words that cover the whole spiritual life. See below on Mt 25.14–17.

252. This overly literal interpretation of *contra* is taken from Fortunatianus, bishop of Aquileia, *Comment. in Evang.* 2 (CCSL 9, 368–69).

253. Cf. Mt 11.29.

254. Cf. Lk 19.33. Cf. Homily 81 in FOTC 57, 169.

selves. When they have seen that the true Lord and his servants had come, who had been sent to untie them, they do not dare to resist. Now as for what the donkey and the colt of the donkey stand for, we can explain in what is added.

21.4–5. *Now this was done that what was spoken through the prophet might be fulfilled, saying: "Tell daughter Zion: Behold, your king comes to you, meek, sitting upon a donkey and a colt, the foal of her that is used at the yoke."* This is written in the prophet Zechariah.[255] I will speak in more detail about this passage in its proper place, if I live long enough.[256] For the present I will briefly say that literally speaking, it is impossible to sit on two animals for a short journey like this. For either he sat on the donkey, and the colt was without a rider, or possibly the colt (which is more suitable) was improperly used for sitting, and the donkey was led freely along. Therefore, since the historical narrative contains either an impossibility or a disgrace, we are transferred to a deeper significance.[257] Thus under the figure of the donkey the synagogue is understood, which was under a yoke, untamed, and which dragged the yoke of the Law. The donkey's rather frisky and free colt represents the people of the Gentiles, on whom Jesus sat. He sent his two disciples to them both, one to the circumcision and the other to the Gentiles.[258]

21.6–7. *And the disciples went and did as Jesus commanded them, and they brought the donkey and the colt and they placed their garments on them, and they made him sit upon them.* Before the coming of the Savior, this colt and donkey were bare on which the apostles spread their garments so that Jesus may sit more comfortably.[259] And although many claimed lordship over them, they were cold and without a covering. But after they received the apostolic clothing, they became more beautiful, now that they had the Lord for a rider. Now the apostolic clothing can be understood of the teaching of the virtues, the explanation of the Scriptures, or the various kinds of ecclesiastical dogmas. If the

---

255. Cf. Zec 9.9.
256. Cf. Jerome, *In Zach.* 2.9.9–10.
257. Cf. Homily 81 in FOTC 57, 171.
258. Cf. Origen, *In Matth.* 16.15; Gal 2.7–8.
259. Cf. Origen, *In Matth.* 16.15.

soul has not been instructed and adorned in these, it does not deserve to have the Lord as its rider.

21.8. *Now a very great crowd spread their garments on the road.* See the distinction of the various persons involved here. It is the apostles who place their garments upon the donkey. The crowd, on the other hand, which is inferior, spreads their garments at the feet of the donkey, lest it should anywhere strike a stone, step on a thorn, or fall into a ditch.

21.8. *But others cut branches from the trees and spread them on the road.* They cut branches from the fruit-bearing trees that grow on the Mount of Olives. They spread them on the road in order to make the rough places straight and the uneven ground level.[260] Thus Christ, the victor over demons and vices, enters more directly and securely into the hearts of believers.

21.9. *But the crowds that went before and that followed shouted and said: "Hosanna to the son of David; blessed is he who will come in the name of the Lord. Hosanna in the highest."* Since the historical narrative is manifest, let us follow a spiritual sequence in our explanation. Crowds had gone out from Jericho and followed the Savior and his disciples. When they saw the donkey's colt untied, which previously had been bound, and that it was adorned with the clothing of the apostles, and when they saw the Lord Jesus sitting on it, they put their own garments under it and spread on the road branches from the trees. And when they had done all these deeds, they offer the testimony of their voice as well.[261] Those who went before and those who followed resound not with a brief and silent confession, but with a very loud outcry: "Hosanna to the son of David; blessed is he who will come in the name of the Lord." Now the words: "The crowds that went before and that followed," point to both peoples, those who believed in the Lord before the Gospel, and those who believed after the Gospel. They both praise Jesus with a harmonious voice of confession. This accords with the example of the parable above, where those who work varying numbers of hours receive one recompense of faith.[262] As for what follows further: "Hosanna to the

260. Cf. Is 40.4.
261. Cf. Homily 81 in FOTC 57, 171; Origen, *In Matth.* 16.18.
262. Cf. Mt 20.1–16.

son of David," I recall having spoken about its meaning many years ago in a brief letter to Damasus, who was at that time bishop of the city of Rome.[263] Yet I shall briefly touch upon it now. In the one hundred seventeenth Psalm, which is plainly written about the coming of the Savior, among other things we read this as well: "The stone which the builders rejected has become at the head of the corner. This has been done by the Lord, and it is marvelous in our eyes. This is the day that the Lord has made, let us exult and be glad in it."[264] And immediately it is added: "O Lord, save me; O Lord, give success; blessed is he who will come in the name of the Lord; we have blessed you from the house of the Lord," etc.[265] At the place where the seventy interpreters have: "O Lord, save me," we read in the Hebrew: *Anna Adonai osi anna.* Symmachus[266] translated this more plainly, saying: "I beseech [thee], Lord, save me, I beseech [thee]." Therefore, let no one think that the wording has been composed from two words, namely, from a Greek word and a Hebrew word. Rather, the entire wording is Hebraic and signifies that the coming of Christ is the world's salvation.[267] This is also why it follows: "Blessed is he who will come in the name of the Lord." For the Savior too confirms the same thing in the Gospel: "I have come in the name of my Father, and you have not received me; another will come in his own name, and you will receive him."[268] And besides, what is added: "Hosanna (that is, salvation) in the highest," clearly shows that the coming of Christ is the salvation not merely of men, but of the entire world, with those on earth joining those in heaven, "that every knee may bow to him of those that are in heaven and on earth and in the infernal regions."[269]

21.10. *And when he had entered Jerusalem, the whole city was disturbed, saying: "Who is this?"* When Jesus enters with the crowd, the whole city of Jerusalem is disturbed, marveling at the multitude, ignorant of the truth, and saying: "Who is this?" In another passage, we read that the angels said this: "Who is this king

---

263. Cf. *Ep.* 20 to Damasus; Origen, *In Matth.* 16.19.
264. Ps 118.22–24.   265. Ps 118.25–26.
266. For Symmachus, see on Mt 6.11, n. 174.
267. Cf. Homily 81 in FOTC 57, 172.
268. Jn 5.43.   269. Cf. Phil 2.10.

of glory?"[270] Now while some are in doubt and raise questions, the insignificant common people make a confession. They begin with the lesser matters and arrive at greater things and say:

21.11. *"This is Jesus the prophet from Nazareth of Galilee."* [They confess that] he is *the* prophet like Moses, whom Moses himself had said was coming.[271] This is written properly in Greek with the article. He is "from Nazareth of Galilee," since he was raised there. Thus the flower of the field was nourished among the flower of the virtues.[272]

21.12–13. *And Jesus entered into the Temple of God, and he drove out all those selling and buying in the Temple, and he overturned the tables of the money-changers and the seats of those selling doves, and he said to them: "It is written: 'My house shall be called a house of prayer, but you have made it a den of thieves.'"* Accompanied by the crowd of believers that had spread their garments in order that the colt might enter with an unhurt foot, Jesus goes into the Temple. He expels all who were selling and buying in the Temple and he overturns the tables of the money-changers. He scatters the seats of those selling doves, and he spoke to them, bringing forth a testimony from the Holy Scriptures,[273] that his Father's house must be a house of prayer, not a den of thieves, or as is written in another evangelist, a house of business.[274] In the first place, we need to know that in accordance with the commandments of the Law, especially on feast days, innumerable sacrifices of bulls, rams, and goats were offered in the Temple of the Lord, which was the most venerated in the whole world. This took place when the Jewish people gathered there from nearly all countries. The poor offered the chicks of doves and turtle-doves,[275] lest they should be without a sacrifice. Very often it came to pass that those who had come from afar did not have victims to sacrifice. Therefore, the priests thought out how they could plunder the people. They sold all kinds of sacrificial

---

270. Ps 24.8. Origen made this connection; cf. *In Matth.* 16.19.

271. Cf. Dt 18.15.

272. Cf. Song 2.1; Jerome, *De interpr. hebr. nom.*, p. 62, line 24; *Ep.* 46.12. "*Nazara* means flower": Homily 75 in FOTC 57, 129.

273. Cf. Is 56.7; Jer 7.11.   274. Cf. Jn 2.16.

275. Cf. Lv 5.7.

animals to anyone who needed them, that these people in turn could sell to those who did not have any. Thus they would receive back again what had been bought. The frequent lack of resources of those who came caused this contrivance of theirs to spread more widely. For the people lacked money for their expenses. Not only did they not have sacrifices, but they lacked the means to buy even birds and common small gifts. Consequently [the priests] stationed money-changers who exchanged the money at a high rate. Now it had been commanded in the Law that no one should take interest.[276] Yet there was no advantage in loaning money that brought no profit, since sometimes it lost its capital. So they thought out another technique to make bankers *(collybistas)* out of the money-changers. The Latin language does not express the proper meaning of this word. Among the Jews *collyba* refers to what we call desserts, or common little gifts, for example, chilled chickpea and raisins and fruit of various kinds. Well, since the *collybistae,* who had lent money at interest, were unable to receive interest, they received various kinds of things in place of interest. Their aim was to exact by means of these things that are purchased with coins that which was not lawful to exact in coin. As if Ezekiel had not warned in advance about this very thing when he said: "You will not receive interest and superabundance"![277] The Lord, seeing this kind of business, or rather thievery, going on in the Father's house, was stirred up by the ardor of his spirit in accordance with what was written in the sixty-eighth Psalm: "The zeal of your house has consumed me."[278] He made a whip for himself from cords,[279] and he ejected from the Temple a very great multitude of men, saying: "It is written: 'My house shall be called a house of prayer, but you have made it a den of thieves.'" For a man is a thief, and converts the Temple of God into a den of thieves, who seeks after financial gain from religion. His worship is not so much the worship of God as a pretext for business. The foregoing has been said as pertaining to the historical narrative. But according to the mystical understanding,[280] Jesus daily en-

---

276. Cf. Lv 25.37; Dt 23.19.   277. Ezek 22.12.
278. Ps 69.9.   279. Cf. Jn 2.15.
280. Cf. Origen, *In Matth.* 16.22; 16.27.

ters the Temple of the Father and expels from his own Church all such bishops, priests, and deacons, as well as laymen and the whole crowd.[281] He holds them all guilty of a single crime, namely, of selling and buying. For it is written: "Freely you have received, freely give."[282] He also overturns the tables of the money-changers. Observe that on account of the greed of the priests the altars of God are called the tables of the money-changers. And he overturns the seats of those selling doves, that is, of those who sell the grace of the Holy Spirit[283] and who do everything in order to devour the people subject to them. Of these it is said: "Those who devour my people as they eat bread."[284] According to the simple understanding, the doves were not on the seats but in cages,[285] unless perhaps the salesmen of the doves were sitting on the seats, which is completely absurd, since in the "seats" of the teachers, greater dignity is indicated.[286] But this dignity is reduced to nothing since it is mixed with profits. Now let each one understand also concerning himself what we have said about the churches. For the apostle Paul says: "You are the temple of God, and the Holy Spirit dwells in you."[287] May there not be business in the house of our heart. May there not be the commerce of selling and buying. May there not be desire for donations, lest an angry and stern Jesus enter and cleanse his own temple in no other way but with a whip that he administers in order to make a house of prayer out of a den of thieves and a house of business.

21.14. *And the blind and the lame came to him in the Temple, and he healed them.* If he had not overturned the tables of the money-changers and the seats of those selling doves, the blind would not have merited to receive the ancient light, and the lame would not have deserved to receive the ability to take vigorous steps.

21.15–16. *But when the chief priests and scribes saw the wonder-*

---

281. Cf. Homily 83 in FOTC 57, 183.
282. Mt 10.8.
283. The dove is associated with the Holy Spirit in Mt 3.16.
284. Ps 14.4.
285. Cf. Homily 83 in FOTC 57, 181.
286. Cf. Mt 23.2.
287. 1 Cor 3.16–17; 2 Cor 6.16.

ful things that he did and the children crying out in the Temple and saying: "Hosanna to the son of David," they were indignant and said to him: "Do you hear what they are saying?" Most people think that the greatest sign is that Lazarus was raised from the dead,[288] that the man blind from birth received the light,[289] that the Father's voice was heard at the Jordan,[290] that he was transfigured on the mountain and showed the glory of the triumphant one.[291] But to me it seems that among all the signs that he did, this one is more wonderful,[292] that one man, who was at that time so contemptible and lowly that he was later crucified, could expel such a great multitude at the crack of a single whip, with the scribes and Pharisees raging against him, seeing that their profits were ruined; that one man could overturn their tables and wreck their chairs and do the other things that an infinite army could not have done. For some sort of heavenly fire was radiating from his eyes,[293] and the majesty of divinity was shining in his face. And though the priests do not dare to set a hand on him, yet they malign his conduct and they convert into a malicious charge the testimony of the people and children, who were calling out: "Hosanna to the son of David," namely, that this should not be said except to the only Son of God. Therefore, let the bishops and all holy men consider with what great danger they would allow these things to be said to them. For these things were being spoken truthfully about the Lord (since the faith of the believers was not yet solid), and yet it is flung at him as a criminal charge.

21.16. *But Jesus said to them: "Certainly; have you never read: 'Out of the mouth of babes and sucklings you have perfected praise'?"* How moderately has he tempered his judgment! His response moves against both alternatives and does not allow the malicious charge to stand. He did not say what the scribes wanted to hear: "These children are doing a good thing when they offer testimony for me"; nor again: "They are in error; they are children; you ought to ignore them on account of their age." Rather, he brings forth a citation from the eighth Psalm.[294] Thus, while the Lord is si-

---

288. Cf. Jn 11.43.   289. Cf. Jn 9.7.
290. Cf. Mt 3.17.   291. Cf. Mt 17.2.
292. Cf. Homily 83 in FOTC 57, 180.   293. Cf. Rv 1.14.
294. Cf. Ps 8.2.

lent, the testimony of the Scriptures confirms the words of the children.

21.17. *And leaving them, he went out of the city to Bethany, and he stayed there.* He left the unbelievers and departed from the city of those who were speaking against him. He went to Bethany, which is translated "house of obedience."[295] Even at that time he was prefiguring the calling of the Gentiles.[296] And he stayed there, since he could not stay permanently in Israel. And this too should be understood, that he was of such great poverty and was so little doted on by anyone that in such a great city he found no host, no dwelling place. Instead, he stayed at a little farm with Lazarus and his sisters; for Bethany is their village.[297]

21.18–20. *In the morning, as he was returning to the city, he was hungry. And seeing one fig tree by the wayside, he went to it, and found nothing on it but leaves only. And he said to it: "May no fruit ever come from you in eternity!" And the fig tree withered at once. And when his disciples saw it, they marveled, saying: "How did it wither at once?"* The night's darkness had been dispelled by the radiant morning light and by the approach of midday, at which time the Lord would illuminate the world by his Passion.[298] When he returned to the city, he was hungry. This shows both the reality of his human flesh and the fact that he was hungry for the salvation of believers.[299] But he is seething over the unbelief of Israel. And when he had seen one tree, which we understand as the synagogue, the meeting place of the Jews, by the wayside (for though it had the Law, it was "by the wayside" because it did not believe in the Way),[300] he went to it. This shows that it was standing there immobile and did not have the feet of the Gospel.[301] And he found nothing on it except leaves only. This refers to the rustling of the promises, the Pharisaical traditions, their boasting in the Law, and the outer display of words without any fruit of

295. Cf. *De interpr. hebr. nom.*, p. 60, line 27; Homily 81 in FOTC 57, 170; Origen, *In Matth.* 16.26.
296. Cf. Homily 82 in FOTC 57, 174.
297. Cf. Jn 11.1.
298. Cf. Mt 27.45.
299. Cf. Homily 82 in FOTC 57, 174.
300. Cf. Jn 14.6; see above on Mt 20.29–31.
301. Cf. Rom 10.15; Na 1.15.

truth. And this is why another evangelist says: "For it was not yet the time,"[302] which refers either to the fact that the time of the salvation of Israel had not yet come, because the people of the Gentiles had not yet entered in,[303] or that the time of faith had passed by, since, though he came to Israel first, he was spurned by them and passed on to the nations.[304] "And he said to it: 'May no fruit ever come from you,'" either "'in eternity'" or "in the age," for the Greek word αἰών signifies both. "And the fig tree withered." This means that it did not have the nourishment that the Lord desired when he was hungry. But the leaves withered in such a way that the trunk itself remained. And though the branches were broken off,[305] the root was still alive. At the end of time, if they want to believe, this root will sprout the shoots of faith.[306] Then the Scripture will be fulfilled that says: "There is hope for a tree."[307] Now according to the letter, since the Lord was about to suffer among the people and endure the scandal of the cross, he had to strengthen the hearts of the disciples by the anticipation of a sign. This is why the disciples are amazed and say: "How did it wither at once?" By this same power, then, the Savior could have likewise withered his enemies, had he not been awaiting their salvation through repentance.

21.21. *But Jesus answered and said to them: "Amen I tell you: If you have faith and do not waver, you will not only do what has been done to the fig tree, but also, if you say to a mountain: Take up and cast yourself into the sea, it will be done."* Gentile dogs[308] bark at us in their books, which they have left behind as a memorial of their impiety. They assert that the apostles did not have faith, because they were unable to move mountains.[309] We shall respond to them as follows. According to the testimony of the evangelist John, the Lord did many signs for which, if they were written down, the world would not have room.[310] This does not mean

---

302. Mk 11.13.
303. Cf. Rom 11.25; cf. Homily 82 in FOTC 57, 177.
304. Cf. Jn 1.11–12.   305. Cf. Rom 10.19.
306. Rom 10.23–26.   307. Jb 14.7.
308. Cf. Porphyry, *Adv. Christianos, fragm.* 3, 70.
309. See above at 17.20.
310. Cf. Jn 21.25.

that the world would not have room for the books. For no matter how much books are multiplied, one more chest[311] or one more case for scrolls has room for them. Rather, it means that it could not bear the magnitude of the signs on account of the miracles and on account of unbelief. Therefore, we believe that the apostles did these things as well, but they were not written down, lest a greater pretext for contradicting be given to unbelievers. Apart from these considerations, we will ask them whether or not they believe in these signs that the writings *do* narrate. And when we find out that they are incredulous, we shall prove as a consequence that those who refused to believe in the lesser ones would not have believed in the greater ones. This is directed against the above-mentioned [Gentile dogs]. But as we have already said earlier,[312] we should understand this mountain as the devil, who is arrogant and vaunts himself against his own Creator.[313] He is called a "corrupted mountain" by the prophet.[314] And when he takes possession of a man's soul and becomes rooted in it,[315] he can be removed by the apostles and by those who are like the apostles. It is moved "into the sea," that is, into salty and bitter places that are full of waves, which do not have the sweetness of God. This is precisely what we read in the Psalms: "We will not fear, though the earth be troubled and the mountains be removed into the heart of the sea."[316]

21.23. *And when he came to the Temple, the chief priests and elders of the people came up to him as he was teaching and said: "By what authority are you doing these things, and who gave you this authority?"* With different words they are constructing the same malicious charge that they spoke above when they said: "By Beelzebub the prince of demons he expels demons."[317] For when they say: "By what authority are you doing these things?" they are in doubt

---

311. This word is used in the very last sentence of the Preface.

312. See above on Mt 17.20.

313. Cf. Is 14.13–14.

314. Cf. Jer 51.25; Zec 4.7. Cf. Homily 18 on Ps 86 (87) in FOTC 48, 136.

315. In Jerome's interpretation he blends Matthew's text with the parallel passage in Lk 17.6, which, in place of a mountain being cast into the sea, speaks of a sycamine tree being "uprooted" and planted in the sea.

316. Ps 46.2.

317. Mt 12.24.

about the authority of God, and they want it to be understood that what he is doing is of the devil. And by adding: "Who gave you this authority?" they are very openly denying that he is the Son of God. For they think that he is doing signs not by his own power, but by that of another.

21.24–25. *Jesus answered and said to them: "I also will ask you one question, which if you will tell me, I too will tell you by what authority I am doing these things. The baptism of John, where did it come from? From heaven or from men?"* etc. This is what is commonly said: For a tree with a hard knot, a hard nail or wedge must be driven in.[318] The Lord could have refuted the malicious charge of his tempters by an open response, but he prudently asks a question. Thus they are condemned either by their silence or by their judgment. For if upon thorough investigation they had answered that John's baptism was from heaven, being so wise in their malice, the logical answer to this would be: Why, then, were you not baptized by John? On the other hand, if they had wanted to say that John's baptism was concocted as a human deception and had nothing divine about it, they would fear a popular uprising. For the entire multitude that had come together had received John's baptism and thus regarded him as a prophet. And so, for the purpose of making adjustments to their plots, this very impious sect responded and made use of the language of humility: they say that they do not know.

21.27. *And he said to them: "Neither do I tell you by what authority I am doing these things."* In answering that they did not know, they lied. Consequently, it was in accordance with their response for the Lord too to say: Neither do I know, but the truth cannot lie; and he says: "Neither do I tell you." By this he shows both that they know, but they are unwilling to give the answer; and that he knows, and the reason he does not tell is because they are being silent about what they know. And immediately he adds a parable by which he convicts them of impiety and teaches that the kingdom of God is to be transferred to the Gentiles.

21.28–32. *"But what does it seem to you? A man had two sons. He*

318. This ancient proverb, according to the *Adages* of Erasmus of Rotterdam (I, ii, 5), is used "whenever we blunt the power of something bad by malignity of the same kind."

approached the first one and said, 'Go, today, and work in my vine-
yard.' But that one said in response: 'I will not'; but afterward, moved
by penitence, he went. And going up to the other one, he said the same.
But that one said in response: 'I am going, sir,'[319] *but he did not go."*
These are the two sons who are also described in a parable in
Luke.[320] One is temperate and the other is luxurious. Zechariah
the prophet says of them: "I took unto me two rods; one I called
Beauty, and the other I called a Cord; and I fed the flock."[321]
First of all, through their knowledge of natural law, it is said to
the people of the Gentiles: "Go and work in my vineyard," that
is: What you do not want done to you, do not do to another.[322]
They responded haughtily: I will not; but afterward at the coming of the Savior they did penance and worked in the vineyard
of God. Thus they made up for the defiance of their words by
means of labor. Now the second son is the people of the Jews
who responded to Moses: "Everything that the Lord has said, we
will do."[323] But they did not go into the vineyard. For when the
son of the householder had been killed, they reckoned themselves to be the heir.[324] Now others[325] think that the parable is
not about Gentiles and Jews, but simply about sinners and the
just, as the Lord himself also explains what he later sets forth:
"Amen I say to you, that the tax collectors and the harlots are
preceding you into the kingdom of God." He says that because
they who by their evil deeds had refused to serve God afterward received the baptism of repentance from John, whereas
the Pharisees, who made a profession of justice and who were
boasting that they were doing God's Law, did not do God's commands. For they held John's baptism in contempt. This is why
he says: "For John came to you in the way of justice, and you did
not believe him; but the tax collectors and the harlots believed."
One should know that with respect to what follows: "Which of
the two did the father's will? And they said: 'the last,'" the au-

319. Or "lord" (*domine*).
320. Cf. Lk 15.11–32.
321. Zec 11.7.
322. Cf. Tb 4.16; Origen, *ComRom* 2.9.1 (M892).
323. Ex 24.3.   324. Cf. Mt 21.38–39.
325. Who?

thentic copies[326] do not have "the last" but "the first." Thus they are condemned by their own judgment. Now if we want to read "the last," the interpretation is plain. We would say that the Jews indeed understand the truth, but they are evasive and do not want to say what they think. In the same way they also know that John's baptism is from heaven, but they were unwilling to say so.[327]

21.33. *"Hear another parable. There was a householder who planted a vineyard, and set a hedge around it, and dug a wine press in it, and built a tower, and leased it to farmers, and went abroad."* What the Lord meant has been taken from a proverb: "It is hard to kick against the goad."[328] The chief priests and the elders of the people who asked the Lord: "By what authority are you doing these things, and who gave you this authority?" and who had wanted to catch Wisdom in a word are overcome by their own artifice. They hear in parables what they did not deserve to hear in clear language. This householder is the very same man who had two sons.[329] In another parable he hired workers for his vineyard.[330] "He planted a vineyard," of which Isaiah speaks in great detail in a song, adding at the end: "The vineyard of the Lord of hosts is the house of Israel."[331] Moreover, in the Psalm it says: "You have transferred the vineyard from Egypt, you have expelled nations and planted it."[332] "And he set a hedge around it": this refers to either the city's wall or the help of angels. "And he dug a wine press in it": this refers either to the altar or to those "wine

326. The textual transmission of the parable of the two sons is very confused. See Metzger, *Textual Commentary,* 55–56.

327. Cf. Mt 21.25–27. According to Jerome, the first son says "No," but afterwards repents. The second son says "Yes," but does nothing. Jesus asks, Which one did the will of the father? The Jews answer: "The last." Jerome thinks that the Jews recognized that this parable was directed against them and chose to give an evasive reply rather than to remain silent. Jerome's primary interpretation may be too subtle and is rejected by many modern commentators. He does support it, however, by the immediate context and by what he considers to be the authentic textual reading, which happens to be the most difficult textual reading (the one that modern textual critics usually consider authentic).

328. Cf. Acts 26.14; some MSS of Acts 9.4; Euripides, *Bacc.* 794; Julian, *Or.* 8.246b.

329. Cf. Lk 15.11.

330. Cf. Mt 20.2.

331. Is 5.7.

332. Ps 80.8.

presses" that are mentioned in the title words of three Psalms: the eighth, the eightieth, and the eighty-third.[333] "And he built a tower": it is scarcely to be doubted that this refers to the Temple, of which it is said through Micah: "And you, cloudy tower of the daughter Zion."[334] "And he leased it to farmers": Elsewhere he named them the workers of the vineyard who had been hired at the first hour, the third hour, the ninth, and eleventh.[335] "And he went abroad." This is not done by means of changing his residence, for where can God not be present, who fills all things and who says through Jeremiah: "I am a God who is near and not far off, says the Lord"?[336] But he seems to go away from the vineyard so that he might leave the free choice for laboring to the vine-dressers.

21.34–35. *"Now when the time of fruits drew near, he sent his servants to the farmers, that they might receive the fruits that were his. And the farmers seized his servants, one they beat, another they killed, and another they stoned."* He had given the Law to them and had commanded them to labor in this vineyard that they might exhibit the fruit of the Law by their works. Later he sent servants to them, whom they seized and beat, such as Jeremiah,[337] or killed, such as Isaiah,[338] or stoned, such as Naboth[339] and Zechariah, whom they killed between the sanctuary and the altar.[340] Let us read Paul's letter to the Hebrews and out of it learn in great detail which of the Lord's servants have endured what sorts of things.[341]

21.37, 36. *"But last of all he sent his own son to them, saying: 'They will respect my son.'"* In what we read higher up: "Again he sent other servants, more than the first, and they did the same to them,"[342] he shows the patience of the householder. For he sent quite frequently so that he might provoke the evil tenants to penitence, but they treasured up wrath for themselves on the day of wrath.[343] What is further added: "They will respect my

333. Cf. Ps 8.1; Ps 81.1; Ps 84.1.   334. Mi 4.8.
335. Cf. Mt 20.1, 3, 5, 6.   336. Jer 23.23.
337. Cf. Jer 37.14.
338. Cf. Heb 11.37; *Mart. Is.* 5.11–14.
339. Cf. 1 Kgs 21.13.
341. Cf. Heb 11.34–37.   340. Cf. Mt 23.35; 2 Chr 24.22.
343. Cf. Rom 2.5.   342. Mt 21.36.

son," does not imply that he was ignorant [of the outcome]. For what would the householder not know, since in this passage he represents God the Father? But God is always *said to be* uncertain, so that free will in man may be preserved. Let us put a question to Arius and Eunomius. Behold, the Father is said to be ignorant. He delays his decision, and as far as it pertains to us, it is proven that he has lied. Whatever answer they give on the Father's behalf, let them understand this answer as well on behalf of the Son, who claims to be ignorant of the day of the consumation.[344]

21.39. *"And taking him, they cast him outside of the vineyard, and they killed him."* The apostle as well says that the Lord was crucified outside the gate.[345] But we can also understand it in another way, that he was cast outside of the vineyard and was killed there. Thus when the Gentiles receive him, the vineyard can be leased to others.

21.40. *"Therefore, when the Lord of the vineyard comes, what will he do to those tenants?"* etc. The Lord asks them, not because he is ignorant of what they will respond, but so that by their own response they may be condemned. Now the vineyard is leased to us, but it is leased on the condition that we give back to God the fruit at the proper time and that at each and every time we know what we ought to say or do.

21.42. *Jesus said to them: "Have you never read in the Scriptures: 'The stone which the builders rejected, this has become the head of the corner; this was done by the Lord; this is marvelous in our eyes'?"*[346] The same themes are being woven together by means of a variety of parables and a diversity of words. For those whom he had above named workers and vine-dressers and farmers, now he calls builders, that is, stonemasons. This is why the apostle says: "You are God's field, God's building."[347] Therefore, just as the vine-dressers receive the vineyard, so these stonemasons have received the stone, which they either lay in the foundations, according to the architect Paul,[348] or in the corner, that it may join together two walls, that is, two peoples. This stone was rejected

344. Cf. Mt 24.36; 28.20.   345. Cf. Heb 13.12.
346. Cf. Ps 118.22–23.   347. 1 Cor 3.9.
348. Cf. 1 Cor 3.10.

by them and became the head of the corner; and this was done by the Lord, not by human strength, but by the power of God. Concerning this stone of help,[349] Peter too speaks boldly: "This is the stone that was rejected by you builders, which has become the head of the corner";[350] and Isaiah says: "Behold, I will lay in the foundations of Zion a chosen, precious, cornerstone, and he who believes in it will not be confounded."[351]

21.43. *"Therefore, I tell you that the kingdom of God will be taken away from you and given to a nation producing the fruits of it."* Several times I have said[352] that the kingdom of God refers to the Holy Scriptures, which the Lord took from the Jews and handed down to us so that we might produce their[353] fruits. This is the vineyard that is handed over to the farmers and vine-dressers. Those who have not labored in it, since they have merely the name of the Scriptures, are going to lose the fruits of the vineyard.

21.44. *"He who falls on this stone will be broken to pieces; but when it falls on anyone, it will crush him."* It is one thing to offend Christ by evil deeds, another to deny him. He who is a sinner and yet believes in him indeed falls upon the stone and is broken to pieces, but he is not entirely crushed. For by patience he is preserved unto salvation.[354] But the one upon whom it falls, is the one whom the stone smashes. He completely denies Christ, and it so crushes him that not even a potsherd remains with which to scoop up a bit of water.[355]

21.45–46. *And when the chief priests and the Pharisees heard his parables, they knew that he was speaking about them. And seeking to seize him, they feared the crowds, because they considered him to be a prophet.* However hard-hearted and dull they were toward the Son of God on account of their unbelief and impiety, yet they were unable to deny evident conclusions. They understood that all the Lord's judgments were directed against them. Therefore, they wanted to kill him, but they feared the crowds, be-

---

349. Cf. 1 Sm 7.12.   350. Acts 4.11; cf. 1 Pt 2.7.
351. Is 28.16.
352. See on Mt 12.28; *Ep.* 53.10 to Paulinus.
353. "Their" is feminine here, referring to the Scriptures.
354. Cf. Lk 21.19.   355. Cf. Is 30.14.

cause "they considered him to be a prophet." A crowd is always fickle. It does not persist with a resolved will, and like waves and diverse winds it is drawn here and there.[356] The one whom they now venerate and worship as though he were a prophet, later they cry out against him: "Crucify, crucify" such a man.[357]

Chapter 22

22.1–3. *And in response Jesus spoke to them in parables, saying: "The kingdom of heaven is like a man who was a king who made a marriage for his son and sent his servant to call those who were invited to the marriage, and they would not come."* The Pharisees understood that the parables were being said about them and sought to seize him and kill him. The Lord knows that this was their will, yet he rebukes those who are furious [with him]. He is not overcome with a fear that would keep him from convicting sinners. This king who made the marriage for his son is the omnipotent God. Now he makes a marriage for our Lord Jesus Christ and the Church,[358] which has been gathered from Jews as well as from Gentiles. He sends his servant to call those who are invited to the marriage. It is scarcely to be doubted that this refers to Moses, through whom he gave the Law to those who were invited. But if we read "servants"[359] as the majority of copies have, it is to be referred to the prophets, because those who were invited by them to come despised the invitation.

22.4. *"Again he sent other servants, saying: 'Tell those who are invited: Behold, I have made ready my dinner, my bulls and my fatted calves are killed, and everything is ready; come to the marriage.'"* As for the servants who were sent second, it is better that they be un-

---

356. Cf. Eph 4.14.

357. Jn 19.6, 15. This form of the text, *Crucifige talem,* is not found in the Gospel, but it is found frequently in Jerome. Cf. *In Jonam* 1.3.

358. Cf. Eph 5.29–32.

359. Jerome seems to prefer the reading "servant" in the singular (cf. Mt 22.3, 12, 22), but he knows that the majority of copies have the plural "servants," which is probably the correct reading. The textual error may have arisen as a correction to make Matthew agree with Lk 14.17. Origen comments on the plural, *In Matth.* 17.15.

derstood as the prophets than as the apostles, on the condition, however, that above this we read "servant." But if you read the former passage as "servants," then here the second group of servants should be understood as referring to the apostles. In the dinner made ready, and the bulls and the fatted calves slaughtered, either the royal wealth is being described metaphorically, so that spiritual things are understood from fleshly things; or at least the greatness of dogmas and the very detailed learning from God's law can be understood.

22.5–6. *"And they went away, one to his farm, another to his business; but the others seized his servants, treated them shamefully, and killed them."* There is great diversity among those who do not receive the truth of the Gospel. For the ones who are occupied in other matters and do not want to come are guilty of a lesser crime than those who despise the friendliness of the one who invited them and turn humanity into cruelty and who seize the king's servants, and either treat them shamefully or kill them. In this parable the killing of the bridegroom[360] is left unmentioned. Contempt for the marriage is shown by the killing of the servants.

22.7. *"Now when the king had heard of it, he was enraged."* Up above he had said of him: "The kingdom of heaven is like a man who was a king." In regard to his inviting to the marriage and doing works of clemency, the term "man" is added. But now, when it comes to vengeance, "man" is left unmentioned and only "king" is said.

22.7. *"And he sent his armies and destroyed those murderers and burned their city."* His armies are either his avenging angels, of whom it is written in the Psalms: "He sent through destructive angels";[361] or we may understand the Romans under the leadership of Vespasian and Titus, who killed the people of Judea and set fire to the sinful city.

22.8–9. *"Then he said to his servants: 'The marriage indeed is ready, but those who were invited were not worthy; go therefore to the outlets of the roads, and as many as you find invite to the marriage.'"*

360. Cf. Mt 9.15.
361. Ps 78.49.

The people of the Gentiles were not on the roads but on the outlets of the roads. Now it is asked how it could be that some good ones are found among these who were on the outside and among the bad. The apostle treats this topic more fully in the letter to the Romans. He says that Gentiles who do naturally the things that are in the Law will condemn the Jews who did not do the written Law.[362] Among the pagans too there is an infinite diversity. For we know that some are inclined to vices and rush off toward evils, but others for the sake of integrity of character devote themselves to the virtues.

22.11–12. *"But the king entered to see those who were reclining, and he saw there a man not clothed with a wedding garment. And he said to him: 'Friend, how did you enter here without a wedding garment?' But he was silent."* Those who had been invited to the marriage from the hedges and corners and streets[363] and diverse places had filled the king's dining hall. But later, when the king came to see those who were reclining at his own feast, that is to say, when on the day of judgment he visits the guests who were resting, as it were, in his faithfulness, and he discerns the merits of each one,[364] he finds one who was not clothed with a wedding garment. That one represents all who are associated with evil. The wedding garments are the Lord's commands and the works that are fulfilled from the Law and the Gospel.[365] These become the clothing of the new man.[366] If anyone with the name of Christian, therefore, is found at the time of the judgment who does not have the wedding clothing, that is, the garment of the heavenly man from above,[367] but has a polluted garment, that is, the hide of the old man, he is immediately reprimanded, and it is said to him: "Friend, how did you enter here?" He calls him "friend" because he had invited him to the wedding. He convicts him of impudence because he had defiled the purity of the wedding feast with a filthy garment.[368] "But he was silent." For at that time there will be no room for impudence nor the capability of denying, since all the angels and the world itself will be a witness against sinners.

---

362. Cf. Rom 2.14.　　363. Cf. Lk 14.23.
364. Cf. Rv 2.23. Cf. Origen, *In Matth.* 18.24.
365. Cf. Rv 19.6.　　366. Cf. Col 3.10.
367. Cf. 1 Cor 15.48–49.　　368. Cf. Rv 3.4.

22.13. *"Then the king said to the attendants: 'Bind his hands and feet, and cast him into the outer darkness; there, there will be weeping and gnashing of teeth.'"* The hands and feet are bound; the eyes weep; the teeth gnash together. Understand these things as confirmation of the truth of the resurrection. Or possibly it means that the hands and feet are bound in order to halt the doing of evils that would run on to the point of the shedding of blood. Also, in the weeping of the eyes and the gnashing of the teeth, he shows through the metaphor of the bodily members the magnitude of the torments.

22.14. *"For many are called, but few are chosen."* He summarizes all the parables with this brief little maxim. For in the laboring in the vineyard and the building of the house and in the wedding feast, it is not the commencement that is sought, but the completion.

22.15–16. *Then the Pharisees went away and took counsel how they might catch him in his words, and they sent their disciples with the Herodians, saying.*[369] Shortly before this, under Caesar Augustus, after Judea had been subjected to the Romans, a census had been conducted of the whole world, and tributes were exacted. At that time there was a great sedition among the people. Some said that tribute must be paid out for the sake of security and calm, since the Romans carried out military operations on behalf of all. The Pharisees, on the other hand, who were applauding themselves for their own justice,[370] supported the contrary view. They said that the people of God were not obligated to be subject to human laws. For they paid tithes and gave firstfruits and the other things that were written in the Law. Caesar Augustus had appointed as king of the Judeans Herod, son of Antipater, who was foreign-born and a proselyte. He was in charge of the tributes and complied with the Roman authorities. This explains why the Pharisees send their disciples with the Herodians, that is, the soldiers of Herod, or rather with those whom the Pharisees were mockingly calling Herodians,[371] since they paid tribute to the Romans and were not supportive

---

369. Cf. Origen, *In Matth.* 17.25–26.
370. Cf. Lk 18.9–12.
371. The term "Herodian" was an embarrassment to Origen; cf. *In Matth.* 17.

of the divine worship. Some Latins[372] ridiculously think that the Herodians believed that Herod was the Christ, which we have never read at all.

22.16–17. *"Teacher, we know that you are a truthful teacher and you show the way of God in truth and care for no man; for you do not regard the person of men. Tell us, then, what it seems to you: Is it permitted to give tax to Caesar, or not?"* The flattering and fraudulent question to the matter at issue is intended to provoke him.[373] They want him to respond that one should fear God more than Caesar, and to say that tribute must not be paid. The result of this would be that at once the Herodians, upon hearing it, would seize him as the leader of sedition against the Romans.

22.18. *But Jesus, aware of their malice, said: "Why do you tempt me, hypocrites?"* The premier virtue seen in his response is his awareness of the mind of his interrogators and his calling them not disciples but tempters. One is called a hypocrite, then, who is one thing, but pretends to be something else; that is, he does one thing in his conduct and alleges something else with his words.

22.19. *"Show me the coin of the tax." And they brought him a denarius.* Wisdom always acts wisely. Thus the tempters are confuted chiefly by their own words. "Show me," he says, the denarius. This kind of coin had the value of ten sesterces and bore the image of Caesar.

22.20. *And Jesus said to them: "Whose image and inscription is this?"* Let those who think that the Savior's question indicates ignorance, and not foresight, learn from the present passage that Jesus assuredly knew whose image was on the coin. He asks the question in order to give a fitting response to their words.

22.21. *They said to him: "Caesar's." Then he said to them: "Render therefore to Caesar the things that are Caesar's, and to God the things that are God's."* We should not think that Augustus Caesar is being signified, but Tiberius,[374] his stepson, who was the successor

372. Cf. Tertullian, *De praescript.* 45; Ps. Tertullian, *Adv. omnes haereses* 1.1; Philaster of Brescia, *Diversarum hereseon* 28. Jerome's vacillation is revealed in the fact that he himself proposes the interpretation that he here calls "ridiculous" in *Dial. adv. Lucif.* 23 (PL 23: 178B).

373. Cf. Origen, *In Matth.* 17.26.

374. Tiberius Julius Caesar (47 B.C.–37 A.D.) was the son of Tiberius Clau-

of his adoptive father, under whom the Lord also suffered. Now all the Roman rulers were called Caesars from the first Caesar, Gaius, who had seized power. Further, what he says: "Render to Caesar the things that are Caesar's," refers to coins, tribute, and money; "and to God the things that are God's": here we should think of tithes, first-fruits, offerings, and victims. Just as he himself had rendered tribute for himself and Peter,[375] so he rendered to God the things that are God's by doing the Father's will.[376]

22.22. *When they heard it, they were amazed.* Those who should have believed in the presence of such great wisdom were amazed that their cunning had not devised the occasion for their conspiracy.

22.22. *And they left him and went away,* reporting their unbelief equally with the miracle.

22.23. *On that day the Sadducees came to him, who say that there is no resurrection.* There were two sects among the Jews: one of the Pharisees and the other of the Sadducees. The Pharisees preferred the justice of traditions and observances, which they call *deuterōsis.*[377] This is why the people called them "the separated ones." The Sadducees, which is translated "the just ones," also claimed for themselves what they were not in reality. While the former confessed and believed in the resurrection of the body and the soul and in angels and the spirit, the latter, according to the Acts of the Apostles,[378] denied all these things. These are the two houses about which Isaiah shows very clearly that they would strike against the stone of stumbling.[379]

---

dius Nero and Livia. He entered into the imperial family when Octavian (the later Augustus Caesar) married his mother. Tiberius reigned from 14–37 A.D.

375. Cf. Mt 17.20.

376. Cf. Jn 6.38.

377. *Deuterōsis* = δευτέρωσις. Cf. *Comm. in Is.* Jerome probably originally recorded the Greek word, which means "second source" or "second tradition" and refers to the interpretation of the Torah or the oral laws.

378. Cf. Acts 23.8.

379. Cf. Is 8.14. In Isaiah the two houses that strike against the stone of stumbling are Israel and Judah. Jerome applies this to the Pharisees and Sadducees. Elsewhere, in his *Comm. in Is.* 3.11–15 (CCSL 73, 115–16), he notes that the Nazareans see in this the two families of Shammai and Hillel.

22.23–25. *And they asked him a question, saying: "Teacher, Moses said: 'If a man dies without a son, his brother should marry his wife and raise up seed for his brother.' Well, there were seven brothers among us, and the first married the wife and died,"* etc. Those who did not believe in the resurrection of the body thought that the soul perished with the body.[380] They fabricate a story proper to this, which exposes the ridiculous dreams of those who assert the resurrection of the dead. Now it is possible that this story actually happened at some time in their nation.[381]

22.28. *"In the resurrection, then, whose wife of the seven will she be? For they all had her."* They bring forward this base story in order to deny the truth of the resurrection.[382]

22.29. *Jesus responded and said to them: "You are in error, knowing neither the Scriptures nor the power of God."* The reason they are in error is that they do not know the Scriptures; and since they do not know the Scriptures, consequently they do not know the power of God, that is, Christ, who is the power of God and the wisdom of God.[383]

22.30. *"For in the resurrection they will neither marry nor be married."* Latin usage does not correspond to the Greek idiom. For, properly speaking, women *marry*, and men *lead wives in marriage*. But we should understand the statement simply, that "to marry" is written with respect to men, and "to be married" concerns women. Thus in the resurrection they will neither marry nor be married; therefore, the bodies, which are able to marry and be married, will rise again. Now obviously, no one says of a stone and a tree and of these things that do not have genital organs that they neither marry nor are married, but of these who, though they can marry, nevertheless do not marry for another reason.[384] Now in what is added:

---

380. Cf. Origen, *In Matth.* 17.30.   381. Cf. Tb 3.8.
382. Cf. Origen, *In Matth.* 17.33.
383. Cf. 1 Cor 1.24.

384. Jerome's point here is an anti-Origenist one, that without the presence of the organs of generation, there is no real resurrection. The very text on which the Origenists based their denial of sexual differentiation in the risen body is used by Jerome to prove the opposite. Cf. *Ep.* 108.22. A discussion is found in J. P. O'Connell, *The Eschatology of Saint Jerome*, 50–51.

22.30. *"But they are like the angels of God in heaven";* there is the promise of a spiritual way of life.

22.31–32. *"But concerning the resurrection of the dead, have you not read what God said to you: 'I am the God of Abraham and the God of Isaac and the God of Jacob'? He is the God not of the dead but of the living."* He could have used other far clearer examples to prove the truth of the resurrection.[385] For example, there is the following: "The dead shall be raised and those who are in their tombs shall rise again."[386] Another passage says: "Many of those sleeping shall rise from the dust of the earth: some to life, others to shame and eternal confusion."[387] Consequently, people ask why the Lord wanted to bring forth this testimony for himself: "I am the God of Abraham and the God of Isaac and the God of Jacob."[388] This passage seems ambiguous and not sufficiently to the point about the truth of the resurrection. And then, as though he had proven what he wanted to prove by bringing forth this testimony, he immediately added: "He is the God not of the dead but of the living." The crowds who were standing around were even astonished at the learning of his answer, since they recognized the mystery of the matter. Above we said[389] that the Sadducees, who confessed neither angel nor spirit nor the resurrection of bodies, also preached the destruction of souls. They received only the five books of Moses and rejected the predictions of the prophets.[390] It would have been foolish, then, to bring forth testimonies [from the prophets], whose authority the Sadducees did not follow. Further, in order to prove the eternity of souls from the writings of Moses, he offers the citation: "I am the God of Abraham and the God of Isaac and the God of Jacob." Then he immediately adds: "He is the God not of the dead but of the living." Thus, when he proved that souls continue after death—for were they not subsisting at all, it could not be the case that God would be their God—the resurrection of bodies was introduced by way of logical inference.

---

385. Cf. Origen, *In Matth.* 17.36.   386. Is 26.19.

387. Dn 12.2.   388. Ex 3.6.

389. See on Mt 22.23.

390. Jerome is developing Origen's explanation concerning the books accepted by the Sadducees. Cf. Origen, *In Matth.* 17.36.

For the bodies carried out good or evil together with the souls. The apostle Paul pursues this subject more fully in the last section of the first letter to the Corinthians.[391]

22.34–37. *When the Pharisees heard that he had silenced the Sadducees, they came together. One of them, a teacher of the Law, asked him a question, to test him. "Teacher, which is the great commandment in the Law?" Jesus said to him: "You shall love the Lord your God with all your heart,"* etc. What we read about Herod and Pontius Pilate, that they made their peace when they killed the Lord,[392] this too now we perceive concerning the Pharisees and the Sadducees. Among themselves they are adversaries, but they agree to think alike when it comes to testing Jesus. Those then who had already been silenced above when the denarius was shown to them, and who had seen the faction of the opposing party undermined, had to be warned by an example to prevent them from undertaking further plots. But malevolence and envy feed impudence. One of the teachers of the Law asks a question, not with the desire to know, but in order to test him, to see whether the one who had been asked knew the answer to the question, namely, what is the greater commandment. He is not asking about the commandments, but that which is the first and great commandment. Thus, since everything that God commands is great, whatever Jesus might respond would create a pretext for bringing a malicious charge. For Jesus would be asserting that one was great out of very many. Therefore, whoever knows and asks a question, not with the wish to learn, but out of a zeal to find out whether the one who is to respond knows, he approaches not as a learner but as a tempter,[393] in imitation of the Pharisees.

391. Cf. 1 Cor 15.35–38. Cf. Origen, *In Matth.* 17.29.
392. Cf. Lk 23.12.
393. Cf. 19.16.

BOOK FOUR (MATTHEW 22.41–28.20)

OW WHILE THE PHARISEES were gathered together, Jesus asked them a question, saying: "What does it seem to you about the Christ? Whose son is he?" They said to him: "David's." He said to them: "How is it, then, that David, in the Spirit, calls him Lord, saying: 'The Lord said to my Lord, Sit at my right hand, till I put your enemies as a footstool of your feet'?" (22.41–44) Those who had gathered to tempt Jesus and who were endeavoring to ensnare the Truth by their fraudulent question offered an opportunity for their own confutation and are asked about the Christ, "Whose son is he?" The question of Jesus still helps us today against the Jews. For even those who confess that Christ is going to come assert that he will be a mere human being and a holy man from the family of David. As those who have been taught by the Lord, then, let us ask them: If he is simply a man and merely David's son, how is it that David calls him his own Lord? And he calls him this, not by an uncertain error, nor in his own will, but in the Holy Spirit. Now the testimony that he cited was taken from the one hundred ninth Psalm.[1] Therefore, he is called David's Lord, not according to the fact that he was born from him, but in accordance with the fact that, having been born from the Father, he has always existed,[2] preceding the very father of his flesh.[3] To elude the truth of the question, the Jews fabricate many frivolous things. They claim that that text refers to Abraham's home-born slave, whose son was Eliezer of Damascus,[4] and that the Psalm was written under his persona. For (they say) that after the slaughter of the five kings,[5] the Lord God said to Abraham his lord: "Sit at my right hand, until I put all your en-

---

1. Ps 110.1.
2. Cf. Jn 8.58: "Before Abraham was born, I am."
3. Cf. Rom 4.1. 4. Cf. Gn 15.2.
5. Cf. Gn 14.17.

emies as a footstool of your feet." Let us ask them: How is it that God said to Abraham the things that follow: "With you is the rulership in the day of your strength in the brightness of your saints; from the womb before the day star I have begotten you"[6] and: "The Lord has sworn and he will not repent it: You are a priest forever according to the order of Melchizedek"?[7] Let us indeed compel them to explain how Abraham was born before the day star and became a priest according to the order of Melchizedek, for whom Melchizedek offered bread and wine and from whom he received a tithe of the booty.[8]

22.46. *And no one was able to answer him a word, nor did anyone dare from that day to ask him any more questions.* The Pharisees and Sadducees were seeking to find a pretext for a malicious charge and some word that would expose him to their treacherous plot. They ask no further questions because they have been put to silence by his words. Yet they very openly hand him over to the Roman authority, once they have him arrested. From this we learn that the poison of envy can indeed be overcome, but it is put to rest with difficulty.

Chapter 23

23.1–3. *Then Jesus spoke to the crowds and to his disciples, saying: "The scribes and Pharisees sit on Moses' seat; therefore, observe and do everything that they tell you, but do not do according to their works; for they say, and do not do."* What could be gentler, what could be more kind than the Lord? He is tempted by the Pharisees, their plots are wrecked, and according to the Psalmist: "The little children's arrows have become their wounds."[9] Nonetheless, on account of the priesthood and the dignity of their office he exhorts the people to be subject to them and to take into consideration their teaching, but not their works. Now, as for what he says: "The scribes and Pharisees sit on Moses' seat," by "seat" he is pointing to the learning of the Law. Therefore, we ought to understand this as referring to learning both what is said in

6. Ps 110.2–3.   7. Ps 110.4.
8. Cf. Gn 14.18–20.   9. Ps 64.7.

the Psalm: "He does not sit on the seat of pestilence,"[10] and: "He overturned the seats of those selling doves."[11]

23.4. *"They bind heavy burdens hard to bear and lay them on men's shoulders, but they are unwilling to move them with their finger."* This has general application to all teachers who command grand things but do not do lesser things. Now one should note that the shoulders, finger, burdens, and chains with which the burdens are bound are to be understood spiritually.

23.5. *"But all their works they do in order to be seen by men."* Therefore, whoever does anything in order to be seen by men is a scribe and a Pharisee.

23.5–7. *"For they make their phylacteries broad and their fringes long, and they love the first places at feasts and the first seats in the synagogues and salutations in the market places and being called rabbi by men."* Woe to us wretched ones to whom the vices of the Pharisees have passed! The Lord, when he gave the commandments of the Law through Moses, added at the end: "You will bind these on your hand and they will be unmoved before your eyes."[12] And this is the meaning: My precepts are in your hand that they might be fulfilled in conduct. Let them be before your eyes for you to meditate on them day and night. The Pharisees, interpreting this perversely, wrote on small parchments the Decalogue of Moses, that is, the ten words of the Law. Folding them up, they even bound them to their forehead and made a crown, so to speak, on their head, so that they would always be moving before their eyes. The Indians and Babylonians do this up to the present day, and among the people the one who has this crown is judged as religious. Moses had commanded something else too, that in the four corners of the robes they should make crimson fringes[13] to distinguish the people of Israel. Thus just as circumcision gives the sign of the Jewish nation in the bodies, so their clothing has some differentiation. Superstitious teachers who were desirous of publicity among the people and seeking a profit from little women[14] made their fringes long and bound very sharp thorns to them. They did this, evi-

---

10. Ps 1.1.   11. Mt 21.12; Mk 11.15.
12. Dt 6.8.   13. Cf. Nm 15.38–40.
14. Cf. 2 Tm 3.6.

dently, so that as they walked about and sat down they might at times be pricked, and by this reminder as it were they would be drawn back to their duties toward God and ministries in his service. When the Lord had said: "All their works they do in order to be seen by men," he was making a general accusation. But now he divides it into parts. They called those little depictions of the Decalogue "phylacteries" because whoever had them had his own protection and fortification as it were.[15] Now the Pharisees did not understand that these things need to be carried in the heart, not in the body. But chests and boxes hold books and do not have the knowledge of God. Among us there are superstitious little women who keep doing this up to the present day with little Gospels and with the wood of the Cross and with things of this sort. They have a zeal for God, to be sure, but not according to knowledge.[16] Straining out a gnat, they swallow a camel.[17] There was a small and short fringe of this sort that had been commanded from the Law. That woman who had the flowing of blood touched it on the Lord's robe,[18] but she was not pricked by the superstitious thorns of the Pharisees; rather, she was healed by contact with him. And since they make their phylacteries broad and their fringes long in vain, since they desire glory from men, they are exposed in the remaining matters. Why do they seek the first places at dinners and the first seats in the synagogues? Why do they pursue gluttony and glory in public? Why are they called "rabbi" by men? In the Latin language "rabbi" means "teacher." Finally, he adds:

23.8–10. *"But you are not to be called rabbi, for one is your Teacher, and do not call anyone your father on earth, for one is your Father, who is in heaven, nor shall you be called teachers, for your Teacher is one, the Christ."* No other should be called "teacher" or "father" except God the Father and our Lord Jesus Christ: Father, because from him are all things;[19] Teacher, because through him are all things, or because by his dispensation in the flesh we have all been reconciled to God.[20] It is asked why, in contradiction to

---

15. The Greek word *phylassō* means "to protect."

16. Cf. Rom 10.2.   17. Cf. Mt 23.24.

18. Cf. Mt 9.20; Lk 8.44; Mk 5.27.   19. Cf. 1 Cor 8.6; Col 1.16.

20. Cf. Rom 5.8.

this command, the apostle claims that he is the "teacher" of the Gentiles;[21] or how it is that in common language, especially in the monasteries of Palestine and Egypt, they call one another Fathers. This is resolved in the following manner: It is one thing to be a father or teacher by nature, something else to be one by tender feeling. If we call a man "father," we are conferring honor to his age; we are not pointing out the Creator of our life. One is called a "teacher," too, by one's association with the true Teacher. And lest I repeat things without end, just as the one God and the one Son by nature does not prejudice others from being called gods and sons by adoption,[22] so also one Father and Teacher does not prejudice others from being called fathers and teachers in an improper sense.

23.13. *"Woe to you, scribes and Pharisees, hypocrites! because you shut the kingdom of heaven before men; you neither enter yourselves, nor do you allow those entering to enter."* The scribes and Pharisees have knowledge of the Law and the prophets. They know that Christ is the Son of God; they are not unaware that he was born of a virgin. Yet so long as they seek to exploit the people subject to them, they do not enter the kingdom of heaven themselves, nor do they permit those who were able to enter. This is the accusation that the prophet makes in Hosea: "The priests have hidden the way, they have killed Shechem";[23] and again: "The priests have not told where the Lord is."[24] Or, at least, every teacher who scandalizes his disciples by his evil works shuts the kingdom of heaven before them.

23.15. *"Woe to you, scribes and Pharisees, hypocrites! for you go round about the sea and dry land to make one proselyte, and when he becomes one, you make him twice as much a son of Gehenna as yourselves."* We do not preserve things that have been sought with the same zeal with which we seek them. The scribes and Pharisees went around the whole world on account of business negotiations and various profits that they desired from their disciples so earnestly that they were able, under the appearance of sanctity, to proselytize from the Gentiles through their image of

21. Cf. 1 Tm 2.7.   22. Cf. Jn 10.34; Rom 8.14.
23. Hos 6.9.   24. Jer 2.8.

zeal for holiness, that is, to integrate into the people of God an uncircumcised foreigner. But he who previously while he was a pagan was simply lost and was a son of Gehenna once, when he sees the vices of the teachers and understands that they ruin by their conduct what they were teaching by their words, he returns to his vomit.[25] And this one, who had become a member of the household, now as a transgressor will be worthy of greater punishment. But he is called a son of Gehenna in the same way that he speaks of a son of perdition[26] and a son of this age.[27] For each one is called a son of that thing whose works he carries out.

23.16–22. *"Woe to you, blind guides, who say, 'If any one swears by the Temple, it is nothing; but if any one swears by the gold of the Temple, he is bound by his oath.' You blind fools! For which is greater, the gold or the Temple that sanctifies the gold? And [you say]: 'If any one swears by the altar, it is nothing; but if any one swears by the gift that is on it, he is bound by his oath.' You are blind! For which is greater, the gift or the altar that sanctifies the gift? Therefore, he who swears by the altar, swears by it and by everything on it; and he who swears by the Temple, swears by it and by him who dwells in it; and he who swears by heaven, swears by the throne of God and by him who sits upon it."* We explained above,[28] as it seemed to us, what was the meaning of the tradition of the Pharisees who say: "Whatever from me would be a benefit to you is a gift."[29] Now here, a twofold tradition of the Pharisees is being condemned, which also brings in its wake an occasion for greed. Thus they are convicted of doing everything for the sake of profit and not for the love of God. For just as by their lengthened phylacteries and fringes the reputation of sanctity was striving to acquire glory and was seeking profits through the occasion of glory, so another ruse invented from the tradition exposes the teachers of impiety. If anyone in a dispute or in some quarrel or in a disputed case swore by the Temple and afterward was convicted of lying, he was not held to be responsible for the charge. But if he swore by the gold and money that was offered in the Temple to the priests, at once he

25. Cf. Prv 26.11; 2 Pt 2.22.
27. Cf. Lk 16.8.
29. Mt 15.5.
26. Cf. Jn 17.12.
28. See on Mt 15.5.

was compelled to pay what he swore on oath. Again, if anyone swore by the altar, no one held him as guilty of perjury; but if he committed perjury by the gift or the offerings, that is, by the sacrifice or victims, and by other similar things, which are offered to God on the altar, they very zealously demanded payment of these things. Therefore, the Lord exposes both their folly and fraudulence. For the Temple is much greater than the gold that is sanctified by the Temple, and the altar is greater than the sacrifice that is sanctified by the altar. But everything they did was not for the fear of God but for the desire of wealth.

23.23. *"Woe to you, scribes and Pharisees, hypocrites! for you tithe mint and dill and cumin, and have neglected the weightier matters of the law, justice, mercy, and faithfulness; it was necessary to do these things and not to omit those things."* There are many precepts in the Law that hold forth types of future things. Some are clear, according to the Psalmist, who says: "The command of the Lord is lucid, illuminating the eyes."[30] Some call for works at once, for instance: "You shall not commit adultery, you shall not steal, you shall not speak false testimony," etc.[31] Now the Lord had given a precept for the support of priests and Levites whose portion was the Lord,[32] namely, a tithe of all things offered in the Temple[33] (for the moment we should forego the mystical interpretation of this precept). But the Pharisees were zealous for this one precept, namely, the accumulation of what had been commanded. Other things that were of greater importance mattered little to them. They did not care whether anyone did them or not. And so, he accuses them of greed on this point, that they zealously exact a tithe even of common herbs, yet they neglect justice in business disputes, and mercy toward poor orphans and widows, and faithfulness to God, which are great matters.

23.24. *"Blind guides, straining out a gnat, but swallowing a camel!"* In this context and in view of the importance of the precepts, I think that the camel refers to justice, mercy, and faith; the gnat, on the other hand, refers to the tithe of mint, dill, and cumin, and of the other common herbs. Contrary to God's precept, we devour and neglect these things that are great. Un-

---

30. Ps 19.8.   31. Ex 20.14–16.
32. Cf. Nm 18.20.   33. Cf. Nm 18.17.

der the impression of being religious, we show diligence toward trivial matters that bring a profit.

23.25–26. *"Woe to you, scribes and Pharisees, hypocrites! for you cleanse the outside of the cup and of the plate, but inside you are full of rapacity and uncleanness. You blind Pharisee! First cleanse the inside of the cup and of the plate, that the outside also may be clean."* With different words, but with the same sense as above, he accuses the Pharisees of pretense and lying. For they show one thing outwardly to men, but at home they do something else. It is not that their superstition lingered in the cup and the plate, but that they were showing their sanctity outwardly to men, by their dress, speech, phylacteries, fringes, the length of prayers, and other things of this sort. Yet inwardly they were filled with the defilements of vices.

23.27. *"Woe to you, scribes and Pharisees, hypocrites! for you are like whitewashed tombs, which outwardly appear beautiful to men, but within they are full of dead men's bones and all filth."* What he pointed out in regard to the cup and the plate, that they were fine on the outside but inwardly filthy, he now repeats this in the example of the tombs. Just as tombs are smoothed over on the outside with chalk, adorned with marble, and distinguished with gold and colors, but inside they are full of dead men's bones, so also are bad teachers. They teach one thing and do something else. They may show purity in the quality of their clothing and in the humility of their words, but inwardly they are full of all filth, avarice, and lust. Finally, he expresses this same thing more openly when he adds:

23.28–31. *"So you also outwardly appear just to men, but within you are full of hypocrisy and iniquity. Woe to you, scribes and Pharisees, hypocrites! for you build the tombs of the prophets and adorn the monuments of the just, and you say: 'If we had lived in the days of our fathers, we would not have taken part with them in [shedding] the blood of the prophets.' Thus you witness against yourselves, that you are sons of those who murdered the prophets."* He exposes them to be sons of murderers with a very skillful syllogism. Under the reputation of goodness and glory among the people, they build the tombs of the prophets whom their forefathers killed. They say: If we had lived at that time, we would not have done the things that our fathers did. But even this they speak by their conduct, if they do not say it in words, from the fact that they ambitiously and magnificently build memorials of those who were murdered, whom they do not deny were cut down by their own fathers.

23.32. *"And you fill up the measure of your fathers."* Let it be taken as proven from the preceding statements that they were sons of murderers and of those who killed the prophets. He now sums up what he meant and records, as it were, the last part of the syllogism:[34] "And you fill up the measure of your fathers." That is to say: What they left out, you fill in; they killed the servants, you crucify the Lord; they killed the prophets, you kill the one who was predicted by the prophets.

23.33. *"Serpents, brood of vipers, how shall you escape from the judgment of Gehenna?"* This is exactly what John the Baptist had also said.[35] So then, just as vipers are born from vipers, so you murderers, he says, are born from your murderous fathers.

23.34. *"Therefore, behold, I am sending to you prophets and wise men and scribes; some of them you will kill and crucify, and some of them you will scourge in your synagogues and persecute from city to city."* We said earlier that the words: "You fill up the measure of your fathers" apply to the person of the Lord, because he was to be killed by them. But these words can also refer to the disciples. For now he says about them: "Behold, I am sending to you prophets and wise men and scribes; some of them you will kill and crucify and scourge in your synagogues and you will persecute from city to city." Thus you fill up the measure of your fathers. At the same time, observe that according to the apostle, as he writes to the Corinthians,[36] there are diverse gifts of the disciples of Christ. Some are prophets who predict things to come; others are wise men who know when they should bring forth words; others are scribes, very learned in the Law. Stephen was one of these [disciples] and was stoned.[37] Paul was killed; Peter was crucified.[38] In the Acts of the Apostles disciples were scourged,[39] and they persecuted them from city to city, expel-

---

34. See above on Mt 23.28–31.   35. Cf. Mt 3.7–10; cf. Lk 3.7.
36. Cf. 1 Cor 12.1, 8–10.   37. Cf. Acts 7.58.
38. Cf. Eusebius, *HE* 2.25.   39. Cf. Acts 5.40.

ling them from Judea so that they moved on to the people of the Gentiles.

23.35–36. *"That upon you may come all the just blood that has been shed on earth, from the blood of just Abel to the blood of Zechariah the son of Barachiah, who was murdered between the sanctuary and the altar. Amen I say to you, all these things will come upon this generation."* There is no doubt that Abel is the one killed by his brother Cain.[40] He is acknowledged as just not only by the Lord's judgment, but by the testimony of Genesis, where his gifts are described as having been accepted by God.[41] But we do need to ask who this Zechariah son of Barachiah is. For we read about many Zechariahs. He even removes the possibility of error for us by adding: "whom you killed between the sanctuary and the altar." I have read diverse things in diverse sources, and I ought to record the opinions of each of these. Some[42] say that Zechariah son of Barachiah is the eleventh of the twelve prophets. The name of his father is in agreement with this,[43] but the Scripture does not say when he was killed between the sanctuary and the altar, chiefly since in his time there were scarcely even ruins of the Temple. Others[44] want this Zechariah to be understood as the father of John.[45] They approve of certain daydreams from apocryphal writings that say that he was killed because he had predicted the Savior's advent.[46] Since this view does not have the authority of the Scriptures, it is rejected with the same facility with which it is approved. Others[47] want this Zechariah to be the one who was killed between the sanctuary and the altar by Joash king of Judea, as the history of Kings narrates.[48] But one should

40. Cf. Gn 4.8.   41. Cf. Gn 4.5.

42. Cf. Origen, *In Matth. comm. series*, 25.

43. Cf. Zec 1.1.

44. Cf. Origen, *In Matth. comm. series*, 25.

45. Cf. Lk 1.5, 13.

46. Cf. Origen, *In Matth. comm. series*, 25; Epiphanius, *Haer.* 26.12.1–4. The apocryphal writing in question is the *Genna Marias* or "Birth of Mary," also called *The Protevangelium of James*, which records that Zechariah, father of John the Baptist, was murdered by the same Herod who ordered the slaughter of the babies at Bethlehem. Probably this legend was suggested by the reference in Matthew's text. See Hennecke-Schneemelcher, *NTA* 1, 344–45; ANF 8, 366.

47. Cf. Origen, *In Matth comm. series*, 25.

48. Cf. 2 Chr 24.22.

observe that that Zechariah was not the son of Barachiah, but the son of Jehoiada the priest.[49] This is why the Scripture relates: "Joash did not remember the good deeds of Jehoiada his father, which he had done for him."[50] Since, then, we should also retain Zechariah and the place of the killing is in agreement, we need to ask why he is called the son of Barachiah, and not of Jehoiada. Barachiah means "blessed of the Lord" in our language, and the justice of the priest Jehoiada is shown in the Hebrew language.[51] In the gospel that the Nazarenes use,[52] in place of "son of Barachiah" we have found it written: "son of Jehoiada." Rather simple brothers point out reddish stones among the ruins of the sanctuary and the altar, or at the exits of the gates which lead to Siloam. They think that these were stained by the blood of Zechariah. We should not condemn their error, because it arises from their pious faith and from the malice of the Jews. We should briefly explain what he means when he says that the blood of just Abel until Zechariah son of Barachiah is required from this generation, seeing that [this generation] has put neither of them to death. The pattern of the Scriptures is to record two [kinds of] generations, [namely,] those who are good or those who are evil; that is, each generation is noted for the one or the other. Let us consider examples of the good: "Who ascends on the mountain of the Lord, or who rests on his holy mountain?"[53] And since he has described very many who would ascend the mountain of the Lord, who lived in various ages, afterward he adds: "This is the generation of those who seek the Lord, of those who seek the face of the God of Jacob."[54] And in another passage it speaks of all the saints: "The generation

---

49. Cf. 2 Chr 24.20. H. Ridderbos, *Matthew*, Bible Student's Commentary (Grand Rapids: Zondervan, 1987), 433, thinks that the best explanation is to assume that the name of the prophet Zechariah's father was added later by an uninformed copyist.

50. 2 Chr 24.22.

51. Cf. *De interpr. hebr. nom.*, p. 60 and p. 39.

52. See Pref., n. 6. It is interesting that immediately above this Jerome can condemn Origen (anonymously) for citing an apocryphal writing with approval, and then shortly thereafter cite one himself.

53. Ps 24.3.

54. Ps 24.6.

of the just will be blessed."[55] But of the evil it speaks as in the present passage: "A generation of vipers," and "all things will be required of this generation." And in Ezekiel, when he had described the sins of the land, the prophetic words added: "If Noah and Job and Daniel were found there, I would not forgive the sins of this land."[56] By Noah, Job, and Daniel, he wants all the just to be understood, who are like them in their virtues. Therefore, even those who committed deeds against the apostles similar to [those of] Cain and Joash are referred to as being of a single generation.

23.37. *"Jerusalem, Jerusalem, you that kill the prophets and stone those who have been sent to you, how often have I wanted to gather your sons as a hen gathers her chicks under her wings, and you were unwilling."* By Jerusalem he does not mean the stones and buildings of the city, but its inhabitants. He laments for it with the feeling of a father, just as also in another passage we read that when he saw it, he wept.[57] Now his words: "How often have I wanted to gather your sons," testify to the fact that all the prophets in the past had been sent by him. We even read a similitude of a hen gathering her chicks under her wings in the song of Deuteronomy: "Just as an eagle protected her nestlings and longingly desired her chicks, spreading her wings, she has taken them up and borne them upon her pinions."[58]

23.38. *"Behold, your house will be left to you deserted."* Earlier he had already said this very thing under the persona of Jeremiah: "I have left my house; I have abandoned my inheritance; my inheritance has become to me like the den of a hyena."[59] We can prove with our eyes that the house of the Jews was deserted, that is, that Temple that was previously shining, inspiring awe. For it destroyed the one who dwelled in it, Christ, and, being eager to seize the inheritance, it killed the heir.[60]

23.39. *"For I say to you: You will not see me from now on until you say: 'Blessed is he who comes in the name of the Lord.'"* He is speaking to Jerusalem and to the people of the Jews. Now the little verse is the one that the little children and nursing infants used

---

55. Ps 112.2.
57. Cf. Lk 19.41.
59. Jer 12.7–8.

56. Ezek 14.14.
58. Dt 32.11.
60. Cf. Mt 21.38.

at the entry of the Lord and Savior into Jerusalem, when they said: "Blessed is he who comes in the name of the Lord. Hosanna in the highest."[61] He took it from the one hundred seventeenth Psalm, which is manifestly written about the coming of the Lord.[62] And he wants his words to be understood as follows: Unless you do penance[63] and confess that I am he of whom the prophets sang, the Son of the Almighty Father, you will not see my face. The Jews have a time given to them for repentance. Let them confess as blessed he who comes in the name of the Lord, and they will see the face of Christ.[64]

Chapter 24

24.1–2. *And having left the Temple, Jesus went away. And his disciples came to him to show him the building of the Temple. But he answered and said to them: "Do you see all these things? Amen I say to you: Not a stone shall be left here upon a stone which will not be destroyed."* The meaning of the historical narrative is manifest. As the Lord was leaving the Temple, all the buildings of the Law and the construction of the commandments were destroyed in such a way that nothing could be fulfilled by the Jews. Once the head was removed, all the members fight among themselves.

24.3. *Now as he was sitting on the Mount of Olives, the disciples came to him privately, saying: "Tell us, when will these things be and what will be the sign of your coming and of the consummation of the world?"* He is sitting on the Mount of Olives where the true light of knowledge was arising.[65] The disciples come to him privately. They were longing to know mysteries and revelation about the future. And they ask three questions: At what time is Jerusalem to be destroyed, when is Christ going to come, and when is the consummation of the world going to happen?

24.5. *"For many will come in my name, saying: 'I am the Christ,'*

61. Mt 21.9.
62. Cf. Ps 118.26. Cf. Homily 94 in FOTC 57, 253.
63. Cf. Lk 13.3.
64. Cf. 2 Cor 2.10; 4.6.
65. The Mount of Olives suggests the theme of light because the ancients used olive oil in their lamps.

and they will seduce many." One of these is Simon the Samaritan, of whom we read in the Acts of the Apostles. He claimed to be the great power of God.[66] Among other things, he left the following written statements in his books: "I am the Word [*Sermo*] of God, I am the Beautiful, I am the Paraclete, I am the Omnipotent, I am God's All."[67] But John the apostle says in his epistle: "You have heard that the Antichrist is coming, but now there are many antichrists."[68] I am of the opinion that all heresiarchs are antichrists and teach things in the name of Christ that are contrary to Christ.[69] It is not surprising that we see some seduced by them, since the Lord said: "And they will seduce many."

24.6. *"For you will hear of wars and rumors of wars. See to it that you are not alarmed; for these things must happen, but the end is not yet."* When we see these things happening, then, we should not think that the day of judgment is imminent. Rather, it is reserved for that time, whose sign is clearly recorded in what follows.

24.7–8. *"For nation will rise against nation, and kingdom against kingdom, and there will be pestilences and famines and earthquakes in various places. All these things are the beginning of the sorrows."* I do not call into question that these things that are written down are indeed predictions of future things according to the letter. But it seems to me that "kingdom against kingdom" and "pestilences" can be understood more of those whose words creep in like a cancer.[70] The famine is the one for hearing the word of God.[71] The shaking of the whole earth and the separation from the true faith occur among the heretics. By battling against one another, they assure victory to the Church. But what he has said: "But these are the beginning of the sorrows," is better translated "of the birth-pains." Thus the coming of the Antichrist should be understood as a kind of conception, but not a bringing to birth.

24.9. *"Then they will hand you over to tribulation and they will kill*

---

66. Cf. Acts 8.10.

67. Cf. Epiphanius, *Haer.* 21.

68. 1 Jn 2.18.

69. In spite of this statement, Jerome does not deny that there will also be an Antichrist who will come at the end of the world, namely, a man in whom the devil will dwell. Cf. *In Dan.* 7.8; *In Abacuc.* 2.15; *Ep.* 121.11. See J. P. O'Connell, *The Eschatology of Saint Jerome,* 25.

70. Cf. 2 Tm 2.17.

71. Cf. Am 8.11.

you." The persona of all believers is designated by the apostles. For at that time no apostles will be found in the flesh.

24.12. *"And because iniquity has abounded, the love of many will grow cold."* He has not denied the faith of all, but of many.[72] "For many are called, but few are chosen."[73] For among the apostles and those like them, love will endure. Of love it is written: "Much water cannot quench love."[74] And Paul himself says: "Who shall separate from the love of Christ? Tribulation or anguish?" etc.[75]

24.14. *"And this Gospel of the kingdom will be preached in the whole world as a testimony to all nations, and then the consummation will come."* The sign of the Lord's coming is the proclamation of the Gospel in the whole world. Thus no one will have an excuse. We perceive that this is either already completed or will be completed in a short time. For I do not think any nation remains that is ignorant of the name of Christ. Even if it does not have a proclaimer, yet it cannot be ignorant of the report of the faith [coming] from the surrounding nations.[76]

24.15. *"Therefore, when you see the abomination of desolation, which was spoken of by Daniel the prophet, standing in the holy place, let the reader understand."* Whenever we are summoned to understanding, what has been said is shown to be mystical. Now, we read it in Daniel in this way: "And for half a week my sacrifice and libations will be removed, and in the Temple there will be an abomination of desolations until the consummation of the time, and the consummation will be given over the devastation."[77] The apostle also speaks of this, that the man of iniquity and the ad-

---

72. J. P. O'Connell, *The Eschatology of St. Jerome*, 27, attempts to synthesize Jerome's understanding of the great apostasy of which Christ has spoken here by suggesting that for Jerome the departure of which Paul speaks (2 Thes 2.3) is identical with this religious defection, and it will be realized in a political defection of the Antichrist from the Roman Empire. Cf. *In Dan.* 7.25; *Ep.* 121.11.

73. Mt 20.16; 22.14.   74. Song 8.7.

75. Rom 8.35.

76. J. P. O'Connell, *The Eschatology of Saint Jerome*, 26, observes: "Jerome must have been unaware of the vast extent of pagan lands still to be evangelized. For he felt that already in his time there was hardly a portion of the earth that had not heard of Christ."

77. Dn 9.27.

versary is to be lifted up against everything that is called God or that is worshiped. He will dare to stand in the Temple of God and show that he himself is God,[78] that his coming in accordance with the working of Satan destroys them,[79] and that it reduces those who received him to a devastation, void of God.[80] Now this can be interpreted either literally of the Antichrist, or of the image of Caesar that Pilate placed in the Temple, or of the equestrian statue of Hadrian, which stands to the present day in the very location of the holy of holies.[81] According to the old Scripture,[82] an "abomination" is also called an "idol," and this is why "of desolation" is added, because an idol will be placed in the desolated and destroyed Temple.

24.16–18. *"Then let those who are in Judea flee to the mountains, and let the one who is on the housetop not go down to take anything from his house, and let him who is in the field not turn back to take his tunic."* The "abomination of desolation" can also be understood of all perverted doctrine. When we see it standing in the holy place, that is, in the Church, and showing itself as God, we should flee from Judea to the mountains; that is, when the letter that kills[83] and Judaic depravity have been abandoned, let us draw near to the eternal mountains[84] from which God illumines marvelously. Let us be on the housetop and in the home where the flaming arrows of the devil[85] cannot reach. Let us not go down and take anything from the house of our former way of life, nor seek the things that are below.[86] Rather, let us sow in the field of the spiritual Scriptures, that we might receive fruit from it. Let us not take another tunic, which the apostles are forbidden to have.[87] Concerning this passage, that is, the "abomination of desolation" that is spoken of by the prophet Daniel as standing in the holy place, Porphyry in the thirteenth volume of his work wrote many blasphemous things against us.[88] Eusebius

---

78. Cf. 2 Thes 2.3–4. 79. Cf. 2 Thes 2.8–9.
80. Cf. Lv 26.31; Jer 25.18. 81. Cf. Origen, *fragm.* 469.
82. That is, the Old Latin (the Latin translation of the LXX).
83. Cf. 2 Cor 3.6. 84. Cf. Ps 76.4.
85. Cf. Eph 6.16; Ps 76.3. 86. Cf. Col 3.1–2.
87. Cf. Mt 10.10.
88. In the prologue of his *Commentary on Daniel* (PL 25: 491A; CCSL 75A, 771), Jerome indicates that Porphyry wrote his *twelfth* volume (not thirteenth,

the bishop of Caesarea responded to him in three volumes: the eighteenth, nineteenth, and twentieth. Apollinaris also wrote on this subject in great detail. And it is a superfluous endeavor to wish to discuss in one little section a question on which disputations of so many thousands of lines have been written.

24.19. *"And woe to pregnant women and nursing mothers in those days."* Woe to those souls that have not brought their offspring through to the point of being the perfect man.[89] They have the beginnings of the faith but in such a way that they lack the nourishment[90] of teachers. This can also be explained in the following manner. During the persecution of the Antichrist or of the Roman captivity, pregnant women and nursing mothers, being weighed down by the burden in their womb or of their children, will be unable to escape very easily.[91]

24.20. *"Pray that your flight may not be in winter or on a sabbath."* If we want to take this of the captivity of Jerusalem when it was captured by Titus and Vespasian, the meaning is that they should pray that their flight will not be in winter or on a sabbath. For in the former season, the harshness of the cold hinders from traveling in the wastelands and hiding in the mountains and deserts. On the sabbath either it is a transgression of the Law if they wanted to escape, or there would be imminent death if they remain. But if it is understood of the consummation of the world, he is commanding that our faith in and love for Christ not grow cold, and that on the sabbath of the virtues we may not grow torpid and lazy in the work of God.[92]

24.22. *"And if those days had not been shortened, no flesh would be saved, but on account of the elect those days will be shortened."* The days are shortened, not in accordance with the delusions of

---

as here) of his great work, *Contra Christianos,* against the prophecy of Daniel. Since Porphyry's work is not extant, it is not possible to determine in which volume of Porphyry the allegations occur.

89. Cf. Col 1.28.

90. "Nourishment" (*enutritio*) is cognate with "nursing mothers" (*nutrientibus*) in the lemma.

91. Jerome interprets Jesus' saying both literally of the time of the Antichrist and allegorically, as he also does in *Ep.* 121.4.

92. Notice again that Jerome has offered both a literal and an allegorical interpretation.

some[93] who think that the motion of time is altered. They forget the Scripture that says: "The day abides by your appointment."[94] Rather, we ought to understand this in terms of the quality of time; that is, they are shortened not in measure but in number. Thus, just as in the benediction it is said: "I will fill him with the length of days,"[95] so also now days are understood to be shortened in order to prevent the faith of believers from being shaken by the delay of time.

24.23. *"Then if anyone says to you, 'Behold, here is the Christ!' or: 'There he is!' do not believe it."* At the time of the Judaic captivity, many leaders rose up who claimed to be the Christ. This occurred to such an extent that when the Romans were conducting their siege, there were three factions within [Jerusalem].[96] But it is understood better of the consummation of the world.

24.24–25. *"For false Christs and false prophets will arise and will give great signs and prodigies, so that even the elect, if it were possible, would be led into error. Behold, I have told you ahead of time."* As I said earlier,[97] the passage here ought to be explained in a threefold way, either concerning the time of the Roman siege, or concerning the consummation of the world, or concerning the battle of the heretics and antichrists of that sort against the Church, who fight against Christ under the pretext of false knowledge.[98]

24.26. *"So then, if they say to you: 'Behold, he is in the desert,' do not go out; 'Behold, he is in the inner rooms,' do not believe it."* If anyone promises you that Christ is staying in the desert of the Gentiles and in the doctrine of the philosophers, or in the inner rooms of the heretics who promise "the secret things of God," do not go out; do not believe it. Or, since at the time of persecution and anguish, false prophets always find an opportunity for deceiving, if anyone wants to vaunt himself under the name of Christ, you should not at once put faith in him.

24.27. *"For just as lightning comes out of the east and appears as*

---

93. Cf. Ambrosiaster, *In Matth.* (= Clavis Patr. Lat., n. 186); Augustine, *Ep.* 199.30.

94. Ps 119.91.   95. Ps 91.16.

96. The leaders of these factions were named John, Eleazer, and Simon. Cf. Josephus, *BJ* 5.1.2.

97. See above on Mt 24.7–8.   98. Cf. 1 Tm 6.20.

far as the west, so will be the coming of the Son of man." Do not go out; do not believe that the Son of man is either in the desert of the Gentiles or in the inner rooms of the heretics. Believe rather that faith in him shines in the Catholic churches from the east as far as the west. The following should also be said: that the second coming of the Savior will be manifested not in humility, as the first, but in glory.[99] And so, it is foolish to look in a small or hidden place for him who is the light of the whole world.[100]

24.28. *"Where the body is, there the eagles will be gathered."* We are being instructed in the mystery of Christ from a natural example that we see every day. Eagles, and vultures likewise, are said to sense carcasses across seas and to be gathered for food of this sort. If, then, irrational birds by a natural feeling, though separated by such great stretches of land and by the waves of the sea, sense where a small carcass is lying, how much more ought we and the entire multitude of believers hasten to him whose lightning flash goes out from the east and appears as far as the west. The Latin word *cadaver* expresses more clearly the meaning of the word body, that is, πτῶμα. For through the death of the body, it falls *(cadat)*.[101] This term refers to the Passion of Christ, to which we are summoned, so that whenever the Passion is read in the Scriptures, we are gathered together, and through it we can come to the Word of God. This is expressed, for instance, in the following words: "They have pierced my hands and feet,"[102] and in Isaiah: "like a lamb led to the slaughter,"[103] and other similar things. Now it is the saints who are called "eagles." Their youth is renewed like an eagle's,[104] and according to Isaiah they have feathers and take up wings[105] that they may come to the Passion of Christ.

24.29. *"But immediately after the tribulation of those days the sun will be darkened, and the moon will not give its light; then the stars of*

99. Cf. *Ep.* 121.11.

100. Cf. Jn 8.12.

101. Jerome's etymology is also sustained in the Greek, since πτῶμα is derived from πίπτω ("fall").

102. Cf. Ps 22.16.   103. Cf. Is 53.7.

104. Cf. Ps 103.5.   105. Cf. Is 40.31.

heaven will fall from heaven, and the powers of heaven will be shaken. "The sun and moon will be darkened and will not give their light. The other stars will fall from heaven and the powers of the heavens will be shaken. This is not going to happen by a lessening of light, for elsewhere we read that the sun will have seven times its light.[106] Rather, the meaning is that in comparison with the true light,[107] all things will seem dark.[108] And so, that sun that now grows red throughout the whole world, and the moon that illuminates in the second place, and the stars that are aflame as a solace to the night, and all the powers, which we understand as the multitudes of angels, will be reckoned as darkness at the coming of Christ. If this is so, let the arrogance of those be struck down who regard themselves as saints[109] and have no fear of the presence of the Judge.

24.30. *"And then the sign of the Son of man will appear in heaven."* The sign here refers either to the Cross, just as according to Zechariah and John, the Jews will look upon the one they have pierced;[110] or it is the banner of victory of the triumphant one.

24.30. *"Then all the tribes of the earth will mourn."* Those will mourn who did not have a home and citizenship in heaven, but who were enrolled on the earth.[111]

24.31. *"And he will send his angels with a trumpet."* The apostle also speaks of this trumpet.[112] We read about it in the Apocalypse of John,[113] and in the Old Testament he commands trumpets to be made that are hammered out thin from gold, bronze, and silver.[114] The reason for this is that they will resound deep mysteries of doctrines.[115]

24.32–33. *"From the fig tree, learn the parable. As soon as its branches become tender and its leaves have sprouted, you know that summer is near,"* etc. By the example of the tree, he has taught

---

106. Cf. Is 30.26.   107. Cf. Jn 1.9.

108. Elsewhere (*In Naum* 1.5), Jerome interprets the physical phenomena that occur at Christ's second coming literally, while still admitting a figurative interpretation.

109. Cf. Lk 18.9.   110. Cf. Zec 12.37; Jn 19.10.

111. Cf. Heb 12.23.   112. Cf. 1 Cor 15.52; 1 Thes 4.16.

113. Cf. Rv 8.5.

114. Cf. Nm 10.2; 8.4. See *In Joelem* 2.1.

115. Jerome does not say whether or not the trumpet is to be taken literally.

the coming of the consummation. Just as, he says, when the little stalks in the fig tree become tender and the bud bursts forth into flower and the bark produces leaves, you understand the coming of summer and the commencement of the west wind and of spring; so when you see all these things that are written, do not think that the consummation of the world is already here. On the contrary, certain preludes and precursors are coming in order to show that it is near and at the gates.

24.34. *"Amen I say to you, that this generation will not pass away until all these things happen."* We have said above[116] that the generations of both the good and the evil are distinct. Therefore, either he is indicating the entire human race, or the race of the Jews in particular.

24.35. *"Heaven and earth shall pass away, but my words will not pass away."* Heaven and earth will pass away by being changed, not by being annihilated.[117] Otherwise, how will "the sun be darkened, and the moon not give its light, and the stars fall"?[118] For this would be impossible if the heaven and the earth did not exist, since this is where these things are located.

24.36. *"But of that day and hour, no one knows, neither the angels of heaven, save only the Father alone."* In some Latin manuscripts is added: "nor the Son," though in the Greek copies,[119] and especially those of Adamantius[120] and of Pierius,[121] this addition is not found. Yet because it is read in some, it seems necessary to

---

116. See on Mt 23.35–36. 117. Cf. *In Is.* 51.6; 65.18.
118. Mt 24.29.

119. Jerome is apparently referring to the Greek copies to which he had access. In reality, the reading "nor the Son" is well attested in the Greek manuscript tradition and should be read. In fact, Jerome essentially adopts this reading below. The words "nor the Son" were probably omitted because of the doctrinal difficulty they presented. See Metzger, *Textual Commentary*, 62.

120. The name Adamantius refers to Origen. Cf. Eusebius, *HE* 6.14.10; Jerome, *Ep.* 43. Origen's text does in fact have the words "nor the Son" (GCS 38.2.126–27), so Jerome must be thinking of other references in Origen's writings that omit these words.

121. Pierius was an eminent priest of Alexandria, famous for his voluntary poverty, his philosophical knowledge, and his public expositions of Scripture. For his eloquence he was known as the younger Origen. He ruled the catechetical school of Alexandria under the bishop Theonas, and afterwards lived in Rome. See Photius, *Bibl.* (PG 103: 400); Jerome, *De viris ill.* 76; *DCB* 4.396.

discuss it. Arius and Eunomius rejoice, as if the ignorance of the teacher is the glory of disciples. They say: He who knows and he who does not know cannot be equal. The following things need to be said briefly against these men. Since Jesus, that is, the Word of God, made all time, for "all things were made through him, and without him nothing was made,"[122] but the day of judgment is included among all time, by what consistency can he be ignorant of a part of which he knows the whole? This too should be said: What is greater, knowledge of the Father or of the judgment? If he knows the greater, how is he ignorant of the lesser? We read that it is written: "All things that are the Father's have been given to me."[123] If all things of the Father are the Son's, by what account has he reserved for himself the knowledge of a single day and been unwilling to communicate it with his Son? But the following should be added as well. If he is ignorant of the last day of time, he is ignorant also of the penultimate day, and of all the days in back of it. For it is impossible that one who is ignorant of the first would know which is the second. Therefore, since we have proven that the Son is not ignorant of the day of consummation, the reason needs to be given for why he is said not to know. The apostle writes of the Savior: "In whom are all the treasures of wisdom and knowledge hidden."[124] Therefore, all the treasures of wisdom and knowledge are in Christ, but they are hidden. Why hidden? After the Resurrection, when asked by the apostles about the day, he answered openly: "It is not yours to know the times and moments that the Father has set by his authority."[125] When he says: "It is not yours to know," he shows that he himself knows, but it is not expedient for the apostles to know.[126] Thus, since they are always uncertain about the coming of the Judge, they will live every day in such a way as though they will be judged on another day. Finally, even the following words of the Gospel compel this interpretation, when he says that the Father alone knows. In the Father he has comprehended also the Son; for to speak of a father is always to name a son.[127]

122. Jn 1.3. 123. Mt 11.27.

124. Col 2.3. 125. Acts 1.7.

126. Cf. Homily 84 in FOTC 57, 187.

127. Lit., "for every father is the name of a son" (*omnis enim pater filii nomen est*). See below on Mt 26.29. Cf. Homily 8 on Ps 74 (75) in FOTC 48, 61.

24.37–38. *"But just as in the days of Noah, so also will be the coming of the Son of man. For just as in the days before the flood they were eating and drinking, marrying and giving in marriage,"* etc. It is asked, How is it that above this it is written: "For nation will rise up against nation and kingdom against kingdom, and there will be pestilences and famines and earthquakes,"[128] and now he mentions future things that are indications of peace? But one must consider this in accordance with the apostle: After the conflicts, dissensions, pestilences, famines, earthquakes, and the other things by which the human race is devastated, a brief peace is going to ensue, which promises a complete period of peace. In this way the faithfulness of believers will be tested to see whether they will hope for the coming of the Judge when the evils have passed. For this is what we read in Paul: "When they say: Peace and security, then sudden destruction will come upon them as the pain of a woman in labor, and they will not escape."[129]

24.40–41. *"Then there will be two in a field; one will be taken, and one will be left. Two women will be grinding at the mill; one will be taken, and the other will be left."* Then, he says, there will be two in a field. When? Namely, at the time of the consummation and judgment: Two will be found equally in a field, doing the same labor and sowing the same seed, as it were. But they do not receive the same fruit from their labor. Likewise, two women will be grinding together; one will be taken, the other will be left. By the two men who are lingering in the field and the two women who are equally grinding, understand the synagogue and the Church. For they would seem to be grinding together at the Law. From the same Scriptures they seem to crush the same flour of God's precepts. Or understand the other heresies that seem to grind the flour of their doctrines either from both Testaments or from one of them.[130] Though they have the intention of having the

---

128. Mt 24.7.   129. Cf. 1 Thes 5.3.

130. For example, the Marcionite sect rejected the Old Testament in its entirety and drew its doctrine from a badly mutilated form of the New Testament (parts of Luke and ten of Paul's letters). Other heresies, such as Valentinian Gnosticism, used both the Old and New Testaments in eclectic fashion. Jerome seems to be conceding, however, that certain heretical sects will be received into the kingdom, and others will be rejected.

name of Christian, they will not receive the same reward. For some of them will be taken and others forsaken.

24.42. *"Watch, therefore, for you do not know at what hour your Lord will come."* He is clearly showing why he had said above: "But concerning that day no one knows, neither the Son of man,[131] nor the angels, save only the Father alone."[132] It is not expedient for the apostles to know this. Thus they will always believe that he is coming with the uncertainty of an imminent expectation. For they do not know when he will come. And he did not say: "For *we* do not know at what hour the Lord will come," but: "*you* do not know." He had spoken earlier about this in the example of the householder.[133] Now he shows more manifestly why he is silent about the day of consummation, saying:

24.44–46. *"Be ready, because you do not know at what hour the Son of man is coming. Who, do you think, is the faithful and wise servant whom his master has appointed over his household that he should give them food at the proper time? Blessed is that servant whom his master when he comes will find so doing."* He impresses more fully and he repeats the reason why he said earlier that neither the angels nor he himself knows about the day and hour of the consummation, but only the Father: because it is not expedient for the apostles to know. And he introduces the example of the householder, that is, himself, and of the faithful servants, that is, the apostles, as an encouragement to solicitous minds. With the expectation of receiving rewards, they are to serve their fellow servants the food of doctrines at the proper time.

24.48–49. *"But if that wicked servant says in his heart: 'My master is delayed,' and he begins to beat his fellow servants,"* etc. These words depend on what precedes. Just as a solicitous servant and one who is always expecting the coming of his master gives food to his fellow servants at the proper time, and afterward he is appointed over all the goods of the householder, so on the contrary he who does not think that his master will come soon becomes rather secure and he takes it easy with feasting and

131. Notice that now Jerome reads "neither the Son of man" as the authentic text of Matthew's Gospel. See his discussion above under Mt 24.36.

132. Mt 24.36.

133. Cf. Mt 21.33–41.

luxury. This agrees with Ezekiel who says: "That will happen in a long time."[134] In the householder he will encounter not leniency but a most severe judge.

24.50–51. *"The master of that servant will come on a day that he does not expect, and at an hour he does not know, and he will divide him and put his share with the hypocrites."* He teaches the same thing, that they might know that the Lord is going to come at a time when he is not being thought of. He admonishes the stewards to vigilance and solicitude. What he says further, "He will divide him," does not mean that he will cut him in two with a sword. Rather, it means that he will separate him from an allotment with the saints and put his share with the hypocrites, namely, with those who were in the field and who were grinding[135] and nevertheless were left behind. We have often said[136] that a hypocrite *is* one thing, but *shows* something else. In this way he too was seen in the field and at the millstone doing the same thing that the man of the Church was doing, but the outcome showed that they were of different wills.

Chapter 25

25.1–2. *"Then the kingdom of heaven will be like ten virgins who took their lamps and went out to meet the bridegroom and the bride;[137] five of them were foolish and five were wise,"* etc. To some[138] this parable, that is, similitude, of the ten virgins, foolish and wise, is interpreted literally of virgins. According to the apostle,[139] some are virgins in both body and mind; others, preserving the virginity of their body only, either do not have other works that are

---

134. Ezek 12.22.   135. Cf. Mt 24.40–41.

136. Cf. Mt 6.2, 16; 7.3; 22.18.

137. The omission of "and the bride" in many ancient manuscripts (and in the modern versions) may have been due to the belief that these words were incompatible with the Pauline (cf. Eph 5.29–32) and Johannine (cf. Rv 21.2) view that Christ, the Bridegroom, would come to fetch his bride the Church. Jerome's reading could easily be the right one.

138. Cf. John Chrysostom, *In Matth. Hom.* 78 (79).1. This is also the interpretation Jerome gives in *Ep.* 22.5 to Eustochium.

139. Cf. 1 Cor 7.34.

similar by their own intention, or, having been preserved by the protection of their parents, nonetheless have married in their minds. But from what precedes, it seems to me that the meaning expressed is different. The comparison applies not to virginal bodies but to the whole human race. For above he spoke of the two in the field and the two grinding at the mill as representing two peoples,[140] that of the Christians and that of the Jews, or that of the saints and that of sinners. The latter indeed seem to be established in the Church, and they seem to be plowing and grinding, but they do everything in hypocrisy. In the same way now the ten virgins embrace all men who seem to believe in God. They congratulate themselves for their possession of the Holy Scriptures. For members of the Church do this, and so do the Jews and the heretics. The reason they are all called virgins is that they boast in the knowledge of the one God, and their mind is not violated[141] by the mob of idolatry.[142] The virgins who have oil are those who are adorned with works as well as with faith. Those who indeed seem to confess the Lord with similar faith, but who neglect the works of the virtues, do not have oil. In the *five* wise and *five* foolish virgins, we can interpret the *five* senses. Some of the senses hasten to heavenly things and desire the things above;[143] others cast longing eyes at earthly corruption and do not have the solace of the truth by which they may illuminate their hearts. For the Scriptures speak of sight, sound, and touch in a spiritual sense, for example: "What we have seen, what we have heard, what we have beheld with our eyes and our hands have touched."[144] Concerning taste it says: "Taste and see that the Lord is good."[145] Concerning smell we find: "We run after the fragrance of your ointments";[146] and: "We are the good fragrance of Christ."[147]

---

140. See above on Mt 24.40.

141. Lit., "is not raped" (*non constupratur*).

142. This is a dominant theme in the prophets: when they reproach Israel for idolatry, they accuse them of adultery and compare the people of God to a prostitute. Cf. Ezek 16–23; Jer 3.6–13.

143. Cf. Col 3.2.   144. 1 Jn 1.1.

145. Ps 34.8.   146. Song 1.3.

147. 2 Cor 2.15.

25.5. *"But when the bridegroom was delayed, they all slumbered and slept."* For no small amount of time passes between the first and the second coming of the Lord. "They all slumbered": that is, they died, since the death of saints is called sleep.[148] It is consistent that it is said, "They slept," since later they will be roused.[149]

25.6. *"But at midnight there was a cry: 'Behold, the bridegroom is coming; go out to meet him.'"* For suddenly, as if in the dead of night and with everything secure, when slumber is deepest, the coming of Christ will resound with the shout of angels and the trumpets of the powers that will precede him.[150] We should say something that may perhaps be useful to the reader. According to Jewish tradition, the Christ will come at midnight. This correlates with the time in Egypt when the Passover was celebrated, the destroyer came, the Lord passed over the tabernacles, and the fronts of our doorposts were consecrated with lamb's blood.[151] I think this is also why the apostolic tradition continued that on the day of the Passover vigil it is not permitted to dismiss the people before midnight, as they await the coming of Christ. Once that time has passed, the safety of all who celebrate the feast day is assured. This is also why the Psalmist said: "I rose at midnight to give praise to you for the judgments of your justice."[152]

25.7. *"Then all those virgins rose and adorned their lamps."* All the virgins rose and each of them adorned her lamp. The lamps stand for the senses by means of which they received the oil of knowledge. Thus do they nourish the works of the virtues that shine forth before the true Judge.

25.8. *"But the foolish ones said to the wise: 'Give us some of your oil, because our lamps are going out.'"* Those who complain that their lamps are going out show that they are shining in part. Yet they do not have an unfailing light or perpetual works. If any-

---

148. Cf. Acts 7.60; 1 Thes 4.13. See *Vita Pauli* 11; *Contra Vig.* 6; *Ep.* 127.14.

149. J. P. O'Connell, *The Eschatology of St. Jerome*, 74, comments: "The resurrection, therefore, is Jerome's reason for using sleep as a figure of death." Cf. *Contra Vig.* 6.

150. Cf. 1 Thes 4.16; Mt 26.64.   151. Cf. Ex 12.3–23.

152. Ps 119.62.

one therefore has a virginal soul and is a lover of chastity, he should not be content with mediocre things which quickly fade. For when the heat rises, they become dry.[153] On the contrary, let him pursue the perfect virtues that he may have eternal light.

25.9. *"The wise answered and said: 'No, for perhaps then there would not be enough for us and for you.'"* They give this response not out of greed but out of fear. For each one will receive a reward for his works,[154] nor can the virtues of some remove the vices of others on the day of judgment. And just as at the time of the captivity in Babylon, Jeremiah was unable to help sinners, and it was said to him: "Do not pray for this people,"[155] so that day will be dreadful, when each one will be concerned for himself.

25.9. *"Go rather to the dealers and buy for yourselves.'"* This oil, which we understand as consisting in alms and in all the virtues and counsels of the teachers, is sold and bought at a great price, and it is acquired with difficult effort.

25.10. *"But while they were going to buy, the bridegroom came."* In their apparent wisdom they give the counsel that they must not meet the bridegroom without oil in their lamps. But because the time of buying had now passed and the day of judgment was approaching, there was no opportunity for repentance. As the Psalmist says: "Who will confess to you in the underworld?"[156] They are compelled to pay the account for the past deeds, not to accomplish new works.

25.10. *"The bridegroom came, and those who were ready went in with him to the marriage, and the door was shut."* After the day of judgment, the opportunity for good works and for justice will disappear.[157]

153. Cf. Mt 13.6; Jb 30.30. 154. Cf. 2 Cor 5.10.
155. Jer 7.16. 156. Ps 6.5.

157. J. P. O'Connell, *The Eschatology of Saint Jerome*, 11–12, notes that during the Origenist quarrel there is little mention of death (as opposed to the future day of judgment) as the end of the Christian's opportunity to do good works and earn merit, because this was not the precise point of Origen's teaching on which the controversy turned. The present passage, however, is of relevance: "Our author [Jerome] seems here to say that the end of a Christian's opportunity to merit is not death but the last judgment. . . . Jerome many times speaks as though he were completely unaware of what happens between death and the last judgment. However, the interpretation of such texts . . . allows no

25.11. *"But at last the other virgins came also, saying: 'Lord, Lord, open to us.'"* To be sure, this is an illustrious confession in the title of the Lord, and it is a repeated indication of their faith. But what benefit is there in calling upon him with your voice when you deny him by your deeds?

25.12. *"But he responded and said: 'Amen I say to you: I do not know you.'"* "The Lord knows those who are his,"[158] and "he who does not know will be unknown."[159] The Lord does not know the workers of iniquity.[160] Though they are virgins, and in two senses they are honored, for the purity of their body and for their confession of the true faith, yet, since they do not have the oil of knowledge, it is sufficient for their punishment that they are not known by the Bridegroom.

25.13. *"Watch therefore, because you do not know the day or the hour."* I always warn the wise reader not to subscribe to superstitious interpretations and those that are spoken "line by line"[161] by people who fabricate things by their own arbitrary will. Instead, let the reader consider what precedes, what is in the middle, and what follows. And let him connect to one another all the things that are written.[162] And therefore, everything that he said can be understood from added words: "Watch, because you do not know the day or the hour." This applies to the two who are in the field, to the two women grinding,[163] to the householder who entrusted his property to his servant,[164] and to the ten virgins.[165] The reason the parables were given first was so that we might carefully prepare the light of good works for ourselves, since we men do not know the day of judgment.[166] Otherwise, the Judge may come when we do not know it.

---

grounds for a denial that death is the end of the Christian's chance to merit." Elsewhere, Jerome makes clear that the soul enjoys its reward immediately after death, which implies that death is the end of the Christian contest.

158. 2 Tm 2.19.   159. 1 Cor 14.38.
160. Cf. Mt 7.23.

161. Lat., *commatice.* A cognate of this word (*commaticum*) is used in the Preface (4) to describe one of Origen's works on Matthew. Jerome probably has Origen in mind in this section.

162. This text is important for appreciating Jerome's method of biblical interpretation.

163. Cf. Mt 24.40–41.   164. Cf. Mt 24.45.
165. Cf. Mt 25.1–12.   166. Cf. Mt 25.7.

25.14–15. *"For just as when a man going on a journey called his servants and delivered to them his goods and to one he gave five talents, to another two, but to another one."* Doubtless this human householder is none other than Christ. When he was about to ascend to the Father as a victor after the Resurrection, he called the apostles and delivered to them the evangelical doctrine.[167] It was not on account of lavishness and stinginess that he gave more to one and less to another, but on account of the abilities of those who receive. This correlates with what the apostle also says, that he fed milk to those who were incapable of taking in solid food.[168] After all, he receives with a similar joy both him who had made ten talents from five and him who had made four from two. He did not consider the size of the profit but the intention of their zeal. In the five, two, and one talents, we should understand either diverse graces, which have been delivered to each one; or, in the first, all the senses that have been examined [above],[169] in the second, understanding and works, and in the third, reason, by which we men are separated from the beasts.

25.16. *"He who had received the five talents went off and put them to work. He gained another five."* By using the earthly senses that he had received, he doubled the knowledge of the heavenly things for himself. He understood the Creator from the creatures,[170] incorporeal things from those with bodies, invisible things from visible ones, eternal things from things that are ephemeral.

25.17. *"He who had received two gained another two."* In proportion to his abilities, whatever he had learned in the Law, he doubled it in the Gospel. Or: he understood that knowledge and works of the present life are types of the future blessedness.

25.18. *"But he who had received one went away and dug in the ground and hid his master's money."* The wicked servant neglected and defiled God's commands by earthly works and by the pleasure of the world. In another evangelist it is written that he

---

167. Cf. Mt 28.19.

168. Cf. 1 Cor 3.2.

169. He means the (five) senses of sight, hearing, taste, touch, smell. See under Mt 25.1–2.

170. Cf. Rom 1.20.

wrapped it in a napkin;[171] that is, he took the vigor out of the doctrine of the householder by living softly and delicately.[172]

25.19. *"But after a long time the master of those servants came."* The time between the Savior's Ascension and his second coming is great. Now if the apostles are going to render an account and rise up with fear of the Judge, what ought we to do?

25.21. *"The lord said to him: 'Well done, good and faithful servant; since you were faithful over a few things, I will appoint you over many things. Enter into the joy of your master.'"* As I have already said earlier,[173] the householder speaks affectionately to the two servants with the same words, both to the one who from five talents made ten, and to the one who from two made four. And one should note that all things that we have in the present, though they may seem great and many, nevertheless are small and few compared with future things. He says, "Enter into the joy of your master," and receive "the things that neither eye has seen nor ear heard nor have ascended into the heart of man."[174] Now what greater thing could be given to the faithful servant than to be with the master[175] and to see the joy of his master?

25.24–25. *"But he also who had received one talent approached and said: 'Lord, I know that you are a hard man; you reap where you have not sown, and you gather where you have not scattered; so I was afraid and went off and hid your talent in the ground. Behold, you have what is yours.'"* Truly, the words of Scripture: "to make excuses to excuse sins"[176] apply to this servant as well, as he adds the crime of arrogance to his laziness and negligence. For the one who ought to have confessed his inactivity and to have pleaded with the householder speaks evil instead. He claims that he has acted by wise counsel and that he was afraid of endangering the capital while seeking to make a profit on the money.

25.26–28. *"But his master answered and said to him: 'You wicked and lazy servant! You knew that I reap where I do not sow, and gather where I have not scattered? Then you ought to have invested my money with the bankers, and at my coming I would have received what was my own with interest. So take the talent from him and give it to him who*

171. Cf. Lk 19.20.
173. See on Mt 25.14–15.
175. Cf. Phil 1.23.
172. Cf. Lk 15.13.
174. 1 Cor 2.9.
176. Ps 141.4.

has ten talents.'" What he thought he had said as an excuse is turned into a charge against him. The servant is called "wicked" because he maligns his master, "lazy" because he was unwilling to double the talent. Thus he is condemned for arrogance on the first point and for negligence on the second. If, he says, you knew that I am hard and cruel, that I run after other people's things and reap where I have not sown, why did this consideration not strike fear into you? You should have known that I was going to seek what was mine more diligently. Then you would have put my money, or silver, with the bankers. For the Greek word ἀργύριον means both. It says: "The things spoken by the Lord are pure utterances, silver examined and proven by fire, purified of earth seven times."[177] Therefore, the money and silver refer to the preaching of the Gospel and the divine words which must be given to the bankers and money-changers. These latter may refer to other teachers, for this is exactly what the apostles did in each province when they ordained priests and bishops. Or they may refer to all believers who can double the money and render it with interest, as they fulfill in deed whatever they have learned in words. But the talent is taken away and given to him who had made ten talents. We can understand this to mean that, although the master's joy in the labor of each one is equal, that is to say, both for him who doubled the five into ten and for him who made two into four, yet the reward owed is greater to him who had labored more with the Lord's money. This is exactly why the apostle says: "Honor the priests who are truly priests, especially those who labor in the word of God."[178] From what the wicked servant has dared to say: "You reap where you have not sown, and you gather where you have not scattered," we understand that the Lord accepts the good life even of the Gentiles and philosophers. He regards those who behave justly one way, and those who behave unjustly in another way. Those who neglect the written law will be condemned in comparison with the one who serves the natural law.[179]

25.29. *"For to everyone who has, it will be given and he will abound, but to him who does not have, even what he seems to have will be tak-*

---

177. Ps 12.6.   178. 1 Tm 5.17.
179. Cf. Rom 2.12, 27.

en away from him." Many are wise by nature and have an acute
natural intelligence. But if they become negligent and corrupt
the good of nature by idleness, they can lose the good of nature
and seem to pass the reward that had been promised to them
to others, namely, to those who in comparison with them had
by labor and diligence compensated somewhat tardily for what
they had less of to begin with. It can also be understood in this
way: The good judge will give to him who has faith and a good
will in the Lord, even if, being human, he has something less in
works; but he who does not have faith will lose even the other
virtues that he seemed to possess by nature. And it is elegantly
said: "what he *seems* to have will be taken from him." For whatever is apart from faith in Christ ought not be imputed to him
who has badly abused it, but to him who gave the good of nature even to the wicked servant.

25.30. *"And cast the useless servant into the outer darkness; there
shall be weeping and gnashing of teeth."* The Lord is light.[180] He
who lacks the true light is sent outside by him. Above[181] we have
discussed what the weeping and gnashing of teeth refer to.

25.31–33. *"Now, when the Son of man comes in his majesty, and
all the angels with him, then he will sit on the throne of his majesty,
and before him will be gathered all the nations, and he will separate
them one from another as a shepherd separates the sheep from the goats.
And he will place the sheep at his right hand, but the goats at the left."*
Being about to celebrate the Passover after two days and to be
handed over to the cross and mocked by men and given a drink
of vinegar and gall, he rightly promises the glory of the triumphant one. He wants to compensate for the stumbling blocks
that are about to follow with the reward of promise. We should
note that he who is to be seen in majesty is the Son of man. And
as for what follows: "He will place the sheep at his right hand,
but the goats at the left," understand it in accordance with what
you read elsewhere: "The heart of a wise man is on his right
hand, and the heart of a fool is on his left."[182] Also, above in this
same Gospel it says: "Do not let your left hand know what your
right hand is doing."[183] The sheep are commanded to stand to

---

180. Cf. Jn 1.4, 9; 9.5.
182. Eccl 10.2.
181. See on Mt 22.13.
183. Mt 6.3.

the right on the side of the just; the goats, that is, sinners, to the left. In the Law goats are always offered for sin.[184] He did not say "she-goats." These can have young, and "when shorn they come up from the washing all bearing twins, and not one among them is sterile."[185] Instead he said "goats," a lascivious animal, apt to butt, and always burning for intercourse.

25.34. *"Come, O blessed of my Father, possess the kingdom prepared for you from the foundation of the world."* This is to be understood in accordance with the foreknowledge of God, with whom future things are already done.[186]

25.40. *"Amen I say to you: As you did this to one of the least of these brothers of mine, you did it to me."* The interpretation is clear. The hungering Christ was fed in each of the poor; thirsting, he received drink; a guest, he was invited in under the roof; naked, he was clothed; weak, he was visited; shut up in prison, he had the solace of a visitor. As for the words that follow: "When you did it to one of the least of these brothers of mine, you did it to me," it does not seem to me that he said this generally of the poor, but of those who are poor in spirit.[187] For it was to them that he reached out his hand and said: "My brothers and my mother are those who do the will of my Father."[188]

25.46. *"And they will go into eternal punishment, but the just into eternal life."* Wise reader, pay attention to the fact that the punishments are eternal,[189] and that, from that time on, the perpetual life has no fear of falling away.[190]

---

184. Cf. Ex 12.5. 185. Song 4.2.

186. Cf. 1 Pt 1.2 (Greek, not RSV). Jerome follows the Greek interpreters in explaining predestination as foreknowledge of merit. Augustine was alone among the Fathers in rejecting election according to foreseen merits.

187. Cf. Mt 5.3. 188. Cf. Lk 8.21; Mt 12.50.

189. This text is the strongest one in Jerome's writings that appears to affirm that once being a Christian is not an absolute assurance of final entrance into heaven. Jerome reminds his Christian readers here that eternal punishments await those whom Christ, at the general judgment, will be able to accuse of a lack of charity during this life. There is not the slightest evidence to suggest that those who are so accused must also lack faith. In spite of this seeming clarity, J. P. O'Connell, *The Eschatology of Saint Jerome,* 175, persists in his view that Jerome was probably a mercyist (see note on 5.29), and that this present text "is not irrefutably anti-mercyist."

190. Jerome is probably directing this second clause against Origen's teach-

Chapter 26

26.1–2. *And it came about that when Jesus had finished all these words he said to his disciples: "You know that after two days the Passover is coming, and the Son of man will be handed over to be crucified."* Let them[191] blush who think that the Savior feared death and that it was out of dread of suffering that he said: "Father, if it is possible, let this cup pass from me."[192] He was about to celebrate the Passover after two days. He knew that he was going to be handed over to be crucified; and yet, he does not avoid the plots, nor does he flee out of terror. To such an extent is he intrepid that he goes on, even when the others are unwilling to go, as when Thomas says: "Let us go, that we too might die with him."[193] And wanting to put an end to the fleshly festivity, and to restore the truth, as the shadow of the Passover passes away, he said: "With desire I have desired to eat this Passover with you before I suffer."[194] "For Christ our Passover has been sacrificed,"[195] if we eat it "with the unleavened bread of sincerity and truth."[196] As for what he says further: "After two days the Passover will come," let us search for what is holy and leave aside the literal understanding. After two days of the clearest light (of the Old and New Testaments), the true Passover is celebrated for the world. In Hebrew the Passover is called *Phase*. The name derives not from the word *passion (passio)*,[197] as the majority think, but from *passing (transitus)*, because the destroyer, upon seeing the

---

ing, which admitted the possibility of falling away in the next life. See on Mt 6.10. St. Thomas Aquinas, following St. Augustine, recognized as Origen's principal error his failure to understand correctly the volitional power of the damned. Cf. *De malo* 16.5; *De ver.* 24.10; *S.T.* I, 64.2.

191. M. Simonetti, *Matthew 1b* (ACC), p. 236, thinks that Jerome's adversaries here are pagans, specifically Porphyry, who used Jesus' request that his cup be taken from him to maintain that he could not have been of a divine nature. Jerome may also have the heretics Arius and Eunomius in mind. See below at 26.37.

192. Mt 26.39.   193. Jn 11.16.
194. Lk 22.15.   195. 1 Cor 5.7.
196. 1 Cor 5.8.

197. According to this commonplace but mistaken Greek etymology, *Phase* is derived from *paschein*, to suffer. Cf. Melito of Sardis, *Peri Pascha* (SC 123, 84); Tertullian, *Adv. Judaeos* 10.18.

blood on the doors of the Israelites, passed through and did not strike them.[198] Or it was because the Lord himself offered his help to the people and walked above them. Read the book of Exodus. I will discuss this in greater detail if life permits.[199] Now our passing, that is, *Phase*, is thus celebrated if we hasten toward heavenly things, leaving earthly things and Egypt behind.

26.3–4. *Then the chief priests and elders of the people were gathered in the palace of the high priest, who was called Caiaphas. And they took counsel that they might seize Jesus by means of deceit and kill him.* With the Passover near, those who should have been preparing victims, making smooth the walls of the Temple, sweeping the pavement, cleansing the vessels, and purifying themselves in accordance with the rite of the Law,[200] that they might become worthy to eat the lamb, are gathered together and enter into counsel to determine how to kill the Lord. They do not fear a tumult, as the literal words show, but they are on guard, lest [Jesus] be removed from their hands with the help of the people.

26.6. *Now when Jesus was in Bethany in the house of Simon the leper.* He was about to suffer for the whole world and to redeem all nations by his blood. He stays in Bethany, "the house of obedience,"[201] which at one time belonged to Simon the leper. It is not that he remained a leper even at that time, but that he was formerly a leper and afterward was cleansed by the Savior. His original name remained with him in order that the power of the one who cured him might appear. For even in the list of apostles, though Matthew is called a tax-collector[202] according to his former vice and duty, he had certainly ceased being a tax-collector. Some[203] want the house of Simon the leper to be understood as that portion of the people that believed in the Lord and was cured by him.[204] Simon, too, is himself called "the one who obeys." According to another understanding his name can be translated "clean." It was in his house that the Church was healed.

26.7. *A woman came to him, holding an alabaster jar of precious*

---

198. Cf. Ex 12.13.

199. Jerome never composed this commentary on Exodus.

200. Cf. Lv 23.3–5; Nm 28.16.

201. Cf. *De interpr. hebr. nom.*, p. 60, line 27.

202. Cf. Mt 10.3.   203. Who?

204. Cf. Homily 84 in FOTC 57, 189.

ointment, and she poured it on his head as he was reclining. Let no one think that she who poured ointment on his head and she who poured it on his feet are the same woman. For the latter also washes them with her tears and wipes them with her hair and is openly called a prostitute.[205] But no such thing is written about this woman.[206] For a prostitute could not at once become worthy of the Lord's head. Another evangelist recorded "pure nard"[207] for "an alabaster jar full of precious ointment." (Alabaster is a kind of marble.) "Pure" *(pisticus)* means "true" and "without deceit." Thus the other evangelist is showing the faith *(pistis)* of the Church and of the Gentiles.[208]

26.8–9. *But when the disciples saw it, they were indignant, saying: "Why this waste? For this could have been sold for a large sum and given to the poor."* I know that some[209] criticize this passage and ask why another evangelist said that Judas alone was angry, for he held the purse and was a thief from the beginning,[210] whereas Matthew writes that *all* the apostles were indignant. These critics are unaware of a figure of speech called σύλληψις, which is customarily termed "all for one and one for many."[211] For even the apostle Paul in his epistle that is written to the Hebrews (although many Latins have doubts about this),[212] when he described the sufferings and merits of the saints, added: "They were stoned, they were tested, they were sawn in two, they died by being cut down by the sword."[213] And yet, the Jews assert that only one prophet, namely, Isaiah, was cut in two.[214] We can also

205. Cf. Lk 7.37–46.
206. Cf. Homily 84 in FOTC 57, 189.
207. Cf. Jn 12.3.
208. Cf. Homily 84 in FOTC 57, 189.
209. Who?
210. Cf. Jn 12.4–7.
211. Above on Mt 12.40 Jerome uses συνεχδοχιχῶς ("by synecdoche") for a similar figure of speech. We call this synecdoche, which consists in taking a part for the whole or the whole for a part. See also below on Mt 27.44.
212. In antiquity there were doubts about the Pauline authorship of the letter to the Hebrews. In the East these doubts did not hinder the acceptance of the letter into the New Testament canon, but in the West the full acceptance of Hebrews came only at the beginning of the fifth century.
213. Heb 11.37; cf. Origen, *fragm.* 522.
214. Cf. *Mart. Is.* 5.

explain it in another way: The apostles truly are indignant for the sake of the poor, but Judas was indignant for the sake of his own profits. This is why his grumbling is recorded along with his misdeeds. For he did not care about the poor but wanted to provide for his own thievery.

26.10–11. *But Jesus, aware of this, said to them: "Why do you trouble the woman? A good work has been done to me; for you always have the poor with you, but you will not always have me."* Another question arises: Why did the Lord after the Resurrection say to the disciples: "Behold, I am with you always until the consummation of the world,"[215] but now he says: "But you will not always have me"? It seems to me that he is speaking in this passage of his bodily presence, which will not be with them after the Resurrection, as it is now in all companionship and intimacy. The apostle was mindful of this matter when he said: "And if we knew Jesus Christ according to the flesh, but now we no longer know him."[216]

26.12. *"For in pouring this ointment on my body, she did it for my burial."* What you think of as a waste of ointment is a duty for burial. No wonder if she gave the good fragrance of her faith to me, since I am going to pour out my blood for her.

26.13. *"Amen I say to you: Wherever this Gospel is preached in the whole world, even what she did will be told in memory of her."* It is not so much this woman as the Church that is preached in the whole world,[217] because she buried the Savior, because she anointed his head. And notice his knowledge of the future, that he who is about to suffer and die after two days knows that his Gospel will be celebrated in the whole world.

26.15. *And he said to them: "What are you willing to give to me and I will hand him over to you?" And they decided upon thirty silver pieces for him.* Wretched Judas! He wants to compensate for the loss that he believed he had incurred at the outpouring of the ointment[218] with the price of his master. And yet, he does not demand a definite sum so that at least the betrayal would have appeared lucrative. But as if handing over a vile slave to the authority of the buyers, he proposed an amount that was as

215. Mt 28.20.   216. 2 Cor 5.16.
217. Cf. Mt 24.14.   218. Cf. Jn 12.6.

much as they were willing to give. "They decided upon thirty silver pieces for him." Joseph was sold not for twenty gold pieces, as many think, in accordance with the LXX,[219] but, according to the Hebrew truth, for twenty silver pieces.[220] For the slave could not have more value than the Master.

26.17. *Now on the first day of Unleavened Bread the disciples came to Jesus, saying: "Where will you have us prepare for you to eat the Passover?"* The first day of the Unleavened Bread is the fourteenth day of the first month, when the lamb is sacrificed and the moon is fullest and the leaven is cast out.[221] Now I think that Judas the traitor was also among these disciples who came to the Lord, asking: "Where will you have us prepare for you to eat the Passover?"

26.18. *But Jesus said: "Go into the city to a certain man."* The new Scripture preserves the usage of the Old Testament. We read frequently: "He said to that one"; and: "In this place and that," which in Hebrew is said as *phelmoni* and *helmoni,* without the names of the persons and places being recorded. "And you will find," he says, "a certain man carrying a jar of water."[222] The reason their names have been omitted is so that a free opportunity of festivity might be opened up for *all* who are going to celebrate the Passover.

26.19. *And the disciples did as Jesus instructed them, and they prepared the Passover.* In another evangelist it is written that they found a large upper room, furnished and cleansed, and they made preparations for him there.[223] It seems to me that the upper room stands for the spiritual law, which emerges from the confined places of the letter and receives the Savior in a lofty place. Paul says the same thing, that he despised as offscourings and refuse the things that he previously considered as gain, that he might prepare a worthy guest room for the Lord.[224]

26.20. *Now when evening came, he was reclining with the twelve disciples.* In this way Judas does everything in such a way that the suspicion of his being a traitor might be removed.

---

219. Lit., "seventy translators" (*LXX interpretes*).
220. Cf. Gn 37.28.   221. Cf. Ex 12.1–6.
222. Mk 14.13.   223. Cf. Lk 22.12.
224. Cf. Phil 3.7–8; Phlm 22.

26.21. *And while they were eating, he said: "Amen I say to you that one of you is going to hand me over."* The one who had predicted his suffering also predicts his betrayer. He was giving room for repentance, so that when he had understood that Jesus knew his thoughts and secret plans, he might repent of his deed. And yet Jesus does not specifically point him out. For he might have become more impudent, had he been manifestly exposed. He casts the charge against the group, that the one who is aware of it might do penance.

26.22. *And being very saddened, they each began to say: "Is it I, Lord?"* At least eleven apostles knew that they were thinking no such thing against the Lord, but they believe the Master more than themselves. They fear their own weakness and ask him sorrowfully about the sin of which they did not have awareness.

26.23. *But he answered and said: "He will hand me over who dips his hand in the dish with me."* How admirable is the Lord's patience! First he said: "One of you is going to hand me over."[225] The betrayer perseveres in his malice. Jesus exposes him more openly but does not reveal his proper name. While the others are saddened and are retracting their hands and are keeping food from their mouths, Judas, with the temerity and impudence by which he was going to commit the betrayal, even puts his hand in the dish with the Master. Thus he feigns a good conscience by this audacity.

26.24. *"The Son of man goes indeed as it is written about him, but woe to that man by whom the Son of man will be handed over."* Judas does not retrace his steps, even after being rebuked for his treachery not one time but twice. Instead, the Lord's patience feeds his impudence, and he treasures up wrath for himself on the day of wrath.[226] Punishment is predicted, that the threatened penalties might correct the one whom shame did not conquer. As for what follows:

26.24. *"It would be[227] good for that man if he had not been born";* it is not to be thought on account of these words that he existed prior to his birth, on the grounds that it could not be well for any-

---

225. Mt 26.21.
226. Cf. Rom 2.5.
227. Using the variant reading, *esset;* see CCSL 77, 250, note on line 1125.

one except for one who existed.[228] Instead, it has been spoken literally, that it is much better not to exist than to exist badly.

26.25. *But Judas, who handed him over, answered and said: "Is it I, Rabbi?" He said to him: "You have said it."* The others were sad and had very sorrowfully asked: "Is it I, Lord?" Thus, lest he seem to betray himself by his silence, Judas himself asks in similar fashion: "Is it I, Rabbi?" He who had boldly put his hand in the dish was stung in his conscience. But in his words he adds either the affection of a flatterer[229] or the sign of unbelief. For the others who were not going to betray say: "Is it I, Lord?" But he who was going to betray calls him not "Lord" but "Teacher." It is as if he would have an excuse if he betrayed at most a teacher, having denied that he was Lord. "And he said to him: 'You have said it.'" The betrayer is put to silence with the same response by which [Jesus] would later answer Pilate.[230]

26.26–27. *Now while they were eating, Jesus took bread and blessed and broke it, and he gave it to his disciples and said: "Take and eat, this is my body." And taking the cup, he gave thanks and gave it to them, saying,* etc. After the figurative Passover had been fulfilled and he had eaten the flesh of the lamb with the apostles, he took bread, which strengthens the heart of man,[231] and passed over to the true mystery of the Passover. Thus, just as Melchizedek had done, the priest of the Most High God, when he offered bread and wine in the prefiguration of him,[232] he too would present it in the truth of his own body and blood. In Luke we read of two cups that he passed on to the disciples.[233] One was for the first month and the other for the second. Thus the one who could not eat lamb among the saints in the first month could eat goat among the penitents in the second month.[234]

228. This may be directed against an Origenist interpretation that would affirm the pre-existence of souls.

229. See above on Mt 11.26.   230. Cf. Mt 27.11.

231. Ps 104.15.   232. Cf. Gn 14.18; Heb 7.

233. Cf. Lk 22.17, 20.

234. In Nm 9.1–14, God provided for Israelites who had been unclean during the Passover and were unable to eat of it. On a fixed day one month later they could celebrate it with a sheep. But Ex 12.5 says that it was permitted to take the lamb from the goats. Jerome finds this to be a prefiguration of future mysteries.

26.29. *"But I say to you: I will not drink from now on from this fruit of the vine until that day when I drink it with you anew in the kingdom of my Father."* He passes from fleshly things to spiritual things. The vine transplanted from Egypt is the people of Israel,[235] to whom the Lord speaks through Jeremiah: "I planted you as a true vine; how is it that you have changed into the bitterness of a foreign vine?"[236] And Isaiah the prophet sings of it in his song to his beloved.[237] Indeed, all Scripture testifies of it in various passages. Therefore, the Lord says that he is not going to drink from this vine ever again except in the kingdom of his Father. I think that the kingdom of the Father refers to the faith of believers. For the apostle,[238] too, confirms the same thing: "The kingdom of God is within you."[239] Therefore, when the Jews receive the kingdom of the Father (note what he says: "of the Father," not "of God"; every father is the name of a son);[240] since, I say, they will believe in God the Father, and the Father will bring them to the Son, then the Lord will drink from their vine, and in the likeness of Joseph reigning in Egypt, will be made merry[241] with his brothers.[242]

26.30. *And when they had sung a hymn, they went out to the Mount of Olives.* This is what we read in a certain Psalm: "All the sleek of the earth have eaten and worshiped."[243] According to this citation, the one who has been filled with the Savior's bread and made merry[244] with his cup can praise the Lord and ascend the Mount of Olives, where there is refreshment from labors and solace from grief and there is knowledge of the true light.[245]

26.31. *Then Jesus said to them: "All of you will suffer a scandal at me on this night."* He predicts what they are going to suffer, so that when they suffer it, they might not despair of salvation, but by doing penance may be delivered. And he has expressly

---

235. Cf. Ps 80.8.   236. Jer 2.21.

237. Cf. Is 5.1–7.

238. He means "the Lord" unless he is referring to the evangelist Luke as an apostle.

239. Lk 17.21.   240. See above on Mt 24.36.

241. Lit., "will be inebriated" (*inebriabitur*).

242. Cf. Gn 43.34.   243. Ps 22.29.

244. Lat., *inebriatus fuerit.* Cf. nn. 241 and 246.

245. See above on Mt 21.1–3.

added: "on this *night* you will suffer a scandal." For just as those who get drunk[246] get drunk *at night*,[247] so also those who suffer a scandal in the night also endure it in the darkness. But as for us, let us say: "Night has passed and the day has approached."[248]

26.31. *"For it is written: 'I will strike the shepherd, and the sheep of the flock will be scattered.'"* This is written in different words in the prophet Zechariah, and, unless I am mistaken, it is said to God under the persona of the prophet: "*Strike* the shepherd and *let* the sheep be scattered."[249] Yet the sixty-eighth Psalm, the whole of which the Lord has just sung, agrees with this meaning: "Because they have persecuted him whom you have struck."[250] Now the good shepherd is struck, that he may lay his life down for his sheep and that from many flocks of strays there may come one flock and one shepherd.[251] We have spoken in more detail about this testimony in the little book that we wrote on the best method of translating.[252]

26.33. *But Peter answered and said to him: "Even if all are scandalized, I will never be scandalized."* This is said not by temerity or falsehood; rather, it shows the faith of the apostle Peter and his burning affection for his Lord and Savior, of which we have spoken above.[253]

26.34. *Jesus said to him: "Amen I say to you that on this night before the cock crows, you will deny me three times."* Peter made the promise out of the ardor of his faith, but the Savior, as God, knew the future. Note also that Peter denies at night, and he denies three times; but after the cock crowed and the approaching light is declared, as the darkness diminishes, he converts and weeps bitterly, washing away the filth of his denial with tears.[254]

26.36. *Then Jesus went with them into a place called Gethsemane, and he said to his disciples: "Sit here while I go there and pray."* Gethsemane is interpreted as "very fertile valley." He commanded

---

246. Lat., *inebriantur.* See nn. 241 and 244, above.

247. Cf. 1 Thes 5.7.   248. Rom 13.12.

249. Zec 13.7.   250. Ps 69.26.

251. Cf. Jn 10.16.

252. He means his *Ep.* 57.7 to Pammachius, where Jerome assembles many inexact references to the Old Testament made by the evangelists.

253. See under Mt 14.28.

254. Cf. Mt 26.69–75.

the disciples to sit there for a little while and to await his return, while the Lord prayed alone for everyone.

26.37. *And when he had taken Peter and the two sons of Zebedee, he began to be sorrowful and grieved.* What we said above about passion and pre-passion[255] is also shown in the present section. To prove the truth of the humanity he had assumed, the Lord is truly sorrowful, but lest passion should be dominant in his soul, he *began* to be sorrowful through pre-passion. For it is one thing to be sorrowful, another *to begin* to be sorrowful. But he was sorrowful not out of fear of suffering. For he had come to this point in order to suffer, and he had rebuked Peter for fearfulness. Rather, he is sorrowful on account of the most wretched Judas, and the falling-away of all the apostles, who were scandalized, and the rejection of the people of the Jews, and the overturning of pitiful Jerusalem. This is also why Jonah is sorrowful over the withering of the gourd, or ivy.[256] He was unwilling that his own dwelling place should ever perish.[257] But if the heretics[258] interpret the sadness of his soul not as the Savior's affection for those who are going to perish but as a passion, let them respond: How do they explain what is said by Ezekiel under the persona of God: "And in all these things you made me sorrowful"?[259]

26.38. *Then he said to them: "My soul is sorrowful even to death; remain here and watch with me."* It is his soul that is very sorrowful; and it is very sorrowful not *on account of death,* but "even to death," until he delivers his apostles by his Passion. As for his command: "Remain here and watch with me," he is not forbid-

---

255. See above on Mt 5.28, n. 136. Simonetti, *Matthew 1b* (ACC), 255, comments: "To explain Jesus' agitation, Jerome resorts to the medical distinction between *pathos* (*passio*, 'disease') and *propatheia* (*propassio*, 'beginning/anticipation of disease'). *Pathos* in the moral sense is considered evil, while *propatheia* signifies the beginning of the agitation, not yet morally wrong because voluntary assent is lacking."

256. Cf. Jon 4.8.

257. As did Jesus himself (cf. Mt 12.40), Jerome sees in Jonah a prefiguring of Christ. This time it is Jonah's sorrow that anticipates Christ's. Cf. *Commentary on Jonah* 4.6 (SC 43, 109–13).

258. He seems to have Arius and Eunomius in mind.

259. Ezek 16.43 (LXX). God says this to Jerusalem. Jerome's point then seems to be that if God himself knows this sorrow, then the sorrow of Jesus is not a human sorrow, but divine.

ding sleep, for it was not the time for sleep, since the critical moment was imminent, but he forbids the sleep of unfaithfulness and the drowsiness of the mind. Let those[260] who suspect that Jesus took up an irrational soul say how he is very sorrowful and knows the time of sorrow. For although even brute animals grieve, yet they do not know the reasons for their grief or the duration of time in which they must be very sorrowful.

26.39. *And going a little farther he fell on his face, worshiping and saying: "My Father, if it is possible, let this cup pass from me; nevertheless, not as I will, but as you will."* Having commanded the apostles to remain and watch with the Lord, going a little farther he falls on his face, and shows the humility of his mind by the disposition of his flesh. And he says affectionately: "My Father." He asks that if it is possible the cup of the Passion might pass from him, concerning which we have spoken above.[261] But he asks not out of fear of suffering but from mercy for the first people, that he should not drink the cup offered by them. This is also why he did not expressly say: "Let the cup pass from me," but: "*this* cup," that is, the one belonging to the people of the Jews. For they can have no excuse for their ignorance if they kill me, since they have the Law and the prophets who predict me every day. And yet, returning to himself, that which he had refused with trepidation from his human persona, he confirms from the persona of the Son of God: "nevertheless, not as I will but as you will." He is saying: This "Let it be done": I am saying this not out of human feeling, but because it was by your will that I have come down to earth.

26.40. *And he came to the disciples and found them sleeping, and he said to Peter: "So, could you not watch with me one hour?"* Peter had said above: "Even if all are scandalized at you, I will never be scandalized."[262] But now he cannot conquer sleep from the greatness of his grief.

26.41. *"Watch and pray that you not enter into temptation."* It is impossible for a human soul not to be tempted. This is why in

260. Perhaps Apollinaris of Laodicea.
261. See on Mt 26.37.
262. Mt 26.33. Notice that the words "at you" (*in te*) are missing from the Mt 26.33 lemma.

the Lord's prayer we say: "Lead us not into temptation"[263] that
we are unable to bear.[264] We are not refusing to face temptation
altogether, but praying for the strength of endurance in temptation. Therefore, in the present passage he does not say: "Watch
and pray" that you not be tempted, but "that you not enter into
temptation," that is, that temptation not overcome and conquer
you and hold you in its nets. For instance, a martyr who sheds
his blood for the confession of the Lord is tempted, to be sure,
but he is not bound in the nets of temptation. But the one who
denies[265] falls into the nets of temptation.[266]

26.41. *"The spirit indeed is willing, but the flesh is weak."* This
is directed against those rash people who think that whatever
they believe, they can attain. And so, however much we trust in
the ardor of our mind, so too we should fear the frailty of the
flesh. And yet, according to the apostle, the works of the flesh
are mortified by the spirit.[267]

26.42. *Again, a second time he went away and prayed, saying: "My
Father, if this cup cannot pass unless I drink it, let your will be done."*
He prays a second time that if Nineveh cannot otherwise be
saved except that the gourd be withered,[268] let the will of the Father be done, which is not contrary to the will of the Son, since
he himself says through the prophet: "I have willed to do your
will, my God."[269]

26.43. *And he came again and found them sleeping; for their eyes
were heavy.* Alone he prays for all, just as also alone he suffers
for all. But the eyes of the apostles were weak and were overwhelmed by the denial that was near.

26.45. *Then he came to his disciples and said to them: "Sleep now
and rest; behold, the hour is at hand."* He prayed for the third time
so that every word be established by the mouth of two and three
witnesses.[270] Thus he procured that the fear of the apostles

---

263. Mt 6.13; Lk 11.4.   264. Cf. 1 Cor 10.13.
265. Cf. Mt 10.32–33.

266. In this paragraph Jerome uses three different words for "nets": *cassis,
rete,* and *plaga.*

267. Cf. Rom 8.13.

268. Cf. Jon 4.8. See above on Mt 26.37.

269. Ps 40.8.

270. Cf. Dt 19.15. Here the witnesses are the three apostles.

should be corrected by subsequent repentance. After this, he is secure concerning his own suffering and goes on toward his persecutors. Of his own accord he offers himself to be put to death, and he says to his disciples:

26.46. *"Rise, let us go; behold, the one who is going to hand me over is at hand."* Let them not find us as ones who are afraid and withdrawn. Let us go to death of our own accord, that they may see the confidence and joy of the one about to suffer.[271]

26.48. *Now, the one who handed him over had given a sign to them, saying: "Whomever I kiss is the one; seize him."* Judas is pitiful, and yet he is not worthy of pity. He handed over his Master and Lord with the same unbelief by which he was thinking that the signs that he had seen the Savior doing were done not by divine majesty but by magic arts. And because he had happened to hear him when he was transfigured on the mountain,[272] he was afraid that he might slip away from the hands of the servants by a similar transformation. Therefore, he gives a sign that they might know that the one whom he reveals with the kiss is he.

26.49. *And at once approaching Jesus, he said: "Hail, Rabbi," and he kissed him.* What an impudent and criminal confidence! To call him Teacher and to give a kiss to the one he was handing over! Yet he still has some shame from being a disciple. For he does not hand him over to the persecutors openly, but through the sign of the kiss. This is the sign that God put on Cain, that whoever found him would not kill him.[273]

26.50. *And Jesus said to him: "Friend, what have you come for?"* The word "friend" should be understood ironically,[274] or at least according to what we have read above: "Friend, how did you enter here without a wedding garment?"[275]

26.51. *And behold, one of those who were with Jesus stretched out his hand and drew his sword, and striking the servant of the high priest he cut off his ear.* In another Gospel[276] it is written that Peter did this, with the same ardor of mind by which he did other things.[277] It is also stated that the servant of the high priest was

271. Cf. Heb 12.2.   272. Cf. Mt 17.2.
273. Cf. Gn 4.15.
274. Κατὰ ἀντίφρασιν; lit., "according to an anti-phrase."
275. Mt 22.12.   276. Cf. Jn 18.10.
277. See above on Mt 14.28, 31; 26.34.

named Malchus and that the ear that he cut off was the right one. In passing one should say that Malchus, that is, "king," represents the former people of the Jews. It became a servant of impiety and of the voracity of the priests, and it lost its right ear. Thus it hears all the contemptibleness of the letter with its left ear. But among those who were willing to believe from the Jews, the Lord gave back the right ear and made the servant a royal and priestly race.[278]

26.52. *Then Jesus said to him: "Return your sword into its place; for all who take the sword will perish by the sword."* Even if he does not bear the sword in vain who is placed as an avenger of the Lord's wrath against the one who works evil,[279] nevertheless whoever takes the sword will perish by the sword.[280] But which sword does he mean? By that one, of course, which turns fiery before Paradise,[281] and by the sword of the Spirit that is described in the armor of God.[282]

26.53–54. *"Or do you think that I am not able to ask my Father at once to put at my disposal more than twelve legions of angels? How then will the Scriptures be fulfilled that say it must happen this way?"* I, who can have twelve legions of the angelic army, do not need the help of twelve apostles, even if all were to defend me. Among the ancients one legion was comprised of 6000 men. Due to the lack of time, we will not start to explain the number. Let it suffice only to say that it is a symbol: twelve legions come to 72,000 angels. This is how many nations of men into which the languages were divided.[283] His appended statement shows how ready his spirit was to suffer. For the prophets would have prophesied in vain if the Lord had not preserved the truth of their words by means of his suffering.

26.55. *At that hour Jesus said: "As against a thief have you come out with swords and clubs to arrest me? Daily I sat among you teaching in the Temple, and you did not seize me."* It is folly, he says, with swords and clubs to seek him who of his own accord hands him-

---

278. Cf. 1 Pt 2.9.
280. Cf. Gn 9.6.
282. Cf. Eph 6.17.

279. Cf. Rom 13.4.
281. Cf. Gn 3.24.

283. Cf. Dt 32.8. In the LXX, this passage reads: "When the Most High divided the nations, when he separated the sons of Adam, he set the bounds of the nations according to the number of the angels of God."

self over to your hands, and by means of a traitor to track him down in the night, as though he is keeping himself hidden and is staying away from your eyes, a man who teaches daily in the Temple. But the reason you have gathered against me in the darkness is because your power is in the darkness.[284]

26.56. *"But all this has happened that the scriptures of the prophets would be fulfilled."* Which "scriptures of the prophets" does he mean? "They pierced my hands and feet";[285] and elsewhere: "Just as a sheep is led to the slaughter";[286] and in another passage: "He was led to death because of the iniquities of my people."[287]

26.57. *But those who had seized Jesus led him to Caiaphas the chief priest, where the scribes and elders had convened.* Upon God's order, Moses had prescribed that high priests should succeed their fathers and a line of descent should be woven among priests.[288] Josephus records that this Caiaphas had purchased the high priesthood at a price from Herod for one year only.[289] It is no wonder, then, if an unjust high priest judges unjustly.

26.58. *But Peter was following him at a distance.* He who was about to deny the Lord was following him at a distance.

26.58. *And having entered inside he was sitting with the attendants to see the end.* Either out of a disciple's love or from human curiosity, he was longing to know what the high priest would judge concerning the Lord, whether he would condemn him to death or release him to be lacerated with whips. And in this, there is a difference between the ten apostles and Peter. They flee, whereas he follows the Savior, though at a distance.

26.60–61. *At last two false witnesses came and said: "He said: 'I am able to destroy the Temple of God and after three days to build it.'"* In what sense are they false witnesses, if they say the things that we have read above that the Lord had actually said?[290] Well, a

284. Cf. Lk 22.53.
286. Is 53.7.
288. Cf. Ex 29.28–44.

285. Ps 22.16.
287. Is 53.8.

289. Cf. Josephus, *AJ* 18.2.2; cf. 18.4.3. There is confusion here. According to Josephus, it was Gratus, the predecessor of Pilate, who deposed successively the three predecessors of Caiaphas, namely, Ananus, Ismael, and Eleazar. It was Eleazar who was deprived of the office after holding it for one year. Jerome's haste in composing this commentary has cost him some factual errors.

290. Cf. Jn 2.19.

false witness is one who does not understand statements in the same sense in which they are said. For the Lord had spoken of the temple of his body.[291] Moreover, even in the very words they use to accuse him falsely, they added and changed a few things, thus making it a "fair" false accusation, as it were. For the Savior had said: "Destroy this temple."[292] But they change this to say: "*I can* destroy the Temple of God." Jesus had said: *You* destroy, not I. For it is forbidden for us to lay a hand upon ourselves.[293] Then they convert his words to: "and after three days to build it." They wanted to make it seem that he had really spoken of the Jewish Temple. But the Lord wanted to point to the living and breathing temple and had said: "And in three days I will raise it up."[294] It is one thing to build, another to raise up.

26.62–63. *The chief priest stood up and said to him: "Do you answer nothing to the things that they are testifying against you?" But Jesus was silent.* Finding no material for a false charge, rash anger and impatience jolted the priest from his seat. Thus he displays the insanity of his mind by the movement of his body. The more Jesus kept silent before the false witnesses and wicked priests who were unworthy of his response, the more the high priest, overcome by fury, challenges him to respond. He wanted to find material for an accusation by some pretext in his words. Nonetheless, Jesus is silent. For, being God, he knew that whatever response he had given, they would have twisted it into a false charge.

26.63. *And the chief priest said to him: "I adjure you by the living God to tell us if you are the Christ, the Son of God."* Why do you adjure, most wicked of priests? Is it to accuse him, or that you might believe in him? If it is in order to accuse him, others will convict him; so condemn him in his silence. But if it is that you might believe in him, why were you unwilling to believe in him when he admits it?

26.64. *Jesus said to him: "You have said it."* The response to Pilate and to Caiaphas is similar.[295] Thus they are condemned by their own pronouncement.

---

291. Cf. Jn 2.21.   292. Jn 2.19.
293. Jerome also condemns suicide in strong terms in *Ep.* 39.3.
294. Jn 2.19.   295. Cf. Mt 27.11.

26.65. *Then the chief priest tore his robes saying: "He has blas-phemed. Why do we still need witnesses?"* The one whom fury had jolted from his priestly seat is provoked by the same madness to tear his garments. He tears his robes to show that the Jews have lost the glory of the priesthood, and that the high priests have a vacant seat. But it is also a Jewish custom to tear their garments, when they hear something blasphemous and contrary to God, as it were. In fact we read that Paul and Barnabas did this when they were honored in Lycaonia with the worship due to the gods.[296] In contrast, Herod did not give honor to God but acquiesced to the immoderate favor of the people and was at once struck down by an angel.[297]

26.67. *Then they spat in his face and struck him with blows.* This was to fulfill what is written: "I gave my cheeks to slaps, and I did not turn away my face from the shame of spitting."[298]

26.67–68. *But others slapped him on the face, saying: "Prophesy to us, Christ; who is it that hit you?"* It would have been foolish to respond to those who were beating him and to prophesy as to who had given the blow. For the madness of the one who had struck him was openly manifest. But just as he did not prophesy this to you, so he most clearly predicted the fact that Jerusalem would be surrounded by an army and that there would not be left a stone upon a stone in the Temple.[299]

26.69. *But Peter was sitting outside in the courtyard.* He was sitting outside to see the outcome of the affair. He did not draw near to Jesus, lest some suspicion should arise among the servants.

26.72. *And again he denied it with an oath: "I do not know the man."* I know that some[300] out of pious feeling for the apostle Peter have interpreted this passage to the effect that Peter did not deny God but "the man." They say that the meaning is: I do not know the man, because I know that he is God. A prudent reader knows how frivolous this interpretation is. By defending the apostle in this way, these people make the Lord guilty of ly-

---

296. Cf. Acts 14.10–14.   297. Cf. Acts 12.21–23.
298. Is 50.6; cf. Lam 3.30.   299. Cf. Lk 19.43–44.
300. Cf. Hilary, *In Matth.* 32.4 (PL 9: 1071B); Ambrose, *In Luc.* 10.82 (SC 52, 184).

ing. For if Peter did not deny him, then the Lord lied when he said: "Amen I say to you that on this night before the cock crows, you will deny me three times."[301] Observe what he says: "You will deny *me*," not *the man*.

26.73. *"Truly you also are one of them, for even your speech makes you known."* It is not that Peter spoke another language or that he was from an outside nation. For they were all Hebrews, both those who were accusing him and he who was being accused. Rather, they say this because each province and region has its own characteristics and could not avoid a vernacular sound of speaking. This is also why in the book of Judges the Ephrathites could not pronounce σύνθημα.[302]

26.74. *Then he began to invoke a curse on himself and to swear that he did not know the man. And immediately a cock crowed.* In another Gospel we read that after Peter's denial and the crowing of the cock, the Savior looked at Peter, and by his gaze he provoked him to bitter tears.[303] For it was impossible for one on whom the Light of the world had looked to remain in the darkness of denial.

26.75. *And he went out and wept bitterly.* While sitting in the courtyard of Caiaphas, he could not do penance. So he goes outside from the council of the impious[304] in order to wash away the filth of a cowardly denial with bitter weeping.

Chapter 27

27.1–2. *But when morning came, all the chief priests and elders of the people took counsel against Jesus, in order to hand him over to death. And they brought him bound and handed him over to Pontius Pilate the governor.* He was led not only to Pilate but also to Herod. Thus both men mocked the Lord. And notice the care with which the priests do evil. They stayed awake all night in order to commit a murder. "And they handed him over, bound, to Pilate." For by their custom, anyone they had condemned to death they handed over, bound, to the judge.

301. Mt 26.34.
302. Cf. Jgs 12.6. Jerome uses the LXX translation of the Hebrew word "shibboleth."
303. Cf. Lk 22.60–62.   304. Cf. Ps 1.1.

27.3–4. *Then, when Judas, who had handed him over, saw that he had been condemned, he was led by penitence to bring back the thirty silver pieces to the chief priests and elders, saying: "I have sinned in handing over just blood."* The burden of his impiety excluded the strength of his avarice. When Judas saw the Lord condemned to death, he returned the price to the priests, as if it were in his own power to change the verdict of the persecutors. And so, although he may have changed his will, nevertheless he did not change the outcome of the initial will. But if he who handed over just blood sinned, how much more did they sin who had paid for the just blood and who had provoked the disciple by offering a price for the betrayal? Let those who attempt to introduce [the doctrine of] diverse natures[305] and who say that Judas became a traitor by his evil nature, and that he was unable to be saved by his election to the apostleship, explain how an evil nature could have repented.

27.4–5. *But they said: "What is that to us? You see to it." And when he had thrown down the silver pieces in the Temple, he withdrew and going away he hanged himself with a noose.* It was of no benefit to have done an act of penance by which he was not able to correct the sin. If at some time a brother sins against a brother in such a way that he is able to amend the sin he committed, it can be forgiven him. But if the works remain, it is in vain that a penance is taken on with words. This is what is said in the Psalm about this same most wretched Judas: "And may his prayer be turned to sin."[306] Thus he was not only unable to amend the crime of betrayal, but to the first act of wickedness he added as well the sin of his own suicide. The apostle speaks of this sort of thing in the second letter to the Corinthians: "Lest the brother be overwhelmed by excessive grief."[307]

27.6. *But the chief priests took the pieces of silver and said: "It is not lawful to put them in the treasury* (corbana) *since it is the price for blood."* They truly strained out a gnat and swallowed a camel![308] For if the reason they do not put money into the *corbana,* that is,

---

305. See above on Mt 5.45; 7.18. Gnostics and Manichaeans seem to have tried to verify their predestinarian doctrine by the case of Judas, whom Christ called a "son of perdition" (Jn 17.12).

306. Ps 109.7.   307. 2 Cor 2.7.

308. Cf. Mt 23.24.

into the treasury and gifts of God, is because it is the price for blood, why is the blood itself poured out?

27.7. *So they took counsel and bought with them the potter's field as a burial place for strangers.* To be sure, they did this with another intention. Thus they left behind an eternal monument to their impiety by the purchase of the field. But still, we who were strangers from the Law and the prophets adopted their faulty zeal for salvation. For we are at rest at the price of his blood. Now it is called the potter's field because our Potter is Christ.[309]

27.9–10. *Then was fulfilled what was spoken through Jeremiah the prophet, saying: "And they took the thirty pieces of silver, the price of him on whom a price had been set by the sons of Israel, and they gave them for a potter's field, just as the Lord appointed for me."* This testimony is not found in Jeremiah.[310] Something similar is recorded in Zechariah, who is nearly the last of the twelve prophets.[311] Yet both the order and the wording are different, although the sense is not that discordant. Recently I read something in a certain little Hebrew book that a Hebrew from the Nazarene sect[312] brought to me. It was an apocryphon of Jeremiah in which I found this text written word for word.[313] Yet it still seems more likely to me that the testimony was taken from Zechariah by a common practice of the evangelists and apostles. In citation they bring out only the sense from the Old Testament. They tend to neglect the order of the words.[314]

27.11. *Now Jesus stood before the governor. And the governor asked*

309. He is a potter in the sense that all things were made by Christ; cf. Jn 1.3; Col 1.16. God is compared with a potter in Gn 2.7; Is 45.9; Jer 18.2.

310. Cf. Homily 11 on Ps 77 (78) in FOTC 48, 83.

311. The citation is from Zec 11.12–13 combined with the idea of purchasing a field suggested by Jer 32.6–15. This is linked with Jeremiah's description of a potter in Jer 18.2–4; 19.1–2.

312. See above on Mt 12.13; 13.53–54; 22.23 n; 23.35–36.

313. Although this sounds like an authentic autobiographical incident in Jerome's recent past, G. Bardy, "Jérôme et ses maîtres hébreux," *Revue Bénédictine* 46 (1934): 161, thinks that Jerome has fabricated the story based on Origen's conjecture (*In Matth. comm. series*, 117) about the existence of this apocryphal text. It seems possible that Jerome was inspired by Origen's reference to consult a "Hebrew from the Nazarene sect."

314. Jerome gives this same solution to the present difficulty in *Ep.* 57.7 to Pammachius.

him, saying: "Are you the king of the Jews?" The Jews are convicted of impiety when Pilate asks nothing else concerning the crime except whether he is king of the Jews. For they could not even find a false accusation to raise against the Savior.

27.11. *Jesus said to him: "You say so."* He responds in such a way that he both speaks the truth and his words are not open to a false charge. And notice that he did say something in response to Pilate, at least in part, who brought out the sentence of judgment against his will, but he was unwilling to respond to the priests and elders. For he judged them to be unworthy of his words.[315]

27.13. *Then Pilate said to him: "Do you not hear how many things they are testifying against you?"* Doubtless the one who condemns Jesus is a pagan, but he refers the case to the people of the Jews. "Do you not hear how many things they are testifying against you?" But Jesus was unwilling to respond anything. For had he explained away the charge, he would have been released by the governor, and the benefit of the cross would have been postponed.

27.16. *Now at that time he had a notorious prisoner, who was called Barabbas.* In the Gospel that is written according to the Hebrews,[316] his name is translated as "son of their teacher."[317] On account of sedition and murder he had been condemned. Now Pilate offers to them the option of releasing whomever they want, the thief or Jesus. He did not doubt that Jesus deserved to be chosen, but he knew that he had been handed over on account of envy. Therefore, the cause of the cross is manifestly envy.

27.19. *Now while he was sitting before the tribunal, his wife sent to him, saying: "Have nothing to do with that just man; for I have suffered many things today in a vision on account of him."* Note that dreams are frequently revealed by God to Gentiles, and that in Pilate and his wife, who confess that the Lord is just, there is testimony of the Gentile people.

---

315. Cf. Mt 26.62–63.

316. For other references to this apocryphal gospel, see Preface, Mt 6.11.

317. For a discussion of this reading, see Hennecke-Schneemelcher, *NTA* 1, 142.

27.22–23. *Pilate said to them: "What then shall I do about Jesus, who is called Christ?" They all said: "Let him be crucified." But the governor said to them: "Why, what evil has he done?" But they shouted all the more, saying: "Let him be crucified."* Pilate gave multiple opportunities for freeing the Savior: first by offering a thief for a just man; then by adding: "What then shall I do about Jesus who is called Christ?" that is, who is your king. And when they answered: "Let him be crucified," he did not at once acquiesce, but in accordance with his wife's suggestion, when she commanded: "Have nothing to do with that just man," he too responds: "Why, what evil has he done?" In saying this, Pilate absolved Jesus. "But they shouted all the more, saying: 'Let him be crucified.'" This was to fulfill what was said in the twenty-first Psalm: "Many dogs have surrounded me; a gathering of the malicious has beset me";[318] and in Jeremiah: "My heritage has become to me like a lion in the forest; they have raised their voice against me."[319] Isaiah too is in agreement with this judgment: "And I expected that they would practice judgment, but they did iniquity; and not justice, but an outcry."[320]

27.24. *So when Pilate saw that he was gaining nothing but rather that a riot was beginning, he took water and washed his hands before the people, saying: "I am innocent of the blood of this just man; see to it yourselves."* Pilate took water in accordance with the following prophecy: "I will wash my hands among the innocent."[321] Thus, in the washing of his hands, the works of the Gentiles are cleansed, and in some manner he estranges us from the impiety of the Jews who shouted: "Crucify him."[322] For he contested this and said: I certainly wanted to set the innocent man free, but because a sedition is arising and the crime of treason against Caesar is being attached to me:[323] "I am innocent of the blood of this man." The judge who is compelled to bring a verdict against the Lord does not condemn the one offered, but exposes those who offered him; he pronounces that he who is to be crucified is just. "See to it yourselves," he says; I am a minister of the laws; it is your voice that is shedding his blood.

318. Ps 22.12.   319. Jer 12.8.
320. Is 5.7.   321. Ps 26.6.
322. Cf. Mk 15.13–14.   323. Cf. Jn 19.12.

27.25. *And all the people answered and said: "His blood be upon us and upon our children.*"[324] This imprecation upon the Jews continues until the present day. The Lord's blood will not be removed from them. This is why it says through Isaiah: "If you wash your hands before me, I will not listen; for your hands are full of blood."[325] The Jews have left the best heritage to their children, saying: "His blood be upon us and upon our children."

27.26. *Then he released for them Barabbas; but he had Jesus scourged, and handed him over to them to be crucified.* Barabbas the thief, who made seditions among the crowds, who was the author of murders, was released to the people of the Jews. He stands for the devil, who reigns in them until today. It is for this reason that they are unable to have peace. But Jesus, having been handed over by the Jews, is absolved by the wife of Pilate, and is called a just man by the governor himself. Even a centurion confesses that he is truly the Son of God.[326] Let the learned reader ask: How is it consistent that Pilate washed his hands and said: "I am innocent of the blood of this just man," and afterward had Jesus scourged and handed him over to be crucified? One should know that he was the administrator of Roman laws according to which it was enacted that one who is crucified must first be beaten with whips. And so, Jesus was handed over to the soldiers to be beaten. They cut with a whip that most holy body and breast that contained God. But this was done since it was written: "Many are the scourgings of sinners."[327] By that scourging, we were delivered from being beaten, since the Scripture says to the just man: "A scourge has not drawn near to your tent."[328]

27.27–29. *Then the soldiers of the governor took Jesus into the praetorium. They gathered the whole cohort before him, and having stripped him they put a scarlet cloak upon him, and plaiting a crown of thorns they put it on his head, and put a reed in his right hand. And kneeling before him they mocked him, saying: "Hail, king of the Jews."* There are soldiers indeed, since he had been named the king of the Jews, and the scribes and priests had hurled the charge at him that

324. Mt 27.25.
326. Cf. Mt 27.54; Mk 15.39.
328. Ps 91.10.

325. Is 1.15.
327. Ps 32.10.

he was usurping power for himself among the people of Israel. They do this mockingly. Thus in place of the red fringe that
ancient kings used, they cover with a scarlet cloak the one they
had stripped of his original clothes. For a diadem they place on
him a crown of thorns; for a royal scepter they give him a reed;
and they do him homage as if he were a king. But we should understand all these things mystically. For just as Caiaphas said: "It
is necessary that one man die for all,"[329] not knowing what he
was saying, so also whatever these men did, even though they
did it with a different frame of mind, nevertheless they were giving mysteries to us who believe. In the scarlet cloak Jesus carries
the blood-stained works of the Gentiles; in the crown of thorns
he dissolves the ancient curse;[330] with the reed he kills poison-
ous beasts; or he held the reed in his hand in order to write
down the sacrilege of the Jews.[331]

27.30. *And spitting on him, they took the reed and struck his head.*
At this time was fulfilled: "I have not turned away my face from
the shame of spitting."[332] And yet, though they are striking his
head with a reed, he endures everything patiently. Thus he
shows the truth of Isaiah's prophecy, who said: "A bruised reed
he will not break."[333]

27.31. *And after they had mocked him, they stripped him of the cloak
and put his own clothes on him, and they led him away to crucify him.*
When Jesus is scourged and spat upon and mocked, he is not
wearing his own clothing, but that which he had taken on account of our sins; but when he is crucified and the spectacle of
both the mockery and derision has passed, at that time he takes
his original clothes and assumes his own dress. And at once the
elements are disturbed, and the creation gives testimony to the
Creator.

329. Cf. Jn 11.50.
330. Cf. Gn 3.18.
331. Cf. Origen, *In Matth. comm. series,* 125. Jerome uses two words for "reed":
in his translation of the scriptural lemmata, verses 29 and 30, as well as in his
comment on v.30, he chooses *harundo,* the same noun as that which occurs in
the Isaiah text (see n. 333). In his comment on v.29, however, he employs the
noun *calamus,* probably for the sake of his image of Christ writing.
332. Is 50.6.
333. Is 42.3.

27.32. *But while going out, they found a man from Cyrene named Simon; this man they compelled to take up his cross.* Let no one think that the narrative of the evangelist John contradicts this passage. For he says that the Lord carried his own cross while he was going out of the praetorium.[334] But Matthew reports that they found a man from Cyrene named Simon, upon whom under compulsion they placed the cross of Jesus. Now we should understand this as follows: while going out of the praetorium, Jesus himself carried his own cross; but afterward he encountered Simon, upon whom they placed the cross to be carried. Now, there is a mystical interpretation *(anagōgē)* here: the nations take up the cross of Jesus, and an obedient foreigner carries the Savior's disgrace.[335]

27.33. *And they came to the place that is called Golgotha, which is the place of the skull* (Calvariae locus). I have heard[336] that someone has explained that "place of the skull" is the place where Adam is buried and that the reason it is so named is because the head of that ancient man is laid there.[337] They relate this to what the apostle says: "Awake, you who sleep, and arise from the dead, and Christ shall enlighten you."[338] This interpretation is attractive and soothing to the ear of the people, but it is not true. For outside the city and outside the gate there are places in which the heads of the condemned are cut off. This is where they took the name "of the skull" *(Calvariae);* that is, it refers to the skulls of the decapitated. But the reason the Lord was crucified there was so that where there was once a site of the condemned, there the banner of martyrdom would be raised; and just as he was made a malediction for us on the cross[339] and was scourged and crucified, so he is crucified as if a guilty man

334. Cf. Jn 19.17.

335. In *De interpr. hebr. nom.*, p. 71, line 4, Jerome says that Simon means "obedient."

336. Cf. Origen, *In Matth. comm. series,* 127; Jerome, *In Ephes.* 5.14.

337. According to A. Plummer, *An Exegetical Commentary on the Gospel According to Matthew,* 394, this tradition is not likely to have been pre-Christian, but was no doubt Jewish-Christian, to bring the first Adam into contact with the Second.

338. Eph 5.14.

339. Cf. Gal 3.13.

among the guilty for the salvation of all. But if anyone should wish to contend that the reason the Lord was crucified there was so that his blood might trickle down on Adam's tomb, we shall ask him why other thieves were also crucified in the same place. From which it appears that Calvary signifies not the tomb of the first man, but the "place of the decapitated." Thus where sin abounded, grace would super-abound.[340] But in the book of Joshua the son of Nave we read that Adam was buried near Hebron and Arba.[341]

27.34. *And they gave him wine to drink mingled with gall, and when he had tasted it, he was unwilling to drink it.* God says to Jerusalem: "I planted you as a true vine; how did you turn into the bitterness of a foreign vine?"[342] A bitter vine makes bitter wine. Bitter wine is administered to the Lord Jesus so that what is written may be fulfilled: "They gave gall for my food, and for my thirst they gave me vinegar to drink."[343] Now as for the words: "When he had tasted it, he was unwilling to drink it," this indicates that he did indeed taste the bitterness of death for us,[344] but on the third day he rose again.

27.35. *But after they crucified him, they divided his garments, casting lots.* This too had been prophesied in the same Psalm: "They divided my garments among themselves and cast lots for my clothing."[345]

27.36. *And sitting down, they kept watch over him.* The vigilance of the soldiers and priests is beneficial to us. Thus the power of the Resurrected One appears greater and more manifest.

27.37. *And above his head they put the written charge: "This is Jesus king of the Jews."* I cannot express my astonishment in a way

340. Cf. Rom 5.20.
341. Cf. Jos 14.15 (cf. LXX). The RSV translates: "Now the name of Hebron formerly was Kiriath-arba ['city of Arba']; this Arba was the greatest man [Heb., *adam*] among the Anakim." But Jerome's Vulgate translation reads: "The name of Hebron before was called Cariath-Arbe: Adam the greatest among the Enacims was laid there" (Douay-Rheims translation). Jerome's version probably mistranslates the Hebrew. In fact, Scripture does not say where Adam is buried.
342. Jer 2.21.   343. Ps 69.21.
344. Cf. Heb 2.9.
345. Ps 22.18. Actually, this is not the same Psalm. A slip of the memory on Jerome's part?

that is equal to the magnitude of this event. Though false witnesses had been paid, and the wretched people had been incited to sedition and shouting,[346] they found no charge for his execution other than that he was king of the Jews.[347] Perhaps they did this mockingly and with ridicule. At any rate, even Pilate responds to the unwilling: "What I have written, I have written."[348] Whether willing or unwilling, O Jews, the whole crowd of the Gentiles responds to you: Jesus is the king of the Jews; he is the ruler of those who believe and confess.

27.38. *Then two thieves were crucified with him, one on the right and one on the left.* If Golgotha is the tomb of Adam[349] and not the place of the condemned, and the reason the Lord is crucified there is that he might raise up Adam, why are two thieves crucified in the same place?

27.39. *But those passing by were blaspheming him, moving their heads.* They were blaspheming because they were passing by the "way"[350] and were unwilling to walk on the true road of the Scriptures. They were moving their heads because they had already previously moved their feet and were not standing on the rock.[351] The foolish people insult him by saying the very same thing that the false witnesses had fabricated.[352]

27.42. *"He saved others, he cannot save himself."* Even against their will the scribes and Pharisees confess that he saved others. And so, your own judgment condemns you. For assuredly, he who had saved others could have saved himself, if he had wanted.

27.42. *"Let him come down now from the cross, and we will believe in him."* What a fraudulent promise! Which is greater? For a man still living to come down from a cross, or for a dead man to rise from the grave? He rose, and you do not believe. In like manner, then, even if he were to come down from the cross, you would not believe. But it seems to me that demons are guiding

---

346. Cf. Mt 27.20.
347. Cf. Origen, *In Matth. comm. series,* 130.
348. Jn 19.22.   349. See on Mt 27.33.
350. Cf. Jn 14.6.
351. Cf. Origen, *In Matth. comm. series,* 132, citing Ps 40.2: "You set my feet on the rock." See also Mt 7.24–27.
352. Cf. Mt 27.40; 26.61.

this. For immediately when the Lord was crucified, they sensed the power of the cross and understood that their strength was broken. They do this that he might come down from the cross. But the Lord knows the plots of his adversaries and remains on the gibbet in order to destroy the devil.[353]

27.44. *And the thieves who were fastened with him were reviling him in the same way.* Here, by a figure of speech called σύλληψις,[354] both thieves, instead of one, are introduced as having blasphemed. Luke, however, asserts that while one was blaspheming, the other made a confession and even rebuked the one who was blaspheming.[355] It is not that the Gospels have discrepancies, but that at first both were blaspheming; then when the sun took flight, when the earth quaked, and when the rocks were split and when the darkness was falling, one of them believed in Jesus and amended his initial denial by a subsequent confession. In the two thieves, there are represented the two peoples, that of the Gentiles and that of the Jews. At first they both blasphemed the Lord. Afterward, one of them became terrified by the greatness of the signs and did penance, and until the present day he rebukes the blaspheming Jews.

27.45. *But from the sixth hour darkness came over the whole land until the ninth hour.* Those who have written against the Gospels[356] suspect that Christ's disciples, through ignorance, have interpreted an eclipse of the sun in connection with the Lord's Resurrection. Now these customarily happen at certain set times, though an eclipse of the sun ordinarily occurs only during a new moon.[357] But there is no doubt that at the time of the Passover the moon was completely full. And lest perhaps it should seem that the earth's shadow or the moon's orb was in opposition to

353. Cf. Heb 2.14.

354. In Jerome's usage this figure is also known as synecdoche, in which a part is named for the whole, or the whole for a part. See above on Mt 12.39–40; 26.8–9.

355. Cf. Lk 23.39–40.

356. Jerome has in mind Porphyry, *Contra Christianos, fragm.* 14, and Celsus. In Origen, *Contra Celsum* 2.33, Celsus explains the darkness of Calvary by proposing an eclipse of the sun. In *In Matth comm. series,* 134, Origen rejects the rationalizing hypothesis of an eclipse of the sun.

357. Lit., "at the rising of the moon" (*ortu lunae*).

the sun and created a brief, twilight-like darkness, it is recorded that the duration was three hours. Thus every pretext for other explanations is removed. And this occurred, in my opinion, that the prophecy might be fulfilled which says: "The sun shall set at midday, and light will become dark on the earth";[358] and in another place: "The sun set when it was still midday."[359] It seems to me that the clearest light of the world, that is, the "greater luminary,"[360] withdrew her rays either in order to avoid seeing the Lord hanging there, or to prevent impious blasphemers from enjoying her light.

27.46. *And about the ninth hour Jesus cried with a great voice, saying: "Eli, Eli, lema sabacthani?" that is, "My God, my God, why have you forsaken me?"* He has used[361] the beginning of the twenty-first Psalm.[362] Moreover, he leaves out what is read in the middle of the little verse: "Look upon me."[363] For in the Hebrew it reads: "My God, my God, why have you forsaken me?" Therefore, they are impious[364] who think that this Psalm was spoken under the persona of David, or of Esther and Mordecai. For the evangelists understand the testimonies taken from it of the Savior, as for example: "They divided my garments among themselves and cast lots for my clothing";[365] and elsewhere: "They have pierced my hands and my feet."[366] Do not marvel at the humility of the words and the complaint of the forsaken one. For by knowing the "form of a servant,"[367] you see the scandal of the cross.

27.47. *And some of the bystanders, hearing it, said: "He is calling Elijah."* It does not say that all, but "some," thought this. I think they were the Roman soldiers, who did not understand the peculiar nature of the Hebrew language. From his words: "Eli,

---

358. Am 8.9.   359. Jer 15.9.
360. Cf. Gn 1.16.

361. Lat., *abusus est.* Jerome's language seems provocative, since *abutor* carries a double sense in Latin, "use" and "misuse."

362. Cf. Ps 22.1.

363. Ps 22.1. In Jerome's version of the Hebrew (see the Douay-Rheims version), the phrase "Look upon me" occurs between: "O God, my God" and "why have you forsaken me?"

364. Jerome is opposing contemporary Jewish interpretation of this Psalm.

365. Ps 22.18.   366. Ps 22.16.
367. Phil 2.7.

Eli," they were thinking that he had invoked Elijah. Now, if you prefer to understand that it was the Jews who said this, they are doing even this by their accustomed habit. They insultingly accuse the Lord of weakness, since he is praying for the help of Elijah.[368]

27.48. *And immediately one of them ran and took a sponge, filled it with vinegar, and put it on a reed, and gave it to him to drink.* These things happened that the prophecy might be fulfilled: "In my thirst they gave me vinegar to drink."[369] Up to the present day the Jews and all who disbelieve in the Lord's Resurrection give Jesus vinegar and gall to drink. And they give him wine mixed with myrrh that they might put him to sleep, and he might not see their evil deeds.

27.50. *But when Jesus had cried out again with a great voice, he sent forth the spirit.* To send forth the spirit is an indication of divine power, as he himself had also said: "No one can take my life[370] from me, but I lay it down of my own accord that I might take it up again."[371]

27.51. *And the curtain of the Temple was torn in two parts from top to bottom.* The curtain of the Temple was torn, and all the mysteries of the Law that were previously woven together were made known and passed to the Gentile people.[372] In the gospel that we have frequently mentioned,[373] we read that the upper lintel[374] of the Temple, which was of immense size, was broken and split in two. Josephus, too, reports that the angelic powers, the former guardians of the Temple, equally cried out at that time: "Let us pass from this dwelling place."[375]

368. The Gospel text provides interesting evidence for the contemporary Jewish belief that the living could prayerfully invoke the help of departed saints.

369. Ps 69.21.   370. Or "soul" (*anima*).

371. Jn 10.18.

372. Cf. Homily 66 on Ps 88 (89) in FOTC 57, 68; *Ep.* 120.8.2.

373. I.e., the *Gospel of the Nazarenes.* Jerome also mentions this gospel "written in Hebrew letters" in *Ep.* 120.8 to Hedibia. In the present work see Pref.; 12.13; 13.53–54; 22.23 n; 23.35–36; 27.9–10. Cf. Hennecke-Schneemelcher, *NTA* 1, 150.

374. Lat., *superliminare.* The lintel is the horizontal architectural member spanning and usually carrying the load above an opening.

375. Josephus places this prodigy before the destruction of Jerusalem in 70

27.51–52. *The earth trembled, and the rocks were split, and the graves were opened.* Doubtless what the great signs signify literally is that both heaven and earth and all things were showing that their Lord was crucified. But it seems to me that the earthquake and the other things bear a type of believers, namely, that those who were formerly like tombs of the dead, when their former errors and vices are abandoned and their hardness is softened, afterward they recognize the Creator.

27.52–53. *And many bodies of the saints who had fallen asleep were raised, and coming out of the tombs after his resurrection, they went into the holy city, and they appeared to many.* Just as the dead Lazarus was resurrected,[376] so also many bodies of the saints were resurrected. Thus they showed the Lord rising again. And yet, though the tombs were opened, they were not resurrected before the Lord was resurrected. Thus he was the firstborn of the resurrection from the dead.[377] Now we should understand the holy city in which they were seen when they were being resurrected either as the heavenly Jerusalem, or this earthly one which was previously holy. Just as Matthew is called a tax-collector, not because as an apostle he continued to be a tax-collector,[378] but because he retains his former title, so the city of Jerusalem was called "holy" on account of the Temple and the Holy of Holies,[379] and in order to distinguish it from other cities in which idols were worshiped. But when it is said: "They appeared to many," it is shown that this was not a general resurrection that appeared to all, but a special one to many. Thus those who deserved to behold it saw it.[380]

27.54. *But a centurion and those who were with him guarding Jesus, when they saw the earthquake and the things that were happening, they feared greatly, saying: "Truly he was the Son of God."* The cause of the miracle of the centurion after the earthquake is ex-

---

A.D. Cf. *BJ* 6.5.3. The same reference to Josephus is found in *Ep.* 46.4 from Paula and Eustochium to Marcella. See also Jerome's *Ep.* 120.8 to Hedibia; *Commentary on Isaiah.*

376. Cf. Jn 11.44.   377. Cf. Col 1.18; 1 Cor 15.20.
378. See above on Mt 26.6.   379. Cf. Is 52.1.
380. For the thought of being deserving of participating in the resurrection, see Lk 20.35.

plained more clearly in another Gospel, which says that when he saw him dismiss the spirit, he said: "Truly he was the Son of God."[381] For no one has authority to dismiss his spirit except the one who is the Creator of souls. Now in this passage we should understand "spirit" for "soul," either because the spirit is what makes the body spiritual and living, or because the spirit is the substance of the soul itself, according to what is written elsewhere: "You will remove their spirit, and they will fail."[382] And the following ought to be taken into consideration: in the presence of the cross, at the very scandal of the Passion, the centurion confesses that he is truly the Son of God. Yet in the Church Arius preaches that he is a creature!

27.55. *Now there were also many women there [looking on] from afar, who had followed Jesus from Galilee, ministering to him.* There was a Jewish practice, and as an ancient custom of the nation it was not regarded as offensive, that women provided food and clothing for teachers out of their own substance. Paul records that he has set aside this custom, because it could cause a scandal among the Gentiles: "Do we not have authority to lead about women as sisters, as the other apostles also do?"[383] Now they were providing for the Lord out of their own substance. Thus he was reaping material things from them, while they were reaping spiritual things from him.[384] It is not that the Lord was in need of the food of his creatures, but to show a type for teachers, that they should be content with food and clothing from their disciples. But let us see what sort of companions he had: Mary Magdalene, from whom he had expelled seven demons;[385] Mary the mother of James and Joseph, who was the Savior's own maternal aunt, the sister of Mary the Lord's mother; and the mother of the sons of Zebedee, who a little earlier had asked for the kingdom for her sons;[386] and others whom we read about in the other Gospels.

27.57. *When it was evening, there came a certain rich man from Arimathea by the name of Joseph. He was himself a disciple of Jesus.* He is referred to as "rich" not because the writer wanted to boast

---

381. Cf. Mk 15.37–39.
383. 1 Cor 9.5.
385. Cf. Lk 8.2; Mk 16.9.

382. Ps 104.29.
384. Cf. Rom 15.27.
386. Cf. Mt 20.21.

and report that a noble and very rich man had been a disciple of Jesus. Rather, it was to show the reason why he was able to procure from Pilate the body of Jesus. For a poor and unknown man could not have gained access to Pilate, the representative of Roman power, and procured the body of a crucified man. In another evangelist, Joseph is called a βουλευτής, that is, a counselor.[387] Some[388] think that the first Psalm was composed about him: "Blessed is the man who does not go in the counsel of the impious,"[389] etc.

27.59. *And having taken the body of Jesus, he wrapped it in clean linen.* The ambition of the rich is condemned through the simple burial of the Lord. They are unable to be without their wealth, even among tombs. But we can also understand this according to the spiritual understanding. The Lord's body is wrapped not in gold and jewels and silk, but in a pure linen shroud. This signifies that he wraps Jesus in clean linen who receives him with a pure mind.

27.60. *And he placed it in his own new tomb, which he had hewn from rock; and he rolled a great stone over the entrance of the tomb, and he went away.* He is placed in a new tomb lest after the Resurrection, while the other bodies remain, it would be fabricated that a different body had been raised. But the new tomb can also point to the virginal womb of Mary. And the stone placed at the entrance, indeed a great stone, shows that the tomb could not have been opened without the help of many.

27.61. *Mary Magdalene and the other Mary were there, sitting opposite the tomb.* Though the others had abandoned the Lord, the women persevered in their duty, awaiting what Jesus had promised. This is why they merited to be the first to see the Risen One. For "the one who perseveres to the end shall be saved."[390]

27.64. *"Therefore, give orders to guard the tomb until the third day, lest perchance his disciples come and steal him away."* It would not have sufficed for the chief priests and scribes and Pharisees to have crucified the Lord and Savior without also guarding the

---

387. Cf. Lk 23.50.
388. Cf. Tertullian, *De spectaculis* 3.4.
389. Ps 1.1.
390. Cf. Mt 10.22; 24.13.

tomb, taking a cohort, sealing the stone, and resisting with all their might the one who was rising again. Thus did their diligence advance our faith.[391] For the more [the tomb] is guarded, so much the more is the power of the Resurrection shown. This is also why he was laid in a new tomb that had been cut in rock. For if it had been built out of many stones, it could have been said that he was removed by theft, once the foundations of the mound had been dug under. That he had to be placed in a tomb is a testimony of the prophet who says: "He dwelt in a deep cave of very strong rock."[392] And at once, after two little verses, follows: "You will see the king with glory."[393]

Chapter 28

28.1. *Now on the evening of the sabbath, at dawn on the first day of the week, Mary Magdalene and the other Mary came to see the tomb.* The fact that different times for these women are described in the Gospels is not a sign of falsehood, as the impious object. Rather, [it shows] the duties of diligent visitation. For they were going away and returning frequently and they could not endure to be absent from the Lord's tomb even for a short while.

28.2–3. *And behold, there was a great earthquake; for an angel of the Lord descended from heaven and coming near rolled away the stone, and he was sitting upon it; but his appearance was like lightning, and his clothing was like snow.* Our Lord is one and the same Son of God and Son of man. According to both natures, divinity and flesh, he shows signs, now of his greatness, now of his humility. This is why in the present passage, though it is a man who was crucified, buried, and shut in the tomb, whom a stone holds back in opposition, nevertheless the things that are done outside show him to be the Son of God: the sun takes flight, darkness falls, the earth quakes, the curtain is torn, the rocks split, the dead are raised, there are services of angels, which even from the beginning of his birth proved that he was God.[394] For ex-

---

391. Cf. Homily 87 in FOTC 57, 219.
392. Is 33.16.   393. Is 33.17.
394. Cf. Mt 1.23.

ample, Gabriel comes to Mary,[395] an angel speaks with Joseph,[396] it announces the same thing to shepherds;[397] afterward a choir of angels is heard: "Glory to God in the highest and on earth peace to men of good will."[398] He is tempted in the desert and immediately after his victory angels serve him.[399] Now, too, an angel comes as a guard of the Lord's tomb. By his bright clothing he expresses the glory of the triumphant one. And what is more, when the Lord ascends to heaven, two angels are seen on the Mount of Olives, promising the Savior's second coming to the apostles.[400]

28.4–5. *And for fear of him the guards were terrified and became like dead men. And the angel answered and said to the women: "Do not be afraid; for I know that you are seeking Jesus who was crucified."* The guards are completely terrified with fear.[401] They lie there stupefied like dead men, and yet the angel consoles not them but the women: "Do not be afraid." Let them be afraid, he says. Panic persists in those in whom abides unbelief. But as for you, since you are seeking the crucified Jesus, hear this: he has been resurrected and has fulfilled his promises.

28.6–7. *"Come and see where he had been placed."* Thus, if you do not believe my words, you should believe the empty tomb. Go with quick steps and announce to his disciples that he has risen. And he is going ahead of you into Galilee, that is, into the quagmire[402] of the Gentiles, where previously there was error and slipperiness, and where previously he did not place his footprint with a firm and stable foot.

28.8. *And they departed quickly from the tomb with fear and great joy, running to announce to his disciples.* Two different feelings occupied the minds of the women: fear and joy. The former came from the greatness of the miracle, the latter from their longing for the Resurrected One. And yet both feelings quickened their feminine steps. They went to the apostles so that through them the seedbed of the faith would be scattered.

---

395. Cf. Lk 1.26.
396. Cf. Mt 1.20.
397. Cf. Lk 2.10.
398. Lk 2.14.
399. Cf. Mk 1.13; Mt 4.11.
400. Cf. Acts 1.11.
401. Cf. Origen, *fragm.* 567.
402. This word is used in 2 Pt 2.22 of a pig's mire.

28.9. *And behold, Jesus met them, saying: "Hail!"* Those who were seeking in this way, those who were running in such a way, merited to meet the risen Lord and to be the first to hear: "Hail!" Thus the curse of the woman Eve was broken among women.[403]

28.9. *But they came and held his feet and worshiped him.* They come and hold his feet, for they worshiped him. But she who was seeking the living among the dead[404] and who still did not know that the Son of God had risen, deservedly hears: "Do not touch me, for I have not yet ascended to my Father."[405]

28.10. *Then Jesus said to them: "Do not be afraid."* Both in the Old and in the New Testament[406] the following should always be observed: When a more majestic vision appears, at first fear is expelled. Thus, when the mind has been made calm in this way, the things that are said can be heard.

28.10. *"Go, announce to my brethren that they should go to Galilee. They will see me there."* He also spoke to these brethren in another passage: "I will announce your name to my brethren."[407] It is not in Judea that they see the Savior, but in the multitude of the Gentiles.

28.12–14. *And when they had assembled with the elders and taken counsel, they gave a generous sum of money to the soldiers, saying: "Say that his disciples came by night and stole him away while we were asleep. And if this comes to the governor's ears, we will convince him and keep you out of trouble."* The guards confess the miracle, return agitated to the city, announce to the chief priests what they saw, the events that they had seen.[408] Those who should have converted to repentance and sought the risen Jesus persevere in their malice. They convert the money that had been given for the Temple's use into a payment for a falsehood, just as they had previously given thirty pieces of silver to Judas the betrayer.[409] Therefore, all who misappropriate the donations of the Temple and those that are given for church use for other matters by

---

403. Cf. Hilary, *In Matth.* (PL 9: 1076B).

404. Cf. Lk 24.5.   405. Jn 20.17.

406. Lat., *instrumentum*. This term is common in Tertullian and Origen as well.

407. Ps 22.22.   408. Cf. Origen, *fragm.* 569.

409. Cf. Mt 26.15.

which they satisfy their own will, are like the scribes and priests who purchased a falsehood and who paid money for the Savior's blood.

28.16. *Now the eleven disciples went to Galilee, to the mountain that Jesus had appointed for them.* After the Resurrection Jesus is seen on a mountain in Galilee, and he is worshiped there, though some doubt, and their doubt increases our faith. Then he manifests himself more openly to Thomas, and he shows his side wounded by a spear and his hands pierced by nails.[410]

28.18. *And Jesus came and spoke to them, saying: "All authority in heaven and on earth has been given to me."* Authority has been given to him who a little earlier was crucified, who was buried in a tomb, who lay there dead, who afterward was resurrected. But authority has been given "in heaven and on earth." Thus he who was previously reigning in heaven reigns on earth through the faith of believers.

28.19. *"Go therefore, teach all nations, baptizing them in the name of the Father, and of the Son, and of the Holy Spirit."* First they teach all nations, then they dip in water those who have been taught. For it is not possible that the body receives the sacrament of Baptism unless the soul first receives the truth of the faith. Now they are baptized in the name of the Father, and of the Son, and of the Holy Spirit. Thus there is one gift from those whose divinity is one.[411] And the name of Trinity is one God.[412]

28.20. *"Teaching them to observe all things whatsoever I have commanded you."* The sequence is extraordinary. He has commanded the apostles first to teach all nations, then to dip them in the sacrament of faith, and after faith and baptism they are to instruct them in the things that must be observed. And lest we think that the things that are commanded are light matters, he added the few words: "all things whatsoever I have commanded you." Thus those who believe, who are baptized in the Trinity, must do everything that has been taught.

28.20. *"And behold, I am with you all the days until the consum-*

---

410. Cf. Jn 20.27.
411. Cf. Origen, *fragm.* 572.
412. Cf. Homily 69 on Ps 91 (92) in FOTC 57, 92.

mation of the age. " He promises to be with his disciples until the consummation of the age. He shows that they will always be victorious and that he will never depart from believers. But he who promises his presence until the consummation of the world is not ignorant of that day on which he knows he will be with his apostles.[413]

413. See above on Mt 24.36; 24.42; 24.44–46.

INDICES

GENERAL INDEX

This index includes Latin words cited. The letter "n" refers to a footnote, but footnotes are not always indicated. The Introduction is referenced by page numbers separated by commas; Jerome's Preface ("pref") is referenced by section number. Jerome's Commentary is referenced by the chapter and verse (or verses), with numerals separated by a period and designating the lemmata of Matthew's Gospel.

INDEX OF HOLY SCRIPTURE

References to Jerome's work follow the colon in each item. The letter "n" refers to a footnote. Jerome's Preface ("pref") is referenced by section number, and Jerome's Commentary is referenced by the chapter and verse (or verses), with numerals separated by a period and designating the lemmata of Matthew's Gospel. This index does not include the Introduction.

Old Testament

New Testament

INDEX OF GREEK WORDS CITED

The lemmata of the Gospel of Matthew are designated by numerals referring to chapter and verse.